# Form and Value in Modern Poetry

The long and distinguished career of R. P. Blackmur falls into two phases. From 1928 to 1940, Mr. Blackmur was a free-lance poet and critic. In 1940 the second phase began, when he became affiliated with Princeton University. He has been at Princeton ever since in various capacities: as a member of the Institute for Advanced Studies (1944–48), as a fellow (resident fellow, 1940–43 and 1946–48, and Hodder fellow, 1944), and as a member of the faculty of the university, where he is now Professor of English.

Mr. Blackmur's many books are central in the body of American poetry and criticism. They are: *The Double Agent* (1935), *From Jordan's Delight* (1937), *The Expense of Greatness* (1940), *The Second World* (1942), *The Good European* (1947), *Language as Gesture* (1952), and *The Lion and the Honeycomb* (1955). His essays appear frequently in literary magazines and journals.

The seventeen essays which appear here under the title *Form and Value in Modern Poetry* are selected from *Language as Gesture,* which was originally published in hardcovers by Harcourt, Brace and Company.

# Form and Value in Modern Poetry

## R. P. BLACKMUR

Doubleday Anchor Books
Doubleday & Company, Inc.
Garden City, New York

COVER BY LEONARD BASKIN

TYPOGRAPHY BY EDWARD GOREY

Anchor Books edition: 1957

# Contents

Form and Value in Modern Poetry

# 1. The Shorter Poems of Thomas Hardy

Both for those who enjoy the bulk of Thomas Hardy's poems and for those whose genuine enjoyment of a few poems is almost overcome by a combination of depression and dismay at the bulk, the great need is some sort of canon—a criterion more for exclusion than for judgment. At the general enjoyers this essay is not directly aimed; nor is it meant to be as irritating as it will seem because it names what it discards more clearly than it specifies what it keeps. It is meant rather to be a help—a protection, a refuge—for those who see in Hardy's poetry a great art beaten down, much of it quite smothered to death, by the intellectual machinery by means of which Hardy expected it to run and breathe free.

However abnormal, the condition is far from unusual. If we may say that in Shelley we see a great sensibility the victim of the early stages of religious and philosophical decay in the nineteenth century, and that in Swinburne we see an even greater poetic sensibility vitiated by the substitution of emotion for subject matter, then it is only a natural step further to see in Hardy the consummate double ruin of an extraordinary sensibility that had been deprived of both emotional discipline and the structural support of a received imagination. Hardy was a free man in everything that concerns the poet; which is to say, helpless, without tradition; and he therefore rushed for support into the slavery of ideas whenever his freedom failed him. The astonishing thing is—as with Shelley and Swinburne to a lesser degree—that he was able to bring so much poetry with him into a pile of work that shows, like a brush heap, all the disadvantages of the nineteenth-century mind as it affected poetry, and yet shows almost none of the difficulties—whether overcome, come short of, or characteristic—belonging to the production or appreciation of poetry itself. The poetry is there—permanently; and it is our business to get at it. What obstructs us is man-made, impermanent, and need not have been there at all. It is a thicket of ideas, formulas, obsessions, indisciplined compulsions, nonce insights, and specious particularities. That is, it is accidental, not substantial, and can be cleared away; then we can come at the feeling, the conviction, the actuality, that are there, not underneath, but throughout the body of poetry.

Everybody who has read a volume of Thomas Hardy's verse retains a secure impression, like the smart of a blow, of what it was like. Everybody who has read the Apology prefixed to *Late Lyrics* knows that Hardy and many of his reviewers disagreed as to what made the blow smart. The reviewers referred to unrelieved pessimism; Hardy insisted he was no pessimist, was applying ideas to life, and that the smart came from "exacting a full look at the worst." That the reviewers were right on instinct, ignorantly and with the wrong slogan, and that Hardy was also right, with an equivalent ignorance and a misapprehension of *his* slogan, is a part of what these notes are meant to show as a basis for exclusion. We are committed then to a study of ignorance in poetry. Specifically, we are bound to segregate examples of those ideas which Hardy applied, like inspection stickers, to those stages of activity which most appealed to him as life, and then to see what happened to the poetry as a consequence.

What Hardy meant by his submission to Arnold's phrase about poetry's being a criticism of life—and that is what his own phrase amounts to—is neither always clear nor always consistent. But he did use ideas and did apply them, and we may provisionally say what the practice amounted to. Hardy seems to have used the word *idea* to represent a pattern of behavior, judgment, or significance. He wrote as if his ideas had an authority equal to their availability, and as if that authority were both exclusive and sufficient. If you had the pattern everything else followed and followed right. Pattern was the matrix of experience. If you could show experience as pattern, you showed all that could be shown; what would not fit, what could not be made to fit the pattern, did not count. Further, Hardy's idea-patterns were not heuristic, not designed to discover, spread, or multiply significance, but were held rather as rigid frames to limit experience so far as possible and to substitute for what they could not enclose. This is the absolutist, doctrinaire, as we now call it totalitarian, frame of mind: a mind of great but brittle rigidity, tenacious to the point of fanaticism, given when either hungry or endangered to emotion: a mind that seems to require, whether for object or outlet, eventual resort to violence. For only by violence, by violation, can experience be made to furnish it satisfaction.

We are familiar with the consequences of this frame of mind in religion, in politics, and in what passes for philosophy. We should also be familiar with it in the chores of daily life: the life we get over with as so much blind action, but which yet needs its excuse, its quick, quibbled justification. We are not familiar with it in the works of rational imagination—at least not as a dominant value or as a source of strength. When we see it, we see it as weakness, as substitution, precisely as work not done: as, at its best, melodrama, and at its worst, dead convention or the rehearsal of formula; and that is what we see in the great bulk of Hardy's verse. The very frame of mind that provided the pattern of his writing provided also, and at once, the terms of its general failure: leaving success, so far as his conscious devotions went, an accident of escape from the governing frame. Concern is in the end with the success, and will show it no accident; in the meantime with the considerations that make it seem so.

It is worth mentioning that the effect of the great liberating ideas of the nineteenth century upon Hardy's ideas was apparently restrictive and even imprisoning. The inductive ideas—the opening areas of experience—associated with the names of Huxley and Mill and Darwin and Arnold, Maxwell and Kelvin, Acton, Lecky, Bellamy, and Marx; all this affected Hardy if at all mostly as so much dead deductive limitation: a further measure for the cripplement of human sensibility. It is this effect that we have in mind I think when we refer to Hardy's stoicism, his pessimism, or to any of the forms of his addiction to a mechanically deduced fate. His gain from the impact of the new sciences and the new democracy, and from the destruction of dead parts of religion by the Higher Criticism, was all loss in his work: a loss represented by what we feel as the privation of his humanity. To push the emphasis an inch, it sometimes seems that his sensibility had lost, on the expressive level, all discrimination of human value, human dignity, and the inextricability in the trope of human life, of good and evil. It was a terrible privation for his work, and he bore it—that was his stoicism—without ever either the smile or the revulsion of recognition; he bore it, as a practical writer, by making various mechanical substitutions: keeping the violence without the value, the desperation without the dignity, the evil without the good—so far as these operations could be performed without mortality —as the basis of substitution.

It is in these substitutions that we find the obsessive ideas that governed the substance and procedure of the great bulk of the poems. Some of these obsessions—for they lost the pattern-character of ideas and became virtually the objects of sensibility rather than the skeleton of attention— have to do with love, time, memory, death, and nature, and have to do mainly with the disloyalty, implacability, or mechanical fatality of these. Some are embedded in single words and their variations; some in tones of response; some in mere violence of emotion; some in the rudimentary predictive pattern of plot; again many in complications of these. The embedded forms, in turn, largely control by limitation, by asserting themselves as principles of exclusion more than by their force as agents of selection, what is actually noted, observed, represented in the poem in question. Were one master of the counters Hardy uses, one could, so much does the production of his poems follow the rules, once the poem was begun, play the hand out for him to the end. Almost the only objective influence consistently exerted upon his verse is the influence of meter; from which indeed his happiest and some of his most awkward effects come. There remain, of course, besides, neither objective nor otherwise, but pervasive, the fermenting, synergical influence of words thrown together, and the primary influence of the rhythm of his sensibility; that double influence in language used, which a skillful poet knows how to invoke, and which *is* invoked in just the degree that he has the sense of the actuality wanted already within him, when it shows as the very measure of his imagination and the object of his craft, but which, in the poet who, like Hardy, has violated his sensibility with ideas, comes only adventitiously and in flashes, and shows chiefly as the measure of imagination missed.

Neither what is adventitious nor what is missed can be dealt with at length. Our waking concern must be with what is plotted, excreted, left as sediment—with what is used. In running over the thousand odd pages of Hardy's verse, feeling them as mass if not as unity, we wake at once, under the obsessive heads listed above, especially to the obsession of what will here be called crossed fidelities as of the commanding, determining order for the whole mass—though not of the poems we most value. By crossed fidelities I mean the significant subject matter of all those poems dealing with love, young, mature, or married, or with the conventional forms of illicit sexual passion, in which at least one and often all the represented characters commits, has committed, or longs to commit fraud upon the object of fidelity, or else loses the true object by mischance, mistake, or misunderstanding, or else discovers either in the self or the object through mere lapse of time or better acquaintance some privy devastating fault. Surely no serious writer ever heaped together so much *sordid* adultery, so much *haphazard* surrender of human value as

Hardy did in these poems, and with never a pang or incentive but the pang of pattern and the incentive of inadequacy, and yet asked his readers to consider that haphazard sordor a full look at the worst—a tragic view of life —exacted with honesty and power.

How it came about is I suppose simple. Hardy had a genuine insight into the instability of irresponsible passion and the effect upon it of conventional and social authority. *Jude* was his clearest expression of that insight, and *Tess* the deepest, though neither touches for imaginative strength and conviction, for expensiveness of moral texture as opposed to cheapness, *Cousine Bette*, *Madame Bovary*, or *Anna Karenina*. But he had the insight, and saw it strike home; therefore he applied it. Unfortunately, he had to a great degree what can only be characterized as a scandalous sensibility. Seeing or guessing the vast number of disorderly, desperate marriages in the world he knew, he applied his combination of insight and observation almost solely to the scandalous pattern—precisely as Antony and Cleopatra, Solomon and Sheba, are heard of in smoking rooms and country stores, only without the dirt or the relish, just the pattern. The pattern as it is repeated more and more barely becomes at first cynical and then meretricious. Hardy mistook, in short, the imaginative function of insight just as he fell short of the imaginative value of convention. Insight is to heighten the significance *of* something; it reveals the pattern *in* the flesh, the trope or forward stress of life. Convention is to determine how the value of that forward stress, so embedded, so empatterned, is received. In works of imagination they make a dichotomy where if either branch is dead the vitality of the tree is impaired. You cannot express, you cannot dramatize human life unless your insight and your convention—your simplifications of substance—are somehow made to seem the very form of that life. Your handy formula will not do, unless you every time, by the persuasive force of your drama, carry it back to the actual instance of which, in your case of instruments, it is the cheap abstraction. That, again, is the skill of the artist; that he knows how to invest any formula, however barrenly presented—like that of *Lear*, say—with enough of the riches of direct sensibility to make it actual and complete for sense and interest; when insight and convention and formula become, as they properly ought to be, all afterthought.

Here is a handy juncture to introduce an image from the early Hardy, before he undertook to substitute his own formulas for those traditionally available, and leant naturally upon the strength of his predecessors to buttress his effects. One of the earliest dated poems is the series of four Shakespearean sonnets called "She to Him." They are facile in mood and mode: it is the jilted lover addressing the beloved after the fashion of Shakespeare or Sidney or Drayton in easy iambics stretched out for meter and rhyme and composed largely on the *when* and *then* scheme. We have the Sportsman Time, Life's sunless hill and fitful masquerade, and we have a good deal of desolated martyrdom supporting a deathless love—all properties so dear because so adequately ominous to the young sensibility, and all used well enough to make, for the reader, a good journeyman's exercise, and show, in the poet, positive promise. What we see in these sonnets is, with one exception, the traditional body of poetry absorbing, holding, expressing the individual apprentice until, if he does, he finds the skill and the scope to add to that body. The exception leaps out: one of the best tropes Hardy ever produced and perhaps the only one of similar excellence in its kind.

> Amid the happy people of my time
> Who work their love's fulfilment, I appear
> Numb as a vane that cankers on its point,
> True to the wind that kissed ere canker came: . . .

Grant its point, which is universally easy, and the metaphor is inexhaustible: it stretches, living, in every direction through its theme. The lines are well enough known and have been quoted before, for example in Symons' early essay on Hardy's verse, and too much ought not to be made of them here, yet they are so startling in Hardy's general context that it seems plausible to look for some other explanation of their appearance than the accidental.

The theory of accidents in poetry like that of idiopathy in medicine is only a cloak for inadequate observation and explains nothing. Language in the form of poetry is as objective as a lesion of the meninges; only we get at the objectivity by different jumps of the inspecting imagination. The appearance of Hardy's trope, if it was not accidental, was, let us say, due to the fertility of the form which he was practicing; the form dragged it out of him. Not the metrical form alone, not any aspect of it separately, but the whole form of the Elizabethan sonnet taken as a mode of feeling and the composition of feeling—that was the enacting agent. The generalized trope of the mind was matrix for the specific trope of sensibility. Precisely as we are able, as readers, to respond to the form—the energizing pattern of music and meaning—of this special type of sonnet as something felt, so Hardy in this figure was able to work from his own feelings into the form *as a poet:* he made something, however fragmentarily, *of* the form. The test of manufacture is that both speed and meaning are absolute, at once in terms of themselves and in terms of the form they exemplify. The tautology between form and significance is absolute within the limits of language and inexhaustible within the limits of apprehension. It might be put that Hardy was here almost only the transmitting agent of an imaginative event that occurred objectively in the words and the pattern of the words; when the true or ultimate agency might be thought of as lying in the invoked reality of the whole form. It is the tradition not only at work, but met, and used. Doubtless Hardy had read a good deal of Elizabethan and Jacobean poetry, and got from his reading the themes as well as the means of his early poems; certainly in this poem, for two lines, he got the full authority of the form at once as a cumulus and as a fresh instance. Authority, then, is the word of explanation that we wanted, and we may take it in two senses: as the principle of derived right and as the very quality of authorship which has as its perfection the peculiar objective virtue of anonymity. That is one's gain from tradition: anonymous authority. We shall come at it later in these notes otherwise and expensively derived.

Meanwhile it is a good deal of weight to heap on two lines; the pity is that it cannot be generally heaped over the whole body of Hardy's verse. That is the privative fact about most of Hardy's verse: he dispensed with tradition in most of his ambitious verse; it is willful where it should be authoritative, idiosyncratic where it should be anonymous; it is damaged—Mr. Eliot would say it is damned— by the vanity of Hardy's adherence to his personal and crotchety obsessions. It is so by choice, but not exactly by discrimination; rather choice by a series of those chances to whose operation in the moral field Hardy was so warmly addicted. (We might risk it parenthetically that Hardy was incapable of the act of choice precisely as he was incapable of discerning the ideal which would have made choice necessary.) Hardy never rejected the tradition of English poetry; probably, indeed, if he thought about it at all, he thought he followed it and even improved it by his metrical experiments. What he did was more negative than rejection. He failed to recognize and failed to absorb those modes of representing felt reality persuasively and credibly and justly, which make up, far more than meters and rhymes and the general stock of versification, the creative habit of imagination, and which are the indefeasible substance of tradition. Put another way, it is the presence of that achieved tradition which makes great poems resemble each other as much as they differ and even "sound" so much alike; and to its absence is due both the relative unreality and incompatibility of minor poetry—especially in its failures. But, to return to Hardy in relation to the major modes of tradition, no poet can compose the whole of his poetry himself, and if he does not go for help to poetic authority he will go elsewhere, substituting the extra-poetic for the poetic as much as may be necessary all along the line just to get the poem on paper. Hardy's elsewhere was not far off: it was in his own head: in his own ideas taken as absolute and conceived as persuasive by mere statement.

The result was that he was relieved of the responsibilities of craft; and the worse result for the reader is that, lacking the persuasiveness of craft—lacking objective authority—the validity of the poems comes to depend on the validity of the ideas in that vacuum which is the medium of simple assertion. What we have is the substitution of the authoritarian for the authoritative, of violence for emotion, frenzy for passion, calamity by chance for tragedy by fate.

Hardy, of course, could not have accepted any such description of his intellectual behavior toward his verse. What he thought he did was, to repeat, to apply his ideas pretty directly to life; and it probably never occurred to him that his practice involved any substitution—or thereby any weakening, any diminution of either life or idea—of intellectual or emotional predilection for actual representation. Judging by his practice he did not know what substitution was, and evidently felt that he quickened the life and heightened the reality of his poems by making their action —what they were meant to show—so often hinge upon an unrepresented, a merely stated idea. In short, and this is what we have been leading up to, what Hardy really lacked was the craft of his profession—technique in the wide sense; that craft, which, as a constant, reliable possession, would have taught him the radical necessity as it furnished the means, of endowing every crucial statement with the virtual force of representation. The availing fount of that enabling craft springs from the whole tradition of poetry. Just as we say that his mastery of the particular, limited tradition of seventeenth-century metaphysical poetry enabled Henry King to compose his "Exequy," so we may say that every poet writes his poetry only as his poetry embodies what is necessary of the whole tradition. The same is true of reading poetry, but on a lesser level; where we often call the mastery of tradition the cultivation of taste, and ought sometimes to call it just getting used to what a poem or body of poetry is about. In Hardy's case, the interesting fact is that he sometimes possessed the tradition and sometimes did not; and the fertile possibility is that possession or lack may explain what otherwise seems the accident of success or failure.

To his ideas as such, then, there is no primary objection. The objection is to his failure to absorb them by craft into the representative effect of his verse. Indeed, from a literary point of view, all that is objectionable in Hardy's ideas would have been overcome, had they been absorbed; for they would have struck the reader as consequences instead of instigators of significance. It is the certification of craft, that what it handles it makes actual: objective, authoritative, anonymous. The final value of a poet's version of the actual is another matter, which literary criticism may take up but with which it ought not to be preoccupied. The standards engaged in the discernment of value cannot be exclusively literary standards. Here, at least for the moment, let us stick to those values which can be exemplified in terms of craft.

Some of Hardy's best effects—which should be kept in mind while looking at his worst—come when his triple obsession with death, memory, and time makes by mutual absorption something of a trinity. It is an absorption which excludes both that "full look at the worst" which he wanted his poems to exact, and also the mechanical crux of what we have called crossed fidelities. Then the business of the poet proceeded free of the violation of ideas, and the ideas became themselves something seen or felt. Here is the nubbin of what is meant, from the poem "One We Knew."

She said she had often heard the gibbet creaking
    As it swayed in the lightning flash,
Had caught from the neighbouring town a small child's
    shrieking
    At the cart-tail under the lash. . .

With cap-framed face and long gaze into the embers—
    We seated around her knees—
She would dwell on such dead themes, not as one who
    remembers,
    But rather as one who sees.

There is a dignity of tone, and a sense of release in the

language, in the poems of this order, which give them a stature elsewhere beaten down: the stature of true or fundamental poetic piety. Since the effect is produced as the series of details, it needs to be shown in the full length of such a poem as "She Hears the Storm."

> There was a time in former years—
>   While my roof-tree was his—
> When I should have been distressed by fears
>   At such a night as this!
>
> I should have murmured anxiously,
>   "The pricking rain strikes cold;
> His road is bare of hedge or tree,
>   And he is getting old."
>
> But now the fitful chimney-roar,
>   The drone of Thorncombe trees,
> The Froom in flood upon the moor,
>   The mud of Mellstock Leaze,
>
> The candle slanting sooty wick'd,
>   The thuds upon the thatch,
> The eaves-drops on the window flicked,
>   The clacking garden-hatch,
>
> And what they mean to wayfarers,
>   I scarcely heed or mind;
> He has won that storm-tight roof of hers
>   Which Earth grants all her kind.

The true piety here exemplified consists in the celebration of the feeling of things for their own sake and not for the sake of the act of feeling; and the celebration becomes poetic when the things are so put together as to declare their own significance, when they can be taken to mean just what they are—when the form, the meter, the various devices of poetry merely provide the motion of the meaning. In this poem and in others of its class, Hardy obtains objective and self-sufficient strength precisely by *reducing* his private operative means to a minimum, by getting rid of or ignoring most of the machinery he ordinarily used altogether. Instead of applying ideas to life—instead of turning the screws to exact meaning—he merely took what he found and let the words it came in, put it together. Doubtless, if asked, he would have said that the poem came on inspiration, and would have valued it less highly as craft for that reason. He evidently preferred to assault his material with an emotion, preferably violent, and an idea, preferably distraught, in either hand. At any rate, something such was his regular practice, so long continued—over sixty years—that it seems certain he could never have noticed that his poems produced more emotion and even developed more nearly into ideas, when he came to them, as it were, quite disarmed.

This is no argument for what is called inspired writing, as inspiration is commonly understood. It would be a better account of the matter to say that there was more work, far more attention to the complex task of uniting diverse and disparate detail, in the preparation of "She Hears the Storm," or in a single line like "My clothing clams me, mire-bestarred," than in a whole handful of those poems deliberately critical of life. It is simply that Hardy was unaware of the nature of poetic work, or of how much he did in spite of himself, or of how vastly much more was done for him in those remote, impressionable, germinal areas of the sensibility—that work which transpires, almost without invocation and often beyond control, to show as both fresh and permanent in what we choose to call *our* works of imagination. The final skill of a poet lies in his so conducting the work he does deliberately do, that the other work—the hidden work, the inspiration, the genius—becomes increasingly available not only in new poems but in old poems re-read.

The only consistent exhibition of such skill in the last century is in the second half of the career of W. B. Yeats. In prose there are others—Mann, James, Gide, possibly Proust, and perhaps Joyce. But these are not our concern and we need not think of them except to buttress the force with which we come back to the example of Yeats as it sits beside the example of Hardy. Yeats was addicted to magic, to a private symbolism, in much the same way, and for similar reasons, that Hardy was addicted to his set of ideas. Each had been deprived by his education, or the lack of it, of an authoritative faith, and each hastened to set up a scaffold out of the nearest congenial materials strong enough and rigid enough to support the structure imagination meant to rear. It was, and remains, a desperate occupation for each; for the risk was that the scaffold might become so much more important than the poetry as to replace it, and the mere preliminary labor come to be the sum of the work done. Such is indeed the condition of most ambitious poetry seriously regarded, and not only in our own day with its invitation to privation but even in the ages of faith. The poetic imagination is seldom able either to overcome or to absorb the devices by which alone it undertakes its greater reaches. Shakespeare is perhaps the only poet in English whose work habitually overcame its conscious means; which is why we say it is so good a mirror looked at generally, and why, looked at specifically, we say it is all in the words. None of it, where it is good, transcends anything or is about anything: it is itself, its own intention as well as its own meaning. Hence the evident fact that it cannot be imitated except ruinously. You can use Shakespeare but you cannot imitate him; for the imitable elements in his work are either vestigial or unimportant. Yeats's poetry rarely overcame its means, but it usually absorbed them in his best work so that they became part of its effect. The devices of his private symbolism can be discriminated but they cannot be disengaged from the poems where he used them; the devices, that is, are partly what the poems are about, and to the degree that they are discriminated, whether for or against, they limit the vitality—the meaning—of the poems in which they occur. You need to know beforehand what Yeats meant to do, and that knowledge delimits the poem and makes it precarious. It is the key that may be lost. With the key, the poetry of Yeats may be both used and imitated; for the discriminated symbolism, once made objective in Yeats's poems, can be put to similar use elsewhere. Hardy's poetry, relatively, almost never either overcame or absorbed its means. On the contrary, the more ambitious the poem, the more the means tend to appear as the complete substitute for the poem; so that what should have been produced by the progression of the poem never appears except in the form—or formula—of intention. Thus Hardy's ambitious poetry may be imitated, and often is, but cannot be used, which is why the imitations are bad. For in the class of poems we speak of, the imitable elements—all that goes by rote, by declaration, by formula, all that can be re-duplicated—constitute almost all that is actually in the words. The rest—what Hardy wanted to write about—is only imputedly present and never transpires except as the sympathetic reader, entertaining similar intentions and inviting identic emotions, finds himself accepting the imputed as actual. It may be observed that such readers are common and inhabit all of us to the great detriment of our taste but to the great benefit, too, of our general sensibility; which brings us to the problem of approach central to all our reading, not only the reading of poets like Hardy where it is necessary to show great good will, but also poets like Yeats where it is less necessary, and poets like the best of Shakespeare where it may impede reading in the proper sense.

If we were not initially ready to accept an author's formula we could never discover what he had done with or in spite of it. There is the benefit. The evil lies in that sloth of mind which finds acceptable only those formulas which are familiar, or violent, and which insists on recognizing just what was expected—or "desired"—and nothing else. In this confusion of good and evil—of good will and sloth—lies one aspect of the problem of approach. As Hardy himself did not know, neither does the reader know how far in a given poem sloth or good will is responsible for the initial effect. We look at a poem that has all the airs and makes all the noises of setting considerable matters in motion. Does it so? or is it merely about the business of searching for a subject to use the airs and noises on? If the latter, does it after all succeed, by divine accident, in catching the subject by the throat or tail? or is it windmill fighting—a whirling, a whirring, and all gone? Certainly the fine lines and passages that vein bad poetry are come at—written and read—somewhat that way; and we need not value them less for that—though we need not thereby value more the slag in which they occur. The economical writ does not run in our experience of poetry, as any library or the best anthology will show. We put up with what we get, no matter what the expense and wastage, in order to use what little we can discover.

Discovery is judgment, and the best judgment is bound to falter, either allowing the poem too little through a deficiency of good will, or accepting as performance what was only expected through undiscriminated sloth, or on both sides at once by overlooking the poem's stretches of plain good writing—writing in the language that, as Marianne Moore says, "cats and dogs can read." Take Hardy at his face value and you may falter in the first or second fashion, depending on whether his machinery repels or fascinates you. Take him seriously, and you are liable to the third error; he gets in his own way so much of the time, you do not notice when his poems go straight, or if you do you think the instances not his but anonymous and ignore them when for that very reason you ought to value them most. Anonymity is the sign of the objective achieved at the blessed expense of the personal, whether in the poet or the reader, and is just what to look for when the bother is done. It is only in its imperfections, which distract us as revery or literary criticism, that good poetry fails to reach the condition of anonymity. Only then can there be anything like unanimity between the poem and its readers. For it is a curious thing that when the author pokes his head in so does the reader, and straightway there is no room for the poem. It is either cramped or excluded.

Fortunately for purposes of elucidation, Hardy gives us many versions of his favorite themes. Most of them appear on aesthetically impoverished levels, but occasionally there is a version, enriched both aesthetically and morally, that reaches into the anonymous and objective level. Let us take, for example, a group of poems occurring in *Satires of Cir-*

*cumstance,* all coming pretty much together in the book, and all on Hardy's principal obsessed theme of crossed fidelities. If we select the appropriate facts to emphasize about them, we should have some sort of standard, a canon of inclusion as well as exclusion, to apply roughly throughout the mass of Hardy's work. The poems chosen are called "The Telegram," "The Moth-Signal," "Seen by the Waits," "In the Days of Crinoline," and "The Workbox."

All these deal one way or another with conflicting loyalties—crossed fidelities—in the double field, as Hardy commonly takes it to be, of love and marriage. The skeleton in the closet of marriage is love, and is often articulated in the light of the honeymoon. Thus in "The Telegram" the bride either deliberately or distractedly declares to the groom that her true love is not for him but for someone else who, she has just learned by telegram, lies ill and perhaps dying. The bride, stung by the roused apprehension of death, shows her falsity by proving an anterior allegiance to which, in turn, by the fact of marriage, she had already been false. To any wakened sensibility the situation cries out for treatment, promising from the riches of feeling involved, a tragic perspective brought to the focus of emotion. I will not say Hardy preferred, but at any rate he used the violence of ill-chosen circumstance as the sole agent of discovery and engine of emotion. The fatalized, which is to say mechanized, coincidence of the telegram and the honeymoon, seizes on precisely its capacity for riches and no more. It is one of those instances where everything depends on the joint operation of the reader's good will and sloth. If he accepts beforehand the first five stanzas of the poem as somehow both equivalent to Hardy's intention and a furnishing forth of his (the reader's) general store of emotion, then the sixth stanza—what Hardy *made* of the poem—will seem a sufficient delivery of riches. It is the groom who speaks:

What now I see before me is a long lane overhung
With lovelessness, and stretching from the present to the
      grave.

And I would I were away from this, with friends I knew
  when young,
    Ere a woman held me slave.

On the other hand, if he persuades his taste to operate—if
he is interested in the creation or sedimentation of poetic
emotion rather than the venting of his own—he will reject
not Hardy's formula but what Hardy did with it, or more
exactly he will reject what the formula did to the possibility
of a poem. It let the poem down, up to the last stanza—let
it down in all but a line or so to about as low a level of
writing as a poem can touch and survive at all. The two
passably good lines, it may be observed, have no intimate
connection with the movement of the poem but merely
serve to give a setting: representing a kind of objective circumstance as compared to the chosen circumstance of the
telegram.

—The yachts ride mute at anchor and the fulling moon is
  fair,
And the giddy folk are strutting up and down the smooth
  parade, . . .

In short, it would seem that where Hardy felt his formula
at work he apparently felt no need to employ more than the
most conventional stock phraseology. Yet where the formula
did not apply he was quick to write as a poet should.
Coming now to the last stanza, quoted above, we see that
it cheats the sensibility that it ought to have enriched. It
is neither guaranteed by what went before, nor does it itself, working backward, pull the poem together. It is something added, not something made; something plainly a substitute for what, whatever it was, ought to have been there.
There is no quarrel with the generalness of its statement;
its rhythm is strong and invigorates the worn imagery; but
it plainly misses with its lame last line any adequate relation to the emotion the poem was meant to construct. Because it would serve as well as an appendage to some other
poem as it serves for this, it fails here. Without any intention
of rewriting Hardy's intended poem, but just to tinker with
the poem as it is, let us try altering the last line to read:

"Ere a man had made me slave"; which would give the words to the bride instead of the groom, and makes poetic sense if not a good verse. Better still would be the deletion of the last line and the substitution of plural for singular personal pronouns in the remaining three lines of the stanza. Either of these stanzas would compel the final stanza both to work back into and draw sustenance from the rest of the poem. Neither change, nor any similar change, could redeem the plain bad writing, but at least all six stanzas would then make an effect of unity for the written aspect of the poem. The unwritten poem—the undeclared possibility—must be left to those with so much superfluous sloth of good will as to *prefer* their poems unwritten.

"The Moth-Signal," the next poem on our list, shows in its first half the immediate advantage of being relatively well-written as verse, and therefore, just in that well-writtenness, shows the parts of the poem yoked together in a proper poetic conspiracy up to the very end. Here a husband reads, a moth burns in the candle flame, a wife waits and watches. After a light word or two, the wife goes out to look at the moon while the husband goes on with his reading "In the annals of ages gone,"—a phrase which prepares for what follows objectively, as the *idea* of the burned moth (not the image, which is imperfect) prepares for what follows symbolically and dramatically. At that point, as the quality of the thought begins to strain a little, the quality of the writing begins to slip.

> Outside the house a figure
>     Came from the tumulus near,
> And speedily waxed bigger,
>     And clasped and called her Dear.
>
> "I saw the pale-winged token
>     You sent through the crack," sighed she.
> "That moth is burnt and broken
>     With which you lured out me.
>
> "And were I as the moth is
>     It might be better far
> For one whose marriage troth is
>     Shattered as potsherds are!"

The metaphor, with straining, becomes inexact with relation to the emotion; both fall mutually out of focus, as that point of strain where inner tension snaps is reached; and the poem ends, like "The Telegram," inadequately to its promise—which is to say awkwardly.

> Then grinned the Ancient Briton
> From the tumulus treed with pine:
> "So, hearts are thwartly smitten
> In these days as in mine!"

It is a question, perhaps, whether "The Moth-Signal" is one of those poems that "exact a full look at the worst" or rather instances one of those humorous poems which Hardy said he put in to lighten the burden of that look. There is a tradition, however poor in itself yet honored because ancient, that allows the humorous poet to overlook what would have otherwise been the exigencies of his craft; so that if this is a humorous poem, then it is plain why the rhyme-sounds were allowed to knock both sense and motion out of kilter in the second half of the poem. Perhaps the second half decided to be humorous. Perhaps only the last stanza. If the poem is not to be taken as humorous but as serious with a quality of levity—or low-level poetic wit—meant to tie it together in the reader's response, then one or two suggestions may be made about the order in which the units of perception are arranged. The grinning Briton ought not to be where he is; if anywhere, he should appear after the first stanza quoted above. The reader may try the transposition and see. But then the poem would lack an ending, a rounding off? Not at all, the ending already exists, occupying a place where it does no good but merely kills time while the wife leaves the house. It is the stanza preceding the stanzas quoted above. If it is shifted to its natural terminal position, the poem will come to a proper end with the transposed Briton even deeper in mind. In its present situation the first line of the stanza reads, "She rose," that is, to go out. Now we want her back among her potsherds, so we will put it merely:

[When she returned, unheeding]
Her life-mate then went on
With his mute and museful reading
In the annals of ages gone.

The point is not that these tinkerings and transpositions actually improve the poems—they may, or may not—but that the poems so lack compositional strength, which is what is meant by inevitability, that they lay themselves open to the temptation of re-composition.

The next poem, "Seen by the Waits," carries the moral progress of this order of Hardy's poetry one step further backward—into the arms of deliberate, unvarnished anecdote. A wait, it should be said, is a band of musicians and singers who play and sing carols by night at Christmas and the New Year in the expectation of gratuities. There are many waits in Hardy's poems, put there partly because he loved them and their old music, and partly because they made excellent agents of observation and even better foils to what they observed. The observation was the gratuity. In this poem the waits play by moonlight outside the manorlady's window, and looking up see her image in a mirror dancing "thin-draped in her robe of night," making "a strange phantasmal sight." The poem ends:

She had learnt (we heard when homing)
That her roving spouse was dead:
Why she had danced in the gloaming
We thought, but never said.

Here again the sloth of good will can accept the manufactured observation as genuine if it likes. There is indeed a kind of competence about the poem, as about so many of Hardy's poems based upon his obsessive formulas, that strikes as more astonishing the more you realize what it misses or overlooks: the competence, precisely, of the lyric exercise joined *mechanically* to a predetermined idea, without that attention to language—the working of words among themselves—that makes competence mastery and the mechanical juncture organic. It is not a quibble but a conviction that you cannot, without sublime inspiration, make out of bad writing—"glancing to where a mirror leaned . . . robe of night" or, in the context, the word "gloaming"—out of such verbal detritus you cannot make a good poem.

"In the Days of Crinoline" is another case in point, but from a slightly different angle. If "Seen by the Waits" remains an unactualized anecdote because carelessly written, "In the Days of Crinoline" remains at its low poetic level because no amount of competence could have raised the conception as taken, the *donnée* from which it springs, to a higher level. It remains versification because there was nothing in it to make poetry of. The *donnée* is on the plain scandal level—almost the limerick level—of the cuckolded vicar, and should have appeared in a bawdier *Punch* or a less sophisticated *New Yorker*, where the pat competence of its rhyme scheme and final smacking gag might shine like mastery. Substance and form are for once indistinguishable (though *not* inextricable) because both are trick, and no more. The vicar complacently lets his wife go off to her lover because she wears a plain tilt-bonnet. Once out of sight she draws an ostrich-feathered hat from under her skirts where she then pins her dowdy hood, reversing the operation when she returns home.

> "To-day," he said, "you have shown good sense,
> A dress so modest and so meek
> Should always deck your goings hence
> Alone." And as a recompense
> He kissed her on the cheek.

What we have been showing is, to repeat, a variety of the ills brought upon Hardy's verse by the substitution of formula for form and of preconceived or ready-made emotion for builded emotion—emotion made out of the materials of the poem. The track through this exhibition has been downward, but it has nevertheless been leading up to the sight of a poem in which the formula is no longer a formula but a genuine habit of seeing, and in which the emotion, however ready-made it may have been for Hardy, yet appears to come out of and crown the poem. The formula discovers the form; the obsession makes the emotion; which

are the preliminary conditions to good poetry where they
affect the matter at all. For the whole emphasis of practical
argument is this: that it is not formula or obsessed emotion
that works evil but the fact of stopping short at them, so
that they substitute for what they actually spring from.
But here is the poem, called "The Workbox," which it would
be unfair not to quote complete.

> "See, here's the workbox, little wife,
>   That I made of polished oak."
> He was a joiner, of village life;
>   She came of borough folk.
>
> He holds the present up to her
>   As with a smile she nears
> And answers to the profferer,
>   " 'Twill last all my sewing years!"
>
> "I warrant it will. And longer too.
>   'Tis a scantling that I got
> Off poor John Wayward's coffin, who
>   Died of they knew not what.
>
> "The shingled pattern that seems to cease
>   Against your box's rim
> Continues right on in the piece
>   That's underground with him.
>
> "And while I worked it made me think
>   Of timber's varied doom;
> One inch where people eat and drink,
>   The next inch in a tomb.
>
> "But why do you look so white, my dear,
>   And turn aside your face?
> You knew not that good lad, I fear,
>   Though he came from your native place?"
>
> "How could I know that good young man,
>   Though he came from my native town,
> When he must have left far earlier than
>   I was a woman grown?"
>
> "Ah, no. I should have understood!
>   It shocked you that I gave

> To you one end of a piece of wood
>   Whose other is in a grave?"
>
> "Don't, dear, despise my intellect,
>   Mere accidental things
> Of that sort never have effect
>   On my imaginings."
>
> Yet still her lips were limp and wan,
>   Her face still held aside,
> As if she had known not only John,
>   But known of what he died.

This is about the maximum value Hardy ever got by the application of this idea—this formula and this obsession—to life; and it amounts, really, in the strictest possible sense of a loose phrase, to a reversal of Hardy's conscious intent: here we have the application to the idea of as much life as could be brought to bear. To define the value is difficult. Like many aspects of poetry it can best be noted by stating a series of negative facts. The poem has no sore thumbs; since its emotion is self-created it maintains an even tone and speed. It is without violence of act and assertion; the details presented are deep and tentacular enough in their roots to supply strength without strain. The coincidence upon which the release of emotion depends seems neither incredible nor willful; because it is prepared for, it is part of the texture of the feelings in the poem, and therefore seems natural or probable. There are no forced rhymes, no wrenchings of sense or meter; there was enough initial provision of material, and enough possible material thereby opened up, to compel—or tempt—the poet to use the full relevant resources of his craft. Put positively, the formula fitted the job of work, and in the process of getting the job done was incorporated in the poem. It is still there; it still counts, and shapes, and limits; but it is not a substitute for any wanted value: it is just the idiosyncrasy of the finished product—the expression on the face—in much the same sense that the character of a wooden box is determined by the carpenter's tools as much as by his skill.

All this is to beg the pressing but craven question of

stature, which requires dogmas that are not literary dogmas to answer, and is therefore not primarily within the province of these notes. In a secondary sense it is not hard to see—one cannot help feeling—that even at its maximum executed value, this formula of production limits the engaged sensibility more than the consequent release is worth; which may be a matter of accident not of principle; for other formulas, when they become habits of seeing and feeling, expand the sensibility in the very terms of the control that the formulas exert. The general formula of ballad-tragedy, for example, as in "The Sacrilege," allows and *demands* a greater scope in music and therefore, possibly, makes a wider range of material available for treatment. Certainly "The Sacrilege," "The Trampwoman's Tragedy" and "A Sunday Morning Tragedy" are poems of wider scope and excite deeper responses than even the best of the crossed-fidelity lyrics, despite the fact that they rest upon substantially similar ideas. The double agency—musical and compositional—of the refrain is perhaps responsible; for the refrain—any agency at once iterative and variable about a pattern of sound—is a wonderful device for stretching and intensifying the process of sensibility. Yeats and Hardy are the great modern masters of refrain; Hardy using it to keep the substance of his ballads—what they were actually about —continuously present, Yeats using it to develop and modify the substance otherwise made present. Returning to the crossed-fidelity formula, it is the difference between the concrete poetic formula—so concrete and so poetic that, like rhyme, it is almost part of the language, an objective habit of words in association—and the abstract intellectual formula, which is a reduction, a kind of statistical index, of the concrete and poetic, and which requires, for success, re-expansion in every instance. Hardy, lacking direct access to all that is meant by the tradition of craft, condemned himself, in a great part of his serious poetry—in over two hundred poems—to the labor of remaking the abstract as concrete, the intellectual as actual. That he had a naturally primitive intelligence, schematized beyond discrimination, only made the labor more difficult. Success—I do not mean greatness but just the possible limited achievement—came about once in ten times. About twenty of these lyrics reach more or less the level of "The Workbox"; none of them reach the level achieved in certain poems which escape the formula altogether. Yet they make—not the twenty but the whole lump of two hundred—the caricature by which Hardy's shorter verse is known; which is why so much space has been here devoted to them. Caricature is the very art of formula.

The true character beneath the caricature and which made the caricature possible—the whole fate of Hardy's sensibility—appears not in these poems where he deliberately undertook the profession of poet, but rather either in those poems where he was overweeningly compelled to react to personal experience or in those poems where he wrote to celebrate an occasion. In neither case was there room for the intervention of formula. It is a satire of circumstance indeed, that for Hardy the wholly personal and the wholly objective could alone command his greatest powers; and it is in this sense that Eliot's remark that Hardy sometimes reached the sublime without ever having passed through the stage of good writing, is most accurate. The clear examples are such poems as those about the loss of the *Titanic*, with its extraordinary coiling imagery of the projected actual, by which the capacity for experience is stretched by the creation of experience; such poems as those on Leslie Stephen and Swinburne, each ending with a magnificently appropriate image, Stephen being joined to the Schreckhorn which he had scaled, and Swinburne joined with the waves—

> Him once their peer in sad improvisations,
> And deft as wind to cleave their frothy manes—

and again such poems as "Channel Firing" and "In Time of 'The Breaking of Nations,'" which need no comment; and finally in such poems as "An Ancient to Ancients" with its dignity and elegance making the strength of old age. But these poems are or ought to be too generally received to permit their being looked at as anything except isolated, like something in the Oxford Book of English Verse. Keeping their special merit in mind as a clue to what we do want, let us look at certain other poems, not yet isolated by familiarity, and perhaps not deserving to be because not as broadly useful, which achieve objectivity on the base of a deep personal reaction. If they can be made to show as part, and the essential, idiosyncratic part, of what Hardy's poetry has to give as value, then we can stop and have done, knowing what to exclude and what to keep close.

The poems chosen have all to do with death, and the first, "Last Words to a Dumb Friend," was occasioned by the death of a white cat and is one of two poems which may, or may not, refer to the same pet animal. The other poem, "The Roman Gravemounds," derives its effect from the collocation of Caesar's buried warriors and the cat about to be buried. Hardy had a perennial interest in Roman relics and used them frequently as furniture for his poems when some symbol of age, time passing, past, or come again, was wanted; and if in "The Roman Gravemounds" he had a definite design it was surely at once to heighten and to stabilize the man's sense of loss.

> "Here say you that Caesar's warriors lie?—
> But my little white cat was my only friend!
> Could she but live, might the record die
> Of Caesar, his legions, his aims, his end!"

But Hardy, oddly enough for him, apparently thought the effect strained or sentimental; for he adds, in the voice of the hypothetical observer of the burial, a superficial, common-sense moral which quite reduces and unclinches the dramatic value of the poem.

> Well, Rome's long rule here is oft and again
> A theme for the sages of history,
> And the small furred life was worth no one's pen;
> Yet its mourner's mood has a charm for me.

Granted the method—the hypothetical observer, the interposition of the stock intellectual consideration, and the consequent general indirectness of presentation—that was about all Hardy could do with the subject. By making it "objective" in the easy sense he made almost nothing of it; which is another way of putting our whole argument about the effect of formula in the crossed-fidelity lyrics.

The true charm of the mourner's mood, only imputed in "The Roman Gravemounds," is made actual in "Last Words to a Dumb Friend" through a quite different set of approaches, all direct, all personal, amounting to the creation or release of objective experience. Let us observe the stages of approach, not to explain the process but to expand our sense of participation in it. First there is the selectively detailed materialization of what it was that died: purrer of the spotless hue with the plumy tail, that would stand, arched, to meet the stroking hand. After the tenderness of immediate memory comes the first reaction: never to risk it again.

> Better bid his memory fade,
> Better blot each mark he made,
> Selfishly escape distress
> By contrived forgetfulness,
> Than preserve his prints to make
> Every morn and eve an ache.

Then come eight lines which envisage what must be done, and the impossibility of doing it, to blot the memory out. All this Hardy supplied, as it were, by a series of directly felt observations; and these, in their turn, released one of those deeply honest, creative visions of man in relation to death which summoned the full imagination in Hardy as nothing else could.

> Strange it is this speechless thing, . . .
> Should—by crossing at a breath
> Into safe and shielded death,
> By the merely taking hence
> Of his insignificance—
> Loom as largened to the sense,
> Shape as part, above man's will,
> Of the Imperturbable.

> As a prisoner, flight debarred,
> Exercising in a yard,

> Still retain I, troubled, shaken,
> Mean estate, by him forsaken;
> And this home, which scarcely took
> Impress from his little look,
> By his faring to the Dim
> Grows all eloquent of him.
>
> Housemate, I can think you still
> Bounding to the window-sill,
> Over which I vaguely see
> Your small mound beneath the tree,
> Showing in the autumn shade
> That you moulder where you played.

Andrew Marvell hardly did better; and the end rises like the whole of Yeats's "A Deep-sworn Vow." You can say, if you like, that all Hardy had to do was to put it down, which explains nothing and begs the question of poetic process which we want to get at. What should be emphasized is, that in putting it down, Hardy used no violence of intellect or predilection; the violence is inside, working out, like the violence of life or light. The burden of specific feeling in the first part of the poem set enough energy up to translate the thought in the second half to the condition of feeling; and the product of the two is the poetic emotion which we feel most strongly as the rhythm, not the pattern-rhythm of the lines, but the invoked rhythm, beating mutually in thought and feeling and syllable, of the whole poem.

Rhythm, in that sense, is the great enacting agent of actuality in poetry, and appears seldom, without regard to good will or application, and is fully operative only when certain other elements are present in combination, but by no means always materializes even then. Perhaps, for the poet, it is what comes when, in Eliot's language, he sees beneath both beauty and ugliness, "the boredom, the horror, and the glory"; what Eliot had in mind, too, when he said that he who has once been visited by the Muses is ever afterwards haunted. However that may be, it involves the power of words to preserve—to create—a relation to experience, passionate quite beyond violence, intense beyond any tension. Hardy's poetry engaged that power now and again, but most purely when responding directly and personally to death or the dead. "Last Words to a Dumb Friend" is only a single example, chosen for the unfamiliar dignity Hardy brought to the subject. The twenty-one poems, written after the death of his first wife, which appear under the motto: *Veteris vestigia flammae,* give, as a unit, Hardy's most sustained invocation of that rhythm, so strong that all that was personal—the private drive, the private grief—is cut away and the impersonal is left bare, an old monument, mutilated or weathered as you like to call it, of that face which the personal only hides. Here, for example, is one of the shorter, called "The Walk."

> You did not walk with me
> Of late to the hill-top tree
>   By the gated ways,
>   As in earlier days;
>   You were weak and lame,
>   So you never came,
> And I went alone, and I did not mind,
> Not thinking of you as left behind.
>
> I walked up there to-day
> Just in the former way;
>   Surveyed around
>   The familiar ground
>   By myself again:
>   What difference, then?
> Only that underlying sense
> Of the look of a room on returning thence.

Like the others in the series, it is a poem almost without style; it is style reduced to anonymity, reduced to riches: in the context of the other twenty, precisely the riches of rhythm.

As Theodore Spencer has remarked (in conversation, but no less cogently for that) Hardy's personal rhythm is the central problem in his poetry. Once it has been struck out in the open, it is felt as ever present, not alone in his thirty or forty finest poems but almost everywhere in his work, felt as disturbance, a pinioning, or a liberation; sometimes present as something just beyond vision, sometimes immanent, sometimes here; sometimes beaten down, mutilated, obliterated by ideas, formulas, obsessions, but occasionally lifting, delivering into actuality, the marks of life lived. If these notes have served any useful purpose it is double: that by naming and examining the obstacles set up by a lifetime of devoted bad or inadequate practice, we are better able both to value what we exclude and to acknowledge—which is harder than to value—the extraordinary poetry which was produced despite and aside from the practice. Hardy is the great example of a sensibility violated by ideas; and perhaps the unique example, since Swift, of a sensibility great enough—locked enough in life—to survive the violation.

1940

## 2. The Later Poetry of W. B. Yeats

The later poetry of William Butler Yeats is certainly great enough in its kind, and varied enough within its kind, to warrant a special approach, deliberately not the only approach, and deliberately not a complete approach. A body of great poetry will awaken and exemplify different interests on different occasions, or even on the same occasions, as we may see in the contrasting and often contesting literatures about Dante and Shakespeare: even a relation to the poetry is not common to them all. I propose here to examine Yeats's later poetry with a special regard to his own approach to the making of it; and to explore a little what I conceive to be the dominant mode of his insight, the relations between it and the printed poems, and—a different thing—the relations between it and the readers of his poems.

The major facts I hope to illustrate are these: that Yeats has, if you accept his mode, a consistent extraordinary grasp of the reality of emotion, character, and aspiration; and that his chief resort and weapon for the grasping of that reality is magic; and that if we would make use of that reality for ourselves we must also make some use of the magic that inspirits it. What is important is that the nexus of reality and magic is not by paradox or sleight of hand, but is logical and represents, for Yeats in his poetry, a full use of intelligence. Magic performs for Yeats the same fructifying function that Christianity does for Eliot, or that ironic fatalism did for Thomas Hardy; it makes a connection between the poem and its subject matter and provides an adequate mechanics of meaning and value. If it happens that we discard more of Hardy than we do of Yeats and more of Yeats than we do of Eliot, it is not because Christianity provides better machinery for the movement of poetry than fatalism or magic, but simply because Eliot is a more cautious craftsman. Besides, Eliot's poetry has not even comparatively worn long enough to show what parts are permanent and what merely temporary. The point here is that fatalism, Christianity, and magic are none of them disciplines to which many minds can consciously appeal today, as Hardy, Eliot, and Yeats do, for emotional strength and moral authority. The supernatural is simply not part of our mental furniture, and when we meet it in our reading we say: Here is debris to be swept away. But if we sweep it away without first making sure what it is, we are likely to lose the poetry as well as the debris. It is the very purpose of a supernaturally derived discipline, as used in poetry, to set the substance of natural life apart, to give it a form, a meaning, and a value which cannot be evaded. What is excessive and unwarranted in the discipline we indeed ought to dismiss; but that can be determined only when what is integrating and illuminating is known first. The discipline will in the end turn out to have had only a secondary importance for the reader; but its effect will remain active even when he no longer considers it. That is because for the poet the discipline, far from seeming secondary, had an extraordinary structural, seminal, and substantial importance to the degree that without it he could hardly have written at all.

Poetry does not flow from thin air but requires always either a literal faith, an imaginative faith, or, as in Shakespeare, a mind full of many provisional faiths. The life we all live is not alone enough of a subject for the serious artist; it must be life with a leaning, life with a tendency to shape itself only in certain forms, to afford its most lucid revelations only in certain lights. If our final interest, either as poets or as readers, is in the reality declared when the forms have been removed and the lights taken away, yet we can never come to the reality at all without the first advantage of the form and lights. Without them we should *see* nothing but only glimpse something unstable. We glimpse the fleeting but do not see what it is that fleets.

So it was with Yeats; his early poems are fleeting, some of them beautiful and some that sicken, as you read them, to their own extinction. But as he acquired for himself a discipline, however unacceptable to the bulk of his readers, his poetry obtained an access to reality. So it is with most of our serious poets. It is almost the mark of the poet of genuine merit in our time—the poet who writes serious works with an intellectual aspect which are nonetheless poetry—that he performs his work in the light of an insight, a group of ideas, and a faith, with the discipline that flows from them, which taken together form a view of life most readers cannot share, and which, furthermore, most readers feel as repugnant, or sterile, or simply inconsequential.

All this is to say generally—and we shall say it particularly for Yeats later—that our culture is incomplete with regard to poetry; and the poet has to provide for himself in that quarter where authority and value are derived. It may be that no poet ever found a culture complete for his purpose; it was a welcome and arduous part of his business to make it so. Dante, we may say, completed for poetry the Christian culture of his time, which was itself the completion of centuries. But there was at hand for Dante, and as a rule in the great ages of poetry, a fundamental agreement or convention between the poet and his audience about the validity of the view of life of which the poet deepened the reality and spread the scope. There is no such agreement today. We find poets either using the small conventions of the individual life as if they were great conventions, or attempting to resurrect some great convention of the past, or, finally, attempting to discover the great convention that must lie, willy-nilly, hidden in the life about them. This is a labor, whichever form it takes, which leads as often to subterfuge, substitution, confusion, and failure, as to success; and it puts the abnormal burden upon the reader of determining what the beliefs of the poet are and how much to credit them before he can satisfy himself of the reality which those beliefs envisage. The alternative is to put poetry at a discount—which is what has happened.

This the poet cannot do who is aware of the possibilities of his trade: the possibilities of arresting, enacting, and committing to the language through his poems the expressed value of the life otherwise only lived or evaded. The poet so aware knows, in the phrasing of that prose-addict Henry James, both the sacred rage of writing and the muffled majesty of authorship; and knows, as Eliot knows, that once to have been visited by the Muses is ever afterward to be haunted. These are qualities that once apprehended may not be discounted without complete surrender, when the poet is no more than a haunt haunted. Yeats has never put his poetry at a discount. But he has made it easy for his readers to do so—as Eliot has in his way—because the price he has paid for it, the expense he has himself been to in getting it on paper, have been a price most readers simply do not know how to pay and an expense, in time and labor and willingness to understand, beyond any initial notion of adequate reward.

The price is the price of a fundamental and deliberate surrender to magic as the ultimate mode for the apprehension of reality. The expense is the double expense of, on the one hand, implementing magic with a consistent symbolism, and on the other hand, the greatly multiplied expense of restoring, through the *craft* of poetry, both the reality and its symbols to that plane where alone their experience becomes actual—the plane of the quickened senses and the concrete emotions. That is to say, the poet (and, as always, the reader) has to combine, to fuse inextricably into something like an organic unity the constructed or derived symbolism of his special insight with the symbolism animating the language itself. It is, on the poet's plane, the labor of bringing the representative forms of knowledge home to the experience which stirred them: the labor of keeping in mind *what* our knowledge is of: the labor of craft. With the poetry of Yeats this labor is, as I say, doubly hard, because the forms of knowledge, being magical, do not fit naturally with the forms of knowledge that ordinarily preoccupy us. But it is possible, and I hope to show it, that the difficulty is, in a sense, superficial and may be overcome with familiarity, and that the mode of magic itself, once familiar, will even seem rational for the purposes of poetry—although it will not thereby seem inevitable. Judged by its works in the representation of emotional reality—and that is all that can be asked in our context—magic and its burden of symbols may be a major tool of the imagination. A tool has often a double function; it performs feats for which it was designed, and it is heuristic, it discovers and performs new feats which could not have been anticipated without it, which it indeed seems to instigate for itself and in the most unlikely quarters. It is with magic as a tool in its heuristic aspect—as an agent for discovery—that I wish here directly to be concerned.

One of the finest, because one of the most appropriate to our time and place, of all Yeats's poems, is his "The Second Coming."

> Turning and turning in the widening gyre
> The falcon cannot hear the falconer;
> Things fall apart; the centre cannot hold;
> Mere anarchy is loosed upon the world,
> The blood-dimmed tide is loosed, and everywhere
> The ceremony of innocence is drowned;
> The best lack all conviction, while the worst
> Are full of passionate intensity.
>
> Surely some revelation is at hand;
> Surely the Second Coming is at hand.
> The Second Coming! Hardly are those words out
> When a vast image out of *Spiritus Mundi*
> Troubles my sight: somewhere in sands of the desert
> A shape with lion body and the head of a man,
> A gaze blank and pitiless as the sun,
> Is moving its slow thighs, while all about it
> Reel shadows of the indignant desert birds.
> The darkness drops again; but now I know
> That twenty centuries of stony sleep
> Were vexed to nightmare by a rocking cradle,
> And what rough beast, its hour come round at last,
> Slouches towards Bethlehem to be born?

There is about it, to any slowed reading, the immediate conviction of pertinent emotion; the lines are stirring, separately and in their smaller groups, and there is a sensible life in them that makes them seem to combine in the form of an emotion. We may say at once then, for what it is worth, that in writing his poem Yeats was able to choose words which to an appreciable extent were the right ones to reveal or represent the emotion which was its purpose. The words deliver the meaning which was put into them by the craft with which they were arranged, and that meaning is their own, not to be segregated or given another arrangement without diminution. Ultimately, something of this sort is all that can be said of this or any poem, and when it is said, the poem is known to be good in its own terms or bad because not in its own terms. But the reader seldom reaches an ultimate position about a poem; most poems fail, through craft or conception, to reach an ultimate or absolute position: parts of the craft remain machinery and parts of the conception remain in limbo. Or, as in this poem, close inspection will show something questionable about it. It is true that it can be read as it is, isolated from the rest of Yeats's work and isolated from the intellectual material which it expresses, and a good deal gotten out of it, too, merely by submitting to it. That is because the words are mainly common, both in their emotional and intellectual senses; and if we do not know precisely what the familiar words drag after them into the poem, still we know vaguely what the weight of it feels like; and that seems enough to make a poem at one level of response. Yet if an attempt is made at a more complete response, if we wish to discover the precise emotion which the words mount up to, we come into trouble and uncertainty at once. There is an air of explicitness to each of the separate fragments of the poem. Is it, in this line or that, serious? Has it a reference?—or is it a rhetorical effect, a result only of the persuasive overtones of words?—or is it a combination, a mixture of reference and rhetoric?

Possibly the troubled attention will fasten first upon the italicized phrase in the twelfth line: *Spiritus Mundi*; and the question is whether the general, the readily available senses of the words are adequate to supply the specific sense wanted by the poem. Put another way, can the poet's own arbitrary meaning be made, merely by discovering it, to participate in and enrich what the "normal" meanings of the words in their limiting context provide? The critic can only supply the facts; the poem will in the end provide its own answer. Here there are certain facts that may be extracted from Yeats's prose writings which suggest something of what the words symbolize for him. In one of the notes to the limited edition of *Michael Robartes and the Dancer*, Yeats observes that his mind, like another's, has been from time to time obsessed by images which had no discoverable origin in his waking experience. Speculating as to their origin, he came to deny both the conscious and the unconscious memory as their probable seat, and finally invented a doctrine which traced the images to sources of supernatural character. I quote only that sentence which is relevant to the phrase in question: "Those [images] that come in sleep are (1) from the state immediately preceding our birth; (2) from the *Spiritus Mundi*—that is to say, from a general storehouse of images which have ceased to be a property of any personality or spirit." It apparently follows, for Yeats, that images so derived have both an absolute meaning of their own and an operative force in determining meaning and predicting events in this world. In another place (the Introduction to "The Resurrection" in *Wheels and Butterflies*) he describes the image used in this poem, which he had seen many times, "always at my left side just out of the range of sight, a brazen winged beast that I associated with laughing, ecstatic destruction." Ecstasy, it should be added, comes for Yeats just before death, and at death comes the moment of revelation, when the soul is shown its kindred dead and it is possible to see the future.

Here we come directly upon that central part of Yeats's magical beliefs which it is one purpose of this poem emotionally to represent: the belief in what is called variously *Magnus Annus,* The Great Year, The Platonic Year, and sometimes in a slightly different symbolism, The Great

Wheel. This belief, with respect to the history of epochs, is associated with the precession of the equinoxes, which bring, roughly every two thousand years, a Great Year of death and rebirth, and this belief, with respect to individuals, seems to be associated with the phases of the moon; although individuals may be influenced by the equinoxes and there may be a lunar interpretation of history. These beliefs have a scaffold of geometrical figures, gyres, cones, circles, etc., by the application of which exact interpretation is secured. Thus it is possible to predict, both in biography and history, and in time, both forward and backward, the character, climax, collapse, and rebirth in antithetical form of human types and cultures. There is a subordinate but helpful belief that signs, warnings, even direct messages, are always given, from *Spiritus Mundi* or elsewhere, which the poet and the philosopher have only to see and hear. As it happens, the Christian era, being nearly two thousand years old, is due for extinction and replacement, in short for the Second Coming, which this poem heralds. In his note to its first publication (in *Michael Robartes and the Dancer*) Yeats expresses his belief as follows:

At the present moment the life gyre is sweeping outward, unlike that before the birth of Christ which was narrowing, and has almost reached its greatest expansion. The revelation which approaches will however take its character from the contrary movement of the interior gyre. All our scientific, democratic, fact-accumulating, heterogeneous civilisation belongs to the outward gyre and prepares not the continuance of itself but the revelation as in a lightning flash, though in a flash that will not strike only in one place, and will for a time be constantly repeated, of the civilisation that must slowly take its place.

So much for a major gloss upon the poem. Yeats combined, in the best verse he could manage, the beliefs which obsessed him with the image which he took to be a specific illustration of the beliefs. Minor and buttressing glosses are possible for many of the single words and phrases in the poem, some flowing from private doctrine and some from Yeats's direct sense of the world about him, and some from both at once. For example: The "ceremony of innocence" represents for Yeats one of the qualities that made life valuable under the dying aristocratic social tradition; and the meaning of the phrase in the poem requires no magic for completion but only a reading of other poems. The "falcon and the falconer" in the second line has, besides its obvious symbolism, a doctrinal reference. A falcon is a hawk, and a hawk is symbolic of the active or intellectual mind; the falconer is perhaps the soul itself or its uniting principle. There is also the apposition which Yeats has made several times that "Wisdom is a butterfly/ And not a gloomy bird of prey." Whether the special symbolism has actually been incorporated in the poem, and in which form, or whether it is private debris merely, will take a generation of readers to decide. In the meantime it must be taken provisionally for whatever its ambiguity may seem to be worth. Literature is full of falcons, some that fly and some that lack immediacy and sit, archaic, on the poet's wrist; and it is not always illuminating to determine which is which. But when we come on such lines as

> The best lack all conviction, while the worst
> Are full of passionate intensity,

we stop short, first to realize the aptness of the statement to every plane of life in the world about us, and then to connect the lines with the remote body of the poem they illuminate. There is a dilemma of which the branches grow from one trunk but which cannot be solved; for these lines have, not two meanings, but two sources for the same meaning. There is the meaning that comes from the summary observation that this is how men are—and especially men of power—in the world we live in; it is knowledge that comes from knowledge of the "fury and the mire in human veins"; a meaning the contemplation of which has lately (April, 1934) led Yeats to offer himself to any government or party that, using force and marching men, will "promise not this or that measure but a discipline, a way of life." And there is in effect the same meaning, at least at the time the poem was written, which comes from a different source and should have, one would think, very different consequences in prospective party loyalties. Here the meaning has its source in the doctrines of the Great Year and the Phases of the Moon; whereby, to cut exegesis short, it is predicted as necessary that, at the time we have reached, the best minds, being subjective, should have lost all faith though desiring it, and the worst minds, being so nearly objective, have no need of faith and may be full of "passionate intensity" without the control of any faith or wisdom. Thus we have on the one side the mirror of observation and on the other side an imperative, magically derived, which come to the conclusion of form in identical words.

The question is, to repeat, whether the fact of this double control and source of meaning at a critical point defeats or strengthens the unity of the poem; and it is a question which forms itself again and again in the later poems, sometimes obviously but more often only by suggestion. If we take another poem on the same theme, written some years earlier, and before his wife's mediumship gave him the detail of his philosophy, we will find the question no easier to answer in its suggested than in its conspicuous form. There is an element in the poem called "The Magi" which we can feel the weight of but cannot altogether name, and of which we can only guess at the efficacy.

> Now as at all times I can see in the mind's eye,
> In their stiff, painted clothes, the pale unsatisfied ones
> Appear and disappear in the blue depths of the sky
> With all their ancient faces like rain-beaten stones,
> And all their helms of silver hovering side by side,
> And all their eyes still fixed, hoping to find once more,
> Being by Calvary's turbulence unsatisfied,
> The uncontrollable mystery on the bestial floor.

I mean the element which, were Yeats a Christian, we could accept as a species of Christian blasphemy or advanced heresy, but which since he is not a Christian we find it hard to accept at all: the element of emotional conviction springing from intellectual matters without rational source or structure. We ought to be able, for the poem's sake, to accept the conviction as an emotional possibility, much as we

*eg. the Spiritus*
*Mundi source*

accept *Lear* or Dostoevski's *Idiot* as valid, because projected from represented experience. But Yeats's experience is not represented consistently on any one plane. He constantly indicates a supernatural validity for his images of which the authority cannot be reached. If we come nearer to accepting "The Magi" than "The Second Coming" it is partly because the familiar Christian paradigm is more clearly used, and, in the last two lines, what Yeats constructs upon it is given a more immediate emotional form, and partly because, *per contra*, there is less demand made upon arbitrary intellectual belief. There is, too, the matter of scope; if we reduce the scope of "The Second Coming" to that of "The Magi" we shall find it much easier to accept; but we shall have lost much of the poem.

We ought now to have enough material to name the two radical defects of magic as a tool for poetry. One defect, which we have just been illustrating, is that it has no available edifice of reason reared upon it conventionally independent of its inspiration. There is little that the uninspired reader can naturally refer to for authority outside the poem, and if he does make a natural reference he is likely to turn out to be at least partly wrong. The poet is thus in the opposite predicament; he is under the constant necessity of erecting his beliefs into doctrines at the same time that he represents their emotional or dramatic equivalents. He is, in fact, in much the same position that Dante would have been had he had to construct his Christian doctrine while he was composing *The Divine Comedy*: an impossible labor. The Christian supernaturalism, the Christian magic (no less magical than that of Yeats), had the great advantage for Dante, and imaginatively for ourselves, of centuries of reason and criticism and elaboration: it was within reason a consistent whole; and its supernatural element had grown so consistent with experience as to seem supremely *natural* —as indeed it may again. Christianity has an objective form, whatever the mysteries at its heart and its termini, in which all the phenomena of human life may find place and meaning. Magic is none of these things for any large fraction of contemporary society. Magic has a tradition, but it is secret,

*available*
*to his readers*

not public. It has not only central and terminal mysteries but has also peripheral mysteries, which require not only the priest to celebrate but also the adept to manipulate. Magic has never been made "natural." The practical knowledge and power which its beliefs lead to can neither be generally shared nor overtly rationalized. It is in fact held to be dangerous to reveal openly the details of magical experience: they may be revealed, if at all, only in arbitrary symbols and equivocal statements. Thus we find Yeats, in his early and innocuous essay on magic, believing his life to have been imperiled for revealing too much. Again, the spirits or voices through whom magical knowledge is gained are often themselves equivocal and are sometimes deliberately confusing. Yeats was told to remember, "We will deceive you if we can," and on another occasion was forbidden to record anything that was said, only to be scolded later because he had failed to record every word. In short, it is of the essence of magical faith that the supernatural cannot be brought into the natural world except through symbol. The distinction between natural and supernatural is held to be substantial instead of verbal. Hence magic may neither be criticized nor institutionalized; nor can it ever reach a full expression of its own intention. This is perhaps the justification of Stephen Spender's remark that there is more magic in Eliot's "The Hollow Men" than in any poem of Yeats; because of Eliot's Christianity, his magic has a rational base as well as a supernatural source: it is the magic of an orthodox, authoritative faith. The dogmas of magic, we may say, are all heresies which cannot be expounded except each on its own authority as a fragmentary insight; and its unity can be only the momentary unity of association. Put another way, magic is in one respect in the state of Byzantine Christianity, when miracles were quotidian and the universal frame of experience, when life itself was held to be supernatural and reason was mainly a kind of willful sophistication.

Neither Yeats nor ourselves dwell in Byzantium. At a certain level, though not at all levels, we conceive life, and even its nonrational features, in rational terms. Certainly there is a rational bias and a rational structure in the poetry we mainly agree to hold great—though the content may be what it will; and it is the irrational bias and the confused structure that we are mainly concerned to disavow, to apologize or allow for. It was just to provide himself with the equivalent of a rational religious insight and a predictable rational structure for the rational imagination that in his book, *A Vision* (published, in 1925, in a limited edition only, and then withdrawn), he attempted to convert his magical experience into a systematic philosophy. "I wished," he writes in the Dedication to that work, "for a system of thought that would leave my imagination free to create as it chose and yet make all that it created, or could create, part of the one history, and that the soul's." That is, Yeats hoped by systematizing it to escape from the burden of confusion and abstraction which his magical experience had imposed upon him. "I can now," he declares in this same Dedication, "if I have the energy, find the simplicity I have sought in vain. I need no longer write poems like 'The Phases of the Moon' nor 'Ego Dominus Tuus,' nor spend barren years, as I have done three or four times, striving with abstractions that substitute themselves for the play that I had planned."

"Having inherited," as he says in one of his poems, "a vigorous mind," he could not help seeing, once he had got it all down, that his system was something to disgorge if he could. Its truth as experience would be all the stronger if its abstractions could be expunged. But it could not be disgorged; its thirty-five years of growth was an intimate part of his own growth, and its abstractions were all of a piece with his most objective experience. And perhaps we, as readers, can see that better from outside than Yeats could from within. I suspect that no amount of will could have rid him of his magical conception of the soul; it was by magic that he knew the soul; and the conception had been too closely associated with his profound sense of his race and personal ancestry. He has never been able to retract his system, only to take up different attitudes toward it. He has alternated between granting his speculations only the validity of poetic myth and planning to announce a new deity. In his vacillation—there is a poem by that title—the rational defect remains, and the reader must deal with it sometimes as an intrusion, of indeterminate value, upon the poetry and sometimes as itself the subject of dramatic reverie or lyric statement. At least once he tried to force the issue home, and in a section of *A Packet for Ezra Pound* called "Introduction to the Great Wheel" he meets the issue by transforming it, for the moment, into wholly poetic terms. Because it reveals a fundamental honesty and clarity of purpose in the midst of confusion and uncertainty the section is quoted entire.

Some will ask if I believe all that this book contains, and I will not know how to answer. Does the word belief, as they will use it, belong to our age, can I think of the world as there and I here judging it? I will never think any thoughts but these, or some modification or extension of these; when I write prose or verse they must be somewhere present though it may not be in the words; they must affect my judgment of friends and events; but then there are many symbolisms and none exactly resembles mine. What Leopardi in Ezra Pound's translation calls that 'concord' wherein 'the arcane spirit of the whole mankind turns hardy pilot'—how much better it would be without that word 'hardy' which slackens speed and adds nothing—persuades me that he has best imagined reality who has best imagined justice.

The rational defect, then, remains; the thought is not always in the words; and we must do with it as we can. There is another defect of Yeats's magical system which is especially apparent to the reader but which may not be apparent at all to Yeats. Magic promises precisely matters which it cannot perform—at least in poetry. It promises, as in "The Second Coming," exact prediction of events in the natural world; and it promises again and again, in different poems, exact revelations of the supernatural, and of this we have an example in what has to many seemed a great poem, "All Souls' Night," which had its first publication as an epilogue to *A Vision*. Near the beginning of the poem we have the explicit declaration: "I have a marvelous thing to say"; and near the end another: "I have mummy truths to tell." "Mummy truths" is an admirable phrase, suggestive as it is of the truths in which the dead are wrapped, ancient truths as old as Egypt perhaps, whence mummies commonly come, and truths, too, that may be unwound. But there, with the suggestion, the truths stop short; there is, for the reader, no unwinding, no revelation of the dead. What Yeats actually does is to summon into the poem various of his dead friends as "characters"—and this is the greatness, and only this, of the poem: the summary, excited, even exalted presentation of character. Perhaps the rhetoric is the marvel and the evasion the truth. We get an impact as from behind, from the speed and weight of the words, and are left with an ominous or terrified frame of mind, the revelation still to come. The revelation, the magic, was in Yeats's mind; hence the exaltation in his language; but it was not and could not be given in the words of the poem.

It may be that for Yeats there was a similar exaltation and a similar self-deceit in certain other poems, but as the promise of revelation was not made, the reader feels no failure of fulfillment. Such poems as "Easter, 1916," "In Memory of Major Robert Gregory," and "Upon a Dying Lady" may have buried in them a conviction of invocation and revelation; but if so it is no concern of ours: we are concerned only, as the case may be, with the dramatic presentations of the Irish patriots and poets, Yeats's personal friends, and Aubrey Beardsley's dying sister, and with, in addition, for minor pleasure, the technical means—the spare and delicate language, the lucid images, and quickening rhymes—whereby the characters are presented as intensely felt. There is no problem in such poems but the problem of reaching, through a gradual access of intimacy, full appreciation; here the magic and everything else are in the words. It is the same, for bare emotion apart from character, in such poems as "A Deep-Sworn Vow," where the words accumulate by the simplest means an intolerable excitement, where the words are, called as they may be from whatever source, in an ultimate sense their own meaning.

Others because you did not keep
That deep-sworn vow have been friends of mine;
Yet always when I look death in the face,
When I clamber to the heights of sleep,
Or when I grow excited with wine,
Suddenly I meet your face.

Possibly all poetry should be read as this poem is read, and no poetry greatly valued that cannot be so read. Such is one ideal toward which reading tends; but to apply it as a standard of judgment we should first have to assume for the poetic intelligence absolute autonomy and self-perfection for all its works. Actually, autonomy and self-perfection are relative and depend upon a series of agreements or conventions between the poet and his readers, which alter continually, as to what must be represented by the fundamental power of language (itself a relatively stable convention) and what, on the other hand, may be adequately represented by mere reference, sign, symbol, or blueprint indication. Poetry is so little autonomous from the technical point of view that the greater part of a given work must be conceived as the manipulation of conventions that the reader will, or will not, take for granted; these being crowned, or animated, emotionally transformed, by what the poet actually represents, original or not, through his mastery of poetic language. Success is provisional, seldom complete, and never permanently complete. The vitality or letter of a convention may perish although the form persists. *Romeo and Juliet* is less successful today than when produced because the conventions of honor, family authority, and blood-feud no longer animate and justify the action; and if the play survives it is partly because certain other conventions of human character do remain vital, but more because Shakespeare is the supreme master of representation through the reality of language alone. Similarly with Dante; with the cumulative disintegration, even for Catholics, of medieval Christianity as the ultimate convention of human life, the success of *The Divine Comedy* comes more and more to depend on the exhibition of character and the virtue of language alone—which may make it a greater, not a lesser poem. On the other hand, it often happens that a poet's ambition is such that, in order to get his work done at all, he must needs set up new conventions or radically modify old ones which fatally lack that benefit of form which can be conferred only by public recognition. The form which made his poems available was only gradually conferred upon the convention of evil in Baudelaire and, as we may see in translations with contrasting emphases, its limits are still subject to debate; in his case the more so because the life of his language depended more than usual on the viability of the convention.

Let us apply these notions, which ought so far to be commonplace, to the later work of Yeats, relating them especially to the predominant magical convention therein. When Yeats came of poetic age he found himself, as Blake had before him, and even Wordsworth but to a worse extent, in a society whose conventions extended neither intellectual nor moral authority to poetry; he found himself in a rational but deliberately incomplete, because progressive, society. The *emotion* of thought, for poetry, was gone, along with the emotion of religion and the emotion of race—the three sources and the three aims of the great poetry of the past. Tyndall and Huxley are the villains, Yeats records in his *Autobiographies,* as Blake recorded Newton; there were other causes, but no matter, these names may serve as symbols. And the dominant aesthetics of the time were as rootless in the realm of poetic import and authority as the dominant conventions. Art for Art's sake was the cry, the Ivory Tower the retreat, and Walter Pater's luminous langour and weak Platonism the exposition. One could say anything but it would mean nothing. The poets and society both, for opposite reasons, expected the poet to produce either exotic and ornamental mysteries or lyrics of mood; the real world and its significance were reserved mainly to the newer sciences, though the novelists and the playwrights might poach if they could. For a time Yeats succumbed, as may be seen in his early work, even while he attempted to escape; and of his poetic generation he was the only one to survive and grow in stature. He came under the influence of the

French Symbolists, who gave him the clue and the hint of an external structure but nothing much to put in it. He read, with a dictionary, Villiers de l'Isle-Adam's *Axel*, and so came to be included in Edmund Wilson's book *Axel's Castle* —although not, as Wilson himself shows, altogether correctly. For he began in the late 'nineties, as it were upon his own account, to quench his thirst for reality by creating authority and significance and reference in the three fields where they were lacking. He worked into his poetry the substance of Irish mythology and Irish politics and gave them a symbolism, and he developed his experiences with Theosophy and Rosicrucianism into a body of conventions adequate, for him, to animate the concrete poetry of the soul that he wished to write. He did not do these things separately; the mythology, the politics, and the magic are conceived, through the personalities that reflected them, with an increasing unity of apprehension. Thus more than any poet of our time he has restored to poetry the actual emotions of race and religion and what we call abstract thought. Whether we follow him in any particular or not, the general poetic energy which he liberated is ours to use if we can. If the edifice that he constructed seems personal, it is because he had largely to build it for himself, and that makes it difficult to understand in detail except in reference to the peculiar unity which comes from their mere association in his life and work. Some of the mythology and much of the politics, being dramatized and turned into emotion, are part of our common possessions. But where the emphasis has been magical, whether successfully or not, the poems have been misunderstood, ignored, and the actual emotion in them which is relevant to us all decried and underestimated, merely because the magical mode of thinking is foreign to our own and when known at all is largely associated with quackery and fraud.

We do not make that mistake—which is the mistake of unwillingness—with Dante or the later Eliot, because, although the substance of their modes of thinking is equally foreign and magical, it has the advantage of a rational superstructure that persists and which we can convert to our own modes if we will. Yeats lacks, as we have said, the historical advantage and with it much else; and the conclusion cannot be avoided that this lack prevents his poetry from reaching the first magnitude. But there are two remedies we may apply, which will make up, not for the defect of magnitude, but for the defect of structure. We can read the magical philosophy in his verse *as if* it were converted into the contemporary psychology with which its doctrines have so much in common. We find little difficulty in seeing Freud's preconscious as a fertile myth and none at all in the general myth of extroverted and introverted personality; and these may be compared with, respectively, Yeats's myth of *Spiritus Mundi* and the Phases of the Moon: the intention and the scope of the meaning are identical. So much for a secular conversion. The other readily available remedy is this: to accept Yeats's magic literally as a machinery of meaning, to search out the prose parallels and reconstruct the symbols he uses on their own terms in order to come on the emotional reality, if it is there, actually in the poems—when the machinery may be dispensed with. This method has the prime advantage over secular conversion of keeping judgment in poetic terms, with the corresponding disadvantage that it requires more time and patience, more "willing suspension of disbelief," and a stiffer intellectual exercise all around. But exegesis is to be preferred to conversion on still another ground, which may seem repellent: that magic, in the sense that we all experience it, is nearer the represented emotions that concern us in poetry than psychology, as a generalized science, can ever be. We are all, without conscience, magicians in the dark.

But even the poems of darkness are read in the light. I cannot, of course, make a sure prognosis; because in applying either remedy the reader is, really, doctoring himself as much as Yeats. Only this much is sure: that the reader will come to see the substantial unity of Yeats's work, that it is the same mind stirring behind the poems on Crazy Jane and the Bishop, on Cuchulain, on Swift, the political poems, the biographical and the doctrinal—a mind that sees the fury and the mire and the passion of the dawn as contrary aspects of the real world. It is to be expected that many poems will fail in part and some entirely, and if the chief, magic will not be the only cause of failure. The source of a vision puts limits upon its expression which the poet cannot well help overpassing. "The limitation of his view," Yeats wrote of Blake, "was from the very intensity of his vision; he was a too-literal realist of imagination, as others are of nature"; and the remark applies to himself. But there will be enough left to make the labor of culling worth all its patience and time. Before concluding, I propose to spur the reader, or inadvertently dismay him, by presenting briefly a few examples of the sort of reconstructive labor he will have to do and the sort of imaginative assent he may have to attempt in order to enter or dismiss the body of the poems.

As this is a mere essay in emphasis, let us bear the emphasis in, by repeating, on different poems, the sort of commentary laid out above on "The Second Coming" and "The Magi," using this time "Byzantium" and "Sailing to Byzantium." Byzantium is for Yeats, so to speak, the heaven of man's mind; there the mind or soul dwells in eternal or miraculous form; there all things are possible because all things are known to the soul. Byzantium has both a historical and an ideal form, and the historical is the exemplar, the dramatic witness, of the ideal. Byzantium represents both a dated epoch and a recurrent state of insight, when nature is magical, that is, at the beck of mind, and magic is natural—a practical rather than a theoretic art. If with these notions in mind we compare the two poems named we see that the first, called simply "Byzantium," is like certain cantos in the *Paradiso* the poetry of an intense and condensed declaration of doctrine; not emotion put into doctrine from outside, but doctrine presented as emotion. I quote the second stanza.

> Before me floats an image, man or shade,
> Shade more than man, more image than a shade;
> For Hades' bobbin bound in mummy-cloth
> May unwind the winding path;

> A mouth that has no moisture and no breath
> Breathless mouths may summon;
> I hail the superhuman;
> I call it death-in-life and life-in-death.

The second poem, "Sailing to Byzantium," rests upon the doctrine but is not a declaration of it. It is, rather, the doctrine in action, the doctrine actualized in a personal emotion resembling that of specific prayer. This is the emotion of the flesh where the other was the emotion of the bones. The distinction should not be too sharply drawn. It is not the bones of doctrine but the emotion of it that we should be aware of in reading the more dramatic poem: and the nearer they come to seeming two reflections of the same thing the better both poems will be. What must be avoided is a return to the poem of doctrine with a wrong estimation of its value gained by confusion of the two poems. Both poems are serious in their own kind, and the reality of each must be finally in its own words whatever clues the one supplies to the other. I quote the third stanza.

> O sages standing in God's holy fire
> As in the gold mosaic of a wall,
> Come from the holy fire, perne in a gyre,
> And be the singing-masters of my soul.
> Consume my heart away; sick with desire
> And fastened to a dying animal
> It knows not what it is; and gather me
> Into the artifice of eternity.

We must not, for example, accept "perne in a gyre" in this poem merely because it is part of the doctrine upon which the poem rests. Its magical reference may be too explicit for the poem to digest. It may be merely part of the poem's intellectual machinery, something that will *become* a dead commonplace once its peculiarity has worn out. Its meaning, that is, may turn out not to participate in the emotion of the poem: which is an emotion of aspiration. Similarly a note of aspiration would have been injurious to the stanza quoted from "Byzantium" above.

Looking at other poems as examples, the whole problem

of exegesis may be put another way; which consists in joining two facts and observing their product. There is the fact
that again and again in Yeats's prose, both in that which
accompanies the poems and that which is independent of
them, poems and fragments of poems are introduced at
strategic points, now to finish off or clinch an argument by
giving it as proved, and again merely to balance argument
with witness from another plane. *A Vision* is punctuated by
five poems. And there is the complementary fact that, when
one has read the various autobiographies, introductions,
and doctrinal notes and essays, one continually finds echoes,
phrases, and developments from the prose in the poems.
We have, as Wallace Stevens says, the prose that wears the
poem's guise at last; and we have, too, the poems turning
backward, re-illuminating or justifying the prose from the
material of which they sprang. We have, to import the
dichotomy which T. S. Eliot made for his own work, the
prose writings discovering and buttressing the ideal, and
we have the poems which express as much as can be actualized—given as concrete emotion—of what the prose
discovered or envisaged. The dichotomy is not so sharp in
Yeats as in Eliot. Yeats cannot, such is the unity of his apprehension, divide his interests. There is one mind employing two approaches in the labor of representation. The
prose approach lets in much that the poetic approach excludes; it lets in the questionable, the uncertain, the hypo-
thetic, and sometimes the incredible. The poetic approach,
using the same material, retains, when it is successful, only
what is manifest, the emotion that can be made actual in a
form of words that need only to be understood, not argued.
If props of argument and vestiges of idealization remain,
they must be felt as qualifying, not arguing, the emotion.
It should only be remembered and repeated that the poet
invariably requires more machinery to secure *his* effects—
the machinery of his whole life and thought—than the
reader requires to secure what he takes as the *poem's* effects; and that, as readers differ, the poet cannot calculate
what is necessary to the poem and what is not. There is
always the debris to be cut away.

In such a fine poem as "A Prayer for My Son," for example, Yeats cut away most of the debris himself, and it is perhaps an injury to judgment provisionally to restore it. Yet to this reader at least the poem seems to richen when it is known from what special circumstance the poem was freed. As it stands we can accept the symbols which it conspicuously contains—the strong ghost, the devilish things, and the holy writings—as drawn from the general stock of literary conventions available to express the evil predicament in which children and all innocent beings obviously find themselves. Taken so, it is a poem of natural piety. But for Yeats the conventions were not merely literary but were practical expressions of the actual terms of the predicament, and his poem is a prayer of dread and supernatural piety. The experience which led to the poem is recounted in *A Packet for Ezra Pound.* When his son was still an infant Yeats was told through the mediumship of his wife that the Frustrators or evil spirits would henceforth "attack my health and that of my children, and one afternoon, knowing from the smell of burnt feathers that one of my children would be ill within three hours, I felt before I could recover self-control the mediaeval helpless horror of witchcraft." The child *was* ill. It is from this experience that the poem seems to have sprung, and the poem preserves all that was actual behind the private magical conventions Yeats used for himself. The point is that the reader has a richer poem if he can substitute the manipulative force of Yeats's specific conventions for the general literary conventions. Belief or imaginative assent is no more difficult for either set. It is the emotion that counts.

That is one extreme to which the poems run—the extreme convention of personal thought. Another extreme is that exemplified in "A Prayer for My Daughter," where the animating conventions *are* literary and the piety *is* natural, and in the consideration of which it would be misleading to introduce the magical convention as more than a foil. As a foil it is nevertheless present; his magical philosophy, all the struggle and warfare of the intellect, is precisely what Yeats in this poem *puts out of mind,* in order to imagine his daughter living in innocence and beauty, custom and ceremony.

A third extreme is that found in the sonnet "Leda and the Swan," where there is an extraordinary sensual immediacy—the words meet and move like speaking lips—and a profound combination of the generally available or literary symbol and the hidden, magical symbol of the intellectual, philosophical, impersonal order. Certain longer poems and groups of poems, especially the series called "A Woman Young and Old," exhibit the extreme of combination as well or better; but I want the text on the page.

> A sudden blow: the great wings beating still
> Above the staggering girl, her thighs caressed
> By the dark webs, her nape caught in his bill,
> He holds her helpless breast upon his breast.
>
> How can those terrified vague fingers push
> The feathered glory from her loosening thighs?
> And how can body, laid in that white rush,
> But feel the strange heart beating where it lies?
>
> A shudder in the loins engenders there
> The broken wall, the burning roof and tower
> And Agamemnon dead.
>                           Being so caught up,
> So mastered by the brute blood of the air,
> Did she put on his knowledge with his power
> Before the indifferent beak could let her drop?

It should be observed that in recent years new images, some from the life of Swift, and some from the Greek mythology, have been spreading through Yeats's poems; and of Greek images he has used especially those of Oedipus and Leda, of Homer and Sophocles. But they are not used as we think the Greeks used them, nor as mere drama, but deliberately, after the magical tradition, both to represent and hide the myths Yeats has come on in his own mind. Thus "Leda and the Swan" can be read on at least three distinct levels of significance, none of which interferes with the others: the levels of dramatic fiction, of condensed insight into Greek mythology, and a third level of fiction and insight combined, as we said, to represent and hide a magical insight. This third level is our present concern. At this level the poem presents an interfusion among the normal terms of the poem two of Yeats's fundamental magical doctrines in emotional form. The doctrines are put by Yeats in the following form in his essay on magic: "That the borders of our mind are ever shifting, and that many minds can flow into one another, as it were, and create or reveal a single mind, a single energy. . . . That this great mind can be evoked by symbols." Copulation is the obvious nexus for spiritual as well as physical seed. There is also present I think some sense of Yeats's doctrine of Annunciation and the Great Year, the Annunciation, in this case, that produced Greek culture. It is a neat question for the reader, so far as this poem is concerned, whether the poetic emotion springs from the doctrine and seizes the myth for a safe home and hiding, or whether the doctrine is correlative to the emotion of the myth. In neither case does the magic matter as such; it has become poetry, and of extreme excellence in its order. To repeat the interrogatory formula with which we began the commentary on "The Second Coming," is the magical material in these poems incorporated in them by something like organic reference or is its presence merely rhetorical? The reader will answer one way or the other, as, to his rational imagination, to all the imaginative understanding he can bring to bear, it either seems to clutter the emotion and deaden the reality, or seems rather, as I believe, to heighten the emotional reality and thereby extend its reference to what we call the real world. Once the decision is made, the magic no longer exists; we have the poetry.

Other approaches to Yeats's poetry would have produced different emphases, and this approach, which has emphasized little but the magical structure of Yeats's poetic emotions, has made that emphasis with an ulterior purpose: to show that magic may be a feature of a rational imagination. This approach should be combined with others, or should have others combined with it, for perspective and reduction. No feature of a body of poetry can be as important as it seems in discussion. Above all, then, this ap-

proach through the magical emphasis should be combined
with the approach of plain reading—which is long reading
and hard reading—plain reading of the words, that they
may sink in and do as much of their own work as they can.
One more thing: When we call man a rational animal we
mean that reason is his great myth. Reason is plastic and
takes to any form provided. The rational imagination in
poetry, as elsewhere, can absorb magic as a provisional
method of evocative and heuristic thinking, but it cannot
be based upon it. In poetry, and largely elsewhere, imagination is based upon the reality of words and the emotion
of their joining. Yeats's magic, then, like every other feature of his experience, is rational as it reaches words; otherwise it is his privation, and ours, because it was the rational
defect of our society that drove him to it.

1936

# 3. W. B. Yeats: Between Myth and Philosophy

The notes that follow are intended to make an extreme case of one aspect of Yeats's poetry. I assume that the reader is pretty familiar with the whole reach of Yeats's work and will accordingly bring my extremity back into proportion without too much irritation; for if he is familiar with Yeats he will know that Yeats combines elements any one of which is disproportionate, even incongruous, taken by itself, and that his unity—what he is taken all together—is an imaginative, a felt unity of disproportions. No poet in recent times, for example, has seemed to base his work on a system, quasi-philosophical, partly historical, and largely allegorical, both so complicated and so esoteric, as the system which Yeats worked out in the two versions of *A Vision*. With the poems which make explicit use of the machinery of that system, these notes have nothing to do, though they include both some of the most fascinating and some of the finest of Yeats's poems, and are those most often dealt with perhaps precisely because the critic is able to catch hold of them by the levers and switches of the machinery. No; here the interest is in those poems where the machinery plays the least explicit part. For with his abstract system and the poetry which it channelized on one side, there is on the other side of Yeats what is also the most concrete, the most independent, perhaps the most personal poetry, in the good sense of the word personal, of our time. One thinks of the ballads, of Burns, of Villon, and of the dramatic aspects of Dante, in looking for archetypes; but one must think of all of them together in order to build up an expectation of great imaginative generalizing power behind or under the concrete images and individual cries of which the poems are made. The system, in short, is still there, but translated back into the actual experience from which it came. How the translation was made, what the compositional habits of the poems are, will make up our interest and the extremity of our case.

It may be risked that in dealing with the structure of poetry thought may be taken as felt assertion, irrelevant to critical analysis, but open to discussion with regard to what it permitted the poet to discover in his poems. Thought becomes metaphor, if indeed it was not already so; from a generalized assertion it becomes in each poetic instance an imaginative assertion that has to do with identity, the individual, the rash single act of creation. We seek to recover the generalized form of the assertion as a clue to what happened to it in the poetry, to find, that is, the spur of the metaphor: an operation which even if failure is an aid to understanding. It gives us something we can verbalize.

So in Yeats, we can detach certain notions which we call basic—though we may mean only that they are detachable —as clues to better reading. At the end of the first version of *A Vision*, Yeats suggests the need of putting myths back into philosophy, and in the "Dedication to Vestigia" in the same version, there is the following sentence: "I wished for a system of thought that would leave my imagination free to create as it chose and yet make all that it created, or could create, part of the one history, and that the soul's." If we take these two notions as sentiments, as unexpanded metaphors, we can understand both what drove Yeats to manufacture his complicated abstract system and the intensity of his effort to make over half of the consequent poetry as concrete as possible. He knew for himself as a poet that the most abstract philosophy or system must be *of* something, and that its purpose must be to liberate, to animate, to elucidate that something; and he knew further that that something must be somehow present in the philosophy. His system, if it worked, would liberate his imagination; and if it worked it must put those myths—the received forms, the symbolic versions of human wisdom—which were its object concretely into his system. A philosophy for poetry cannot be a rationale of meaning, but, in the end, a myth for the experience of it.

I should like to put beside these two notions or sentiments, two more. At different places in his autobiographies and in his letters to Dorothy Wellesley, Yeats quotes one or another version of Aristotle's remark that a poet should "think like a wise man, yet express himself like the common people." It should be insisted that this is a very different thing from what has been lately foisted on us as a model in the guise of Public Speech. To turn poetry into public speech is to turn it into rhetoric in the bad sense or sentimentality in the meretricious sense.

> The rhetorician would deceive his neighbors,
> The sentimentalist himself; while art
> Is but a vision of reality.

If we keep these lines—from one of Yeats's more esoteric poems—well in mind, they will explain for us much of what Yeats meant by the desire to express himself like the common people. He wanted to charge his words to the limit, or to use words that would take the maximum charge upon themselves, in such a way that they would be available to the unlearned reader, and demand of him all those skills of understanding that go without learning. We shall come to an example shortly.

The fourth sentiment that I want brought to mind here is again one found in many places in both prose and verse in Yeats's work. This is his sentiment that a poet writes out of his evil luck, writes to express that which he is not and perforce, for completion or unity, desires to be. Dante required his exile and beggary, the corruption of the Church, the anarchy of Florence, in order to write *The Divine Comedy*, with its vast ordering of emotion, its perspicuous judgment of disorder and corruption. Villon needed his harlots and his cronies at the gibbet. "Such masters—Villon and Dante, let us say—would not, when they speak through their art, change their luck; yet they are mirrored in all the suffering of their desire. The two halves of their nature are so completely joined that they seem to labour for their objects, and yet to desire whatever happens, being at the same instant predestinate and free, creation's very self." So Yeats in his chapter of autobiography called "Hodos Chameliontos"—the path of muddlement, of change, of shift from opposite to opposite. And he goes on, in language characteristic elsewhere of his regard both for his own life and his own works. "We gaze at such men in awe, because we gaze not at a work of art, but at the re-creation of the man through that art, the birth of a new species of man, and it may even seem that the hairs of our heads stand up, because that birth, that re-creation, is from terror." Lastly, in the next paragraph, there is a declaration of exactly what I want to make manifest as the effort in the dramatically phrased poems of the later years. "They and their sort," he writes, and it is still Dante and Villon, "alone earn contemplation, for it is only when the intellect has wrought the whole of life to drama, to crisis, that we may live for contemplation, and yet keep our intensity."

Now I do not believe Yeats felt all these sentiments all the time, for a man is never more than partly himself at one time, and there is besides a kind of outward buoyancy that keeps us up quite as much as the inward drive keeps us going—but I believe that if we keep all four sentiments pretty much consciously in mind we shall know very nearly where we are in the simplest and most dramatic as in the most difficult and most occult of Yeats's poems. With these sentiments for landmarks, he is pretty sure to have taken a two- or a three- or even occasionally a four-point bearing, in setting the course of a particular poem.

To say this smacks of instruments and tables, of parallel rules and compass roses. But only when the waters are strange and in thick weather are thoughts taken as instruments necessary or helpful. With familiarity the skill of knowledge becomes unconscious except in analysis, running into the senses, and all seems plain sailing. As with sailing so with poetry, the greatest difficulties and the fullest ease lie along known coasts and sounds; there is so much more in the familiar to work on with the attention, whether conscious or not. The object of these remarks is to suggest why it is appropriate to research, so to speak, the original perils of certain poems of Yeats—those in which one way or another the intellect has wrought life to drama—and thereby to jolt the reader's attention, on as conscious a level as possible, back to those aids to navigation which long practice safely ignores but which alone made the passage, in the beginning, feasible. In this figure it is the intellect, the imagination, the soul that is sailed. The poem is not the ship, the poem is the experience of sailing, the course run, of which it is possible to make certain entries. It should be insisted, though, that these entries in the log only recount and punctuate the voyage, and in no way substitute for it. The experience of sailing cannot be put in any log, in any intellectual record. There is the sea, and there is language, experienced; there is the sailing and the poetry: there are not only no substitutes for these, there is nothing so important as getting back to them unless it be to begin with them.

Let us begin then, and it is quite arbitrary to begin in this way, and to many minds will seem extreme, by conceiving that there is a play of words in the composition of poetry, which the conscious mind cannot control but of which it must take continuous stock, and which, by holding itself amenable, it can encourage or promote. Let us insist, further, that to equip himself with conscious amenities of this order is the overt training of a poet: remarking that this is one way to consider the acquisition of habits of meter, pattern, phrase, cadence, rhyme, aptitude for trope and image: adding, that without such intellectual training the poet will be quite at a loss as to means of taking advantage of the play of the words as it begins and will write wooden of demeanor, leaden of feet. Let us insist on this because Yeats himself insisted on it. Aubrey Beardsley once told Yeats—and Yeats liked to repeat it—that he put a blot of ink on paper and shoved it around till something came. This is one routine hair-raising practice of the artist of any sort: to invoke that which *had been* unknown, to insist on the apparition, to transform the possible into a vision. The artist poaches most on his resources when ad libbing, when he meets, and multiplies, his perils with, as Yeats said, nonchalance. The rest is cribbing or criticism.

To crib is to find something from which to start—some system, some assumption, some assertion; and to criticize is only to spot the connections, to name the opposite numbers. To crib and criticize together is to get the whole thing back on a concrete or actual basis where it is its own meaning. It is in this sense that art is a realized, an intensified (not a logical or rhetorical) tautology. Art declares its whatness, its self, with such a concreteness that you can only approach it by bringing abstractions to bear, abstractions from all the concrete or actual experience you can manage to focus. That is how art attracts richness to itself and reveals its inner inexhaustibleness; that is how art becomes symbolic, how it lasts, how it is useful, how it is autonomous and automotive—how it puts its elements together so as to create a quite unpredictable self. Different accounts reach similar conclusions; all accounts bring up on the unaccountable fact of creation; this account merely emphasizes ad libbing as a means of getting at the unaccountable, and is meant to invoke the murk—the blot of ink—in which words habitually do their work.

Yeats, as he grew older, wrote a good many of his most effective poems by ad libbing around either some fragment of his "system" or some free assumption or assertion. Often these *donnée's* turn up as refrains. For example, the poem called "The Apparitions" works around the refrain lines:

> *Fifteen apparitions have I seen;*
> *The worst a coat upon a coat-hanger.*

The whole poem is made of three stanzas, of three couplets each, with the refrain added. The first stanza is "about" talking vaguely, implausibly, untrustingly of an apparition. The second is "about" the pleasure of talking late with a friend who listens whether or not you are intelligible. There is no "poem," there is nothing made, so far; the refrain with one repetition seems to hang fire, but there is a sense of fire to come. The blot of ink is beginning, after a move this way and that, after just *possible* movements, to turn itself into a vision; and indeed the third stanza shows itself as the product, backed or set by the first two stanzas, of the vision *and* the refrain. Put another way, the possible is pushed over the edge and into the refrain, so that the refrain is, for the instant, the limit of meaning.

> When a man grows old his joy
> Grows more deep day after day,
> His empty heart is full at length,
> But he has need of all that strength
> Because of the increasing Night
> That opens her mystery and fright.
> *Fifteen apparitions have I seen;*
> *The worst a coat upon a coat-hanger.*

The scarecrow hangs in that closet for good; nobody knows how or why, unless we say by ad libbing around the refrain. That the refrain may in fact have come earlier and required the stanzas, or that the stanzas may in fact have searched for the refrain, makes no difference. Something has been done to the refrain by the progressive interaction between it and the stanzas that has built up a plurisignificance (to borrow Philip Wheelwright's substitute for the Empsonian term Ambiguity) that has not stopped when the poem stops. The astonishing thing is that this plurisignificance, this ambiguity, is deeper than the particular words of the poem, and had as well been secured by other words at the critical places, indeed by the opposite words, so far as superficial, single meanings go. I do not mean to rewrite Yeats; I mean to take a slightly different tack on the course he himself set, and with the same wind in my tail. Ignoring the exigences of rhyme, let us ad lib the stanza quoted above so that instead of joy growing more deep it grows less, so that the full heart grows empty, and remark that he has need of all that room—the room of emptiness, it will be—precisely

> Because of the increasing Night
> That opens her mystery and fright.

But let us not stop there. Could not the night diminish as

well as increase; could it not, for the purposes of the achieved poem, close as well as open? One tends to let poems stay too much as they are. Do they not actually change as they are read? Do they not, as we feel them intensely, fairly press for change on their own account? Not all poems, of course, but poems of this character, which engage possibility as *primum mobile* and last locomotive? Is not the precision of the poem for the most part a long way under the precision of the words? Do not the words involve their own opposites, indeed drag after them into being their own opposites, not for contradiction but for development? After such queries we can return to the poem as it is, and know it all the better so, and know that we have not altered, even tentatively, anything of its actual character by playing with what is after all merely its notation. We have come nearer, rather, to the cry, the gesture, the metaphor of identity, which as it invades the words, and whichever words, is the poem we want.

I bring up this mode of treating a poem, because Yeats more than any recent poet of great ability has written many of the sort that invite the treatment, and because it is that class of his poems which this paper proposes to treat. In these poems he is dealing with a kind of experience which is understood by the unlearned better than, as a rule, by the learned; for the learned tend to stick to what they know, which is superficial, and the unlearned, who should ideally be, in Yeats's phrase for his own ambition, as ignorant as the dawn, have their own skills of understanding immediately available.

That this race of the unlearned, these common readers every poet hopes for, cannot be found in a pure state, whether under the apple tree or the lamplight, is not relevant beyond first thought. There are no poems, only single lines or images, entirely fit for this kind of common reading. There are only poems which move in the direction of such reading—such hearing, I would rather say; and, similarly, there are only readers sufficiently able to rid themselves of their surface, rote expectations to get down to their actual abiding expectations about poetry. It was such readers as well as such poetry that Yeats had in mind when he ended his verses rejecting the embroidered brocade of his early work with the lines:

> For there's more enterprise
> In walking naked.

And it was the poetry which came out of that enterprise made him put this in a letter to Dorothy Wellesley: "When I come to write poetry I seem—I suppose because it is all instinct with me—completely ignorant." The excitement and the difficulty of the enterprise show in another letter: "I have several ballads, poignant things I believe, more poignant than anything I have written. They have now come to an end I think, and I must go back to the poems of civilisation."

To push the process one step further, it was perhaps the contemplation of a combination of both kinds of poetry, that led him to write a month later, with the proof sheets of *A Vision* just done, and with all the burden of that effort, so abstract in frame and so learned in its special rash fashion, so concrete in intention and detail, that he had begun "to see things double—doubled in history, world history, personal history. . . . In my own life I never felt so acutely the presence of a spiritual virtue and that is accompanied by intensified desire. Perhaps there is a theme for poetry in this 'double swan and shadow'. You must feel plunged as I do into the madness of vision, into a sense of the relation of separated things that you cannot explain, and that deeply disturbs emotion."

Yeats as a poet was indeed a double man and the drive of one half was always encroaching upon the drive of the other half, the one richening, quickening, anchoring, disfiguring the other, as the case might be. The one half was always, to come back to our poem, infecting the other with the violence and inevitability of an apparition, proof, as he wrote in "Under Ben Bulben,"

> Proof that there's a purpose set
> Before the secret working mind:
> Profane perfection of mankind.

Let these lines be an example as well as a commentary; and let the example, before we are done, flow back into the whole poem with a kind of extra resilience for our having pulled it out taut. The lines have their prose meaning clear and immediate enough for the purposes of quotation, a meaning that brings up as something of a puzzler only, at first sight, on the word profane. Just what that word signifies here I don't know in any sense that I can communicate. But I am certain that its meanings are plural, and that neither Yeats nor his poem may have intended to apply all of them. It is one of those words which, looked at, gets ahead of all its uses and makes something unexpected of its context, as words in poetry should. As it seems to have in it the theme—that which is held in tension—of the poems I want to discuss, some of the meanings may be elaborated a little.

There are meanings over the horizon, meanings that loom, and meanings that heave like the sea-swell under the bows, and among them, when you think of them all, it is hard to say which is which, since any one gradually passes through the others. There is the traditional association of profane with Sacred and Profane Love. There is profane in the sense of violated, of common in the good sense, of racy rather than austere, of instinctive or passionate rather than inspired. There is profane in the sense of known to everybody, to the uninitiate, known in ignorance without articulation. And there is also profane in the etymological sense, still thriving in Donne, the sense which the other senses only get back to, the sense which has to do with that which is outside or before the temple; and this suggests, of course, profane in the senses of the impious, the disorderly, the random, even the wicked, the lustful: all that is anathema to the absolute or obsessed mind. To elaborate further is vain waste, for with what we have the context begins to draw the meanings in, and begins to illustrate, too, in passing, to what degree the poet using this mode of language cannot help ad libbing, playing, with his most inevitable-seeming words: he cannot possibly control or exclude or include all their meanings.

But to return to the text. Wondering a little whether profane is not alternatively both verb and adjective, we attach it to the word perfection, enhanced or confused as we may have rendered it. Profane perfection! what is that but man's perfection outside the temple of his aspiration, the perfection from which his aspiration sprang, and yet a perfection which cannot be felt except in apposition to the temple. Let all the meanings of profane play in the nexus, here surely is the madness of vision, the "sense of the relation of separated things that you cannot explain," into which, with his double view, Yeats felt he had plunged. But we are not finished; we are not yet concrete enough. If we go back a little in the poem, and remind ourselves that Yeats is only developing his admonition to the sculptor and poet to

> Bring the soul of man to God,
> Make him fill the cradles right,

then the relatedness between profane and perfection becomes almost a matter of sensation; and indeed does become so if we now at last take the lines as they come. We see, as in the Apparitions poem, how the ad libbing of notions and images finally works full meaning out of the final reading of profane perfection.

> Measurement began our might:
> Forms a stark Egyptian thought,
> Forms that gentler Phidias wrought.
> Michael Angelo left a proof
> On the Sistine Chapel roof,
> Where but half-awakened Adam
> Can disturb globe-trotting Madam
> Till her bowels are in heat,
> Proof that there's a purpose set
> Before the secret working mind:
> Profane perfection of mankind.

It should be noted that we have deliberately begun with two poems where the ad libbing is for the most part done with material that may well have been derived from Yeats's system; at least it may all be found outlined in *A Vision* or in the *Autobiographies*. We have plain examples of the system affording the poet's imagination the chance to create what it chose: it gave backing, movement, situation to the intuitive assertions, and the intuitions, working backward, make the rest seem concrete. The reader will not now object, I think, if I insist that here as in the other poem all except the lines quoted separately could have as well been different, most of all could have been their own opposites without injury to the meaning which is under the lines. I believe that this is one of the freedoms of imagination consequent upon having a sufficiently complex system of reference, though I know, as Yeats knew, that there are other ways of securing similar freedom. There is that freedom, for example, which would have come had Yeats set the course of his poem according to the first of the four bearings mentioned above: had there been enough mythology put into this particular patchwork of his system to keep his invention a little nearer the minimum. Thus we can say that as it stands there is a little too much tacking to the poem. The famous sonnet to "Leda and the Swan" gives us the nearly perfect example of the fusion of mythology and system and intuitive assertion so dramatized in crisis as to provide an inexhaustible symbol in contemplation without loss of intensity. This poem I have dealt with elsewhere, and here only add that the circulating presence of the myth, like the blush of blood in the face, brings the underlying richness of meaning nearer the surface, and nearer, if you like, too, to the expectations of the learned reader, than the poems we have just examined. There is less in the meanings but curiously more in the words themselves that could have been different; which is witness that the reality of myth is much further beneath the words in which it happens to appear than mere unmoored philosophy can be.

An example halfway between the two comes to hand in the short poem called "Death," which had it been given but a situation, a place in history, and the man in it a name, would have been a myth in little.

> Nor dread nor hope attend
> A dying animal;

A man awaits his end
Dreading and hoping all;
Many times he died,
Many times rose again.
A great man in his pride
Confronting murderous men
Casts derision upon
Supersession of breath;
He knows death to the bone—
Man has created death.

Here lines five to nine provide out of Yeats's system the *necessary* stuffing to complete the interval between dread and hope and the supersession of breath; they both could be too readily something else and too much invite expansion in terms of Yeats's known field of reference. Yet the splendid word supersession almost makes up for them, almost removes from them their murk of facileness; for supersession, mind you, means both plain stoppage and the condition (here death) of having become superfluous. As it stands, I think it is one of those poems that tremble between on the one hand collapse and on the other hand supreme assertion. It depends on what voice you hear or say the poem in. It allows but does not itself release a great gesture.

The trouble is, generally, that not all a man wishes to write always finds for itself bodily support in existing myth, and that, too, even if it did, most readers would be insufficiently familiar with the machinery of the myth used to understand the development to which it had been pushed without the use of reference books. This has been my experience in a practical way with readers of "Leda and the Swan." The skill of nearly instinctive, deposited understanding of the classic myths has become either mechanical or muddled where it has not disappeared; and without such a skill in his reader the poet cannot use his own, and is driven inward. Specifically, the trouble with Yeats was that the system that he had been driven to invent in despite of both Christianity and rationalism, did not in actuality leave him free to create what he chose more than, say, half the time. Thus as a poet he was left in the dubious position of being unable to believe in his own system more than half the time; he was constantly coming on things which his system could not explain, and which he was yet compelled to turn into poetry.

Yeats's solution was to wipe out of his consciousness the whole middle class, the educated class, the Christian class, the rationalist class, both as subject matter and for direct audience, and write poems addressed to a double-faced class of his own creation, which luckily includes a part of us all, half peasant or fisherman or beggar, half soldier or poet, half lord and half lout. It was as if, groping for Dante's luck he had come suddenly on Villon's, but with the knowledge of Dante in his blood beating in furious aspiration and with the burning indignation of Swift blinding his eyes with light: Dante the "chief imagination of Christendom" and

Swift beating on his breast in sibylline frenzy blind
Because the heart in his blood-sodden breast had dragged
   him down into mankind.

Villon's luck was enough as Yeats used it in the poems I think of—the best of the Crazy Jane poems and the best of his other three groups with a similar ballad-like surface and subterranean symbolism—Villon's luck was enough to make the hair stand up cold on end. This quality is present only in the best of these poems; in others there is a deal of aimless and irredeemable violence, or worst of all an aimlessness without violence. One can say immediately, with this discrepancy in mind, that in the successful poems the machinery is fused in the dramatized symbol, and that in the worst there is not enough machinery—whether from Yeats's system or from the general machinery of the tradition—to bring the symbolism to light, let alone dramatize it. But to say that is to make phrases too easily, and actually to ignore what we pretend to judge. Let us rather exhibit what poetic facts we can in both good and bad examples, and see whether the poems do not render judgment themselves.

There is a kind of general fact involved when in the phrase above the hair is said to stand up *cold* on end; there is a kind of coldness in the sense of remoteness about the best Yeats that we do not find either in Dante or Villon or Swift; the kind of coldness which we associate with the activities of a will incapable of remorse or compunction or humility: the kind of coldness that reverses itself only as the heat of a quarrel, the violence of assault, the fire of the merely tumescent emotions. I do not speak of the man but of the poetry, which he made, as he said, out of his antithetical self: the self which in his old age he called old Rocky Face, that *other* self for which he wrote this epitaph in a moment of rage against Rilke's warmer ideas about death—

> *Cast a cold eye*
> *On life, on death.*
> *Horseman, pass by!*

The coldness of this created self shows most, I think, in the fact that none of the human figures in his poems—most of them nameless, for to name, he thought, was to pin the butterfly—are created as individuals. They are rather types dramatized as if they were individuals. They move as all that is typical must in a separated space. There is a barrier between them an wholly individual being which is set up by the fact that they cannot ever quite overcome the abstractions from which they sprang. Thus when Yeats pushed furthest to escape from his system he was in most peril of collapsing into it, which is what fills his figures—his Crazy Jane, his Bishop, his men and women Young and Old—with the focusing force of dramatic crisis. It is his system precariously dramatized, the abstract felt as concrete: the allegorical simulacrum churned with action. The point is, the system *is* dramatized, the typical figures *are* liberated into action, however precariously, which we can and do experience as actual within their limited focus. And the curiosity is, they are liberated most, seem most nearly individuals crying out, when inspection shows they are in fact most nearly commentaries upon some notion or notions taken out of Yeats's system. Man being man and in his senses, right or wrong, even as a poet, there is vertigo in wondering whether Yeats at bottom is giving us "felt thought" or is giving us a generalized version of what he could grasp of certain fundamental, self-created symbols of love and death. Is it insight or experience that is invoked, or a third thing which is neither but reveals both?

I do not mean to be mystifying—there is enough of that in Yeats—but I find it difficult to ascribe the right quality to such lines as come at the end of the seventh poem in "A Woman Young and Old." It is a dialogue between lovers in three quatrains and a distich called "Parting," and the first ten lines in which the two argue in traditional language whether dawn requires the lover to leave, are an indifferent competent ad libbing to prepare for the end. The stable element or symbol is the singing bird, and it is almost a version of "The bird of dawning singeth all night long," which indeed as a title would have strengthened the poem. It ends:

> *She.* That light is from the moon.
>
> *He.* That bird . . .
>
> *She.*            Let him sing on,
> I offer to love's play
> My dark declivities.

Declivities—my dark downward slopes—seems immediately the word that clinches the poem and delivers it out of the amorphous into form, and does so as a relatively abstract word acting in the guise of a focus for the concrete, delicately in syllable but with a richness of impact that develops and trembles, a veritable tumescence in itself of the emotion wanted. Call it lust and you have nothing, certainly not lust; call it as the poem does and you do have lust as a theme, and life caught in the theme. But the last two lines do not perform that feat by themselves; the situation is needed, the bird, the dawn, the song, and the moon, perhaps the moon most of all. The moon is all machinery, and very equivocal machinery out of Yeats's system. To use John Ransom's terms, does the moon supply structure to the declivities, or does the word declivities supply texture to the moon? Or is there a kind of being set up between the two, a being which is the created value of both? If so, and I think that this is one way of putting it, can we not say that Yeats has created a sort of rudimentary symbol, nameless but deeply recognizable, good in any apt repetition? Is not that what this sort of poetry is for? In what else does its immanent richness consist?

Yeats did the same thing again in "The Lover's Song" from *Last Poems.*

> Bird sighs for the air,
> Thought for I know not where,
> For the womb the seed sighs.
> Now sinks the same rest
> On mind, on nest,
> On straining thighs.

The illuminating, synergizing word here, without which the rest is nothing but maundering, is of course the word sighs; but I am afraid it will not take analysis. Fortunately there is pertinent material from Yeats's letters to Dorothy Wellesley. First, there is a phrase from Yeats's introduction to *The Selected Poems of Dorothy Wellesley,* which has an incipient connection to his own poem: "in the hush of night are we not conscious of the unconceived." Next there is a letter in which Yeats describes the reproductions of pictures on one wall of his bedroom: "Botticelli's 'Spring', Gustave Moreau's 'Women and Unicorns', Fragonard's 'Cup of Life'. . . . The first & last sense, & the second mystery—the mystery that touches the genitals, a blurred touch through a curtain." Evidently these phrases got him going, for the next day he sent the poem quoted in a letter beginning: "After I had written to you I tried to find better words to explain what I meant by the touch from behind the curtain. This morning, this came."

In comparing this poem with "Parting," there is the important difference that here the symbolic line could ride by itself, so that if it were plausible in English to have poems of one line, "For the womb the seed sighs" would be enough, and would make its own work of application wherever apt. English poetry being what it is, we say rather that the line infects the rest of the poem with its symbolic richness. But in saying that, it should not be forgotten that it is not a situation but something as primitive as a pulse that the poem dramatizes.

If the reader objects to the ascription of such qualities as rudimentary and primitive to the symbols in these two poems, I mean them so only relatively and do not at all mean that they lack complexity. Primitive symbols like primitive languages are likely to be more complex than those in which the mind has a longer history at work. This will be clear I think if we look now at the poem called "Crazy Jane Talks With the Bishop" (the second, not the first of that name). In this poem the Bishop tells Crazy Jane she is old enough to die and had better leave off the sin of flesh, but she answers him valiantly in the flesh, ending:

> 'A woman can be proud and stiff
> When on love intent;
> But love has pitched his mansion in
> The place of excrement;
> For nothing can be sole or whole
> That has not been rent.'

This is like the "torn and most whole" symbolism of Eliot's *Ash Wednesday* and of much other religious poetry, but it is also like the sexual symbolism in *Lear* and in Swift's poems, and again is like some of the "lighter" sexual poems of Blake, where the lightness of the verse forms covers profound observation; indeed, it is a fusion, with something added, of all three. Beyond that, as a trope it is an enantiosis, which includes as well as expresses its own opposite. Further, and in fact, it is an enantiodromia, the shocked condition, the turning point, where a thing *becomes* its own opposite, than which there is no place at once more terrifying and more fortifying to find oneself in. Feeling and sensation and intuition and thought are all covertly at work here, and what we see is the sudden insight at the end of a long converging train.

It may be risked that this insight, this symbol, cannot be as easily "used" as those of the two poems just discussed. As there is a great deal more development of all kinds behind this stanza, so a greater stature of response is required of the reader. At first it merely makes the hair stand on end; only later it reveals itself as an object of contemplation. Neither the terror nor the strength will show, nor will they resolve themselves in full symbolic value, unless the reader gets over the shock of the passage and begins to feel, even if he does not analyze, the extraordinary plurisignativeness of the words of the verses, taken both separately and together. I doubt if even in "Sailing to Byzantium" Yeats ever packed so much into the language of his poetry. The words are fountains of the "fury and the mire in human veins." Yet none of the meanings are abstruse or require a dictionary; none of them are derived directly from Yeats's system, but come rather from the whole history of the common language of the mind, or as Yeats calls it of the soul. The reader has been long at home with all these words, yet as he reflects he will perceive that he has never known them in this particular completeness before. It was only the convention of this poem that Yeats invented; the rest was discovery of what had long since been created. The terror is in recognition, the strength in the image which compels assent: a recognition and an assent which it is the proper business of the symbolic imagination to bring about, whether as philosophy or as myth, or as the poetry of either.

Yeats commonly hovered between myth and philosophy, except for transcending flashes, which is why he is not one of the greatest poets. His ambition was too difficult for accomplishment; or his gift too small to content him. His curse was not that he rebelled against the mind of his age, which was an advantage for poetry, considering that mind, but that he could not create, except in fragments, the actuality of his age, as we can see Joyce and Mann and it may be Eliot, in equal rebellion, nevertheless doing. Yeats, to use one of his own lines, had "to wither into the truth." That he made himself into the greatest poet in English since the seventeenth century, was only possible because in that withering he learned how to create fragments of the actual, not of his own time to which he was unequal, but of all time of which he was a product.

To create greatly is to compass great disorder. Yeats suffered from a predominant survival in him of that primitive intellect which insists on asserting absolute order at the expense of the rational imagination; hence his system, made absolute by the resort to magic and astrology, which produced the tragic poetry appropriate to it. But hence, too, when the system failed him, his attempt to create a dramatic, concrete equivalent for it. If the examples we have chosen are fairly taken, he found himself ad libbing—as most poets do—most of the time. But his ad libbing was in the grand manner and produced passages of great and luminous poetry. He was on the right track; "Homer was his example and his unchristened heart"; and more than any man of his time he upheld the dignity of his profession and re-opened the way for those of us who have the fortitude and the ability to follow, and the scope to go beyond him, if as is unlikely any such there be. For our times are of an intolerable disorder, as we can see Yeats's were for him, and will take a great deal of compassing.

> *'I am of Ireland,*
> *And the Holy Land of Ireland,*
> *And time runs on,' cried she.*
> *'Come out of charity,*
> *Come dance with me in Ireland.'*

1942

# 4. Masks of Ezra Pound

## I

The work of Ezra Pound has been for most people almost as difficult to understand as Soviet Russia. Ignorance, distance, and propaganda have about equally brought reaction to violent terms—either of idolatry or frightened antipathy. Enthusiasm and hatred, in matters of literature, are even more injurious than in economy; the chosen emotions seem entirely to obviate the need for a reasoned attitude. Enthusiasm is whole-hearted and hatred instinctive, and their satisfactions, to those who experience them, seem acts of sufficient piety. But what is obviated is only suppressed, never destroyed; and the more work—especially the more Cantos[1]—Mr. Pound publishes the more need there is for an attitude, both less whole-hearted and less instinctive, from which the work can be appreciated.

First statements had better be negative and dogmatic. Mr. Pound is neither a great poet nor a great thinker. Those of his followers who declare him the one only belittle him, and when he writes as the other, he belittles himself. Except where in his belittled forms he has done or received wrong to his verse, this essay is not concerned either with his influence upon others or with the misinterpretations of which

[1] Perhaps it should be said the more available the Cantos become. After years of scarcity and costliness, Farrar and Rinehart of New York published *A Draft of Thirty Cantos* at $2.50, followed by Cantos XXXI-XL. The text for this essay is that of the earlier volume.

he has been the victim. For Mr. Pound is at his best a
maker of great verse rather than a great poet. When you
look into him, deeply as you can, you will not find any extraordinary revelation of life, nor any bottomless fund of
feeling; nor will you find any mode of life already formulated, any collection of established feelings, composed or
mastered in new form. The content of his work does not
submit to analysis; it is not the kind of content that can be
analyzed—because, separated, its components retain no being. It cannot be talked about like the doctrines of Dante
or the mental machinery of Blake. It cannot be deduced
from any current of ideas. It is not to be found in any book
or set of books. Only in a very limited way can Mr. Pound
be discussed as it is necessary to discuss, say, Yeats: with
reference to what is implicit and still to be said under the
surface of what has already been said.

Mr. Pound is explicit; he is all surface and articulation.
For us, everything is on the outsides of his words—of which
there is excellent testimony in the fact that his best work is
his best translation. In reading even his most difficult verse,
such as the Cantos, there should never be any intellectual
problem of interpretation. It is unnecessary to pierce the
verse to understand it, and if by chance the verse is punc-
tured and the substance seems obscure or esoteric it will be
because contact has been lost with the verse itself. The difficulties of the Cantos are superficial and their valuable qualities are all qualities or virtues of a well-managed verbal
surface; which is far from saying that the virtues are superficial or slight.

On the contrary, the kind of surface which Mr. Pound
makes—the type of poetry into which the best parts of his
Cantos fall—is a very important kind of surface and reflects
a great deal of critical labor. His surface is a mask through
which many voices are heard. Ever since he began printing
his poems, Mr. Pound has played with the Latin word *persona. Persona*, etymologically, was something through which
sounds were heard, and thus a mask. Actors used masks
through which great thoughts and actions acquired voice.
Mr. Pound's work has been to make *personae*, to become

himself, as a poet, in this special sense a person through which what has most interested him in life and letters might be given voice.

Such a surface, such a mask, consumes more critical than naively "original" talent; as may be seen when in the Cantos Mr. Pound demonstrates his greatest failures where he is most "original," where he has not remembered to be a mask. That is, the verse which is left after he has selected and compressed what voices he wants to be heard, will be both a result of criticism and a species of criticism itself, and the better the criticism the better the verse. Where the critical labor has been foregone and the other, commonplace kind of personality has been brought in as a substitute, the dull reading of duller gossip in bad verse is the result.[2]

We may accept, then, the thirty-odd published Cantos of Mr. Pound's long poem as a mask which is also a criticism of the men and books and gods whose voices he wishes us to hear. We cannot quarrel with what he chooses to personify any more than we quarrel with Shakespeare for writing about Caesar rather than Socrates—although if it pleases us we may be puzzled and regret missed opportunities. Here, however it may be in writers whose work is differently weighted, we are concerned with a poetry of which the finished surface is to the maximum degree its subject, and the object of criticism will be to see whether it enforces the terms itself exacts.

Before examining the large, unfinished mask of the Cantos, Mr. Pound's two principal finished works—*Hugh Selwyn Mauberley* and *Homage to Sextus Propertius*—may first be considered. The first is Mr. Pound's most nearly, in the ordinary sense, "original" work, and the second, as a translation, the least. The reverse ascriptions are in fact more accurate; and the paradox is verbal not substantial.

[2] The doctrinaire and hortatory sections of Mr. Pound's prose criticism are but the apotheosis of the bad parts of the Cantos. The further he gets from the center of his verse the greater his self-indulgence. In verse and when directly handling the fabric of verse perhaps our most acute critic, he is in his general prose our least responsible.

The substance of *Mauberley,* what it is about, is common-place, but what the translator has contributed to *Propertius* is his finest personal work. In both poems a medium is set up and managed as near perfectly as may be in such qual-ities as phrasing, rhyme (in *Mauberley*), cadence and echo. One indication of the perfection of the medium is that, al-most without regard to content, both poems are excessively quotable. With no compunction as to substantial relevance phrase after phrase comes to mind in a kind of willy-nilly elegance.

*Mauberley* as a whole combines homage to a poet half contemporary and half ninetyish with an attack on the cir-cumstances which make the success of such a poet difficult, and possible. It is the cry of the romantic poet against the world which surrounds him and the cry of a poet choosing a different world in his mind; but the romantic cries are ut-tered with a worldly, even a tough elegance. As a whole, *Mauberley* must be either swallowed or rejected; that is, after reading, one operation or the other will be found to have been made. There is no logic, no argument, in the poem, to compel the reader's mind to adherence; it is a matter for assimilation.[3]

[3] T. S. Eliot in his Introduction to Pound's *Selected Poems* (London: Faber & Gwyer, 1928) expresses very firmly a larger belief. "It is compact of the experience of a certain man in a certain place at a certain time; and it is also a document of an epoch; it is genuine tragedy and comedy; and it is in the best sense of Arnold's worn phrase, a 'criticism of life'." More re-cently, in a group of fifteen Testimonies put out by Farrar and Rinehart to accompany the Cantos, Mr. Eliot goes even further. "I find that, with the exception of *Mauberley,* there is no other contemporary—with disrespect for none, for I include myself—whom I ever want to re-read for pleasure." Against these periods it may not be unilluminating to expose another, equally rigid point of view. Mr. Yvor Winters (*Hound & Horn,* April-June, 1933, p. 538) has this to say of *Mauberley* (he has been speaking of the defect of Romantic irony in the Middle Gener-ation of American writers): "Pound writes a lugubrious lament for the passing of Pre-Raphaelitism, yet deliberately makes Pre-Raphaelitism (and himself) appear ludicrous. The result is a kind of slipshod elegance: the firmness of the secure ironist . . . is impossible." Mr. Eliot presses his acceptance,

However, *Mauberley* need not be taken as a whole; wholeness, preconceived, is a prison into which the mind is not compelled to thrust itself; the parts, taken seriatim, establish parallels, sequences, connections, and conspire, in spite of the prejudiced mind, to produce an aggregate better, that is more useful, than the prison. It is a matter of adding. Here the addition will not be exhaustive, because the task is preliminary, to come at the addition of the Cantos.

The first stanza of the first poem ("Ode pour l'Election de son Sepulchre") sets the subject of which the remaining seventeen poems are variations.

> For three years, out of key with his time,
> He strove to resuscitate the dead art
> Of poetry; to maintain "the sublime"
> In the old sense. Wrong from the start—

"No, hardly," the poem goes on—the rest of *Mauberley* goes on—listing contrasts between the present time and the sublime in the old sense. The next four stanzas contain references to Capaneus, the gods lawful in Troy, Penelope, Flaubert, Circe, The Grand Testament of Villon, and the Muses' diadem. The only difficulties are Capaneus, who appears between semicolons unadorned, and the fact that the Trojan gods are given in Greek; and these difficulties—as will be illustrated later—are typical of all the difficulties in Mr. Pound's work. They are not difficulties in the substance of the poem, but superficial, in the reader's mind. This poet expects the reader to know, or to find out, that Capaneus was one of the seven against Thebes, that he was presumptuous enough to say that Zeus himself could not destroy him, that Zeus did destroy him with appropriate lightning; that, finally, the poet like Capaneus is full of *hubris* and is likely to be himself similarly destroyed. The line about the gods is in Greek script because the syntax of the poem demands it; the substance, perhaps, is in the fact that it is in

---

and Mr. Winters his rejection, too hard; both for reasons outside the poem, so that both end in misconstruction. As the dilemma is false the poem refuses to be impaled.

Greek. In English the lovely rhyme of Τροίη and *leeway* would have been impossible; but that is not the only loss that would have been incurred. In English, "Be the gods known to thee which are lawful in Troy," could never have been "caught in the unstopped ear" (the next line), at least not without considerable circumlocution. The ear would have been stopped, and the Sirens do not sing in English. If the reader protests that he cannot be expected to know Capaneus at first sight and that his knowledge of Greek characters is visual at best, Mr. Pound's retort might well be that the reasons for that protest made the subject of his poem; that anyway, the poem is there and the reader can come at it if he wants to, and that, besides, the reader's ignorance, if he have wit, is likely to be as illuminating as any instruction he can come by.

Without pre-judging either protest or retort, the point here to be emphasized is this: this is the sort of poem Mr. Pound writes when he writes most personally. Nothing is based on sensation, very little on direct feeling or vision, and the emotion is conventional, agreed upon, or given, beforehand. What Mr. Pound does is to support his theme with the buttresses of allusion. This is as true of poems numbered IV and V, which deal with the war and contain only one literary tag ("Died some pro patria non dulce non et decor") as it is true of "Medallion," the last of the group, which is perhaps the most literary. The object is to give conventional, mask-like form, in the best possible verse, to the given attitude or emotion.

> Charm, smiling at the good mouth,
> Quick eyes gone under earth's lid,
>
> For two gross of broken statues,
> For a few thousand battered books

is no better verse and no less conventional than

> The sleek head emerges
> From the gold-yellow frock
> As Anadyomene in the opening
> Pages of Reinach.

What we see is Mr. Pound fitting his substance with a surface; he is a craftsman, and we are meant to appreciate his workmanship. When we try to discern the substance, we find that the emphasis on craft has produced a curious result. Instead of the poem being, as with most poets of similar dimensions, a particularized instance of a plot, myth, attitude, or convention, with Mr. Pound movement is in the opposite direction; the poem flows into the medium and is lost in it, like water in sand. Shakespeare used what are called the sources of *King Lear* to encompass and order a vast quantity of his own experience, and as the play is digested we are left, finally, with Shakespeare's material rather than the source material. With Mr. Pound, we begin with his own experience and end up with the source. The Pound material has been lost sight of; it is no longer necessary or relevant, because it has been generalized into the surface of the poem, and has thus lost its character in the character of the mask.[4] In other words, with a little exaggeration, Mr. Pound behaves as if he were translating; as if there were, somewhere, an original to which *Mauberley* must conform. He is not looking for an objective form to express or communicate what he knows; the objective form is in his mind, in the original, which requires of him that he find and polish only a verbal surface. It is therefore not unnatural that where there is actually an original to control him, he will do his freest, best, and also his most personal work. The *Homage to Sextus Propertius,* if only because it is longer, more complex, and has a more available original, is a better example of his success than "The Seafarer" or "Cathay."

*Propertius* is made up of passages, some as short as three or four lines, one as long as ninety-four, taken from Books II and III of the Elegies. The selections are neither consecutive in the Latin nor complete in themselves; nor does Mr. Pound always give all of the passage chosen. He arranges, omits, condenses, and occasionally adds to, the

---

[4] There may be some connection between this procedure in poetry and Mr. Pound's recent declaration that he is giving up letters and will devote his mind to economics.

Latin for his own purposes: of homage, of new rendering, and of criticism.[5]

What is characteristic of this poem more than its attitudes toward love and toward the poet's profession, is the elegance of the language in which these attitudes are expressed. By elegance is meant—and the meaning may be recovered in the term itself—a consistent choice of words and their arrangement such as to exemplify a single taste; a quality, like Mr. Pound's other qualities, which may be associated with craftsmanship; a quality which can be acquired, and may be retained only with practice. Usually associated with poets of lesser talent, or with the lesser works of greater talent, elegance is commonly taken as an end in itself. Its sustaining, its transforming powers are not seen or are underestimated. Dryden and Pope are sometimes reduced to the level of Gray and Collins for reasons which come very nearly to this: that the elegance of all four poets is taken as equally ornamental and, once appreciated, equally for granted. The truth is that in relation to the subject or inspiration of verse there are contrary sorts of elegance, the sort which enriches because it transforms and the sort which impoverishes because it merely clothes. Gray and Collins, aside from their single successes, exhibit the impoverishing elegance to which an insufficiently mastered taste can lead: too much of their work reads like water and leaves no trace. Dryden and Pope, in their mature work, are always strong, the elegance of their language is powerful enough to sustain and transform any subject however commonplace or weak its surd may be. Mr. Pound's *Propertius* has this quality of tough elegance, and to a degree great enough to surpass what might have been the insuperable difficulties of a loose metrical form and a highly

[5] It may save the interested reader trouble and will certainly clarify Mr. Pound's structural method to list the passages rendered, in the order in which Mr. Pound presents them. III i; II ii; III iii; III xvi; III vi; II x; II i; II xiii; III v; III iv; II xv; II xxviii; II xxix; II xxx; II xxxii; II xxxiv. Omissions, inventions and the minutiae of rearrangement are not given.

conventional subject matter.[6] What and how Mr. Pound transforms in his English Propertius' Latin can only be illustrated by quotation and comparison—from Mr. Pound, from the Latin, and from the prose version of H. E. Butler in the Loeb Library.

> Callimachi Manes et Coi sacra Philetae,
>   in vestrum, quaeso, me sinite ire nemus.
> primus ego ingredior puro de fonte sacerdos
>   Itala per Graios orgia ferre choros.
> dicite, quo pariter carmen tenuastis in antro?
>   quove pede ingressi? quamve bibistis aquam?
> a valeat, Phoebum quicumque moratur in armis!
>   exactus tenui pumice versus eat,—
> quo me Fama levat terra sublimis, et a me
>   nata coronatis Musa triumphat equis,
> et mecum curru parvi vectantur Amores,
>   scriptorumque meas turba secuta rotas.
> quid frustra missis in me certatis habenis?
>   non datur ad Musas currere lata via.
> multi, Roma, tuas laudes annalibus addent,
>   qui finem imperii Bactra futura canent;
> sed, quod pace legas, opus hoc de monte Sororum
>   detulit intacta pagina nostra via.
> mollia, Pegasides, date vestro serta poetae:
>   non faciet capiti dura corona meo
> at mihi quod vivo detraxerit invida turba,
>   post obitum duplici faenore reddet Honos;
> omnia post obitum fingit maiora vetustas:
>   maius ab exsequiis nomen in ora venit.
>
> (Elegies III, i, 1-24.)

Shades of Callimachus, Coan ghosts of Philetas
It is in your grove I would walk,
I who come first from the clear font

---

[6] Readers who have consulted the classics only in metrical translation, must often have been struck with the commonplaceness of great poets. Most poetry is on commonplace themes, and the freshness, what the poet supplies, is in the language. There are other matters of importance in original poetry, but it is the freshness of Mr. Pound's language, not the power of his mind or of a sounder interpretation, that makes his translations excellent poetry.

Bringing the Grecian orgies into Italy,
               and the dance into Italy.
Who hath taught you so subtle a measure,
               in what hall have you heard it;
What foot beat out your time-bar,
               what water has mellowed your whistles?

Out-weariers of Apollo will, as we know, continue their
     Martian generalities.
               We have kept our erasers in order,
A new-fangled chariot follows the flower-hung horses;
A young Muse with young loves clustered about her
               ascends with me into the ether, . . .
And there is no high-road to the Muses.

Annalists will continue to record Roman reputations,
Celebrities from the Trans-Caucasus will belaud Roman
     celebrities
And expound the distentions of Empire,
But for something to read in normal circumstances?
For a few pages brought down from the forked hill
     unsullied?
        I ask a wreath which will not crush my head.
               And there is no hurry about it;
I shall have, doubtless, a boom after my funeral,
Seeing that long standing increases all things
               regardless of quality.
         (*Homage to Sextus Propertius*, I.)

Shade of Callimachus and sacred rites of Philetas, suffer
me, I pray, to enter your grove. I am the first with priestly
service from an unsullied spring to carry Italian mysteries
among the dances of Greece. Tell me, in what grotto did
ye weave your songs together? With what step did ye enter? What sacred fountain did ye drink?

Away with the man who keeps Phoebus tarrying among
the weapons of war! Let verse run smoothly, polished with
fine pumice. 'Tis by such verse as this that Fame lifts me
aloft from earth, and the Muse, my daughter, triumphs
with garlanded steeds, and tiny Loves ride with me in my
chariot, and a throng of writers follows my wheels. Why
strive ye against me vainly with loosened rein? Narrow is
the path that leadeth to the Muses. Many, O Rome, shall
add fresh glories to thine annals, singing that Bactra shall
be thine empire's bound; but this work of mine my pages

have brought down from the Muses' mount by an untrodden way, that thou mayest read it in the midst of peace.

Pegasid Muses, give soft garlands to your poet: no hard crown will suit my brow. But that whereof the envious throng have robbed me in life, Glory after death shall repay with double interest. After death lapse of years makes all things seem greater; after the rites of burial a name rings greater on the lips of men. (Butler, *Propertius*, III, i.)

If the differences rather than the similarities of the three versions are sufficiently emphasized the connections between them become slight. The "original," whatever it was, perhaps equally inspired all three; that is, the Latin itself seems as much a version as either translation. Not only the tone and texture vary, but the intent, the inner burden, of any one is incompatible with either of the others. The prose version is the most poetical, the Latin less, and Mr. Pound's, while the least, is today, whatever it might have been in the first century, the best verse—because its intent is suitable to our own times, and because Mr. Pound carries only the baggage to hold down and firm that intent.

Such general statements require no insight to make and emerge from general reading alone. But support is available and at least a sort of definition possible in an examination of specific words and phrases. "Coan ghosts . . . Grecian orgies . . . mellowed your whistles . . . Martian generalities . . . something to read in normal circumstances . . . expound the distentions of empire . . . a boom after my funeral"—these phrases spring from the same source as Propertius' Latin and Butler's prose; but they have an element common to neither, or at any rate not found in either to the same degree, the element of conversational, colloquial ease used formally, almost rhetorically, to heighten the seriousness of the verse. The words "ghosts, orgies, whistles, normal, distentions, generalities, boom" do not appear either in the Latin or in Butler's English. They make Butler superfluous, for this purpose, and transform Propertius; and they are the result of the operation of a very definite taste.

The matter may become clearer if two lines are taken where the verbal transformations are less obvious and what is called fidelity to the original is greater. "Exactus tenui pumice versus eat" becomes with Butler "Let verse run smoothly, polished with fine pumice" and with Mr. Pound "We have kept our erasers in order." So far as facts go, the words come to the same thing in all three, but the tones are utterly different. Even closer to the Latin "non datur ad Musas currere lata via" is Mr. Pound's "And there is no high-road to the Muses." Butler's "Narrow is the path that leads to the Muses" illustrates the difference between Mr. Pound and Propertius, and points the value of it: the value, that is, in translation, of making a critical equivalent, rather than a duplicate, of the original.

Forgetting now the differences between Propertius and Mr. Pound—forgetting them because once apprehended they no longer matter—it is possible to judge better the likeness. We know better what sort of likeness to look for. We know that this Homage is a portrait not a photograph, the voice a new recital not a dictaphone record. We know, in short, that Mr. Pound begins his work where ordinary translations leave off—with a reduction of English and Latin fractions to a common denominator; he proceeds to a new work built up from that denominator. The denominator was that quality, really, of which examples were given above. The dissimilarity is superficial, in the form of expression, and only by exaggerating the surface difference could the quality be given in English at all. Mr. Pound felt the quality in the Latin, and determined that it was what made Propertius valuable; he therefore concentrated upon rendering that quality very nearly to the exclusion of Propertius' other qualities. Where the quality was lacking, he either omitted the text, condensed, or supplied it himself in his English. Thus he performed both a general and a minutely specific criticism upon Propertius. If the result is not Propertius to the classicist, or only a little of him, it is for the English reader better than Propertius, how much better the reader cannot appreciate unless he compares the passages he likes best with the Latin.

With reference to the Cantos and in comparison to *Mauberley* there are three points of importance about the

*Propertius:* that it is, although a translation, an original poem; that it is a criticism as well as a poem; and that it is exactly as much a mask, a *persona,* as *Mauberley,* though constructed in the opposite direction. The structure, which is to say the secret, if there is one, of the Cantos, is a combination, with variations, of the structure of these two poems. The Cantos ought not to be read without them, and both of them may be considered—and especially the *Propertius* of which even the meter is similar—as themselves part of the Cantos.

Of the three points mentioned, two have already been dealt with: that translation of this order makes new English poetry; and that the critical element—what the translation emphasizes, what it excludes, and in what it differs with relation to the Latin—is as necessary to appreciate as the craftsmanship. The third point needs only to be made explicit to be seized, when it is seen to have a definite connection with the other two points. In *Mauberley,* if the account was correct, all the work flowed into and ended in a convention; the intellectual intent, so far as there was one, was the declaration of a conventional attitude about the poet and his profession. In *Propertius* the convention, and very nearly the same one, was given beforehand, and the work flowed away from it, to illustrate and particularize it. Hence, having a center rather than a terminal, the *Propertius* is a sturdier, more sustained, and more independent poem than *Mauberley.* Craftsmanship may be equally found in both poems; but Mr. Pound has contributed more of his own individual sensibility, more genuine personal voice, in the *Propertius* where he had something to proceed from, than in *Mauberley* where he was on his own and had, so to speak, only an end in view. This fact, which perhaps cannot be demonstrated but which can be felt when the reader is familiar enough with the poems, is the key fact of serious judgment upon Mr. Pound. It establishes his principal limitation and measures his freedom. But the quality of judgment need no more be harsh than humane; it will be judgment of kind and degree; it will help acceptance and rejection. By emphasizing the talents Mr.

Pound possesses, it will perhaps enlighten his defects, and explain his failures as well as his successes; but that is a critical gain more than a loss. It amounts to saying that Mr. Pound is equipped to write one kind of poetry and that when he attempts with the same equipment to write other sorts of poetry, he fails, or, at most, does not write as well.

The superiority of *Propertius* over *Mauberley,* where the craftsmanship is equally skilled, may be seen analogously in Mr. Pound's earlier work. The translations are in every case more mature and more original. "The Seafarer" is better than "N.Y."; and "Cathay" is better than the epigrams in *Lustra,* and so on. That is—and this is the severest form in which the judgment can be framed—lacking sufficient substance of his own to maintain an intellectual discipline, Mr. Pound is always better where the discipline of craftsmanship is enough. And this is especially true of the Cantos.

## II

In the Cantos the reader who is not, at least at first, selective, will be lost, and will mistake, in this packed archipelago, every backwash for a thoroughfare, each turn of the tide for the set of an ocean current. It is the mistake of assuming that the Cantos make a good part of an ordinary, complex, logically and emotionally arrayed long poem, having as a purpose the increasing realization of a theme. The Cantos are not complex, they are complicated; they are not arrayed by logic or driven by pursuing emotion, they are connected because they follow one another, are set side by side, and because an anecdote, an allusion, or a sentence begun in one Canto may be continued in another and may never be completed at all; and as for a theme to be realized, they seem to have only, like *Mauberley,* the general sense of continuity—not unity—which may arise in the mind when read seriatim. The Cantos are what Mr. Pound himself called them in a passage now excised from the canon, a rag-bag.

Hang it all, there can be but the one "Sordello,"
But say I want to, say I take your whole bag of tricks
Let in your quirks and tweeks, and say the thing's an art-
    form,
Your "Sordello," and that the "modern world"
Needs such a rag-bag to stuff all its thought in . . .
                    (*Lustra*. New York, 1917, p. 181.)

These and the following lines from Canto XI together make
an adequate account of the content and one view of the
method of the poem as it has so far appeared.

And they want to know what we talked about?
    "de litteris et de armis, praestantibusque ingeniis,
Both of ancient times and our own; books, arms,
And of men of unusual genius,
Both of ancient times and our own, in short, the usual sub-
    jects
Of conversation between intelligent men."

That is, we have a rag-bag of what Mr. Pound thinks is
intelligent conversation about literature and history. As you
pull out one rag, naturally, so well stuffed is the bag, you
find it entangled with half the others. Since it is a poetical
bag the entanglements are not as fortuitous as they at first
seem, the connections may be examined, and some single
pieces are large and handsome enough to be displayed
alone.

   An exhibition of the principal subject matters in summary
form should give at least the directions the poem takes.
Most of the first Canto is translation from the eleventh
book of the *Odyssey* where Odysseus visits hell, followed
by a few lines, used as an invocation, from the second
Hymn to Aphrodite. The translation is not from the Greek
but from a Latin version. The second Canto, after half a
page of allusions to Browning, Sordello, Aeschylus, the
*Iliad* and the *Odyssey*, proceeds with a translation from the
third book of Ovid's *Metamorphoses* of how Acoetes found
Bacchus. Then, with mixed allusions, the Tyro episode
from the *Odyssey* is taken up again. The third Canto is
mixed: dealing briefly with Venice, the gods, the Cid, and
Ignez da Castro. The fourth Canto is a deliberate combina-

tion, rather than a mixture, of Provençal, Latin, and Japanese mythology. The fifth Canto sets Iamblichus, Catullus, the Provençal poets, the Borgias, and the Medici side by side. The sixth Canto is twelfth-century French history, Provençal poetry and Sordello, with Greek tags. The seventh Canto ties up Eleanor of Acquitaine with Helen of Troy, adds Diocletian's Arena, Ovid, a tournament, Dante, and proceeds with Flaubert and Henry James, and ends with an allusive apostrophe to the murder of Alessandro de' Medici by his cousin Lorenzino. Cantos eight through eleven concern the fifteenth-century Italian despot Sigismondo Malatesta, his friends, loves, learning, and wars. The twelfth Canto is about Baldy Bacon and Jim X, two modern adventurers, and is mostly anecdotal in character. By contrast, the thirteenth Canto is Chinese Philosophy in conversational form. The next three Cantos present an obscene inferno of British money, press, and war lords, with alleviations in the form of war anecdotes. Canto seventeen returns to the classics with interspersed allusions to the Italian Renaissance. A quotation from Marco Polo begins the eighteenth Canto; modern analogues of Marco Polo fill the remainder of this and all the next Canto. The twentieth Canto mixes Provençal, fifteenth-century Italian, philology, a partial résumé of the *Odyssey*, and returns to the Malatesti. The Medici occupy the first part of the twenty-first Canto, classical mythology ends it. Canto twenty-two begins with economics, Indian wars, adventure in the near east, and ends with an anecdote about Florentine sumptuary legislation *circa* 1500. In Canto twenty-three appear the Platonists, modern science, the Malatesti, a poem by Stesichoros in the Greek, Provençal troubadors, and concealed references to the first Hymn to Aphrodite. The twenty-fourth Canto is Italian scraps about the Este and Malatesti dating from 1422 to 1432. Canto twenty-five is mostly Venetian, quotes documents of the fourteenth century, letters by and about Titian of the sixteenth century, with quotations from Tibullus and Homer interlarded. Canto twenty-six centers on the Council of Florence, 1438, adds further material on the Malatesti, Medici, and Este families, quotes letters by

Pisanello and Carpaccio and one about the murder of Alessandro de' Medici. Canto twenty-seven skips over several centuries and tongues and ends with a rather lovely tale about tovarisch, Xarites, and Cadmus. Canto twenty-eight is modern science, business, small wars, and adventure. Canto twenty-nine mixes the contemporary with fourteenth- and fifteenth-century Italian. Canto thirty begins with Artemis and Mars, touches on Ignez da Castro, and ends with the death of Pope Alessandro Borgia in 1503. Subsequent Cantos deal with American statesmen in the first quarter of the nineteenth century, particularly with Jefferson and John and John Quincy Adams.

It ought perhaps to be recalled that the full title of Mr. Pound's poem is *A Draft of XXX Cantos*. That which is a draft is unfinished and may be altered, may gain proportion and assume order; and so sets up a *prima facie* defense against criticism on those scores. But what is deliberately not final, avowedly inchoate, lays itself open, as nothing else, to the kind of criticism in which Henry James—another craftsman—deeply and habitually delighted. James somewhere says that when he read a novel, he began immediately to rework it as he would have written it himself, had the *donnée* been presented to him. Under such an eager light all that is unfeasible in the Cantos luminously declares itself.

Most poets read a good deal and some are immoderately talkative. A draft of a poem of some length might well be written by a poet whose reading was in the sources of Anglo-Saxon law and the marriage customs of the Aleutian Indians, subjects which to the adept may be as exciting as Ovid or the Italian *condottieri*—and no further from the modern reader's experience. The point is an advocate's, forensical, and had better be left in the air.

We had better deal with the Cantos as if they were finished, as if they made samples of the poem to be finished, and hence select from these samples items typical of the whole.

The first thing to notice is that the classical material is

literary—translation and paraphrase; the Renaissance material is almost wholly historical; and the modern material is a composition of the pseudo-autobiographical, the journalistic, and the anecdotal. Excepting the two Cantos—the first and third—which are longish translations, the narrative structure is everywhere anecdotal—and the special technique within the anecdote is that of the anecdote begun in one place, taken up in one or more other places, and finished, if at all, in still another. This deliberate disconnectedness, this art of a thing continually alluding to itself, continually breaking off short, is the method by which the Cantos tie themselves together. So soon as the reader's mind is concerted with the material of the poem, Mr. Pound deliberately disconcerts it, either by introducing fresh and disjunct material or by reverting to old and, apparently, equally disjunct material. Success comes when the reader is forced by Mr. Pound's verbal skill to take the materials together; failure, when it occurs, is when Mr. Pound's words are not skillful enough and the internal dissensions are all that can be seen, or when the reader, as often, is simply ignorant of what is being talked about.

These effects, which may seem willful in the bad sense, are really necessary results of the anecdotal method as used by Mr. Pound. The presumption must always be, in an anecdote, that the subject and its import are known before the story is begun; they cannot be given in the anecdote itself. An anecdote illustrates, it does not present its subject; its purpose is always ulterior or secondary. Thus Mr. Pound's treatment of the *Odyssey* in the first and twentieth Cantos and *passim.*, requires, to be understood, that the reader be previously well acquainted with it. The point of the paraphrase from the Eleventh Book in the first Canto is beyond mere sound acquaintance; is perhaps that a better translation can be made through the old Latin translations than direct from the Greek: the actual subject matter translated has no substantial bearing upon the rest of the Cantos— except in so far as it deals with a divination of the dead and serves as a general invocation. Likewise the invocation to Aphrodite which follows the passage from the *Odyssey* is, very likely, not the succor of the goddess herself, but the fact that Mr. Pound used the same text for both paraphrases: thus that Latin is also a good medium for *The Hymns to the Gods*.[7]

The Malatesta Cantos (VII-XI) make a different illustration of the same method. As a unit they have only the most general relation to the other Cantos. As the Cantos about Jefferson and Adams are representative of the early American Republic, these Cantos are representative of the Italian Renaissance, and the reader is at liberty to compare the two sets. It is their character within themselves that is interesting, however, rather than the external relations in which they may be enfolded. By far the longest and most detailed in treatment of a single figure, this section of the Cantos turns out to require more rather than less anterior knowledge than some of the frankly mixed Cantos (II, IV, or XXIII). The reason for the additional requirement is external to the content of the Cantos and rises from the method used by Mr. Pound in handling that content. This is that allusive method which *must* take it for granted that the object of allusion is known, and is characteristically unable to explain it: a method that cannot take account of the reader's probable state of knowledge. Americans may be expected to know something about Jefferson and the Adamses; that Jefferson and John Adams dissolved their enmity in years of correspondence, that John Quincy Adams kept a monumental diary; at least enough to make any material used by Mr. Pound relevant to the reader's existing knowledge. That is not the state of the American mind with regard to the minor history of fifteenth-century Italy. Yet Mr. Pound writes as if conditions were identical; he writes as if Monticello and the Temple of Isotta were equally present and significant in the reader's mind, and, for example, he refers to the most astonishing and bloody of the legends about Sigismondo as casually and indirectly as he might refer to the Louisiana Purchase: as if a hint and a pun

[7] Documentary evidence for this emphasis may be found in Mr. Pound's *Instigations* (New York, 1920, pp. 334-345) where the texts in question are printed and commented upon.

would awaken complete memory. The reference is brief and
will prove the point in question.

And there was the row about that German-Burgundian
    female
And it was his messianic year, Poliorcetes, but he was being
    a bit too POLUMETIS.

                         (Canto IX)

Poliorcetes was a Macedonian king and his name meant
besieger of cities, and thus might fit Sigismondo who spent
his life besieging cities. POLUMETIS means in the Greek,
possessed of much wisdom and sagacity. The year was
1450, the year of the Jubilee at Rome. The row was because
Sigismondo, finding persuasion ineffectual, stripped, murdered, and raped a Burgundian noblewoman returning
from the Jubilee.

This may be taken as the extreme type of anecdotal allusion: where the meaning is ineluctable without the gloss.
Other examples could be given where the difficulty is of a
contrary character, where, that is, a long catalogue of names
and items appears without any statement being made of the
general event they catalogue. A third type may be illustrated as follows:

        Ye spirits who of olde were in this land
        Each under Love, and shaken,
        Go with your lutes, awaken
        The summer within her mind,
        Who hath not Helen for peer
            Yseut nor Batsabe.

                       (Canto VIII)

This is partly translation, partly modification, of a passage
beginning *O Spreti che gia fusti in questy regny*, from a
long poem written by Sigismondo in honor of Isotta degli
Atti, later his third wife. The loveliness of the verse gains
nothing by recovery of the origin, but the structure and
sense of the Canto gain considerably.

Other parts of this section of the Cantos present none of
these difficulties, and despite inversions of chronology and
telescoped detail read swiftly and straightforwardly, as for

example the first page and a half of Canto IX. The reader has the choice either of reading all the Cantos as if they were similarly straightforward and self-explanatory, or of going behind the verses to the same material, or as much as he can discover of it, that Mr. Pound himself used.[8] The poem the reader seizes will be very different depending on the choice he makes. In the one case, unglossed reading will give him, with many fine lines and lucid passages, the feeling that he has traversed a great deal of material, without having at any time been quite certain what the material was about—and without, perhaps, distinguishing any need to find out. Each person was someone, each letter written, each voice spoken, each deed historical—or each invented; collected, the parts attract each other, and without the cohesive power of obvious design or continuing emotion, cling together, a quilt in the patch work, a string of rags from the inexhaustible bag. To such phrasing might appreciation run.

But an active mind will not always stop short at the uncertain, however persuasive, when the ascertainable is at hand. Then, in the second case, glossed not unreasonably with a little history, these Malatesta Cantos exhibit not greater light but more difficulty. The sum of what is discovered as this or that, as fitting here and there, is only surpassed by what is undiscoverable. Not every word, but every paragraph at least, requires to be situated, expanded, dated, restored or brought up to the plain sense of history.

Not only must the reader know exactly what books Mr. Pound used but must himself use them in the way Mr. Pound used them. When he discovers that "But dey got de mos' bloody rottenes' peace on us" is Mr. Pound's equivalent for Broglio's statement that the Pope imposed a bad peace, he will not be so much pleased with his acumen

[8] The principal sources of the Malatesta Cantos are an unpublished life of Sigismondo by Gaspare Broglio; Clementini, *Raccolto Istorico della Fondatione di Rimini e dell' origine e vite dei Malatesti;* and Yriarte, *Un Condottiere de XVme Siècle.* More available in English is Hutton's *Sigismondo Malatesta.*

as irritated by the probability that many other lines are equally, but undiscoverably, quirky. In short, at the maximum vantage of half-instructed guessing, he will be convinced he was much better off, and the Cantos were better poetry, when he was ignorant of the intricacy of their character; and the conviction will be supported by the reflection that though the Cantos led him to history, the history did not lead him back to the Cantos.

Instruction, instead of diminishing, emphasized the anecdotal character of the poetry. Mr. Pound put together the materials and roused the interest appropriate to a narrative, and then deliberately refused the materials a narrative form, without, however, destroying the interests that expected it. Whether intentionally or not, it is the presence of this defeated expectation which holds these Cantos together. That is the attraction which the parts exert over each other; an attraction which constantly makes the Cantos seem on the point of rearranging themselves in an order quite different from the printed order, and quite different, also, from the historical order upon which the printed order is founded. But this third order is not achieved; there is a clog, a stoppage, at the point of crisis, and the Cantos fall back in the dismay of choices that cannot be made. Climax, what happens when things meet in a form and have ending, is rejected for the inchoate, the anecdotal, the deliberately confused, a jungle.

Jungle:
Glaze green and red feathers, jungle,
Basis of renewal, renewals;
Rising over the soul, green virid, of the jungle,
Lozenge of the pavement, clear shapes,
Broken, disrupted, body eternal,
Wilderness of renewals, confusion
Basis of renewals, subsistence
Glazed green of the jungle; . .
(Canto XX)

These phrases, upon which variations appear at least twice elsewhere in the Cantos, may, in association with the two passages quoted above about rag-bags and the subjects of conversation, be taken as Mr. Pound's declaration of doctrine. They make the "philosophic" basis, itself in anecdotal form, for the theory of sequence and structure observed in the Cantos. If the reader can accept this basis, or something like it, or can substitute for it an analogous feeling for confusion in his own soul, he will be able to accept most of the Cantos on their own terms. They will have become their own subject matter, their own end, and their own "philosophy."[9] Then the only test will be whether a passage put in question was or was not, by a saltatory action of the mind, an extension of the reader's own confusion. This view may appeal to many who take their art as the impact of experience regardless, and to whom the object of appreciation is inarticulate exhilaration. It has the extreme quality of all personal views; a quality whose maximal value is only established by surrender to it. Our concern here is only with Mr. Pound's demand that the view be taken, and we need merely grant a provisional assent to it, in order to judge the Cantos in spite of it.

Confusion, that is, is for Mr. Pound a deliberate element of procedure; but its success—such is the unitary character of language and hence of thought in language—will depend upon how well the things confused are known. Chaos is an absolute bliss which the mind may envisage but cannot reach in affirmation; there is a logic in the wildest association which the mind cannot help seizing when it sees it and which is ineffably irritating when, although suspected, it cannot be seized because it is unseen. The Malatesta Cantos furnish examples of confusion where the objects confused may at least be assumed as discoverable; and it is possible that the assumption is as good as the

[9] Mr. Pound is not a philosopher and the term is put in quotes to represent that something quite the opposite of a philosophy is being used as if it were one. A deep, but vague, feeling is made to act with the controlling power of a rigid, intellectual system. Both the depth and the vagueness are indicated when it is remembered that the Cantos accept Dante, the most orderly and rigidly systematic of poets, and that their object is in some sense analogous to that of the *Divine Comedy:* to array and judge centuries of years and individuals.

fact: the material is recorded history. In the following extract from Canto XXVIII no similar assumption can be made or if made cannot be similarly effective.

> And Mrs. Kreffle's mind was made up,
> Perhaps by the pressure of circumstance,
> She described her splendid apartment
> In Paris and left without paying her bill
> And in fact she wrote later from Sevilla
> And requested a shawl, and received it
> From the Senora at 300 pesetas cost to the latter
> (Also without remitting) which
> May have explained the lassitude of her daughter.

This, so far as can be determined, is one of Mr. Pound's completely personal contributions. He wrote it, or invented it, himself; and it has no probable source in literature or history. It is a pointless thumbnail sketch, one among the thirty-odd which in these Cantos represent our own age. It is Mr. Pound unsupported and insupportable: the pure anecdote; and there is nothing the reader can do about it.

The only assumption that can be made is that the anecdote meant something to Mr. Pound—something he didn't like but was mildly amused by. Seriously, it is a kind of dated journalism about which not enough can be known to make it important and which is not well enough written to permit enjoyment of the medium to replace knowledge of the subject. The subject failed to compel the craftsman and it came out flat. The translation from Ovid (*Metamorphoses* III, 580, ff.) in Canto III is equally anecdotal in treatment but it contains some of Mr. Pound's best writing and it has the existing literary monument to support the writing with subject and point. As soon as we know that it is about Bacchus we are at home and can appreciate as in the *Propertius* what Mr. Pound has done with the text. Mrs. Kreffle we cannot feel at home with because neither in literature nor in history did she give Mr. Pound anything to do.

The moral is plain. As our earlier comparison of *Propertius* and *Mauberley* suggested, Mr. Pound is at his best and most original when his talents are controlled by an existing text; and he is at his worst and, in the pejorative sense, most conventional, when he has to provide the subject as well as the workmanship.

We have examined the extremes of pure literature (the *Propertius* which may be thought of as resembling in this sense Cantos I and III), pure history (the Malatesta Cantos) and the personal contribution (Mrs. Kreffle). There remain certain combinations and modifications of these which exemplify the Cantos in their most interesting and important aspects.

Canto IV begins with an apostrophe to burning Troy, Apollo in his attribute as lord of the lyre (Anaxiforminges), Aurunculeia (the family name of the lady whose wedding is celebrated by Catullus in Carmen LXI), and Cadmus of Golden Prows who, among other things, was supposed to have invented the alphabet. Then follow two combinations of classical and Provençal material. The myth of Itys and Terreus (Ovid *Metam.* VI, 620, ff.) is combined with the story of the death of Cabestan, a Provençal troubadour who flourished about 1196. The story goes that Cabestan loved the lady Soremonda, and that her husband, Sir Raymond, discovering the intrigue, slew Cabestan and brought home his head and heart. The heart he roasted and seasoned with pepper. After his wife had eaten of the dish he told her what it was, showing her the head, whereupon she cast herself down from the balcony. The passage in Mr. Pound's Canto is not a version of this story but a reference to it; and the important thing about the reference is that is completes the references to the myth of Itys with which the Cabestan material is prefaced and concluded. Though description is complicated, Mr. Pound's verses are simple and once the objects of reference are known, immediately apprehensible.

The same Canto proceeds with a combination of the legend of Peire Vidal and the myth of Actaeon and Diana (Ovid, *Metam.* III, 170, ff.). Here the combination is carried further and becomes a uniting. Vidal mutters Ovid and identifies himself with Actaeon; which is perhaps Mr. Pound's explanation of Vidal's recorded behavior. Loving a woman named Loba of Penautier, and being a little mad, Vidal called himself Lop, dressed as a wolf, ran wild in the mountains of Cabaret, where he was hunted down and brought in more dead than alive. Here again it is the comparison, the anthropological identification of different materials that is important rather than the materials *per se*. No one not knowing the original material could appreciate the point of these verses. The allusions are not illustrative but indicative of a subject.

In the next Canto begins Mr. Pound's treatment of the assassination of Alessandro de' Medici by his cousin Lorenzino, which is taken up or referred to throughout the poem. This material is on a different plane and is worked up with a different type of allusion from the two examples above, but the intent is the same: analogous murders are brought to bear on each other as if the verses had an anthropological bias and were at least as much a labor in comparative mythology as Ovid would have made them.

The narration is Mr. Pound's version of Benedetto Varchi's original account. Varchi thinks of Brutus which would have been natural to the contemporary student of Renaissance murder, and Mr. Pound, as a classicist, as naturally thinks of Agamemnon and quotes, in the Greek, from Aeschylus' play parts of two lines dealing with Agamemnon's death. Later appears the Italian phrase *Caina attende*, referring to Dante's *Inferno* (XXXII) where those who commit Cain's sin are found in a lake of ice. Then follows an allusion to the astrological prophecy of the murder made in Perugia by Del Carmine. And so on. The point for emphasis is that the murder itself is not described; nor is more than the favorable and alternative motive of patriotism indicated. What was important for Mr. Pound was what the murder made it possible to allude to. In this instance the connections are comparatively ascertainable, or are superfluous, or can be guessed. The verse, and especially its continuation at the end of Canto VII, is vivid and excellent; the density of reference and the clarity of image together give the effect of immitigable substance, of which the particles, as it were, are in indefinable but necessary association.

This association, this tight cohesiveness, is the characteristic of the Cantos—it is almost their idiosyncrasy—upon which their success depends and from which result their many breaches with success. It is this effect which Mr. Pound uses instead of syllogistic logic, instead of narrative, and instead of plot. He leaves in disuse devices which would by their traditional force have ensured the strong and valuable effect of parade, of things coming one after another in an order more or less predictable by the reader's aroused expectation, and has chosen rather to depend on the device of a single method—the method of free ideogrammatic association.

Freedoms have their limits and invoke their own penalties. The Cantos overstep the one and are apparently oblivious of the other; which, while it may be one of the appropriate attitudes toward experiment, is not an attitude from which a poet can handle his work with any degree of certainty about the result. The helter-skelter appearance of the Cantos, the frequency with which they bring up or drop off short, their sudden leaps and pointless halts—these effects are not only willful but are a necessary consequence of a method which, used exclusively, cannot but be misunderstood both by the poet and by his readers.

Let us examine the limitations as they proceed from a provisional declaration of principle. Mr. Pound wishes to bring together the subjects of intelligent conversation in such a way that their association will make the one significant in terms of the others, will make the one criticize the others, and so satisfy a purpose which amounts to the ethical in the issue of a hierarchy of values. He has himself set up his categories in a letter to *The New English Weekly* (Vol. III, No. 4. 11 May 1933). After denying that his poem has a dualistic basis and asserting that it should establish a hierarchy of values, he concludes: "If the reader wants three categories he can find them rather better in: permanent, recurrent, and merely haphazard or casual." Archetypes would perhaps be the myth of Itys and Terreus, the story of Cabestan, and, say, Mrs. Kreffle. The Malatesta Cantos mix all three categories into a fourth unnamed category. Another, equally useful set of archetypes would be the literary monument (Homer, Ovid, Dante), history (the Medici, the Malatesti), and journalism (Mrs. Kreffle, Baldy Bacon). A third set might be thought, act, and the merely phenomenal. The Cantos furnish evidence for numerous analogous triads. Two phrases quoted at important junctures in the Cantos are: *Formando di disio nuova persona* and *Et omniformis omnis intellectus est,* the first from Cavalcanti and the second from Psellos, each of which implies a triad in itself.

If with such categories in mind Mr. Pound wishes to combine his material as nearly as possible by the method of free association exclusively, it is fair to assume, leaving aside as obvious the questions of interest and ultimate cogency, that each such association should either contain, like the characters in a novel, a satisfying account of its terms, or should be immediately apperceptible to readers in a certain state of cultivation, or should be accompanied by a gloss. With the possible exception of the Malatesta Cantos and the longer translations from Homer and Ovid, Mr. Pound nowhere accounts for his material in the text. The poem, unlike the poems of Homer, Dante, and Milton, is addressed not to the general intelligence of its time, nor to an unusually cultivated class merely, but to a specially educated class alone, a class familiar with exactly the material Mr. Pound uses but does not present. And here the Cantos differ from such works as Joyce's *Ulysses,* the long poems of Blake, or the poetry of Crashaw, in that it is neither the structural framework and some of the ornament, nor the key to the meaning that is hidden in symbolism, complex allusion, and difficult thought, but the substance of the poem itself. The movement of the reader's mind is thus either from the poem as a unit to the verse as such, or from the poem to the material alluded to. Thus the poem is either lost in the original or becomes an attachment to it: it is scholia not poetry.

Yet Mr. Pound must write and his poem must be read

as if the poem were of first and only importance. That is where the limits of Mr. Pound's practice of association begin to exert themselves at least in a negative fashion. Those associations which come, not most readily to the ignorant but most keenly to the instructed mind, are those which—like the combination of Ovidian myth and Provençal biography—are most susceptible to a complete gloss. The obscurity is so easily cleared up that it no longer seems to exist, and the reader comes away with the feeling that elements in his own mind have been so compounded as to add to his sensibility. For different readers different associations will be similarly successful, not so much because of different degrees of intelligence as because of different quantities of information. When the associations seem only to be a series of apostrophes, juxtapositions, and interpolations it will be the lack of appropriate information in the reader's mind that makes them seem so; and no amount of perspicuous good will can make up for that lack. To repeat: it is not the meaning but the very subject of the thing meant that must be hunted down. This is the positive limitation of Mr. Pound's method. The adequacy of his data to the ends he has in view must often depend on improbable accident. Let one example carry the weight of many arguments. At the end of Canto XXIII occur these lines in a context containing references to Troy and Anchises:

> "King Otreus, of Phrygia,
> That king is my father."

From Mr. Pound's point of view the use of this quotation, which in itself contains nothing remarkable and enlists no profound sentiment, is highly illuminating to the association he had in mind. When the exact origin is revealed the subject appears and the association is completed. But conjecture is almost a certainty that the reader not only will not know but will not exactly find out that the quotation comes from the first Hymn to Aphrodite and represents the goddess hiding her identity to Anchises before lying with him and becoming thus the mother of Aeneas. For such a reader the quotation is a breach of limits and the association fails

because its technique demanded certainty of conditions external to the poem and inherently unpredictable: in this
case an intensive and minute familiarity with the Homeric
*Hymns to the Gods.*

Such are the limits that must needs be passed; the penalties of this technique are even more severe and arise from
the same characteristics considered from another angle. As
limitations are external and imposed from without, so penalties are internal and are a direct consequence of germinal character. The forms of expression are not rigid and
their differences are perhaps not primitive. They may be
reduced hypothetically to rudimentary agitations, signs of
recognition or dismay; but the attempt, which Mr. Pound
makes, to use a verbal language ideographically, to think in
English words as if they carried the same sort of burden as
Chinese characters—such an attempt must not only often
fail of objective form but even when it approximates that
form, as in the Ovid-Provençal material, it is incapable of
the higher effects of either kind of expression used singly—
much as hog-latin is incapable of supplication. It is less
that the familiar forms of western logic are done away with
than that they persist in seeming to do work that they are
not meant to do. The western reader—at whom doubtless
the Cantos are aimed—will necessarily expect that the chief
uses to which Mr. Pound puts his language will be similar,
or adjustable, to his own. Neither the reader nor Mr. Pound
can defeat these expectations by the assertion, however deliberate, that different expectations are in order. The intent
may be made clear but the effect cannot transpire. In the
passage from Canto XX about the jungle quoted above,
the reader may appreciate the word "lozenge," can guess
the seriousness of the intent, and will know that the effect
is of lesser dimension than the words demanded. Here, as
elsewhere where important matters are in hand, the conclusion must be that Mr. Pound has described his method,
indicated his material, and used neither in terms of the
other.

It is irrelevant to speculate as to the possible success of

an ideographic method applied to ideographic symbols; Mr. Pound has not made that experiment. He has proved, rather, the impossibility of combining an ideographic structure and a language whose logic is verbal without to a considerable extent vitiating the virtues of both. And his successes may be used against him. Whether his method be called free association, ideography, or something else, where that method is solely in evidence the result is unintelligible, trivial, or vacantly conventional. Where the method is in abeyance, or where in spite of its presence more familiar methods of expression supersede it, Mr. Pound has written passages of extraordinary beauty and clarity. If most of these passages are to be found in translations, or where an original text has been remodeled, it only shows what a terrible penalty Mr. Pound has imposed on work of his own invention by adopting his peculiar method, the penalty, in shortest description, of stultification. And the stultification arises of necessity because Mr. Pound has not seen that the idiosyncrasy of thought in English is established by the idiosyncrasy of the language itself.

The judgment that flows from this essay needs hardly be stated; it is judgment by description. But the description may be recapitulated and will perhaps gather point by condensation. Mr. Pound's poetry has had from the beginning one constant character which qualifies deeply and subordinates to it every other character. It has been deliberately constructed as a series of surfaces or *personae;* it is a mask of Mr. Pound's best craftsmanship through which the voices of old times and our own are meant to be heard. Because the medium is verse, and private, the voices are an integral part of the mask, but whether because of choice or some radical limitation of talent, the voices are as a rule given indirectly, by allusive quotation or analphabetical catalogue, and this is truer of Mr. Pound's original verse than of his translations. That is, the subject matter of his verse is, as it were, behind the mask and apart from it in spite of the intention to the contrary, so that the reader is prevented from contact with the subject matter through the verse.

The success of Mr. Pound's mask depends on the critical labor performed, in which, before the success is apparent, the reader must share. The reader must know the original or enough of it to apprehend the surface Mr. Pound has made for it, exactly as the Roman audience had to know the substance of the myths they heard recounted through the actor's *personae*. For Mr. Pound's verse is not something new, substantially on its own feet, it is a surface set upon something already existing.

When, as in *Mauberley*, the subject begins by being something comparatively his own, a consequence of private experience, it is changed as rapidly as possible, not into something objective and independent, but into something conventional and hidden, wholly dependent for existence upon the surface under which it is hidden. In *Propertius* the procedure is contrary; the subject of what Mr. Pound does in his homage is the criticism of a subject rationally preserved in the verse. The fact of translation and the criticism involved in Mr. Pound's selective, condensing, emphatic method of translation together guarantee the original subject and make it Mr. Pound's own.

The Cantos may be most easily read as a combination, both as to method and subject, of *Mauberley* and *Propertius*. The translations, under this view, secure the greatest success; the summaries such as the Malatesta Cantos rank second and the personal contributions third because the substance criticized, that is, given the form of a mask, is not sufficiently present in the parts which are not translation for the reader to apprehend it.

There is a secondary kind of success when the reader, by private research, is able to re-import the substance—as he may in the Ovid-Provençal episodes. The reader is not always able, and sometimes though able, as in the Malatesta Cantos, cannot grant the poem success because, again, Mr. Pound has not provided a critical enough surface for the substance, however acquired, to fill out. The reward of research cannot be guaranteed and the reader must choose whether or not to risk the work. This is because Mr. Pound while composing a poem of surfaces, a *persona,* has ignored the necessity that every convention have its second party subscribing to the terms on which the convention is laid down. The nature of conventions is agreement between the archetype and the instance and between the poet and his readers. Where a convention was initially successful as in the Medici-Agamemnon episode, failure for most readers was inevitable because of the free association or ideographic method of subsequent treatment, wherein Mr. Pound became himself the victim of a method he could not use.

As suggested above, the stultification of the Cantos as a whole rises from an intellectual attitude either insufficient or foreign to the idiosyncrasy of the English language. If the uses of language include expression, communication, and the clear exhibition of ideas, Mr. Pound is everywhere a master of his medium so long as the matter in hand is not his own, is translation or paraphrase; everywhere else, whether in putting his translations together or in original material, the language has an air of solipsism and bewildered intent. The contrast is too sharp and constant to explain as intermittence of talent, and must rather be due to an essential alteration, occurring when responsibility is removed, in the poet's attitude toward language itself. That is the judgment of this essay—upon which of course it may collapse—that Mr. Pound, however he may have stretched and sharpened his private sensibility, has by his raids upon ideograms and unsupported allusions, limited and dulled that of his poetry: the mask of the Cantos seems too often a camouflage.

There remain—and the pity is the greater because they are remnants—the actually hundreds of magnificent lines and passages. In an earlier version of the Cantos there was a line, now excised, which fits very well the whole poem: "A catalogue, his jewels of conversation." The Cantos are an anthology of such jewels and read as most people read anthologies, as indeed all but a few read any sort of poetry, for the felicity of line and phrase, for strangeness, or for an echoed aptness of sentiment, the reader can afford to forget the promise and ambition of which the poem cheated him. He will have been equally cheated in all but the smallest part of his reading.

1933

# 5. An Adjunct to the Muses' Diadem

*A Note on E. P.*

"In the gloom, the gold gathers the light against it." It does not matter much what source the gloom has in folly and misjudgment and human dark, if within the gloom the gold still gathers the light against it. The line occurs in Pound's eleventh Canto, one of those dealing with Sigismondo Malatesta, written about 1922, and thus, I think, at the heart of that period of Pound's work which shows most light because there was most gold to gather it, the period between 1918 and 1928: the period of Propertius in Pound's remaking, of the translations from the Provençal, of *Hugh Selwyn Mauberley*, and of the first *Thirty Cantos*. Let us see, knowing the dimness is only of time, what is (in Marianne Moore's phrase) "not now more magnificent than it is dim."

Take the line itself once more—"In the gloom, the gold gathers the light against it"; does it not commit itself in the memory by coming at an absolute image, good anywhere the writs of language run, by the most ordinary possible means, the fused sequences of two trains of alliteration, the one guttural and the other dental? Does it not also, and more important, clinch the alliteration and the image by displaying itself, as Pound used to argue all verse ought to display itself, in the sequence, not of the metronome, but of the musical phrase? Do we not come, thus, on a true blank verse line where something, which we here call music, lasts when the words have stopped, and which locks, or gears, the words together when they are spoken? Nobody knows whether the words discover the music or the music discovers the unity in the words; nobody but a craftsman skilled at this particular job of work knows how to make words and music work in common with so little contextual or environmental force; without a drama or a situation; nobody, that is, but a craftsman skilled in the details of other men's work. "In the gloom, the gold gathers the light against it."

In the eighth Canto, there is a running version of Malatesta's own lines beginning *O Spreti che gia fusti in questy regny*, which reads as follows:

> Ye spirits who of olde were in this land
> Each under Love, and shaken,
> Go with your lutes, awaken
> The summer within her mind,
> Who hath not Helen for peer
> Yseut nor Batsabe.

Here again it is composition in the sequence of the musical phrase which lifts this most commonplace and traditional notion to the direct freshness of music, and without, as in songs actually sung, any disfigurement or blurring of the words. We resume, by the skill of the words and their order, not only the tradition but also the feeling that gave rise to the tradition, but we in no way repeat the localized version of the tradition that Malatesta himself used in (what would be) bad English of the twentieth century pretending to be fifteenth. Another example, the "Alba" from *Langue d'Oc*, carries this variety of composition about as far as Pound, as craftsman, could force it. It is again translation.

> When the nightingale to his mate
> Sings day-long and night late
> My love and I keep state
> In bower,
> In flower,
> Till the watchman on the tower
> Cry:
> "Up! Thou rascal, Rise,

> I see the white
>         Light
>     And the night
>             Flies."

Here, it is true, we are nearer both the regular or metro-
nomic pattern and an actual singing tune, but we are there
by exactly the means of musical composition; we have only
to think how Swinburne would have done it, to see the delicacy and absoluteness of Pound's musical phrase, and the
difference is to be named by thinking of what Pound called,
and here made present, the "prose tradition in verse." That
tradition, that verse ought to be at least as well written as
prose, is exemplified, when one has caught its idiosyncrasy
of movement, in passage after passage of the *Homage to
Sextus Propertius,* nowhere better for purposes of quotation than the opening of the sixth selection.

> When, when, and whenever death closes our eyelids,
> Moving naked over Acheron
>         Upon the one raft, victor and conquered together,
> Marius and Jugurtha together,
>
>                         one tangle of shadows.

The third and fourth lines in this passage are not at all the
same thing as what Propertius wrote, nor do they need to
have been for what Pound was doing.

> Victor cum victis pariter miscebitur umbris:
> consule cum Mario, capte Iugurtha, sedes

is magnificent formal Latin with the special kind of finality
that goes with that mode of language and that kind of musical creation in language. Pound used what he could catch
of the mood in Propertius' mind—not the mode of his language—and responded to it with what he could make out
of the best current mood and mode of his own time; that
is why his versions of Propertius are called a Homage, and
that is why they seem written in a mode of language (the
prose tradition combined with composition in the musical
phrase) which is an addition to the language itself. One
more passage should suggest the characteristics of that
mode.

But for something to read in normal circumstances?
For a few pages brought down from the forked hill un-
          sullied?
     I ask a wreath which will not crush my head.
               And there is no hurry about it;
I shall have, doubtless, a boom after my funeral,
Seeing that long standing increases all things
                         regardless of quality.

This and the "Alba" quoted above are the extremes in opposite directions to which Pound brought his special mode;
his very best work, the extreme of his own accomplishment,
comes about when his mode is running in both directions
at once, sometimes in the *Cantos*, sometimes in the two
groups of poems called *Hugh Selwyn Mauberley*, and it
is from these groups that we may select four examples. One
is the fifth and concluding passage from the "Ode pour
l'Election de son Sépulchre."

> There died a myriad,
> And of the best among them,
> For an old bitch gone in the teeth,
> For a botched civilization,
>
> Charm, smiling at the good mouth,
> Quick eyes gone under earth's lid,
>
> For two gross of broken statues,
> For a few thousand battered books.

"In the gloom, the gold gathers the light against it." There
is no better poem of the other war, and it may well come
to be that there is no better poem to herald the war just
over, when we see what has happened in it. One feels like
addressing Pound as Williams addressed the morning star:
"Shine alone in the sunrise, towards which you lend no
part." The central distich, once the context, both that before and the concluding distich, has been mastered, makes
both epitaph and epigraph, both as near breathless and as
near sound as words can be. It is Propertius *and* the poets
of the Langue d'Oc that wrote them, the sequence of the
musical phrase *and* the prose tradition in verse, but leaning
a little more strongly toward Propertius and prose than
Arnaut and music.

A little nearer to Arnaut, but not much, is a quatrain from the preceding section of the same ode, but only by reason of the rhymes. It needs no context:

> Faun's flesh is not to us,
> Nor the saint's vision.
> We have the press for wafer;
> Franchise for circumcision.

It is prose in syntax; generalized or commonplace in thought; but it is prose and commonplace moving into music through a combination of its alliterative sequence—its ear for syllabic relations and their development—and the sequence of the idiomatic phrase. We can see—or hear—this more clearly if we put it next to two quatrains from "Medallion," where the syllabic play is as complex in English as Arnaut or Bertrans in Provençal, and where the rhyming is Pound's own.

> Luini in porcelain!
> The grand piano
> Utters a profane
> Protest with her clear soprano.
>
> The sleek head emerges
> From the gold-yellow frock
> As Anadyomene in the opening
> Pages of Reinach.

Eliot says that we must not be deceived by the roughness of the rhyme in these poems, but I do not see how anybody could see anything rough about a metric and syllabic practice which keep, as these lines do, all their sounds in the ear at once without blur or whir or anything but their own clear creation, as in this:

> Go, dumb-born book,
> Tell her that sang me once that song of Lawes;
> Hadst thou but song
> As thou has subjects known,
> Then were there cause in thee that should condone
> Even my faults that heavy upon me lie
> And build her glories their longevity.
> Tell her that sheds

> Such treasure in the air,
> Recking naught else but that her graces give
> Life to the moment,
> I would bid them live
> As roses might, in magic amber laid,
> Red overwrought with orange and all made
> One substance and one color
> Braving time.

These are the first two stanzas of the "Envoi (1919)" to the first part of *Hugh Selwyn Mauberley*, and they are quoted last in our series of examples because, at least in the context here provided for them, they show almost perfectly the combination wanted—of the prose tradition and the musical phrase; and because, too, with some alteration of the pronouns, they are lines that might well be addressed to Pound himself—except on those occasions when he gave up his song (the subjects he had mastered as music) for the sake of subjects so-called (songs which he had not mastered); for when he tried such subjects his poems are left so many

> Mouths biting empty air,
> The still stone dogs,
> Caught in metamorphosis, were
> Left him as epilogues;

just as when he kept to the songs he knew, he produced "Ultimate affronts to human redundancies"—than which a poet of Pound's class can do nothing more.

But what is Pound's class, and how can it be described without any contemptuousness in the description and without giving the effect of anything contemptible in the class; for it is an admirable class and ought to be spoken of with admiration. Essentially it is the class of those who have a care for the purity of the tongue as it is spoken and as it sounds and as it changes in speech and sound, and who know that that purity can only exist in the movement of continuous alternation between the "faun's flesh and the saint's vision," and who know, so, that the movement, not the alternatives themselves, is the movement of music.

It is the purity of language conceived as the mind's agency for creation or discovery, not merely manipulation or communication, that this class of poet works for; it is, so to speak, a pitch or condition of speech almost without reference to its particular content in a given work. The class is common enough, short of the work; it is the class of those everywhere who talk and read for the sake of talking and reading, the class of spontaneous appreciators; but it is a very uncommon class at the level of active work, and it is the active workers who make appreciation possible by providing immediate examples to train taste. It is executive work; it shows what can be done with the instrument by skill and continuous practice, and it reminds us, in terms of new prospects, of what has been done. But even more than those who read, those who write need the continuous example of poets supreme in the executive class or they would not know either what they ought to do or what it is possible for them to do in the collaboration between their conceptions and their language. Poets like Pound are the executive artists for their generation; he does not provide a new way of looking, and I think Eliot is mistaken in thinking his work an example of Arnold's criticism of life, but he provides the *means* of many ways of looking. If you criticize Pound for what he has said you come on the ancient commonplace refreshed through conventions that are immediately available; without his craftsmanship he would be a "popular" poet in the pejorative sense: the convention is always interposed *between* the actuality and his reaction to it; even his best verse is only applicable to *other* situations, it never creates its own. But that is precisely what makes him so valuable to other poets, both good and bad; his executive example helps them to unite reaction and actuality directly in a convention—the necessary working together—of language and conception, not now a commonplace but a commonplace to come; and his work affords that help because it does not intrude any conception or contortion of conception of its own. Thus he differs from poets like Hopkins or Rimbaud or Swinburne or Whitman, whose innovations represented sometimes weaknesses and sometimes purposes of their own, which when imitated substitute for weaknesses in their imitators. Thus also, he differs from poets like Shakespeare or Dante or Wordsworth, from whom the modern poet learns less the means of his trade than he learns habits of feeling to transpose and habits of insights to translate and habits of architecture—of large composition—of which he will probably be incapable except in intent. He is like, rather, poets like Cavalcanti, Arnaut, Gautier (his own chosen example), Marlowe, Greene, and Herrick; all of whom strike the living writer as immediately useful in his trade, but in no way affecting the life he puts into his trade.

In short, poets of the class in which Pound shines are of an absolute preliminary necessity for the continuing life of poetry. What he meant by composition in the sequence of the musical phrase and by the prose tradition in verse, both as he taught them in his criticism and as he exhibited them in his translations and original verses, were not only necessary in 1912 or 1918, but are necessary now and have always been necessary if the work done by man's mind in verse is not to fall off and forget its possibilities. "In the gloom, the gold gathers the light against it." If the first word in the last line is taken in the opposite sense, as in his easy irony he meant it to be taken, we can apply to Pound once more in our own context, the following verses which he once applied to himself:

> His true Penelope was Flaubert,
> He fished by obstinate isles;
> Observed the elegance of Circe's hair
> Rather than the mottoes on sun-dials.

> Unaffected by "the march of events,"
> He passed from men's memory in *l'an trentiesme*
> *De son eage;* the case presents
> No adjunct to the Muses' diadem.

1946

# 6. T. S. Eliot

*From "Ash Wednesday" to*
*"Murder in the Cathedral"*

If you want a text to head and animate a discussion of Mr. Eliot's work from *Ash Wednesday* to *Murder in the Cathedral*, there is none better—for exactness, for ambiguity, and for a capacity to irritate those unlikely otherwise to respond—than the following sentence drawn from *After Strange Gods*, which summarizes Mr. Eliot's answer to the charge of incoherence between his verse and his critical prose. "I should say that in one's prose reflexions one may be legitimately occupied with ideals, whereas in the writing of verse one can only deal with actuality." Here Mr. Eliot shows his characteristic talent for making statements of position which mislead some, drive others to labored exegesis, but end by seeming self-evident and a piece with the body of his work. In this instance what is misleading is not in the words but in the common and not always tacit assumption that poetry aims to transcend or idealize the actual; which may be so of some poetry, of official poetry for example, but cannot well be so without vitiating it, of poetry like Mr. Eliot's which has a dramatic or moral cast. Conflict of character, mixture of motive, and the declaration of human purpose and being, cannot be presented (however much they may be argued) except in terms of good and evil, which makes the most actual realm we know.

It is the criterion of the actual, of the important orders among it, and the means of approach that differ; and if we call the differences verbal, intending to belittle them, it is because we wish to escape the pressure of imaginative labor inherent in any genuine picture of the actual—as if the actual were free and ascertainable to all comers at the turn of a tap, instead of being, as it is, a remaining mystery even when long ardor has won knowledge of it. The actual, for poetry, or for Mr. Eliot's poetry, resides perhaps among "the deeper, unnamed feelings which form the substratum of our being, to which we rarely penetrate"; a notion, and Mr. Eliot's phrasing of it, to which this essay will return. Now, you might say that for the realm of the actual so conceived the psychoanalysts have a means of approach but no criterion, and the Nazis have a criterion which for their purpose makes means of approach superfluous. Mr. Eliot has a criterion and a means which may be disentangled but which cannot be separated. But it is not a criterion that many can adopt today. As it happens, the three major adequate criteria of the actual—the Church of the great Christians, philosophy as it includes Plato, Montaigne, and Spinoza, and, third, that nameless tradition of the supernatural in daily life which includes folk magic and extra-Christian religion; as it happens all three are in our day either taken as modes of escape or their animating influence is ignored. This is because of the tireless human genius for evasion and the inexhaustible human appetite for facts of the kinds that have use but cannot declare meaning: the satistical facts of science; it has nothing to do with the adequacy of the criteria themselves. Which indicates only that a man must achieve his own criterion individually and that it may appear disguised.

Mr. Eliot's criterion is the Christianity of the Church of England; and he is in the process of achieving it for himself. He provides us with an example of a powerful poetic imagination feeding on a corpus of insight either foreign or stultifying to the imaginative habit of most of us, and sustained by an active and inclusive discipline beyond our conscious needs. He is as far from us as Mr. Yeats, our one indubitable major poet, is with his fairies and lunar phases; and as close, in his best work, as Mr. Yeats in his, in an immitigable grasp of reality. It is a question which is the outsider. Mr. Yeats finds Christianity as unsatisfying for himself, finally, as any Huxley;[1] and Mr. Eliot has emphasized, with reference to Mr. Yeats, that you cannot take heaven by magic, has argued in several places recently that you cannot substitute a private for an institutional religion or philosophy. Both men write verse with the authority and the application of an orthodoxy. It may be that both are outsiders, if we conceive, as it may be fruitful to do, that the prevailing essences of English and American civilization are heterodox—when the mere sight of any orthodoxy, of any whole view, may be entertained as dramatic and profoundly tragic. Some such notion was perhaps tacitly present in Mr. Eliot's mind when he wrote the following sentence: "At the moment when one writes, one is what one is, and the damage of a lifetime, and of having been born into an unsettled society, cannot be repaired at the moment of composition." At least it is in terms derived from such a notion that the spectator can see the tragedy in the lives of such writers as D. H. Lawrence and Hart Crane—perhaps no less in the life of Dante—though the writers themselves may have seen only the pursuit of a task.[2]

Here two interesting and fundamental problems are raised—that of the truth of an orthodoxy and that of the tragedy of an orthodox mind in a heterodox world; one is for theology and the other for imaginative representation; but neither can be here our concern. Our own problem is

---

[1] I hope to consider in another place the extraordinary strength in representing reality which Mr. Yeats derives from his own resort to the supernatural; a strength so great that it corrects every *material* extravagance of his doctrine. Here I merely quote three lines addressed to a modern Catholic.

> Homer is my example and his unchristened heart.
> The lion and the honeycomb, what has Scripture said?
> So get you gone, Von Hügel, though with blessings on
> your head.

[2] It is notable that from another point of view Henry James saw the artist as an interesting theme for fiction only in his guise as a failure; his success was wholly in his work. See the Prefaces to *The Tragic Muse*, *The Author of Beltraffio*, and *The Lesson of the Master*.

no less interesting and I think no less fundamental; the problem of the moral and technical validity of Mr. Eliot's Christianity as it labors to seize the actual for representation in his poetry. Validity is not truth in an ascertainable sense, but amounts to truth in a patent sense. We are faced in Mr. Eliot's recent verse with a new and rising strength patently connected with his Christianity; and the Christian discipline is dominant and elemental in the two plays, *The Rock* and *Murder in the Cathedral*. It might formerly have been thought odd to call attention to a writer's religion as still earlier his religious conformity would have been the final test of his value. Now a man's religion is the last thing we can take for granted about him, which is at it should be; and when a writer shows the animating presence of religion in his work, and to the advantage of his work, the nature of that presence and its linkage deserve at least once our earnest examination. Interest will be clearly seen if the statement can be accepted that there has hardly been a poet of similar magnitude in English whose work, not devotional in character, shows the operative, dramatic presence of Christianity. Many poets have relied, like Wordsworth, upon a religion to which they did not adhere, and many have used such a religion provisionally as a foil from the rack; but there are only rarely examples of poets or poems where deliberate affirmative use is made of religion for dramatic purposes. It is true, after the middle age, in the ages of Faith muddled with reason, the Church would not have tolerated such a use at lay hands. There is Milton unarguably; but I should like to submit that Milton's religious dramatizations are theological in an age of theology and that what I am anxious to discriminate in Mr. Eliot is in the dramatization of the turbulent feelings and the voids beneath the theology. Then there is Blake, whose religion was not Christian and often not religion at all but whose religious convictions permeated his prophetic books; but Blake's religion was self-manufactured as well as self-achieved, with the consequence that it as frequently clogged as freed his insight. Here we are concerned with the operative advantage of an objective religion on the material of dramatic poetry.

That is, the great interest, here as in any domain of criticism, is in the facts that can be stated about the relation between Mr. Eliot's poetry and his religion. No fact requires so much emphasis as the fact that, just as Mr. Yeats's poetry is not magic, Mr. Eliot's poetry is not religion. Religion and magic are backgrounds, and the actual (which may include the experience of magic and religion) is so to speak the foreground for each; the poet is in the area between, and in the light of the one operates upon the other. But there is no way in which, say, the mystery and magic of the Mass can enter directly into the material of poetry; nor on the other hand can poetry alone satisfy the legitimate aspirations of religion. For all I know the Church may hold differently; these propositions are meant to apply from the point of view of poetry alone, which we may think of here as looking for light upon its subject matter. The Church, which is religion embodied, articulated, and groomed, concentrates and spurs the sensibility, directing it with an engine for the judgment of good and evil upon the real world; but it does not alter, it only shapes and guides the apprehension and feeling of the real world. The facts of religion enlighten the facts of the actual, from which they are believed to spring.[3]

The act of enlightening or of being enlightened cannot, except for the great mystic, amount to identification of the object with the light in which it was seen; and in poetry it is only the devotional order which would desire such identification. Mr. Eliot's poetry is not devotional, unless we accept the notion that the love of God is best exercised in the knowledge of his works; a notion which would include Shakespeare as above all a devotional poet since he mir-

[3] The facts of science may similarly enlighten, providing there is a medium of poetic imagination; this although Mr. Eliot finds, correctly, the falsely poetic astronomy of our day quite vitiated. It was, says Mr. Eliot, the eternal *silence* of the immense spaces that terrified Pascal.

rored more of the actual man than any poet we know. But that is not what we mean by devotional poetry and it is ruining the heart of a word to sustain the pretense that we do. We mean as a rule poetry that constructs, or as we say expresses, a personal emotion about God, and I think it requires something approaching a saint to be very often successful in such constructions; and a saint, as Mr. Eliot observes, would limit himself if he undertook much devotional poetry. Otherwise, whatever the sincerity, private devotions are likely to go by rote and intention rather than rise to a represented state; there enters too much the question of what ought to be felt to the denigration (and I should say to God's eye) of what is actually felt—and it is this characteristic predicament of the devout which cripples the development of poets like Hopkins and Crashaw so that we value them most in other, hindered qualities than the devout. It is perhaps indicative in this context of devotional poetry considered as poetry to remember how few from twenty Christian centuries are the great prayers. It would seem that an earnest repetition of the General Confession is a more devout if less emotional act than the composition of a poem.

Mr. Eliot's poetry is not devotional in any sense of which we have been speaking, but, for the outsider—and we are all outsiders when we speak of poetry—it is the more religious for that. It is religious in the sense that Mr. Eliot believes the poetry of Villon and Baudelaire to be religious —only an educated Villon and a healthy Baudelaire: it is penetrated and animated and its significance is determined by Christian feeling, and especially by the Christian distinction of Good and Evil. This feeling and this distinction have in his prose reflections led him to certain extravagances—I remember as superlative a paper contributed to a Unitarian monthly attacking the liberal element, which ended magnificently: "They are right. They are damned." —but in his verse, where he has limited himself, if sometimes obscurely, to the actual, there is no resulting extravagance, but the liberation of increased scope and that strength of charitable understanding which is apparently most often possible through Christian judgment.[4]

That is, the Church is in Mr. Eliot's poetry his view of life; it recognizes and points the issues and shapes their poetic course; it is the rationale of his drama and the witness of its fate; it is, in short, a way of handling poetic material to its best advantage. It may be much more—as there is always life itself beyond the poetry that declares it; here nothing but the poetry is in question. If we consider the series of poems united in *Ash Wednesday* apart from the influence of that view of life we shall be left in as much of a muddle as if we consider them apart from the influence which Mr. Eliot's merely poetic habits exert upon their Christianity. We should have, in the one case, an emotional elegy without much point but human weakness; and in the other, if we recognized the Christianity and nothing else, we should have only a collection of ritual trappings and reminiscences.

I do not know if there have been efforts to appreciate the Christian tags alone; but I know that so intelligent a critic as Mr. Edmund Wilson (in *Axel's Castle*) missed the Christian *significance* in the poem and saw only a revelation of human weakness and an escapist's despair. Mr. Wilson had a non-literary axe to grind. Mr. I. A. Richards, who had, as Mr. Eliot would say, more nearly the benefits of a Christian education, saw, even if he did not share, the Christian light, although that is not what he calls it. Mr. Richards saw what the poem was about; that it was not a revelation of human weakness and an attempt at escape but a summoning of human strength and an effort to extinguish both hope and despair in the face of death. The poem is neither the devotion of a weary soul nor an emotional elegy; it is, like almost all of Mr. Eliot's poetry, a dramatized projection of experience. As it happens the experience has a religious bias; which means that it calls

---

[4] The least charity is moral indifference, and Mr. Eliot's attacks upon it (in *After Strange Gods*) are just, whether you share his Christianity or not; but his principles are not the only ones to secure the end in view.

on specific Christian beliefs to make the projection actual.

That the poem relies on other devices of the poetic imagination is obvious, and that these in their turn make the Christian beliefs actual for the poem—as Shakespeare's devices made Othello's jealousy actual—should be equally obvious. Here I want to emphasize that the abnegation in the first section of the poem is Christian abnegation (it is introduced, after all, by the governing title *Ash Wednesday*, which begins the forty days of fast and penance before the resurrection, and which also commemorates the temptation and triumph in the wilderness); and Christian abnegation is an act of strength not weakness, whereby you give up what you can of the evil of the flesh for the good of the soul. The conception is certainly not limited to Christianity; as an ethical myth it is common to most philosophies and religions; but its most dramatic because most specifically familiar form is certainly that rehearsed by the Christian Church. That Mr. Eliot should make serious use of it, aside from his private religion, is natural; and it ought to have helped rather than hindered the understanding of the fundamental human feelings his poem dramatized. Mr. Wilson should have recognized its presence, and had he done so could not have mistaken the intent of the poem, however much for other reasons he might have judged it inadequate, for many persons, to its theme.

Similarly—if there is need for a further example—in the quoted words of Arnaut Daniel in the fourth section, we should, to gain anything like their full significance, not only be aware of their literary origin in the *Purgatorio*, not only feel the weight of Dante at our backs, but also should feel the force of the Christian teaching which made the words poignant for Dante—and so for Mr. Eliot. This or its equivalent. Knowing such matters for poetry is not so hard as it seems when the process is described; perhaps in this case, if the mind strikes instinctively at all the right attitude, the context of the poem will force the right meaning into the reader's mind once the literal meaning is understood. *Sovegna vos:* Be mindful of me, remember my pain. Arnaut wishes Dante to remember him in the willfully accepted, refining fires of purgatory. It is characteristic of the meaning and integral to the association from which it springs that the words appear in Dante's Provençal. Had Mr. Eliot translated them they would have lost their identity and their air of specific origin; their being a quotation, and the reader knowing them so, commits them to a certain life and excludes other lives; nor could they have brought with them, in bare English, the very Christian context we wish to emphasize.

A different, but associated, effect is secured by the fact that the line which, with variations, opens the first and the last of these poems, appears in Mr. Eliot's English rather than in Guido Cavalcanti's Italian: at least I assume the line would own its source. Cavalcanti's line reads: *"Perch'io non spero di tornar già mai";* Mr. Eliot's first version reads: "Because I do not hope to turn again," and his second: "Although I do not hope to turn again." The difference between "Because" and "Although" is deliberate and for the attentive reader will add much to the meaning. Mr. I. A. Richards has commented on the distinction in *On Imagination.* But the point I wish to make here is not about the general influence of either form of the line; the unwary reader can determine that for himself. My point is smaller, at least initially, and consists in stating two or three facts, and the first fact is very small indeed. *"Perche"* may be rendered either "because" or "although," depending on the context, here supplied by Mr. Eliot. The second fact is a little larger; although Mr. Eliot may greatly admire the Ballata from which the line was taken, it was not its import in that poem which concerned him in his own, so that to have quoted it in the original would either have given a wrong impression of import or have prefaced a serious work with a meretricious literary ornament. The Italian line (with its overtones about turning and renunciation of many orders) gave him material to remodel for his own purposes in his own poem—with yet a sediment, perhaps, of objective source to act as a mooring. As it happens, which is why the line is discussed here at all, it is indissolubly associated in both its forms with the "great" lines in the poem: the prayer—

> Teach us to care and not to care
> Teach us to sit still

This is a Christian prayer (not, as I gather Mr. Wilson would have it, at all mystical) and represents in an ultimate form for poetry one of the great aspects of the Church—its humility. That it also represents, in another interpretation, a great aspect of Confucianism is immaterial; as it is immaterial that by still another interpretation it represents the heart of Roman stoicism. Mr. Eliot came to it through the Church, or his poem did, and he brought Guido's line with him;[5] and the line as used has a dominant Christian flavor which cannot be expunged. There is thus a transformation of tone in this quotation quite different but to be associated with the quotation of Arnaut's phrase. As materials in the poem, one exerted Christian feeling in its own right, and the other was made to carry Christian feeling by the context—and feeling of the deep and nameless order which is the reality of Mr. Eliot's poetry.

The reader may rightly wonder if he is expected to get at Mr. Eliot's reality so indirectly and through the coils of such close-wound ellipsis; and especially will he wonder if he has read Mr. Eliot's assertion that he would like an audience that could neither read nor write, and this because, as he says, "it is the half-educated and ill-educated, rather than the uneducated, who stand" in the poet's way. Well, the uneducated hardly exist with relation to Mr. Eliot's poetry; and very few of his audience can be said to be rightly educated for it—certainly not this writer; most of us come to his poetry very ill-educated indeed. If modern readers did not as a class have to make up for the defects of their education in the lost cause of Christianity— if we did not find Christianity fascinating because strange, and dramatic because full of a *hubris* we could no more emulate than that of Oedipus—there would be neither oc-

---

[5] It is amusing but not inconsistent to reflect that Mr. Eliot has noted that Guido was a heretic.

casion nor point for this particular essay. We have a special work of imaginative recovery to do before we can use Mr. Eliot's poetry to the full. However a later day may see it in perspective, to us Mr. Eliot must be of our time less because he seems to spring from it than because he imposes upon us a deep reminder of a part of our heritage which we have lost except for the stereotypes of spiritual manners. These stereotypes form our natural nexus with the impetus or drive of his poetry; and it is as we see them filled out, refreshed, re-embodied, that his poems become actual for us. Mr. Eliot is perhaps not himself in a position to sympathize with this operation of imaginative recovery; at any rate he rejected the to us plausible statement of Mr. Richards that *The Waste Land* was poetry devoid of beliefs. Mr. Eliot would prefer the advantage of a literal to that of an imaginative faith, immersion to empathy; and he has very much doubted, in his moral judgment of Thomas Hardy, whether what he says could "convey very much to anyone for whom the doctrine of Original Sin is not a very real and tremendous thing." The answer to that is that we do need to know that the doctrine of Original Sin is a reality for Mr. Eliot, and how much so, in order to determine both what light it sheds on Hardy and how to combine it with other insights into Hardy; but we do not need to share Mr. Eliot's conviction of literal application. Indeed, many of us would feel that we had impoverished our belief by making it too easy if we did share the conviction. Here is the crux of the whole situation between Mr. Eliot and those outside the Faith. The literal believer takes his myths, which he does not call myths, as supernatural archetypes of reality; the imaginative believer, who is not a "believer" at all, takes his myths for the meaning there is in their changing application. The practical consequences may be similar, since experience and interest are limited for data to the natural world, but the labor of understanding and the value assigned will be different for each. Thus Mr. Eliot and Mr. Richards are both correct—although neither would accept my way of saying so. *The Waste Land* is full of beliefs (especially, for this essay, a belief in the myth of Gethsemane) and is not limited by them but freed once they are understood to be imaginative. Only Mr. Eliot is correct for himself alone, while Mr. Richards is correct for others as well. Our labor is to recapture the imaginative burden and to avoid the literal like death.

If Mr. Eliot could not accept this notion in the abstract, he employs something very like it in his practical view of poetry, and by doing so he suggests an admirable solution for the reader's difficulties with his own poems and especially the difficulty with their Christian elements. This is the notion of different levels of significance and response. "In a play of Shakespeare," says Mr. Eliot, "you get several levels of significance. For the simplest auditors there is the plot, for the more thoughtful the character and the conflict of character, for the more literary the words and phrasing, for the more musically sensitive the rhythm, and for auditors of greater sensitiveness and understanding a meaning which reveals itself gradually. And I do not believe that the classification of audience is so clear-cut as this; but rather that the sensitiveness of every auditor is acted upon by all these elements at once, though in different degrees of consciousness. At none of these levels is the auditor bothered by the presence of what he does not understand, or by the presence of that in which he is not interested."

I propose to apply a little later the burden of these sentences where they properly belong: to the two plays, *The Rock* and *Murder in the Cathedral*. Meanwhile let us twist the reference slightly and apply it to our present problem: the reader's relation to the Christian element among other elements in such poems as *Ash Wednesday*, merely substituting within the quotation the word readers for audience or auditors. Clearly there are different levels of significance at which the poem can be read; there are the levels responded to by Mr. Richards and Mr. Wilson; and there is the simplest level where there is "only" the poem to consider. But if the formula is applicable with any justice it is because Mr. Eliot's contention is correct that "The sensitiveness of every reader is acted upon by all these elements at once," and because, further, "at none of these levels is the reader bothered by the presence of what he does not understand, or the presence of that in which he is not interested." In that case we must admit that most readers do not count for more than the simplest form of excitement and vicarious mewing; which is the truth—and it is upon that class that the existence of poetry relies. Then there is a class a little higher in the scale, the class that propagates poetry without understanding it in any conscious sense; this is the class Mr. Wilson describes, the class of young poets who, after *The Waste Land* began to sink in, "took to inhabiting exclusively barren beaches, cactus-grown deserts, and dusty attics overrun with rats." Possibly these classes are unconsciously affected by all or almost all the possible levels of significance, including those of which the author was unaware; which makes occasion both for pride and prospective humiliation in the poet. I think the notion has something Christian in it; something that smells of grace; and has very little to do with any conception of popular poetry addressed to an audience that can neither read nor write. However that may be, there remains the class that preserves and supports poetry, a class the members of which unfortunately cannot stop short on the level of their unconscious appreciation but necessarily go on, risking any sort of error and ultimate mistake, until they are satisfied as to what a poem means. This may not be the class for which Mr. Eliot or any poet writes; but it includes that very small sub-class of readers of "greater sensitiveness and understanding" for whom the meaning of a poem reveals itself gradually. It is the class for and by both the good and bad members of which honest literary criticism is written.

And it is this class which, confronted by a sensibility so powerful and so foreign as Mr. Eliot's, is determined to get at the means as well as the meaning. It is in that sense that Mr. Eliot's poetry may be a spiritual exercise of great scope. This class, then, apprehending the dominant presence of Christian doctrine and feeling in Mr. Eliot's work, must reach something like the following conclusions as representing provisional truths. The Church is the vehicle through which human purpose is to be seen and its teachings prod and vitalize the poetic sensibility engaged with the actual and with the substrata of the actual. Furthermore, and directly for poetry, the Church presents a gift of moral and philosophical form of a pre-logical character; and it is a great advantage for a poet to find his material fitting into a form whose reason is in mystery rather than logic, and no less reason for that. It is perhaps this insight into the nature of the Church's authority that brought Mr. Eliot to his most magnificent statement about poetry. "The essential advantage for a poet is not to have a beautiful world with which to deal: it is to be able to see beneath both beauty and ugliness; to see the boredom, and the horror, and the glory."

But since this class of reader is not itself Christian—any more than poetry is itself Christian—it will be to our advantage and to that of poetry to remind ourselves emphatically of what Mr. Eliot has himself several times insisted, that the presence of Christianity does not make a poem good. It is the poetry that must be good. Good Christianity will be a very watery thing adulterated with bad poetry, and good poetry can overcome a good deal of defection in a Christian poet's Christianity—as it does in Dante's hate. In admitting and enforcing the advantage of the Church, we commit ourselves, and before measuring our appreciation, to define the limits, both moral and operative, contained in our admission. There are some orders of charity in moral judgment which the doctrines of the Church cannot encompass; there are some experiences, that is, that the Church cannot faithfully mirror because it has no clues or has not the right clues to the reality involved. Thus we find Mr. Eliot refusing to understand Shelley and *Lady Chatterley's Lover;* and we find him also complaining of Irving Babbitt, whom he admired, that he made too much use of the Eastern Philosophies. I doubt, too, if the Church would be the right docent for an inspection of the drama of personality unfolded by Freudian psychology; it would see a different drama. . . . And we have, too, to decide provisionally what the Church, as a supernatural reference, makes up for, and what—whether we miss it or not—it fails to make up for; which is not at all easy to do. Perhaps we may say that the doctrines of the Church (we are not concerned, in poetry, with ritual worship) idealize a pretty complete set of human aspirations, and do this by appealing to a supernatural order. That is a great deal; but for poetry the Church does more. As these ideals are applied for judgment and light, all human action, struggle, and conflict, and all human feelings, too, gain a special significance. For us, as outsiders, the significance becomes greater if we remember that it is a special, a predicted significance, and that other ideals, would give a different significance or none at all. Taken as a whole, the Church, by insisting on being right, became one of the great heresies of the human mind.

Our final obligation with respect to the Church is our smallest but most specific: to deal with it as an element of metric, only to be understood in composition with the other elements. We shall have emphasized and exaggerated in order to accomplish a reduction. But as the Church is not itself logical neither are the other elements in the composition. We have collections of elements, of qualities, which appear side by side, engaged, or entangled, or separate, of which the product is a whole varying with each combination. And a mind, too, such as we wish to think of as whole, is subject to the "damage of a lifetime," and we must think of the pressure and stress of that damage, omnipresent, agonizing, even though we cannot and would not wish to say what at the moment it is: unless we say vaguely that it is the personality.

To put together indications of the qualities of a mind and of its suffusing personality is a labor for which there are models but no principles; there is no logical structure; and the more plausible the picture made the more likely it is to be untrustworthy. Mr. Eliot's mind, let us say, is a mind of contrasts which sharpen rather than soften the longer they are weighed. It is the last mind which, in this century, one would have expected to enter the Church in a lay capacity. The worldliness of its prose weapons, its security of posture, its wit, its ability for penetrating doubt and destructive definition, its eye for startling fact and talent for nailing it down in flight, hardly go with what we think of today as English or American religious feeling. We are accustomed to emotionalism and fanaticism in religious thought and looseness in religious feeling; the very qualities which are the natural targets of Mr. Eliot's weapons. Possibly it may be that we are unfamiliar with good contemporary Christian writers; they could hardly infect the popular press. Possibly, or even probably, it was these very qualities which, after the demolition of the pretense of value in post-war society, drove him into the Church as the one institution unaffected by the pretense or its demolition. Perhaps the teaching of Irving Babbitt, less by its preliminary richness than by its final inadequacy, was an important influence: we see in Mr. Eliot at least one of the virtues which Babbitt inculcated—Mr. Eliot is never expansive, either in verse or in prose, and expansiveness was a bugaboo to Babbitt.

However that may be, within the Church or not, Mr. Eliot's mind has preserved its worldly qualities. His prose reflections remain elegant, hard (and in a sense easy—as in manners), controlled, urbane (without the dissimulation associated with ecclesiastical urbanity), and foolproof. One would say that the mind was self-assured and might pontificate; but there is a redeeming quality of reserve about the assurance of his rare dogmatic extravagances, a reserve which may be taken as the accompaniment of scrupulous emotion and humility. This is—except the reserve—the shell which a mind must needs wear in order to get along without being victimized, and in order to deal, without escape, with things as they are on the surface. It is the part of a mind which is educable from outside, without regard to its inner bias.

Beneath the shell is a body of feeling and a group of convictions. Mr. Eliot is one of the few persons to whom convictions may be ascribed without also the ascription of fanaticism. Prejudice, which he has, is only a by-product of conviction and need be raised as an issue only when the conviction goes wrong; and intolerance, which he condones, is in the intellectual field only the expected consequence of conviction. With a little skill one learns to allow for prejudice and intolerance in Mr. Eliot's mind as we do for any convicted mind. His convictions are those which stem from the Church, from the history of Christian peoples, and from the classical cultures: including the convictions which represent Sophocles, Dante, and Shakespeare, as well as those which represent Original Sin, the Resurrection, and the sin of Spiritual Pride. However complexly arrived at, and with whatever, as the outsider must think them, tactful evasions in application, his convictions are directly and nobly held. If they enhance narrowness and put some human problems on too simple a plane they yet unflaggingly enforce depth. The mind reaches down until it touches bottom. Its weakness is that is does not always take in what it passes.

But a mind furnished only with convictions would be like a room furnished only with light; the brighter the more barren. Mr. Eliot's convictions light a sensibility stocked with feelings and observations and able to go on feeling and observing, where the feelings are more important than the observations. It is this body of feelings, and not any intermediately necessary intellectualizations of them, which are his ultimate concern; and ours, when we can bear on them. We may note here the frequency in his work of physiological images to symbolize the ways of knowing and the quality of things known; the roots and tentacles and all the anatomical details. Concerned with the material of life actually lived, his convictions only confirm a form for the material, make it available, release contact with it; as I suppose, in the other direction, convictions only confirm a form for the feeling of faith. And for these operations all learning is only a waiting, a reminiscence, and a key. It is the presence of this material, living and seen, if underneath, that makes Mr. Eliot master of the big words which, when directly charged, are our only names for its manifestations as emotion. Both in his poetry when he needs to and in his prose when he cares to, Mr. Eliot is free to use all those large emotional words with absolute precision of contact which your ordinary writer has to avoid as mere omnibuses of dead emotion.

It is natural then, in connection with these remarks, that in his prose writing, whether early or late, whether in essays or controversy, appreciation or judgment, Mr. Eliot is master of the compressed insight, the sudden illumination, the felt comparison, the seminal suggestion, and a stable point of view; and it is equally in course that we should find him master of persuasive and decimating rhetoric rather than of sustained argument and exhaustive analysis. He sees and his words persuade us of the fact that he has seen and of the living aspect of what he saw; but his words hardly touch, directly, the objective validity of what he saw. This explains the scope of his influence. There is no question that he has seen what he asserts; in the field of literature his eye for facts is extraordinarily keen, though like a sharpshooter's it hits only what it is looking for. There is no question, either, if you share his point of view even provisionally, that his weapons of attack penetrate if they do not dispatch their victims. That there is more to be seen, his scruples make him admit. But as for the objects of his attack, not his scruples but his methods leave some of them alive. You cannot kill an idea unless you have first embraced it, and Mr. Eliot is chary of embraces. This explains, too, why some of his followers have turned against him and why others are content to parrot him. He has an air of authority in his prose, an air of having said or implied to the point of proof everything that could be said; when as a matter of fact he has merely said what he felt and demonstrated his own conviction. Conviction in the end is opinion and personality, which however greatly valuable cannot satisfy those who wrongly expect more. Those who parrot Mr. Eliot think they share his conviction but do not understand or possess his personality. Those who have, dissatisfied, turned against him have merely for the most part expected too much. The rest of us, if we regard his prose argument as we do his poetry—as a personal edifice—will be content with what he is.

To argue that the poetry is written by the same mind and intellectually in much the same way as the prose is to show, in this order, all we need to know. It explains what he leaves out and gives a right emphasis to what he puts in; and if we add, once again, that his mind runs almost instinctively to dramatic projections, we understand what kind of organization his work has—and it has one, deeply innervated. And I do not mean to beg the question when I say, as Mr. Eliot said of Shakespeare, that he is himself the unity of his work; that is the only kind of unity, the only circulating energy which we call organization, that we are ever likely to find in the mass of a man's work. We need to remember only that this unity, this effect of organization, will appear differently in works of criticism and works of poetry, and that it will be more manifest, though less arguable, in the poetry than in the criticism. The poetry is the concrete—as concrete as the poet can make it—presentation of experience as emotion. If it is successful it is self-evident; it is subject neither to denial nor modification but only to the greater labor of recognition. To say again what we have been saying all along, that is why we can assent to matters in poetry the intellectual formulation of which would leave us cold or in opposition. Poetry can use all ideas; argument only the logically consistent. Mr. Eliot put it very well for readers of his own verse when he wrote for readers of Dante that you may distinguish understanding from belief. "I will not deny," he says, "that it may be in practice easier for a Catholic to grasp the meaning, in many places, than for the ordinary agnostic; but that is not because the Catholic believes, but because he has been instructed. It is a matter of knowledge and ignorance, not of belief or scepticism." And a little later he puts the advantage for readers of poetry "of a coherent traditional system of dogma and morals like the Catholic: it stands apart, for understanding and assent even without belief, from the single individual who propounds it." That is why in our own context we can understand Mr. Eliot and cannot understand Mr. Pound. The unity that is Mr. Eliot has an objective intellectual version in his Christianity. The unity of

Mr. Pound—if there is one—is in a confusion of incoherent, if often too explicitly declared, beliefs.

Christianity, then, is the emphatic form his sensibility fills; it is an artificial question which comes first. It is what happens to the sensibility that counts; the life lived and the death seen. That is the substantial preoccupation of the poet and the reader's gain. The emotion leans for expression on anything it can. Mr. Eliot's sensibility is typical of the poet's, as that of many poets is not. There is no wastage, little thinning out, and the least possible resort to dead form, form without motion. It is a sensibility that cannot deal with the merely surface report—what we used to call naturalism—and be content, but must deal with centers, surds, insights, illuminations, witnessed in chosen, obsessive images. These, as presented, seize enough of the life lived, the death seen, to give the emotion of the actuality of the rest. These we use as poetry; some will keep and some will wear out, as they continue or fail to strike reality as we can bear to know it.[6]

For opposite reasons, this essay can present texts for study neither of the apposite Christian form nor of the private sensibility that fills it; it merely emphasizes—with as much repetition as the reader is likely to put up with—that knowledge is better than ignorance for the one, and that the other exists to implement the first. There is the Church for inspection and there are the poems to read. There remains the common labor of literary criticism: the collection of facts about literary works, and comment on the manage-

[6] It is perhaps relevant to quote here part of Mr. Eliot's comment on Arnold's "Poetry is at bottom a criticism of life," in the essay on Arnold in *The Use of Poetry*. "At bottom: that is a great way down; the bottom is the bottom. At the bottom of the abyss is what few ever see, and what those cannot bear to look at for long; and it is not a 'criticism of life.' If we mean life as a whole—not that Arnold ever saw life as a whole —from top to bottom, can anything that we can say of it ultimately, of that awful mystery, be called criticism?" Here Mr. Eliot, as he commonly does at important junctures, which are never arguable, resorts to the emotional version of the actual concerned. The "abyss" is one of his obsessive images.

ment, the craft or technique, of those works; and this labor, in so far as it leaves the reader in the works themselves, is the only one in itself worth doing. All that has been said so far is conditional and preliminary and also a postscript to reading. The modern reader is not fitted to appreciate either a mind or its works conceived in relation to Christianity as a living discipline; and the effort to appreciate as dead manners what is live blood is as vain as it is likely to prove repulsive. If I have shown to what degree the reader must perform an imaginative resurrection, I have so far done enough.

For Mr. Eliot does spill blood for ink and his discipline does live. It is a commonplace assertion that Mr. Eliot has shaped both his Christianity and his technique to forward the expressive needs of his mind. Here let us keep to the technique; it involves the other; and say that he has deliberately shaped and annealed and alloyed and purified it: the object being a medium of language to enhold the terms of feeling and the sign of the substance felt so as to arouse, sustain, and transform interest at different levels of response; and that he has done so, besides, under the severest of disciplines, adherence to the standards of the good writing that has interested him. I do not say that he has succeeded altogether. Such a technique is the greatest *practical* ambition possible to secure; it takes long to come by and is slow to direct, since if it is to be adequate it must include the craft of presenting everything that is valuable. Very young poets confuse technique either with tricks, dodges, and devices, which are only a part of it, or with doodabs.

> Ambition comes when early force is spent
> And when we find no longer all things possible.

Perhaps I twist a little Mr. Eliot's implications, but it seems to me that the great temptations to which a poet's technique are exposed are the early temptation of the adventitious—the nearest weapon and the neatest subject—, and the temptation of repetition, which comes later, and of which it is the sin that the result is bound to be meretricious. These are fundamentals for all techniques and there are modifications for each; the whole technique of any one poem can never be the whole technique of any other poem, since, such is the limitation of human experience, a new poem is more likely to represent a growth of technique than a *growth* (I do not say change) of subject matter.

Nor will such a technique, for all readers or perhaps for any, ever be completely achieved except in the sum of the greatest poets. There are too many expectations, just enough in their sincerity, that can neither be gratified nor eradicated. There are those, for an extreme example, who expect an art of happiness. But the fact is that the rest of us, whose expectations are less gross, can hardly ever at a given time get over expecting a technique to show us what is not there; nor can we invariably "let" ourselves see what is there.

Confronted by *The Rock* and *Murder in the Cathedral*, it is at once clear, first, that it is Mr. Eliot's technique rather than his subject matter that has grown, and, second, that this technique, new or old, radically limits the number and kind of our expectations. The scope of his poetry, its final magnitude, is a different matter, and the impurity or bloom of the contemporaneous must be rubbed away before it can be determined. What I mean here is that we get neither the kind nor variety of emotional satisfaction from either of his plays that we get from Noel Coward or Congreve or Shakespeare. We are not titivated or stroked; we do not see society brushed with the pure light of its manners; there is no broad display of human passion and purpose; we get the drama of the Church struggling against society toward God, which is something new (for those who like newness) in English drama; we get the way of the Church against the way of the World. And we get the awful harm as well as the good done men and women in the course of the struggle. It is this harm and this good, this sense of irreparable damage and intransigent glory, as it is in contact with this struggle, that makes the drama actual. It is not spiritual drama; it is not like Dante the drama of damnation, penance, and beatitude; it is the drama of human emotions actualized in the light of spiritual drama.

The spirit is there, and intellect, and theology; but all these through actualized emotions of the experience of good and evil, of fraud and ambition, self-deceit and nobility, and the communal humility of the poor—which is a humility beneath Christian humility. This is what we get most in *Murder in the Cathedral*, and what we crucially fail to get in *The Rock*.

It is the substance of this (the same utter view of life) that we get in another way in "Mr. Eliot's Sunday Morning Service" and "The Hippopotamus"—these the tough anticlerical way; and in still other ways it is the same substance in "Prufrock," "Gerontion," and *The Waste Land*. The substance is permanent; the flux representative. If we take all the poems together with this substance in mind one charge that has been made against them should disappear—that they resent the present and fly into some paradise of the past. On the contrary, they measure the present by living standards which most people relegate to the past. The distinction is sharp; it is between poetry that would have been a shell of mere disillusion and poetry that is alive, and beyond disillusion. As Mr. Eliot himself remarked, *The Waste Land* only showed certain people their own illusion of disillusionment. It is this fundamental identity of substance which marks the unity of his work; that a variety of subjects and diverse approaches conspire to complete, to develop, a single judgment.

The changes—and no one would confuse or wrongly date two of Mr. Eliot's poems—are in the changes and growth of technique. The deliberate principle of growth has been in the direction of appealing to more levels of response, of reaching, finally, the widest possible audience, by attempting to secure in the poetry a base level of significance to which any mind might be expected to respond, without loss or injury to any other level of significance. It is in the light of this re-interpretation that Mr. Eliot's desire for an illiterate audience should be considered. That it is obvious does not make it any less telling, or any less inspiring to work toward, or—remembering the tacit dogma of difficulty held by so many poets—any less refreshing for the prospective reader. That this direction is not a guess on my own part and that he meant his notion of levels of significance in Shakespeare to apply to his own poetry, Mr. Eliot provides a candid text to show. It is at the very end of *The Use of Poetry*. With the great model of Shakespeare, the modern poet would like to write plays. "He would like to be something of a popular entertainer, and be able to think his own thoughts behind a tragic or a comic mask. He would like to convey the pleasures of poetry, not only to a larger audience, but to larger groups of people collectively; and the theatre is the best place to do it. . . . Furthermore, the theatre, by the technical exactions which it makes and limitations which it imposes upon the author, by the obligation to keep for a definite length of time the sustained interest of a large and unprepared and not wholly perceptive group of people, by its problems which have constantly to be solved, has enough to keep the poet's *conscious* mind fully occupied."

The best of Mr. Eliot's paragraph I have omitted: sentences that give the emotion of being a poet. What I have quoted is that part of his prose reflections concerned with the ideal behind the two plays. It is extraordinary how much of what we want to know these three sentences can be made to explain. The only emphasis needed is this: that the obligation to keep an audience interested is only indirectly connected with the real interest of the plays. It is primarily a technical obligation; it points to and prepares for the real interest by seeming to be connected with it; and the great liability or technical danger is that the two interests may be confused without being identified, as the great gain is when the two interests are, in crisis, actually identified.

I do not think that in his two plays Mr. Eliot has realized either the radical limitations of his substance or the insuperable limitations of the theater. The two do not always cooperate and they sometimes overlap. Perhaps it is better so; the comparative failure which says most, like *Hamlet*, is better than the relative success, like *The Coward*, that says least. The elements of failure must be nevertheless pointed out both when they spread rot and when they are surpassed. *The Rock* gives us an example of failure by confusion of interest which is nearly fatal, and *Murder in the Cathedral* gives us an example of success by fusion of interests.

Contrary to custom in English drama, it is the objective, the witnessing, the only indirectly participating, passages in these plays that are the finest poetry and that do the most work. These are the Choruses, in *The Rock* the chorus that represents the voice of the Church, and, in *Murder in the Cathedral,* the chorus of the women of Canterbury. In *The Rock* there are also choruses of the unemployed, of workmen, and some songs used as ritual chorus. In *Murder in the Cathedral* there is a kind of grand chorus of Priests, Tempters, and Chorus proper, which is used once, in the crisis of the first part. Whereas the traditional uses of the chorus are to comment on and to integrate action, here they are the integrity of the action itself, its actuality. Their relation to the "ordinary" version of the action, the rest of the play, is different in the two plays; and the quality of the work they do is different. It is these differences, in the light of the notion of levels of significance and response and in connection with the effort to maintain interest of both orders, that I wish to lay down the bare bones of. They carry the flesh.

*The Rock* is a pageant play, superficially about the difficulties, the necessity, and the justification of building a church in modern London. The pageant is a loose form and condones the introduction of a great variety of material; and so we are shown, upon the recurring focal scene of a church foundation actually in progress, a variety of episodes in the history of London churches. The theme and much of the incident were no doubt set; it is not a promising theme in which to expand a substance as concentrated as Mr. Eliot's, it is too generous and like the form chosen too loose, and too inherently facile of execution. Where almost anything will do passably there is nothing that will do well. The resulting text is not as drama very promising either. It is the sort of thing that, as a whole, depends on lushness of production and the personality of performance. At Sadler's Wells it may have been magnificent, but not because of Mr. Eliot's poetry; and as it is now, a reader's text, what was important and the very life of the performance—the incident, the fun, the church-supper social comment, and the good-humored satire—reduce the effect of the poetry because it points away from the poetry instead of toward it. Bad verse cannot point to good poetry, and there is here the first bad verse Mr. Eliot has allowed himself to print, as well as his first bad jokes. The whole play has an air of following the counsel of the Chorus to the worshipers.

> Be not too curious of Good and Evil;
> Seek not to count the future waves of Time;
> But be ye satisfied that you have light
> Enough to take your step and find your foothold.

It is all satisfied and nearly all spelt in capital letters. Whether the expected nature of the audience was responsible, the form chosen, or whether Mr. Eliot was mistaken about both, the fact is that the level of interest appealed to by the whole play is too low to make passage to the higher levels natural. The general level lacks emotional probability and therefore lacks actuality. It is dead-level writing. The reader satisfied with the dead level can hardly be expected to perceive, even unconsciously, the higher levels; and the reader interested in the higher levels cannot but find his interest vitiated by finding it constantly let down. Take the episode of the Crusades. The conversation between the man and his betrothed is one thing, a flat appeal to stereotyped emotion; the taking of the Cross, with its sonorous Latin dressing, is another, an appeal by the direct use of ritual, on another plane, to the stereotype of the conversation; neither is actualized. The actuality is in the Chorus; but the Chorus is not the same thing in a different form, it is another thing altogether. There is a gap between, which is not crossed, and the relations between the three are disproportional. We hear a distinct voice from another world, which is the real world, and which is the real poem; the actuality of which the other voices are only the substitute and the sham. And the Chorus, in this instance, perhaps loses some of its effect because it comes first, prefacing what it does not perform, and because its phrasing depends on the statements it makes rather than makes the statements.

> Not avarice, lechery, treachery,
> Envy, sloth, gluttony, jealousy, pride:
> It was not these that made the Crusades,
> But these that unmade them.
>
> . . . . . .
>
> Our age is an age of moderate virtue
> And of moderate vice
> When men will not lay down the Cross
> Because they will never assume it.

Mr. Eliot has not here levied enough upon that other actuality, the actuality bred in the fitting of words together; which is not the same thing as fitting notions together. These strictures apply throughout the episodes of the play and to most of the Choruses to the episodes. It is only rarely, in some of the songs and parts of the general choruses, that we get lines like these, when the poetry escapes the Oppressor.

Our gaze is submarine, our eyes look upward
And see the light that fractures through unquiet water.
We see the light but see not whence it comes.

The Oppressor was the misconceived need of expressing the Church at the level of general interest, instead of intensifying the actuality envisaged by the Church in terms of a represented interest.

This last is what Mr. Eliot has done in his second play, *Murder in the Cathedral,* and I think that the play could not have been better constructed with a view to representing in a self-contained form the mutually interrelated play of different levels of significance, from the lowest to the highest. I do not expect to have exhausted anything but its general interest for a long time to come and I do expect its actual significance—its revelation of essential human strength and weakness—to grow the whole time. Yet it deals with an emotion I can hardly expect to share, which very few can ever expect to share, except as a last possibility, and which is certainly not an emotion of general interest at all; it deals with the special emotion of Christian martyrdom. Martyrdom is as far removed from common experience as the state of beatitude to which it leads; and it is much further removed, too, from ordinary interests than is the episodic material of *The Rock*. The view of life is as seriously held in either play, and the emotion is in itself as valid in one as in the other; they are in fact substantially the same. The whole difference between the failure of the first and the success of the second play depends on the lowest level of poetic intensity employed. If anything, the lowest level of significance (that is, the broadest, appealing to more, and more varied minds) is lower in the second play than the first; and this fact is in itself an element of formal strength and a verification of Mr. Eliot's ideal theory. It almost seems as if in *The Rock* Mr. Eliot had confused conventional significance with basic significance, but in his second play had clarified the confusion.

Applying Mr. Eliot's sentences about levels of significance, we can say that there is for everyone the expectation (we can hardly call it a plot) and ominous atmosphere of murder and death; for others there are the strong rhythms, the pounding alliterations, and the emphatic rhymes; for others the conflict, not of character, but of forces characterized in individual types; for others the tragedy or triumph of faith at the hands of the world; and for others the gradually unfolding meaning in the profound and ambiguous revelation of the expense of martyrdom in good *and* evil as seen in certain speeches of Thomas and in the choruses of the old women of Canterbury. It is the *expense* of martyrdom as a supreme form of human greatness, its expense for the martyr himself and for those less great but bound with it, its expense of good and evil and suffering, rather than its mere glory or its mere tragedy, that seems to me a major part of the play's meaning. Greatness of any kind forces to a crisis the fundamental life and the fundamental death in life both for the great themselves and for those who are affected by it. Martyrdom is the Christian form of personal greatness, and as with other forms of greatness, no human judgment or representation of it can fail of a terrible humility and a terrifying ambiguity. It is the limit of actuality in what Mr. Eliot calls the abyss.

I do not expect to prove that the emotional substance of which these remarks are a re-formulation may be found in *Murder in the Cathedral.* There is no proof of the actual but the experience. But if the reader will first realize that the predicament of Thomas Becket is the predicament of human greatness, and that its example affects him, the reader, by reading over the dialogue between Thomas and the Fourth Tempter and Thomas' final speech in Part One, he will at least have put himself in the frame of mind to perceive the higher levels of significance, and the identification of all levels in the six long choruses and the play as a whole. It may be impertinent to point out as a clue or indication, that the Fourth Tempter's last speech repeats, as addressed to Thomas, Thomas' speech on his first appearance in the play, where the words are applied to the Chorus:

You know and do not know, what it is to act or suffer.
You know and do not know, that acting is suffering,
And suffering action. Neither does the actor suffer
Nor the patient act. But both are fixed
In an eternal action, an eternal patience
To which all must consent that it may be willed
And which all must suffer that they may will it,
That the pattern may subsist, that the wheel may turn and
    still
Be forever still.

And it may be superfluous to note that in the last of Thomas' speech at the end of Part One, he addresses you, the reader, you, the audience. Impertinent or superfluous the emphasis will not be amiss.

The Choruses, which flow from the expression of the common necessities of the poor up to, and in the same language, the expression of Christian dogma, may be said to exist by themselves, but their instance is the greatness of Thomas, as the death in them is Thomas' death. Thomas exists by himself, too, and his particular struggle, but both are made actual in relation to the Choruses. They are separate but related; they combine and produce a new thing not in the elements themselves. But the Choruses themselves have interrelated parts which work together by fate because they were rightly chosen and not because, in any ordinary sense, they have natural affinity for each other. The kinds of parts and their proportional bulk are not fixed but vary with the purpose of the particular Chorus; but the predominant elements are the concrete immanence of death and death in life, and the rudimentary, the simple, the inescapable conditions of living, and there is besides the concrete emotion of the hell on earth which is the absence or the losing of God. It is the death and the coming of it, of the Archbishop which measures and instigates all the Chorus has to say; but neither that death, nor its coming, nor its Christian greatness creates its words; rather what it says is the actual experience from which the Christian greatness springs. That is why the chorus is composed of poor women, ordinary women, with ordinary lives and fates and desires, women with a fundamental turbulence of resentment at the expense of greatness.

> What is woven on the loom of fate
> What is woven in the councils of princes
> Is woven also in our veins, our brains,
> Is woven like a pattern of living worms
> In the guts of the women of Canterbury.

It is against this, the common denominator of all experience, that the extraordinary experience of Thomas is seen, and by it made real.

It is shameful to quote for illustration when half the virtue is lost without the context, but I nevertheless quote two passages, one for concreteness of sensual image and as an example of internal rhyme, and the other to show how actual an emotion the expectation of death can be, and how dramatic.

> I have eaten
> Smooth creatures still living, with the strong salt taste
> of living things under sea; I have tasted

The living lobster, the crab, the oyster, the whelk and
  the prawn; and they live and spawn in my bowels,
  and my bowels dissolve in the light of dawn.

*Chorus, Priests and Tempters alternately*

C. Is it the owl that calls, or a signal between the trees?
P. Is the window-bar made fast, is the door under lock and
  bolt?
T. Is it rain that taps at the window, is it wind that pokes
  at the door?
C. Does the torch flame in the hall, the candle in the room?
P. Does the watchman walk by the wall?
T. Does the mastiff prowl by the gate?
C. Death has a hundred hands and walks by a thousand
  ways.
P. He may come in the sight of all, he may pass unseen
  unheard.
T. Come whispering through the ear, or a sudden shock on
  the skull.
C. A man may walk with a lamp at night, and yet be
  drowned in a ditch.
P. A man may climb the stair in the day, and slip on a
  broken step.
T. A man may sit at meat, and feel the cold in his groin.

These are the easy things that come first; but without
them, the other meaning that comes gradually would not
come at all; they are its basis, in poetry as in life. "The
world," says Mr. Eliot, "is trying the experiment of attempting to form a civilised but non-Christian mentality." He believes the experiment will fail; and I think we may be sure
it will fail unless it includes in itself the insight, in Christian
terms or not, of which Mr. Eliot gives an actual representation. Meanwhile he redeems the time.

1935

# 7. Unappeasable and Peregrine

*Behavior and the "Four Quartets"*

## I

It is the actual behavior of things that willy-nilly gets into poetry, and what poetry does to behavior is to give it some sort of order, good for the time, or the life, of the poem. What behavior does in this relation to order is to give the sense, the pressure toward incarnation, of reality greater than can be apprehended. Poetry is something we do to the actual experience of this relation between behavior and order; it is something we do to these partial incarnations. So it is with Eliot's *Four Quartets;* a poem dense with behavior and brimming with order.

The problem is always two-ended in making notes about a live poem: how to begin far enough in to catch on to the momentum of the poem, and how to stop soon enough to let it go on. What is the right point in reading to say, here is the midst of things in motion (what is meant by *in medias res*), and what is the appropriate point to say, now the poem goes of itself? The first point is where the words and the action of the poem seem to be at work on each other in such a way that they *together* look out upon you. The second point is reached perhaps when the composed order of word and action begins to decompose. The order of poetry is achieved between two disorders, the disorder in which feelings and thoughts are found in behavior, and the second disorder in which the order of the poem (what the poem has done to the feelings and thoughts by joining them in an action of the mind) is lost or seems exorbitant. The adventure of poetry is in taking the risk that what has been found in behavior may be lost if it is cared for too much.

Eliot's poetry is full of phrases which exemplify this condition and this risk. In "Gerontion" there are the phrases:

> I have lost my passion: why should I need to keep it
> Since what is kept must be adulterated?

In *Ash Wednesday* there is:

> Terminate torment
> Of love unsatisfied
> The greater torment
> Of love satisfied

In the *Four Quartets* there is the imperative: "Old men ought to be explorers," which being interpreted means, the mind should cry out upon what it finds, for that is the burden of the word "explore," if you will look in the dictionary; and that is the burden of this poem, if you will look into its words. And does Eliot not say it himself, at the beginning of the final passage of the poem?

> We shall not cease from exploration
> And the end of all our exploring
> Will be to arrive where we started
> And know the place for the first time.

To explore is to search into the unknown, known step by step, behavior by behavior, "Through the unknown, remembered gate," and there to cry out upon what is recognized and also to weep. Exploration is the agony of prophecy as the action of the mind upon behavior. The passage goes on to resume, image by image, the order the poem has made, an order now at the point both of disintegration as a human order and of consummation into a divine order. There the poem stops, and there it also goes on.

How did it begin? In the childhood of the poet, where there were the gifts of all later imagination. The poet's labor is re-accession, not to the childhood (which ran free, till brooked) but to the gifts. One's own childhood is where the past experience of the race appears as pure behavior and pure authority. Each season of growth, unless the child die, a new ring of green wood toughens into heart wood. But in the beginning there is the green heart: ever irrecoverable except at the center which never disappears, what we know through the voices of the children in the apple tree.

But there is nothing innocent, in the trivial senses of the word, about this child, this *anima semplicetta;* there is nothing innocent in the quality of its experience. On the contrary it is naive, native, the moving image of the whole burden of experience we want to explore. There is no innocence about it, unless there is a kind of innocence to the authority of experience itself—unless there is innocence in unprotectedness from both good and evil. The child is very near reality, and is in this sense the child in the man, which the man both builds over and seeks to recover, as in this poem the poet seeks to recover the hidden laughter of children among the leaves of the garden.

There is here a relation not only to the image of the simple soul issuing from the hand of him who loves her in *Purgatorio* XVI but perhaps, as Helen Gardner says, also a relation to Kipling's "They": the children in which are "'what might have been and what has been,' appearing to those who have lost their children in the house of a blind woman who has never borne a child." *Vere tu es Deus absconditus.* The mind of the poet and the mind of the reader reach after texts to help in the exploration: reach after analogies, after paths, arrests, traps, betrayals, reversals, and, above all, reach after reminders; for there is today no strict interpretation in these matters, no substitute for either experience or for the full mimesis of experience.

The mind uses what it must. I would suppose that in the voices of these children which reverberate through the *Four Quartets* lie more than echoes of Grimm's tales of *The Juniper Tree* and of *The Singing Bone*. They were present in *Ash Wednesday* and they are present here. In *The Juniper Tree* a woman kills her stepson and by a trick puts the crime upon her own daughter. Of the flesh was made black puddings which the father ate. Of the bones the little girl made a bundle in a silk handkerchief and sat down weeping tears of blood under a juniper tree. "After she had lain down there, she suddenly felt light-hearted and did not cry any more. Then the juniper tree began to stir itself, and the branches parted asunder, and moved together again, just as if some one were rejoicing and clapping his hands. At the same time a mist seemed to arise from the tree, and in the center of this mist it burned like a fire, and a beautiful bird flew out of the tree singing magnificently, and he flew high up in the air, and when he was gone, the juniper tree was just as it had been before, and the handkerchief with the bones was no longer there. Marlinchen, however, was as gay and happy as if her brother were still alive. And she went merrily into the house, and sat down to dinner and ate." Meanwhile the bird proceeds through the world, getting a chain from a goldsmith, red shoes from a shoe-maker, and from a miller a millstone: each in exchange for the identical song:

> My mother she killed me,
> My father he ate me,
> My sister, little Marlinchen,
> Gathered together all my bones,
> Tied them in a silken handkerchief,
> Laid them together beneath the juniper tree,
> Kywitt, kywitt, what a beautiful bird am I!

Then the bird returns to the father's house and sings to all three. Marlinchen laughs and weeps, the mother chatters her teeth and dreads and is on fire, the father goes out to see what bird is singing. The father is given the gold chain; Marlinchen, joyous and dancing, the red shoes; "'Well,' said the woman, and sprang to her feet and her hair stood up like flames of fire, 'I feel as if the world were coming to an end. I, too, will go out and see if my heart feels lighter.'" At that the bird drops the millstone on her head.

In this tale the woman, in Eliot's language, could not bear very much reality; the man did not know reality when he saw it; and the little girl was herself reality in the form of behavior. It is not so very different in the tale of *The Singing Bone*. There is a wild boar, a great terror to the king's lands, and the king offers his daughter to whoso kills it. Two brothers go into the forest from opposite sides, the elder proud, crafty, shrewd; the younger innocent, simple, kindhearted. The younger is given a spear for purity and goodness and with it kills the boar. The elder brother, who could not kill the boar, kills the younger brother and marries the king's daughter. Years later a shepherd found a snow-white bone in the sand of the stream where the body had been thrown and made out of it a mouthpiece for his horn. "Of its own accord" the bone "began to sing":

> Ah, friend, thou blowest upon my bone!
> Long have I lain beside the water;
> My brother slew me for the boar,
> And took for his wife the King's young daughter.

The wicked brother "was sewn up in a sack and drowned. But the bones of the murdered man were laid to rest in a beautiful tomb in the churchyard."

It is images like these that loom through the surface of Eliot's poems. Both the tales are magic formula; are neither sentimental nor didactic; they are precisely means for reaching into behavior under morals and sentiment. Every child knows this; only a mature poetic mind seems to know how to deal with it, or to remember it, or be reminded of it, or put it together.

There is a more abstract way of putting the significance of the presence of these tales in Eliot's poems. As a part of the composition they are a constant reminder of the presence of the barbaric, of other and partial creations within our own creation. Their presence makes a criticism of the Mediterranean tradition, whether in "complete" religion, or in "complete" reason, or in terms of our long heritage of Latin rhetoric as the instrument of interpretation. It seems worse than useless, it is mutilating, to think of this sort of composition as if it were rational allegory, but it would be fatal to our understanding to forget the presence of the old rhetorical allegory. There is, rather, a mutually related transformation of two modes of the mind.

There is a text in Eliot's prose (*Notes Towards a Def-*

*inition of Culture*) which is specially apt to this aspect of all his poetry:

The reflection that what we believe is not merely what we formulate and subscribe to, but that behavior is also belief, and that even the most conscious and developed of us live also at the level on which belief and behavior cannot be distinguished, is one that may, once we allow our imagination to play upon it, be very disconcerting. It gives an importance to our most trivial pursuits, to the occupation of our every minute, which we cannot contemplate long without the horror of nightmare.

Let us say that the presence of the fairy tales in the deserted garden, the earthly paradise unused, in the first part of the first Quartet, gives the effect of belief merging in behavior. The rhymed and formal verses which begin the second part of the same Quartet give the different but related effect of behavior rising into belief, as it were altering the experience of belief if not the belief itself.

> Garlic and sapphires in the mud
> Clot the bedded axle-tree.
> The trilling wire in the blood
> Sings below inveterate scars
> And reconciles forgotten wars.
> The dance along the artery
> The circulation of the lymph
> Are figured in the drift of stars
> Ascend to summer in the tree
> We move above the moving tree
> In light upon the figured leaf
> And hear upon the sodden floor
> Below, the boarhound and the boar
> Pursue their pattern as before
> But reconciled among the stars.

Note that the axle-tree does not move, that inveterate means confirmed by age and hence ineradicable. Note, too, that it is a *drift* of stars: drift is a deep dominance from a force outside knowledge—it is occult knowledge showing—and contrary or across other forces; like a current, like a tide; like what the current brings—strange movements in calm, the debris, the flotsam, in a drift of order. And again, note the two uses of "reconcile," one for something that happens in the blood under scars, the other for something that happens above among the stars. "Reconciled" is the burden word in this passage. It has to do with the means of submission to greater force—to harmony—to wisdom—to unity. It is the means of drawing together again, in a superior drift, which is also, and at the same time, the drift of the fortune which we still tell in the stars.

Let us look at the two aspects of drift together. It is the drift from Mallarmé (in the first line) through the body to Fortuna, Scientia, Man's Will, and the Reason of the Stars (for the stars are our best double image of that which is ordained and that which we can make or reach) to the boarhound and the boar—no doubt in a tapestry, a weaving in beauty together—as well as upon a sodden floor. We see at once the innocent and the native working together; how they work, and with what beside them, the drift of the stars, and with what above or beyond them, what is reconciled among the stars. It is *so*. It is so that we understand the garlic and the sapphires in the mud. We see what the words mean: what is incarnated in them—though it is a partial incarnation: partial ecstasy and partial horror, and it may be we do not grasp what is not incarnated.

II

Here certainly the order of poetry has done something to the apprehension of behavior. The three old modes of the mind—the poetic, rhetorical, dialectical—are here at work synergically in a polarity of the intellectual and the sensual: upon the still point of the turning world and the pressure of behavior into consciousness. It would seem a maxim if not a rule for this sort of poetry, that the more the behavior presses in the more order must be found to take care of it. As Coleridge says, in poetry you have more than usual emotion and more than usual order; and as he does not say, the orders you use are no more yours to come by than is the emotion or the behavior you find. It is in you—in the poet, in the reader—that the old orders and the old emotions become more than usual. Let us now turn to some of the old orders, which Eliot has made unusual, and then return, if we can, to old behavior.

Let decorum be a name for the possession of a good supply of old orders through which we cope with or understand our experience. Ages with a highly developed decorum find verse a relatively easy medium. Recent ages have clearly a low decorum and have run toward prose. This is not a trivial consideration: it has to do with the possibility of getting work done, and it tends to set the level at which the work gets done; also it affects the ease of the reader's access to what has got done. The circumstance of decorum in which Eliot writes led him to declare in Sweden some years ago, that we live in an incredible public world and an intolerable private world. In a public world of low decorum we get many intolerable private worlds; and all the more intolerable to a man like Eliot who preserves in himself the "inveterate scars," the living sore points, of what he takes once to have been a credible public world; the man who, believing, lives in a world which does not believe what he believes, though to him it shows the privation of that belief. Such a man may well feel that he has a one-man job of making a decorum in which the experience of belief can be restored along with the experience of unbelief. His subject may well be rather more the effort than the accomplishment because he will try to sack the whole citadel of old orders whether he has dramatic (or mimetic) need of them or not. But if we remember his burden, as readers we can carry our share of it the more easily.

Eliot took up his burden early and has never been able quite to balance the load. His most important early essay was on "Tradition and the Individual Talent," in which the continuous modifiable whole of all literature was maintained as simultaneously existing. In the 'twenties he made the serious statement that the spirit killeth, the letter giveth life, and a little later, with regard to his conversion, he said he was not one of those who swallow the dogma for the sake of the emotion but put up with the emotion for the sake of the dogma. Again, he remarked that whereas intellectual belief was easily come by, emotional belief was the pursuit of a lifetime. These are the remarks of a man in anguish over the privation of decorum not that of his own time, yet intensely alive in his time. Unwilling to accept as sufficient the commitments visible in his society, yet himself committed to that society, he attempts to express its predicament in terms of the Christian tradition which ought to enlighten it. This is not, for many minds, a tenable position; and to many it seems to have forced Eliot back upon an ancestral utopia. That may be so—though Eliot might say, rather, that he had been forced not back but forward.

What is important is that Eliot has been forced, as none of the religious poetry of other Christian ages has been forced, to make present in his poetry not only Christian dogma and Christian emotion, but also the underlying permanent conditions, stresses, forces with which that dogma and that emotion are meant to cope. That is to say, Eliot as poet is compelled to present the aesthetic, the actual experience *of and under* Christianity at the same time that he uses his faith to understand, or express, that experience. This is the source of the power and influence and also of the weakness of his poetry.

There is no wonder in that. This is the burden which Arnold, better understood than he understood himself, imposed on poetry: not to replace religion but to give the actual experience of it *in its conditions.* It was under this kind of poetic impulse (not then directed toward religion) that Eliot *discovered* (which is why he had neither time nor need to *develop*) the notion that the emotion or feeling in the poetic situation to be expressed needed an objective correlative in the poem or play. It is only a further movement of this impulse that led him to his early argument about the poet as mere catalyst, the mere precipitator of a reaction between order and behavior, and the still further notion that intensity of poetic process was the sign of poetic maturity. It is this, now, in the Quartets, that leads him to say the poetry does not matter. It can be suggested, as a consequence of these observations, that Christian belief—any belief—is susceptible of the state where, if aesthetic experience is not the only possible experience, it is the experience most capable of authority. I do not say that Eliot believes any such thing—assuredly he does not—but in his poetry he is compelled to act as though he did: he has to take up that burden also.

It is for these and similar reasons that though we know what the poetry does as excitement and though we possess the excitement, it is not easy to say what it is about. It gives us the raw force of what it is about, plus something more, but we are not sure of the plus. So, also, though these poems move us, and in a direction among directions, we cannot say whether they have or do not have composition. Only by a decorum we do not possess could they come to have full composition: that is, a decorum with the realm of the ideal felt everywhere in apposition to the real and experienced in the realm of the actual. Meanwhile we rest on so much composition as may be secured by a combination of external form and so much of the traditional decorum as can be made to apply. If this is not enough, it is still a great deal; for it is by this combination that we *know* that we live in an incredible public world and an intolerable private world.

From his version of this knowledge Eliot proceeds in his search for the reality, and makes a kind of excess or aesthetic actuality by resort to what techniques of the mind he can find for making manifestations or epiphanies or incarnations of the real into the actual. We may say that these Quartets, having the *dogma* of the real, are an exemplary vade mecum for Eliot's pilgrimage toward the *emotion* of reality; or we can put it the other way round, that in these poems the actual is the riddle of the real, where the riddle is not so much for solution as for redemption. We begin, then, where pilgrimages should begin, with what we have, in intellect, on the edge of faith—the edge of what we have and the edge of what we have not.

We have a great deal in the intellect, in our citadel of old orders, and in various stages of development and disrepair, all in one way or another reflecting Eliot's one-man job of making a decorum. When listed out they seem more than any poem could stand, but that is because we tend to underestimate the unusual capacity for order that belongs to poetic imagination and because we ignore the tremendous pressure of behavior, or emotion, to fit into a proper order or orders. Here are five fourfold sequences as they apply to the four Quartets.

I. The immediate apprehension of timeless reality. The sickness of the soul when it comes short of timeless reality. The conditions of the soul: the river and the sea of life. The sin of the soul: in pride and humility.

II. The formal garden: the imposition of pattern: human actuality. Pattern as cycle in history: non-human actuality. Metaphorical patterns of the absolute actual: that is, of Annunciation. Metaphorical patterns of rebirth: the meaning of history.

III. The Rose-garden of any place: the present: the chance visit. The Ancestry of the dead: history: where one comes from. The ancestry of the forces showing only in nature: where one grows up; sempiternity. The ancestry and the inheritance by will and contemplation: where one thinks of self: eternity.

IV. The cycle of the elements. Air: the breath of life. Earth: decay and renewal. Water: what is in course and what is in permanence. Fire: of purgation and of love; of consumption and of consummation.

V. The Christian Cycle. Innocence in the garden. The Life of History. The Annunciation. The Incarnation and Crucifixion. Pentecost.

Also running through the poem there are at least three dramatic struggles: with time as the struggle with the pattern of the four elements; the struggle of the Fortune Teller and the Saint; and the struggle with language. All of these are part of the struggle to get at reality. Also, there are at least nine ideas or general notions implicated in this struggle. There is the idea of death in life and life in death: death as the condition of rebirth. The idea of the steps of Humility. The idea of getting at central reality by negative mysticism. The idea of music as the absolute condition of contemplation. The idea of the dance as the absolute condition of action. The idea of the still point: the intersection of time and the timeless. The idea of the sea, over and above any relation to the river. The idea of up and down, and how they are the same. The idea of beginning and end. The idea that the human enterprise is necessarily renewable.

Besides all this, the reminder is offered that each Quartet has in its parts the following five elements. I. A statement and counterstatement of the theme as predicament, given in terms of a scene or a landscape. II. A formal lyric: a birth by forms: with comment and conditions of further statement. III. Movement and action at the level of actual life. IV. A short lyric: an equivalent movement in the medium of music and the dance. V. Resumption and resolution (with consideration of the poet's job in his struggle with language) at the maximum level of statement—the level where the poetry does not matter.

It was looking forward to this sort of conspectus of orders that it was said above that, in a way, Eliot's effort to find his subject *is* his subject. To find the means of poetry is a step toward finding the subject, for the poetry will be its actual form. If you have the poetry the object may be found that corresponds to the subject.

Reflecting on this conspectus can we not sum up as follows? This is Court poetry without the operative aid of a court; religious poetry without the operative aid of a Church; classical poetry without the effective presence of the classics. The presence and aid are all putative. They are there, like orthodoxy in Eliot's phrase, whether anybody knows it or not. This is religious, royalist, classical poetry written for a secular world which has not yet either shown its shape or declared its commitments—without which it cannot have a decorum of its own.

Let us now still further close our summary, at that point where the order is merged in the behavior. "Burnt Norton" is actual innocence and immediate experience. "East Coker" is actual experience and direct history. "Dry Salvages" is the conditions in nature in which innocence and experience take place: epiphanies of the reality which they engage.

"Little Gidding" is the epiphany of the reality—that other, fatal reality—in *human* nature: the river and the sea within, as other and the same as the river and the sea without.

Again, "Dry Salvages" deals with the actual experience of pride and humility without doctrine, and without the ability to cope with them. "Little Gidding" deals with the experience of pride and humility under doctrine or dogma, but in the condition where they are forced into the actual. At this point we see that this man of necessary institutions would restore the ground upon which institutions are built: the ground of our beseeching. That is his actual experience of his institutions, and that is why they are live to him. There is the ground swell of the sea in "Dry Salvages," the ground of our beseeching in "Little Gidding." Both swells are from afar, both from mystery, both from reality. The ground swell is reality manifest in time. The ground of our beseeching is the reality manifest in timeless moments. The ground swell is all that is irredeemable. The ground of our beseeching is the hope of redemption; but there is a pattern of timeless moments which we cannot apprehend except in the ground swell.

## III

It is in this aspect of apprehension that our behavior becomes belief. Apprehension is in the backward look, the backward half-look, into the primitive mystery where things are themselves, what they always were, like the rock in the "Dry Salvages," which is also the Trois Sauvages, and lastly a rock worn by the sea off Cape Ann. That is the outside, ending in the calamitous annunciation. It is not much different (only wholly different) within: as we say that the time of death is every moment. It is only the difference between menace and caress.

The menace and caress of wave that breaks on water; for does not a menace caress? does not a caress menace? It is the difference between the annunciation that becomes death and the Annunciation that becomes Incarnation. In the one life and the one mind and the one prayer ("the hardly, barely prayable prayer") that perceives both, we apprehend in actuality "the impossible union of spheres of existence."

So the order of the poem, for the moment it lasts, fuses the levels of belief and behavior. It would seem that in our institutions we have no means of coping (until the moment of death) with the "daemonic, chthonic powers," except the means of liberation from them. In the things that go toward death, we are driven. In the things that go toward new life, the things within us move us. There are many annunciations but only one Annunciation of Incarnation, "Costing not less than everything."

In this poem—which like other efforts at major poetry is a kind of provisional institution—it is often not possible to tell which annunciation into the actual is being dealt with. That is because of Eliot's own honesty; he cannot himself always tell. Nobody can tell honestly what is lost of the real when it gets into the actual. Meaning withers and is replaced by—either a fresh bloom, or a straw-flower from an older harvest; replaced by a need, or by an error. Thus (in "Little Gidding") the need to forgive both good and bad; and thus the shame at motives late revealed. Nobody can tell a miracle, at sight, from a hallucination; though the one purifies and the other betrays the actual experience. The fuller the faith, the more difficult the task of honesty.

Is not this why in the Dante-like section of "Little Gidding," the "compound ghost both intimate and unidentifiable," is made to represent this final predicament of full faith: that there may be, always (though *I* do not myself believe it), *another* path, *another* pattern of timeless moments; not an anarchy, not a damnation, but another pattern, another revelation. Does not the great sin of human pride, within the forms of Eliot's belief, consist in *putting* God (one's own grasp, or loss, of reality) into first place? One should *find* reality; one cannot create it. Thus "The unknown, remembered gate," and thus "Taking any route." It is not in experience (as in "East Coker") but in prayer (as in "Little Gidding")—it is in the taking of things together, and in beseeching, that there is the sense of having found: "With the drawing of this Love and the voice of this Calling"—where drawing is attraction, and calling is summons.

But Eliot, being a believer, envisaging full faith, having the dogma of vital purpose, ends with the great idiosyncratic assertion—but only at the end. The emotion of the actual lasts up to the end. But the emotion can be *only* actual. It is the idiosyncrasy of Christian reality to be ineffable: a mystery which we do not so much experience as partake of. It is what suffers in us; and perhaps what it suffers, is, in part, the blows of other reality to which belief has not reached. So the poetic imagination sometimes compels us to think. It is eminently natural that, since reality is a mystery, man's institutions, and especially those institutions which are poems, as they cluster about that mystery, must again and again be made to feel the pressure of the real into the actual, lest the institutions lose their grasp of ideal aspiration and become mere formulae. We only *know* the real by what happens to it and to us; which is a true paradox. Man dwells in the actual, between the real and the real.

If this is true for Eliot, then his poem would seem to tell us, with examples, that man's ideals ought to be nourished by the cumulus of manifestations of the real into the actual (and of the actual into the real; for it is a reversible relation), and that these manifestations are enacted by Annunciation and Incarnation—the ideal of the fire to come; and also by Resurrection and the Immanence (or Descent) of the Holy Ghost.

But if this were all, then his poem would be only a set of doctrines out of dogmas, of verses made out of the traditional orders of the mind, put to work manipulating what images came to hand. Luckily there is more, as there is always more in poetry. Poetry by its use of language makes something—is always a *poiesis*—out of the doctrines in exact but unpredictable relation to the orders employed upon it. Poetry is more than usual emotion *and* more than usual order, and this double condition is the very condition of the language of poetry. Our language, as we understand it, purify it, keep it alive, is the great exemplary cumulus of our knowledge of the actual. Language is our memory, which we can partially master, of approximate intrusions of the real into the actual, just as it is also the body of our structures of the actual as it aspires into the real. To use Kenneth Burke's language, for the one, language is *symbolic* action, as for the other it is symbolic *action*. That is why Eliot's poem says of right language, *that it is the complete consort dancing together*. That is also why the poem says the poetry does not matter; the poetry is the way to get into language as a living resource. That is why this poem is a poetry of pattern and recurrence and modified repetition. That kind of poetry will drag more into being, as it is more nearly the condition of the actual, than that terribly deprived deformity of language known as polemic. Here the poetry is the "objective correlative" to the poem's *own* ineffable actual experience. The point is, the poem is not as near full response as the language the poem uses. All poems are imperfect. One cannot say of one's own calling, what one can say of what it aims at.

## IV

Let us now think of the conditions of language where order and behavior work upon each other, but not forgetting the conditions of the mind using the language.

We must be still and still moving
Into another intensity
For a further union, a deeper communion
Through the dark cold and the empty desolation,
The wave cry, the wind cry, the vast waters
Of the petrel and the porpoise. In my end is my beginning.

In these lines, from the end of "East Coker," is an example of everything that needs still to be said. The mind is in a circle and it proceeds by analogy; and the mind needs to know nothing it does not already know except the life in the words that it has not yet apprehended. The petrel is a bird of storm and its name is a diminutive of Peter who walked upon the waters. The porpoise is that creature not a fish of the most beautiful of all motion either in emerging from water or submerging and the motion is single: this porpoise who bore the souls of the dead to Hades and who even now precedes us on our ocean voyages. Thus, as well as analogy and circle we have images which are their own meanings.

In this Pilgrimage—by invocation, prayer, and ritual; all, like rhythm, means of prolonging the contemplation of the moment—in this Pilgrimage toward the emotion of reality (which is also the vision of reality, the meaning of reality) the movement is circular and the medium is allegory. These we will explore, then end on image.

The circle is because things lead into themselves, because experience leads into itself, or back to itself, or to the moment when it confronts itself; and because also the things of experience meet each other at different stages of development or relationship.

The analogy is because the things of experience do not pass out of themselves but into different phases of themselves, and not always at different times, but sometimes together and sometimes disparately, sometimes converging and concentrating, sometimes diverging and dissipating; and because it is by analogy alone, or almost alone, that words record the drift and shift, the sequence and the leap, from phase to phase, which seem the substance of our experience, moving us where we are moved: in our imitation of which is our one act of creation, our one means of expressing something more than was *already* in ourselves.

The circle is the serpent swallowing his own tail; but it is the serpent where no point is anywhere nearer the mouth than the tail. It is also, this circle, the up and the down, the end and the beginning, the sea and the river, the rock and the Incarnation.

The analogy is the correspondence of the members of the circle. It is the congruence, proportion, ratio, equivalence, correlation, but never the identity, of the members. It is in analogy that the action of the mind moves from one to the other, keeping both present; and does this in plurality as well as in duality. It is when we keep analogy in mind, that we see how it is that Eliot's correspondences move both ways, each requiring the other for its own elucidation; each working a little incongruously (with something left over and something left out) on the other; each imitating the other, or as we say, representing or enacting the other. It is the habit of analogy that keeps the circle *in* motion, *in* the actual, *in* a critical state. It keeps the circle from being finished; keeps it inclusive rather than exclusive; keeps it from self-satisfaction. The habit of analogy is the great reminder of what we would like to forget and what we must remember: that no revelation expressed or understood in human terms is total or complete, however we may believe it total beyond our terms of expression and understanding. It is by analogy that we create approximations of the experience we have not had: faith as the substance of things hoped for, and, as it were equally, the substance of things dreaded.

I suspect that this is kin to what Eliot meant by saying that the advantage for the poet was to see beneath both beauty and ugliness (the One and the other than One, order and chaos), to see the boredom, the horror, and the glory. Certainly, at any rate, in the *Four Quartets* it is analogies of these three that in beauty and ugliness we are brought to see. Again, in an older phrase, it is in the context of habitual analogy that we take upon us the mystery of things and become God's spies. Lear himself is a multiple analogy—both in pattern and in image—of the boredom, the horror, and the glory; and the ripeness (which is all) is the ripeness of each phase as it drifts, or crosses the gap, into the other place.

It is because Eliot's mind is both circular and dramatic that it has had to resort so much to analogy; and it is because his mind, as sensibility, is a great onion of analogy that he has had to resort to so many patterns and frames of experience. If you think of the Mediterranean catholic mind, it is one thing, which is not the same as the northern mind, catholic or not. The northern catholic mind would seem to require (since it contains so much more material which has not been incorporated into the Graeco-Christian rationale) a greater recourse to analogy to explain, or express, its own content to itself. This is only a suspicion, and only thrown out. But in any case, the Christian mind is never the whole mind, though the whole mind may aspire to be Christian, and it is one way of construing the Christian poet's task to make something—to make as much as he can—of the struggle of the whole mind to enact that aspiration. That is one way of accounting for what Eliot is up to in these poems. He has to discover what it is in that mind which struggles, and he has to find ways—analogies—by which he can keep his discoveries present. He has to keep present all those creations other than Christian, all those conditions of life other than human, which affect his sensibility and press into his behavior. As a poet, he must know and deal with, what as a Christian he perhaps has only to know and transcend, all that knowledge and experience which is not Christian and which is so much greater in quantity than the Christian. It would seem that in our stage of history, all the phases of the relations between behavior and belief have become live and urgent issues in the action of the mind to a degree that they have not been since the twelfth or thirteenth century. There was a deadness of the mind after Dante that destroyed more than did the Black Death of 1348.

If this sort of consideration is pertinent at all it is more pertinent to the avowedly Christian mind than another: he will see the predicament in greater extremity, and the more especially if, like Eliot, he has also an anti-clerical cast of mind. The war between emotion and belief, and the impurity of that war, will press him hardly. He will be forced to much deliberate and individual creation and re-creation of both image and pattern. He will be forced to attempt what he cannot do, and what, though he knows he cannot do it, he must nevertheless attempt if only because he sees that it is there to do. He must make what he does *stand for* what he cannot do, but he must never permit it (though it will happen, as the inevitable abuse of powers) to substi-

tute for what he cannot do. These considerations seem to
me to explain partially the fragmentary interrupted character of Eliot's composition from "Gerontion" onward, to explain the materials that get into his poems and the ineffable
tensions between them, and also to explain the over-arching
dramatic gestures of analogy by which he unites them.
These considerations perhaps also explain the force of the
poetry: why it is so much of ourselves we find struggling
there—a special case of ourselves, as James would say—and
as much so whether we are with or are without the special
version of belief we take to be his belief. We are engaged
in the same war, with different tokens, and the same substance unknown. We "are the music while the music
lasts," and while the music lasts we make the same pilgrimage toward reality.

Let us look at some examples, in none of which do I wish
to distinguish the circular from the analogic aspects. The
distinction would be merely analytic, and the two aspects
are much better taken in single perception.

In "East Coker" the first line is the motto of Mary Queen
of Scots: but in reversed order; and the last half of the last
line is the same motto but in its original order. We move
from In my beginning is my end, to In my end is my beginning. I take it that this motto is in analogy to the
references to Heraclitus and St. John of the Cross in its first
use, and that in the second use it is joined with the analogy
of earth and sea, and with

The wave cry, the wind cry, the vast waters
Of the petrel and the porpoise. In my end is my beginning.

Here are two chains-of-being in human history (social and
Christian) drawn together and put into relation with the
history which is not human in such a way that all three are
united in a single perception. This perception jumps the
gap into the last iteration of the initial phrase: In my end
is my beginning. This is analogy reaching up to the condition of the medieval anagoge: actually reaching the modern equivalent for it.

Eliot is quite aware of the distinction between the medieval and the modern analogy—and he makes us quite

aware of it in at least two instances in "East Coker," both in the second section. One is in the word "grimpen" which is without meaning in itself, but is a place name, that is to say a word meaning itself entirely, taken from the Great Grimpen Mire in *The Hound of the Baskervilles*. Eliot's line, "On the edge of a grimpen, where is no secure foothold," is inserted in a reference to the deceits made by the patterns imposed by knowledge derived from experience, and has to do with the knowledge so to speak which *is* experience: the grimpen in short, the thing itself with its *own* pattern, new every moment, and perhaps with ultimate deceits, all that must be sought for and shunned, on the way to knowledge beyond experience. That is one instance. The other is in the formal song which begins the second section of "East Coker," together with the verses immediately following in comment on the song. It is a song of the disturbance of things out of season, with flowers of all seasons in bloom at once, and with stars belonging to July and November in constellated wars: it is the condition when the world goes into the dark and into the fire "which burns before the icecap reigns." The flowers are of the senses, the stars are of astronomy and astrology both. The footwork is neat, the meaning is derivable (as any large dictionary will show), and the first seven lines have an analogous relation with the remainder of the song, but the analogy is not vital. That is almost why it is there; for the poem goes on:

That was a way of putting it—not very satisfactory:
A periphrastic study in a worn-out poetical fashion,
Leaving one still with the intolerable wrestle
With words and meanings. The poetry does not matter.

The poetry does not matter, but what does matter must be put in poetry to keep it in place. *That* historical skill has become periphrastic. The language of the stars is no longer a mature language, in the sense that it no longer works, except through the dictionary, and has only the fascination of a dead game, no matter what the astrologers think; it plays something, but we no longer know what. Yet it contributes to, and is in analogy with, the two lines which end this section of "East Coker," two lines with a space between them:

> The houses are all gone under the sea.
>
> The dancers are all gone under the hill.

This section deals with the humiliation *and* the humility that go with the struggle for faith

> On the edge of a grimpen, where is no secure foothold,
> And menaced by monsters, fancy lights,
> Risking enchantment.

And it leads by right into the Dark of the next section, at first a Miltonic dark (O dark dark dark. They all go into the dark) and then the darkness of God of St. John of the Cross. The dark of moonlight becomes the dark of the stars. In the very failure of the equivalence lies the strength of these analogies; the failure is part of the experience of "the intolerable wrestle with words and meanings."

It all comes back to the relation and the struggle between belief and behavior; and this is all the more clearly seen if we move from "East Coker" to the "Dry Salvages," from the history of man to the life of the individual, from human history to the history of the conditions in which humans live: to the river within and the sea all about us: to the gods and to God: to the many annunciations and the one Annunciation: to the sea and the Virgin: and also to the half-guessed, half-understood life which is somehow—not in our old skills of interpretation, not in what we have understood either in our experience or our revelation—which is somehow one Incarnation. There, by the fiat of incarnation, by the images of ultimate behavior actually in the poem,

> The hint half guessed, the gift half understood, is Incarna-
>     tion.
> Here the impossible union
> Of spheres of existence is actual,
> Here the past and the future
> Are conquered, and reconciled. . . .
> We, content at the last

If our temporal reversion nourish
(Not too far from the yew-tree)
The life of significant soil.

Not too far from the yew-tree. Sir Thomas Browne says the yew is "an emblem of Resurrection from its perpetual verdure." In our temporal reversion. Reversion is residue, is going back; in law is the returning of an estate to the grantor or his heirs. Hence the significant soil.

It is these lines, this fiat, at the end of the last part of "Dry Salvages," that establishes the relations, perfects the analogy, back through the other parts to the great sestina of the sea which is in the second part, and the double invocation of the river and the sea in the first part. Thus we understand that the "ragged rock in the restless waters," no matter what else it is, "is what it always was." And thus, also, we understand:

The salt is on the briar rose,
The fog is in the fir trees.

"East Coker" was incarnation in history, and purgation in darkness. "Dry Salvages" is Incarnation in Nature, and, through the Virgin, through the hint *and* the gift, in significant soil. The annunciations—the troubling messages—become the Annunciation, and are included by it.

These, then, are examples of analogies within their circles, and if we think of them together certain questions raise themselves about the relation of the patterns of the analogies to the images which are their elements. Which is the primary element of the correspondence: all the borrowed frames or the found images? The hollyhocks or the stars, the petrel and the porpoise or the ragged rock which is what it always was. There is the question of patterns and that which requires us to find patterns; the question of images (reaches, drifts, in perception) and that which requires us to find images. Perhaps there is a reversible relation; either the images or the patterns renew and change and come to zero, to the fecund still point of the turning world. There is a pattern in the pressing images—if only we could find it. There are images in the pattern—if only we could feel them.

## V

With that effort to find and feel, the remainder of these notes is concerned. That is, we shall deal with poetic composition by the attractive force of images which are neither circular nor analogical, images which are set in the center and draw things to them, compelling the things to declare their own meaning, transforming the things into enclosed tautologies. It is in part five of each quartet that such images are conspicuously found. In "Burnt Norton" there is the form or pattern of the Chinese jar.

> Only by the form, the pattern,
> Can words or music reach
> The stillness, as a Chinese jar still
> Moves perpetually in its stillness.

In "East Coker" there is this:

> Not the intense moment
> Isolated, with no before or after,
> But a lifetime burning in every moment
> And not the lifetime of one man only
> But of old stones that cannot be deciphered.

In "Dry Salvages," there is this:

> For most of us, there is only the unattended
> Moment, the moment in and out of time,
> The distraction fit, lost in a shaft of sunlight,
> The wild thyme unseen, or the winter lightning
> Or the waterfall, or music heard so deeply
> That it is not heard at all, but you are the music
> While the music lasts.

In "Little Gidding," there is this:

> Every phrase and every sentence is an end and a beginning,
> Every poem an epitaph. And any action
> Is a step to the block, to the fire, down the sea's throat
> Or to an illegible stone: and that is where we start.

And again in "Little Gidding," there is this:

> The voice of the hidden waterfall
> And the children in the apple-tree

> Not known, because not looked for
> But heard, half-heard, in the stillness
> Between two waves of the sea.

And this, in its turn, works back upon the following lines in "Dry Salvages," but is also an image for its own sake:

> The sea howl
> And the sea yelp, are different voices
> Often together heard; the whine in the rigging,
> The menace and caress of wave that breaks on water.

All but the last of these images have to do with the poet meditating his job of *poiesis*, meditating as if making an aesthetic: unearthing, discovering, exploring, beseeching a skill which, when he has it, will do the work over which *otherwise* he has no control. This is the skill of inspiration, of invoking the muses by ritual, in short the skill of incantation. It is the skill of skills, the mystery of the craft. It is how you get through the mere skills of poetry (what may be learned and rehearsed) into the skill of language itself (whatever *reality* is there) without losing the mere skills of poetry. It is then that you find that the poetry no longer matters; it matters, but *no longer*.

All of us, some of the time, seem to believe that it is by images like these (in their sequences, relations, triangulations) that Eliot composes his poems. At any rate, we believe that Eliot wants such images to act like compositors— as magic agents of composition. Beliefs of this kind are representatives of a deeper, troubled belief (the stage of belief when it is troubled and exasperated by unbelief—the movement of the exasperated spirit from wrong to wrong), the belief that the mind is not up to the task of responding to what confronts it; the belief that the mind must somehow incorporate into the response part of what confronts it; the belief that there is a failure of rational imagination when it ought least to be expected—at the very center of interest, the identification of the subject (or object) of response. I would say that this troubled belief is a part, but only a part, of Eliot's experience. It is one of the persisting conditions of experience, and a condition which has a relation to the conditions of our experience of poetry and language, what we do with language and what language does itself, what we create in language and what language creates in us. But it is not central; it is an obstacle on the path and it is also a mysterious incentive. It cannot be ignored. It must not be destroyed. It is certainly a corrective. It interrupts and modulates the rhythm of our footfalls, and sometimes seems the substance of the rhythm itself—but only seems. I would suppose then that these images (these closed tautologies) are present as symbolic reminders of the uneven rhythm of the rational imagination; that they operate —where they come—as a very high-level ad libbing habit of the rational poetic imagination; and that they furnish a consciously incomplete additional symbolic form of one persisting pattern of experience: one among many ways of composition: the way from the point of view of which Eliot spoke when he called poetry a mug's game.

It is true that for most of us most of the time any operation belonging to the full intelligence is a mug's game; and for all of us there is the precipice, either just behind us or just ahead of us.

Possibly this mug should be kept in mind whenever inspiration of the muses or ritual are under consideration, for all of these objects are counterparts in the mug's game of the mind. But, with this caution, I prefer to think of these images as primarily concerned with wooing the muse; that wooing which is the steady passion of the poet; and one of the reasons for this preference is that although each of these images seems independent, tautological, and generative, each is also appropriate—or keyed to—the general frame of rational imagination in which it occurs. The Chinese bowl belongs to the children in the apple-tree, to the formal garden. The lifetime of old stones that cannot be deciphered belongs to history and the conditions of human life in history. The music heard so deeply that you are the music while the music lasts, belongs both to the river within us, to the sea that is all about us, and to the vast waters of the petrel and the porpoise, as these are annunciated. And *Every poem an epitaph* belongs to the birth in death, to the death and birth which are *both* perennial and permanent, to the one and the One. It seems to me that seen as *so* keyed, seen as *thus* appropriate, these images become indeed agents of composition.

That is to say they are seen as themselves analogies which by enlightening each other are themselves enlightened, but which never enlighten themselves. The analogies are always pretty much undeclared, they do not say what they are about. They are ungoverned: they do not come *directly* under the head or the power of anything, but only by association. They are incomplete: they always require their parallels, and they always represent more than they state. To understand this, two sets of words from Shelley's "Defense of Poetry" seem useful. Words, says Shelley, "unveil the permanent analogies of things by images which participate in the life of truth." Here the word "participate" is the moving term. Again, Shelley remarks that misery, terror, despair itself, in poetry, create "approximations to the highest good." Here it is the word "approximations" that we want to keep in mind. Shelley seems to have hit on something which if it did not describe his own poetry, yet could not have been more expressly written to describe the poetry of Eliot; as, in another way, at a much fuller extension of his terms, it describes that of Dante.

In Dante the extension is to all the modes of the mind. In Eliot the reduction is to the images or small metaphors as they work and build on one another. In Dante there are many languages of the mind conspicuously and consciously at work. In Eliot, though there are other modes working, a predominance of the work is done in the language of the words themselves. We deal largely with what has got into the language *as* words, relatively little with what the words call on. In Eliot the authority is more direct, more limited, and with greater gaps. We are left with what the words will bear and with reminders of what the language will not bear. There is a radical difference in the *magnitude* of the authority of language as poetry in the two poets, which I believe has something to do with the *magnitude* of *achieved* mind confronted with life. This is not to condemn Eliot but to describe him, and in a sense, since he is writing our poetry, to describe ourselves. It seems, looking back, that with Dante the great rebellious troubles of unbelief fed and strengthened his belief, but that with Eliot there is a struggle between belief and unbelief in which each devours the other, except at the moment of desperation. Eliot has passed through the stages of Montaigne, St. John of the Cross, Pascal, Baudelaire, Mallarmé, and Valéry. It is a destructive process. In St. Francis our little sisters the flowers were left as well as our little sister Death. In Dante the Love still moved the sun and the other stars; and there is everywhere the continuous declaration of indestructible human identity. In Eliot there is the choice of pyre or pyre, of consumption or consummation, in either case a destruction. It would seem that the purgation destroys that which was to have been purged, and that refinement is into nothingness.

At least this is the sort of judgment into which we should be pushed by the "doctrine" of the poem, if we had to accept the doctrine by itself and without benefit of the images of permanent analogy to which it clings and with which it corrects itself. It is the sort of doctrine to which the unimpeded mind of our day turns as if by instinct— and to which the unimpeded part of all minds is drawn, tempted, called. The impediments, what holds us back, brings us up, concentrates us, are in poetry in the images. The impediments are to the point, and *Every poem an epitaph*, from "Little Gidding," is an excellent example; it is beside the doctrine, illuminates the doctrine, redeems the doctrine.

An epitaph is a funeral oration, a commendatory inscription; it gets rid of the dead, understands the dead, rejoins the dead, and also takes off from the dead. Every poem is an epitaph; but an epitaph is a poem, precisely because it has a life of its own which modifies the life of what died, and because it thereby instigates the renewal of the life which never died. It gets us back to the reality from which we started and thereby forward to the reality in which we shall end. It is thus, in Shelley's phrase, that even our despair is an approximation of the highest good;

and in Eliot's mood we have only our despair with which to make an approximation. Thus: "we shall not cease from exploration."

And so on, there is image after image that could be tackled with similar results. Let us, to conclude, take rather a single line from the second part of "Little Gidding," which both has a special interest and generalizes the whole poem: "To the spirit unappeased and peregrine." For the most part Eliot's metaphors of analogy restore us to the under-blows or the cellarage of the primitive in our souls and mind and behavior. But in the Dante-like section from which this line is taken it is everywhere the power of state-ment—the power of the rational imagination at the point of maximum control of the irrational and primitive in behavior —that is at stake. It is a mirror of the mind more like Shake-speare than like Dante. There is a terrible *disinterestedness* here quite different from the terrible *interestedness* of Dante. It is as if Eliot had to write "like Dante," which happens to be in singularly pure traditional blank verse, in order to feel "like Shakespeare." It is as if he had to do this in order to get at his full compound ghost of poet and man. The dark dove with the flickering tongue has gone, the disfigured street remains in the waning dusk and break-ing day. The whole job of man's world is to be done over again and the whole role of man in his world is to be re-created. Yet it is all the same, all perennial and all perma-nent and all unique. "The words sufficed to compel the recognition they preceded."

> the passage now presents no hindrance
> To the spirit unappeased and peregrine
> Between two worlds become much like each other.

Here is the American expatriate; the uprooted man in a given place; the alien making a home; man the alien on earth; man as the wanderer becoming the pilgrim; and the pilgrim returning with the last and fatal power of knowing that what was the pilgrim in him is only the mature and unappeasable state of the first incentive. All this is imme-diately present in the word "peregrine," and it is also gradually present with the aid of a little knowledge, and it is also finally present as something that reveals itself as you let the content of the word work into its surroundings and as you invite what surrounds it to join naturally to the word itself.

In the Republic and the Empire, *Peregrini* were, in Rome, citizens of any state other than Rome, with an implied membership in a definite community. So says the Oxford Classical Dictionary. The Shorter Oxford Dictionary says of "Peregrine": one from foreign parts, an alien, a wanderer; and goes on to say that in astrology (that ironic refuge of Eliot as of Donne and of Dante) a peregrine is a planet situated in a part of the zodiac where it has none of its essential dignity. In Italian the meanings are similar, and the notion of pilgrim is a late development.—Have we not an expatriate looking for a *patria*—an American turned Anglican—a perpetual peregrine at Rome? To clinch it, let us look to Dante (*Purgatorio* XIII, 94-96):

> O frate mio, ciascuna è cittadina
> d'una vera città; ma tu vuoi dire
> che vivesse in Italia peregrina.

> O my brother, each is citizen of a
> true City; but you would say one
> that lived in Italy peregrine.

I do not know how much nearer home we need to come, but if we think of Arnold's Grande Chartreuse poem, surely we are as close to the quick of the peregrine's home as we are likely to come. There looking at the old monastery Arnold felt himself hung between two worlds, one dead and the other powerless to be born. I do not think this is too much to pack into a word, but it is no wonder that it should take the attribute unappeasable, for it is the demands of the peregrine, whether outsider or pilgrim, that cannot be met. I will add that the peregrine is also a hawk or falcon found the world over but never at home: always a migrant but everywhere met; and, wherever found, courageous and swift.

1951

# 8. Examples of Wallace Stevens

The most striking if not the most important thing about Mr. Stevens' verse is its vocabulary—the collection of words, many of them uncommon in English poetry, which on a superficial reading seems characteristic of the poems. An air of preciousness bathes the mind of the casual reader when he finds such words as fubbed, girandoles, curlicues, catarrhs, gobbet, diaphanes, clopping, minuscule, pipping, pannicles, carked, ructive, rapey, cantilene, buffo, fiscs, phylactery, princox, and funest. And such phrases as "thrum with a proud douceur," or "A pool of pink, clippered with lilies scudding the bright chromes," hastily read, merely increase the feeling of preciousness. Hence Mr. Stevens has a bad reputation among those who dislike the finicky, and a high one, unfortunately, among those who value the ornamental sounds of words but who see no purpose in developing sound from sense.

Both classes of reader are wrong. Not a word listed above is used preciously; not one was chosen as an elegant substitute for a plain term; each, in its context, was a word definitely meant. The important thing about Mr. Stevens' vocabulary is not the apparent oddity of certain words, but the uses to which he puts those words with others. It is the way that Mr. Stevens combines kinds of words, unusual in a single context, to reveal the substance he had in mind, which is of real interest to the reader.

Good poets gain their excellence by writing an existing language *as if* it were their own invention; and as a rule success in the effect of originality is best secured by fidelity, in an extreme sense, to the individual words as they appear in the dictionary. If a poet knows precisely what his words represent, what he writes is much more likely to seem new and strange—and even difficult to understand—than if he uses his words ignorantly and at random. That is because when each word has definite character the combinations cannot avoid uniqueness. Even if a text is wholly quotation, the condition of quotation itself qualifies the text and makes it so far unique. Thus a quotation made from Marvell by Eliot has a force slightly different from what it had when Marvell wrote it. Though the combination of words is unique it is read, if the reader knows his words either by usage or dictionary, with a shock like that of recognition. The recognition is not limited, however, to what was already known in the words; there is a perception of something previously unknown, something new which is a result of the combination of the words, something which is literally an access of knowledge. Upon the poet's skill in combining words as much as upon his private feelings, depends the importance or the value of the knowledge.

In some notes on the language of E. E. Cummings I tried to show how that poet, by relying on his private feelings and using words as if their meanings were spontaneous with use, succeeded mainly in turning his words into empty shells. With very likely no better inspiration in the life around him, Mr. Stevens, by combining the insides of those words he found fit to his feelings, has turned his words into knowledge. Both Mr. Stevens and Cummings issue in ambiguity—as any good poet does; but the ambiguity of Cummings is that of the absence of known content, the ambiguity of a phantom which no words could give being; while Mr. Stevens' ambiguity is that of a substance so dense with being, that it resists paraphrase and can be truly perceived only in the form of words in which it was given. It is the difference between poetry which depends on the poet and poetry which depends on itself. Reading Cummings you either guess or supply the substance yourself. Reading Mr. Stevens you have only to know the meanings of the words and to submit to the conditions of the poem. There is a precision in such ambiguity all the more precise because it clings so closely to the stuff of the poem that separated it means nothing.

Take what would seem to be the least common word in the whole of *Harmonium*[1]—funest (page 74, line 6). The word means sad or calamitous or mournful and is derived from a French word meaning fatal, melancholy, baneful, and has to do with death and funerals. It comes ultimately from the Latin *funus* for funeral. Small dictionaries do not stock it. The poem in which it appears is called "Of the Manner of Addressing Clouds," which begins as follows:

> Gloomy grammarians in golden gowns,
> Meekly you keep the mortal rendezvous,
> Eliciting the still sustaining pomps
> Of speech which are like music so profound
> They seem an exaltation without sound.
> Funest philosophers and ponderers,
> Their evocations are the speech of clouds.
> So speech of your processionals returns
> In the casual evocations of your tread
> Across the stale, mysterious seasons. . . .

The sentence in which funest occurs is almost a parenthesis. It *seems* the statement of something thought of by the way, suggested by the clouds, which had better be said at once before it is forgotten. In such a casual, disarming way, resembling the way of understatement, Mr. Stevens often introduces the most important elements in his poems. The oddity of the word having led us to look it up we find that, once used, funest is better than any of its synonyms. It is the essence of the funeral in its sadness, not its sadness alone, that makes it the right word: the clouds are going to their death, as not only philosophers but less indoctrinated ponderers know; so what they say, what they evoke, in pondering, has that much in common with the clouds. Suddenly we realize that the effect of funest philosophers is due to the larger context of the lines preceding, and at the same time we become aware that the statement about

[1] The references are to the new edition of *Harmonium*, New York: Alfred A. Knopf, 1931. This differs from the first edition in that three poems have been cut out and fourteen added.

their evocations is central to the poem and illuminates it. The word pomps, above, means ceremony and comes from a Greek word meaning procession, often, by association, a funeral, as in the phrase funeral pomps. So the pomps of the clouds suggests the funeral in funest.

The whole thing increases in ambiguity the more it is analyzed, but if the poem is read over after analysis, it will be seen that *in the poem* the language is perfectly precise. In its own words it is clear, and becomes vague in analysis only because the analysis is not the poem. We use analysis properly in order to discard it and return that much better equipped to the poem.

The use of such a word as funest suggests more abstract considerations, apart from the present instance. The question is whether or not and how much the poet is stretching his words when they are made to carry as much weight as funest carries above. Any use of a word stretches it slightly, because any use selects from among many meanings the right one, and then modifies that in the context. Beyond this necessary stretching, words cannot perhaps be stretched without coming to nullity—as the popular stretching of awful, grand, swell, has more or less nullified the original senses of those words. If Mr. Stevens stretches his words slightly, as a live poet should and must, it is in such a way as to make them seem more precisely themselves than ever. The context is so delicately illuminated, or adumbrated, that the word must be looked up, or at least thought carefully about, before the precision can be seen. This is the precision of the expert pun, and every word, to a degree, carries with it in any given sense the puns of all its senses.

But it may be a rule that only the common words of a language, words with several, even groups of meanings, can be stretched the small amount that is possible. The reader must have room for his research; and the more complex words are usually plays upon common words, and limited in their play. In the instance above the word funest is not so much itself stretched by its association with philosophers as the word philosophers—a common word with many senses—stretches funest. That is, because Mr. Stevens has used the word funest, it cannot easily be detached and used by others. The point is subtle. The meaning so doubles upon itself that it can be understood only in context. It is the context that is stretched by the insertion of the word funest; and it is that stretch, by its ambiguity, that adds to our knowledge.

A use of words almost directly contrary to that just discussed may be seen in a very different sort of poem—"The Ordinary Women" (page 13). I quote the first stanza to give the tone:

> Then from their poverty they rose.
> From dry catarrhs, and to guitars
> They flitted
> Through the palace walls.

Then skipping a stanza, we have this, for atmosphere:

> The lacquered loges huddled there
> Mumbled zay-zay and a-zay, a-zay.
> The moonlight
> Fubbed the girandoles.

The loges huddled probably because it was dark or because they didn't like the ordinary women, and mumbled perhaps because of the moonlight, perhaps because of the catarrhs, or even to keep key to the guitars. Moonlight, for Mr. Stevens, is mental, fictive, related to the imagination and meaning of things; naturally it fubbed the girandoles (which is equivalent to cheated the chandeliers, was stronger than the artificial light, if any) . . . Perhaps and probably but no doubt something else. I am at loss, and quite happy there, to know anything literally about this poem. Internally, inside its own words, I know it quite well by simple perusal. The charm of the rhymes is enough to carry it over any stile. The strange phrase, "Fubbed the girandoles," has another charm, like that of the rhyme, and as inexplicable: the approach of language, through the magic of elegance, to nonsense. That the phrase is not nonsense, that on inspection it retrieves itself to sense, is its inner virtue. Somewhere between the realms of ornamental sound and representative statement, the words pause and balance, dissolve and resolve. This is the mood of Euphues, and presents a poem with fine parts controlled internally by little surds of feeling that save both the poem and its parts from preciousness. The ambiguity of this sort of writing consists in the double importance of both sound and sense where neither has direct connection with the other but where neither can stand alone. It is as if Mr. Stevens wrote two poems at once with the real poem somewhere between, unwritten but vivid.

A poem which exemplifies not the approach merely but actual entrance into nonsense is "Disillusionment of Ten O'Clock" (page 88). This poem begins by saying that houses are haunted by white nightgowns, not nightgowns of various other colors, and ends with these lines:

> People are not going
> To dream of baboons and periwinkles.
> Only, here and there, an old sailor,
> Drunk and asleep in his boots,
> Catches tigers
> In red weather.

The language is simple and declarative. There is no doubt about the words or the separate statements. Every part of the poem makes literal sense. Yet the combination makes a nonsense, and a nonsense much more convincing than the separate sensible statements. The statement about catching tigers in red weather coming after the white nightgowns and baboons and periwinkles, has a persuasive force out of all relation to the sense of the words. Literally, there is nothing alarming in the statement, and nothing ambiguous, but by so putting the statement that it appears as nonsense, infinite possibilities are made terrifying and plain. The shock and virtue of nonsense is this: it compels us to scrutinize the words in such a way that we see the enormous ambiguity in the substance of every phrase, every image, every word. The simpler the words are the more impressive and certain is the ambiguity. Half our sleeping knowledge is in nonsense; and when put in a poem it wakes.

The edge between sense and nonsense is shadow thin, and in all our deepest convictions we hover in the shadow, uncertain whether we know what our words mean, never-

theless bound by the conviction to say them. I quote the
second half of "The Death of a Soldier" (page 129):

> Death is absolute and without memorial,
> As in a season of autumn,
> When the wind stops,
> When the wind stops and, over the heavens,
> The clouds go, nevertheless,
> In their direction.

To gloss such a poem is almost impertinent, but I wish to
observe that in the passage just quoted, which is the important half of the poem, there is an abstract statement,
"Death is absolute and without memorial," followed by
the notation of a natural phenomenon. The connection between the two is not a matter of course; it is syntactical,
poetic, human. The point is, by combining the two, Mr.
Stevens has given his abstract statement a concrete, sensual
force; he has turned a conviction, an idea, into a feeling
which did not exist, even in his own mind, until he had
put it down in words. The feeling is not exactly in the
words, it is because of them. As in the body sensations are
definite but momentary, while feelings are ambiguous
(with reference to sensations) but lasting; so in this poem
the words are definite but instant, while the feelings they
raise are ambiguous (with reference to the words) and have
importance. Used in this way, words, like sensations, are
blind facts which put together produce a feeling no part of
which was in the data. We cannot say, abstractly, in words,
any better what we know, yet the knowledge has become
positive and the conviction behind it indestructible, because
it has been put into words. That is one business of poetry,
to use words to give quality and feeling to the precious
abstract notions, and so doing to put them beyond words
and beyond the sense of words.

A similar result from a different mode of the use of words
may be noticed in such a poem as "The Emperor of Ice-
Cream" (page 85):

> Call the roller of big cigars,
> The muscular one, and bid him whip
> In kitchen cups concupiscent curds.

Let the wenches dawdle in such dress
As they are used to wear, and let the boys
Bring flowers in last month's newspapers.
Let be be finale of seem.
The only emperor is the emperor of ice-cream.

Take from the dresser of deal,
Lacking the three glass knobs, that sheet
On which she embroidered fantails once
And spread it so as to cover her face.
If her horny feet protrude, they come
To show how cold she is, and dumb.
Let the lamp affix its beam.
The only emperor is the emperor of ice-cream.

The poem might be called Directions for a Funeral, with Two Epitaphs. We have a corpse laid out in the bedroom and we have people in the kitchen. The corpse is dead; then let the boys bring flowers in last month's (who would use today's?) newspapers. The corpse is dead; but let the wenches wear their everyday clothes—or is it the clothes they are used to wear at funerals? The conjunction of a muscular man whipping desirable desserts in the kitchen and the corpse protruding horny feet, gains its effect because of its oddity—not of fact, but of expression: the light frivolous words and rapid meters. Once made the conjunction is irretrievable and in its own measure exact. Two ideas or images about death—the living and the dead—have been associated, and are now permanently fused. If the mind is a rag-bag, pull out two rags and sew them together. If the materials were contradictory, the very contradiction, made permanent, becomes a kind of unison. By associating ambiguities found in nature in a poem we reach a clarity, a kind of transfiguration even, whereby we learn *what* the ambiguity was.

The point is, that the oddity of association would not have its effect without the couplets which conclude each stanza with the pungency of good epitaphs. Without the couplets the association would sink from wit to low humor or simple description. What, then, do the couplets mean? Either, or both, of two things. In the more obvious sense, "Let be be finale of seem," in the first stanza, means, take whatever seems to be, as really being; and in the second stanza, "Let the lamp affix its beam," means let it be plain that this woman is dead, that these things, impossibly ambiguous as they may be, are as they are. In this case, "The only emperor is the emperor of ice-cream," implies in both stanzas that the only power worth heeding is the power of the moment, of what is passing, of the flux.[2]

The less obvious sense of the couplets is more difficult to set down because, in all its difference, it rises out of the first sense, and while contradicting and supplanting, yet guarantees it. The connotation is, perhaps, that ice-cream and what it represents is the only power *heeded*, not the only power there is to heed. The irony recoils on itself: what seems *shall* finally be; the lamp *shall* affix its beam. The only emperor is the emperor of ice-cream. The king is dead; long live the king.

The virtue of the poem is that it discusses and settles these matters without mentioning them. The wit of the couplets does the work.

Allied to the method of this poem is the method of much of "Le Monocle de Mon Oncle." The light word is used with a more serious effect than the familiar, heavy words commonly chosen in poems about the nature of love. I take these lines from the first stanza (page 16):

> The sea of spuming thought foists up again
> The radiant bubble that she was. And then
> A deep up-pouring from some saltier well
> Within me, bursts its watery syllable.

The words foist and bubble are in origin and have remained in usage both light. One comes from a word meaning to palm false dice, and the other is derived by imitation from a gesture of the mouth. Whether the history of the words was present in Mr. Stevens' mind when he chose them is immaterial; the pristine flavor is still active by tradition and is what gives the rare taste to the lines quoted. By employing them in connection with a sea of spuming

[2] Mr. Stevens wrote me that his daughter put a superlative value on ice-cream. Up daughters!

thought and the notion of radiance whatever vulgarity was in the two words is purged. They gain force while they lend their own lightness to the context; and I think it is the lightness of these words that permits and conditions the second sentence in the quotation, by making the contrast between the foisted bubble and the bursting syllable possible.

Stanza IV of the same poem (pages 17-18) has a serious trope in which apples and skulls, love and death, are closely associated in subtle and vivid language. An apple, Mr. Stevens says, is as good as any skull to read because, like the skull, it finally rots away in the ground. The stanza ends with these lines:

> But it excels in this, that as the fruit
> Of love, it is a book too mad to read
> Before one merely reads to pass the time.

The light elegance and conversational tone give the stanza the cumulative force of understatement, and make it seem to carry a susurrus of irony between the lines. The word excels has a good deal to do with the success of the passage; superficially a syntactical word as much as anything else, actually, by its literal sense it saves the lines from possible triviality.

We have been considering poems where the light tone increases the gravity of the substance, and where an atmosphere of wit and elegance assures poignancy of meaning. It is only a step or so further to that use of language where tone and atmosphere are very nearly equivalent to substance and meaning themselves. "Sea Surface Full of Clouds" (page 132) has many lines and several images in its five sections which contribute by their own force to the sense of the poem, but it would be very difficult to attach special importance to any one of them. The burden of the poem is the color and tone of the whole. It is as near a tone-poem, in the musical sense, as language can come. The sense of single lines cannot profitably be abstracted from the context, and literal analysis does nothing but hinder understanding. We may say, if we like, that Mr. Stevens found himself in ecstasy—that he stood aside from himself emotionally—before the spectacle of endlessly varied appearances of California seas off Tehuantepec; and that he has tried to equal the complexity of what he saw in the technical intricacy of his poem. But that is all we can say. Neither the material of the poem nor what we get out of it is by nature susceptible of direct treatment in words. It might at first seem more a painter's subject than a poet's, because its interest is more obviously visual and formal than mental. Such an assumption would lead to apt criticism if Mr. Stevens had tried, in his words, to present a series of seascapes with a visual atmosphere to each picture. His intention was quite different and germane to poetry; he wanted to present the tone, in the mind, of five different aspects of the sea. The strictly visual form is in the background, merely indicated by the words; it is what the visual form gave off after it had been felt in the mind that concerned him. Only by the precise interweaving of association and suggestion, by the development of a delicate verbal pattern, could he secure the overtones that possessed him. A looser form would have captured nothing.

The choice of certain elements in the poem may seem arbitrary, but it is an arbitrariness without reference to their rightness and wrongness. That is, any choice would have been equally arbitrary, and, esthetically, equally right. In the second stanza of each section, for example, one is reminded of different kinds of chocolate and different shades of green, thus: rosy chocolate and paradisal green; chophouse chocolate and sham-like green; porcelain chocolate and uncertain green; musky chocolate and too-fluent green; Chinese chocolate and motley green. And each section gives us umbrellas variously gilt, sham, pied, frail, and large. The ocean is successively a machine which is perplexed, tense, tranced, dry, and obese. The ocean produces sea-blooms from the clouds, mortal massives of the blooms of water, silver petals of white blooms, figures of the clouds like blooms, and, finally, a wind of green blooms. These items, and many more, repeated and modified, at once impervious to and merging each in the other, make up the words of the poem. Directly they do nothing but rouse the small sensations and smaller feelings of atmosphere and tone. The poem itself, what it means, is somewhere in the background; we know it through the tone. The motley hue we see is crisped to "clearing opalescence."

> Then the sea
> And heaven rolled as one and from the two
> Came fresh transfigurings of freshest blue.

Here we have words used as a tone of feeling to secure the discursive evanescence of appearances; words bringing the senses into the mind which they created; the establishment of interior experience by the construction of its tone in words. In "Tattoo" (page 108), we have the opposite effect, where the mind is intensified in a simple visual image. The tone existed beforehand, so to speak, in the nature of the subject.

> The light is like a spider.
> It crawls over the water.
> It crawls over the edges of the snow.
> It crawls under your eyelids
> And spreads its webs there—
> Its two webs.
>
> The webs of your eyes
> Are fastened
> To the flesh and bones of you
> As to rafters or grass.
>
> There are filaments of your eyes
> On the surface of the water
> And in the edges of the snow.

The problem of language here hardly existed: the words make the simplest of statements, and the poet had only to avoid dramatizing what was already drama in itself, the sensation of the eyes in contact with what they looked at. By attempting *not* to set up a tone the tone of truth is secured for statements literally false. Fairy tales and Mother Goose use the same language. Because there is no point where the statements stop being true, they leap the gap unnoticed between literal truth and imaginative truth. It is worth observing that the strong sensual quality of the poem is defined without the use of a single sensual word; and it is that ambiguity between the words and their subject which makes the poem valuable.

There is nothing which has been said so far about Mr. Stevens' uses of language which might not have been said, with different examples, of any good poet equally varied and equally erudite[3]—by which I mean intensely careful of effects. We have been dealing with words primarily, and words are not limited either to an author or a subject. Hence they form unique data and are to be understood and commented on by themselves. You can hardly more compare two poets' use of a word than you can compare, profitably, trees to cyclones. Synonyms are accidental, superficial, and never genuine. Comparison begins to be possible at the level of more complicated tropes than may occur in single words.

Let us compare then, for the sake of distinguishing the kinds of import, certain tropes taken from Ezra Pound, T. S. Eliot, and Mr. Stevens.

From Mr. Pound—the first and third from the *Cantos* and the second from *Hugh Selwyn Mauberley:*

In the gloom, the gold gathers the light against it.

Tawn foreshores
Washed in the cobalt of oblivion.

A catalogue, his jewels of conversation.

[3] See *Words and Idioms,* by Logan Pearsall Smith, Boston: Houghton Mifflin, 1926, page 121. "One of the great defects of our critical vocabulary is the lack of a neutral, non-derogatory name for these great artificers, these artists who derive their inspiration more from the formal than the emotional aspects of their art, and who are more interested in the masterly control of their material, than in the expression of their own feelings, or the prophetic aspects of their calling." Mr. Smith then suggests the use of the words erudite and erudition and gives as reason their derivation "from *erudire* (*E* 'out of,' and *rudis,* 'rude,' 'rough' or 'raw'), a verb meaning in classical Latin to bring out of the rough, to form by means of art, to polish, to instruct." Mr. Stevens is such an *erudite;* though he is often more, when he deals with emotional matters as if they were matters for *erudition.*

From T. S. Eliot—one from "Prufrock," one from *The Waste Land,* and one from *Ash Wednesday:*

> I should have been a pair of ragged claws
> Scuttling across the floors of silent seas.

> The awful daring of a moment's surrender
> Which an age of prudence can never retract.

> Struggling with the devil of the stairs who wears
> The deceitful face of hope and of despair.

The unequaled versatility of Ezra Pound (Eliot in a dedication addresses him as *Il miglior fabbro*) prevents assurance that the three lines quoted from him are typical of all his work. At least they are characteristic of his later verse, and the kind of feeling they exhibit may be taken as Pound's own. Something like their effect may be expected in reading a good deal of his work.

The first thing to be noticed is that the first two tropes are visual images—not physical observation, but something to be seen in the mind's eye; and that as the images are so seen their meaning is exhausted. The third trope while not directly visual acts as if it were. What differentiates all three from physical observation is in each case the non-visual associations of a single word—*gathers,* which in the active voice has an air of intention; *oblivion,* which has the purely mental sense of forgetfulness; and, less obviously, *conversation,* in the third trope, which while it helps *jewels* to give the line a visual quality it does not literally possess, also acts to condense in the line a great many non-visual associations.

The lines quoted from T. S. Eliot are none of them in intention visual; they deal with a totally different realm of experience—the realm in which the mind dramatizes, at a given moment, its feelings toward a whole aspect of life. The emotion with which these lines charge the reader's mind is a quality of emotion which has so surmounted the senses as to require no longer the support of direct contact with them. Abstract words have reached the intensity of thought and feeling where the senses have been condensed into abstraction. The first distich is an impossible statement which in its context is terrifying. The language has sensual elements but as such they mean nothing: it is the act of abstract dramatization which counts. In the second and third distichs words such as *surrender* and *prudence, hope* and *despair,* assume, by their dramatization, a definite sensual force.

Both Eliot and Pound condense; their best verse is weighted—Pound's with sensual experience primarily, and Eliot's with beliefs. Where the mind's life is concerned the senses produce images, and beliefs produce dramatic cries. The condensation is important.

Mr. Stevens' tropes, in his best work and where he is most characteristic, are neither visual like Pound nor dramatic like Eliot. The scope and reach of his verse are no less but are different. His visual images never condense the matter of his poems; they either accent or elaborate it. His dramatic statements, likewise, tend rather to give another, perhaps more final, form to what has already been put in different language.

The best evidence of these differences is the fact that it is almost impossible to quote anything short of a stanza from Mr. Stevens without essential injustice to the meaning. His kind of condensation, too, is very different in character and degree from Eliot and Pound. Little details are left in the verse to show what it is he has condensed. And occasionally, in order to make the details fit into the poem, what has once been condensed is again elaborated. It is this habit of slight re-elaboration which gives the firm textural quality to the verse.

Another way of contrasting Mr. Stevens' kind of condensation with those of Eliot and Pound will emerge if we remember Mr. Stevens' *intentional* ambiguity. Any observation, as between the observer and what is observed, is the notation of an ambiguity. To Mr. Stevens the sky, "the basal slate," "the universal hue," which surrounds us and is always upon us is the great ambiguity. Mr. Stevens associates two or more such observations so as to accent their ambiguities. But what is ambiguous in the association is not the same as in the things associated; it is something new, and it has the air of something condensed. This is the quality that makes his poems grow, rise in the mind like a tide. The poems cannot be exhausted, because the words that make them, intentionally ambiguous at their crucial points, are themselves inexhaustible. Eliot obtains many of his effects by the sharpness of surprise, Pound his by visual definition; they tend to exhaust their words in the individual use, and they are successful because they know when to stop, they know when sharpness and definition lay most hold on their subjects, they know the maximal limit of their kinds of condensation. Mr. Stevens is just as precise in his kind; he brings ambiguity to the point of sharpness, of reality, without destroying, but rather preserving, clarified, the ambiguity. It is a difference in subject matter, and a difference in accent. Mr. Stevens makes you aware of how much is *already* condensed in any word.

The first stanza of "Sunday Morning" may be quoted (page 89). It should be remembered that the title is an integral part of the poem, directly affecting the meaning of many lines and generally controlling the atmosphere of the whole.

> Complacencies of the peignoir, and late
> Coffee and oranges in a sunny chair,
> And the green freedom of a cockatoo
> Upon a rug mingle to dissipate
> The holy hush of ancient sacrifice.
> She dreams a little, and she feels the dark
> Encroachment of that old catastrophe,
> As a calm darkens among water-lights.
> The pungent oranges and bright, green wings
> Seem things in some procession of the dead,
> Winding across wide water, without sound.
> The day is like wide water, without sound,
> Stilled for the passing of her dreaming feet
> Over the seas, to silent Palestine,
> Dominion of the blood and sepulchre.

A great deal of ground is covered in these fifteen lines, and the more the slow ease and conversational elegance of the verse are observed, the more wonder it seems that so much could have been indicated without strain. Visually, we have a woman enjoying her Sunday morning breakfast in a sunny room with a green rug. The image is secured, however, not as in Pound's image about the gold gathering the light against it, in directly visual terms, but by the almost casual combination of visual images with such phrases as "*complacencies* of the peignoir," and "the green *freedom* of the cockatoo," where the italicized words are abstract in essence but rendered concrete in combination. More important, the purpose of the images is to show how they dissipate the "holy hush of ancient sacrifice," how the natural comfort of the body is aware but mostly unheeding that Sunday is the Lord's day and that it commemorates the crucifixion.

From her half-awareness she feels the more keenly the "old catastrophe" merging in the surroundings, subtly, but deeply, changing them as a "calm darkens among waterlights." The feeling is dark in her mind, darkens, changing the whole day. The oranges and the rug and the day all have the quality of "wide water, without sound," and all her thoughts, so loaded, turn on the crucifixion.

The transit of the body's feeling from attitude to attitude is managed in the medium of three water images. These images do not replace the "complacencies of the peignoir," nor change them; they act as a kind of junction between them and the Christian feeling traditionally proper to the day. By the time the stanza is over the water images have embodied both feelings. In their own way they make a condensation by appearing in company with and showing what was already condensed.

If this stanza is compared with the tropes quoted from Pound, the principal difference will perhaps seem that while Pound's lines define their own meaning and may stand alone, Mr. Stevens' various images are separately incomplete and, on the other hand, taken together, have a kind of completeness to which Pound's lines may not pretend: everything to which they refer is present. Pound's images exist without syntax, Mr. Stevens' depend on it. Pound's images are formally simple, Mr. Stevens' complex. The one contains a mystery, and the other, comparatively, expounds a mystery.

While it would be possible to find analogues to Eliot's tropes in the stanzas of "Sunday Morning," it will be more profitable to examine something more germane in spirit. Search is difficult and choice uncertain, for Mr. Stevens is not a dramatic poet. Instead of dramatizing his feelings, he takes as fatal the drama that he sees and puts it down either in its least dramatic, most meditative form, or makes of it a simple statement. Let us then frankly take as pure a meditation as may be found, "The Snow Man" (page 12), where, again, the title is integrally part of the poem:

> One must have a mind of winter
> To regard the frost and the boughs
> Of the pine-trees crusted with snow;
>
> And have been cold a long time
> To behold the junipers shagged with ice,
> The spruces rough in the distant glitter
>
> Of the January sun; and not to think
> Of any misery in the sound of the wind,
> In the sound of a few leaves,
>
> Which is the sound of the land
> Full of the same wind
> That is blowing in the same bare place
>
> For the listener, who listens in the snow,
> And, nothing himself, beholds
> Nothing that is not there and the nothing that is.

The last three lines are as near as Mr. Stevens comes to the peculiar dramatic emotion which characterizes the three tropes quoted from Eliot. Again, as in the passage compared to Pound's images, the effect of the last three lines depends entirely on what preceded them. The emotion is built up from chosen fragments and is then stated in its simplest form. The statement has the force of emotional language but it remains a statement—a modest declaration of circumstance. The abstract word *nothing*, three times repeated, is not in effect abstract at all; it is synonymous with the data about the winter landscape which went before. The part which is not synonymous is the emotion: the overtone of the word, and the burden of the poem. Eliot's lines,

> The awful daring of a moment's surrender
> Which an age of prudence can never retract,

like Pound's lines, for different reasons, stand apart and on their own feet. The two poets work in contrary modes. Eliot places a number of things side by side. The relation is seldom syntactical or logical, but is usually internal and sometimes, so far as the reader is concerned, fatal and accidental. He works in violent contrasts and produces as much by prestidigitation as possible. There was no reason in the rest of "Prufrock" why the lines about the pair of ragged claws should have appeared where they did and no reason, perhaps, why they should have appeared at all; but once they appeared they became for the reader irretrievable, complete in themselves, and completing the structure of the poem.

That is the method of a dramatic poet, who molds wholes out of parts themselves autonomous. Mr. Stevens, not a dramatic poet, seizes his wholes only in imagination; in his poems the parts are already connected. Eliot usually moves from point to point or between two termini. Mr. Stevens as a rule ends where he began; only when he is through, his beginning has become a chosen end. The differences may be exaggerated but in their essence is a true contrast.

If a digression may be permitted, I think it may be shown that the different types of obscurity found in the three poets are only different aspects of their modes of writing. In Pound's verse, aside from words in languages the reader does not know, most of the hard knots are tied round combinations of classical and historical references. A passage in one of the Cantos, for example, works up at the same time the adventures of a Provençal poet and the events in one of Ovid's *Metamorphoses*. If the reader is acquainted with the details of both stories, he can appreciate the criticism in Pound's combination. Otherwise he will remain confused: he will be impervious to the plain facts of the verse.

Eliot's poems furnish examples of a different kind of reference to and use of history and past literature. The reader must be familiar with the ideas and the beliefs and systems of feeling to which Eliot alludes or from which he borrows, rather than to the facts alone. Eliot does not restrict himself to criticism; he digests what he takes; but the reader must know what it is that has been digested before he can appreciate the result. The Holy Grail material in *The Waste Land* is an instance: like Tiresias, this material is a dramatic element in the poem.

Mr. Stevens' difficulties to the normal reader present themselves in the shape of seemingly impenetrable words or phrases which no wedge of knowledge brought from outside the body of Mr. Stevens' own poetry can help much to split. The wedge, if any, is in the words themselves, either in the instance alone or in relation to analogous instances in the same or other poems in the book. Two examples should suffice.

In "Sunday Morning," there is in the seventh stanza (page 93) a reference to the sun, to which men shall chant their devotion—

> Not as a god, but as a god might be,
> Naked among them, like a savage source.
> Their chant shall be a chant of paradise,
> Out of their blood, returning to the sky; . . .

Depending upon the reader this will or will not be obscure. But in any case, the full weight of the lines is not felt until the conviction of the poet that the sun is origin and ending for all life is shared by the reader. That is why the god might be naked among them. It takes only reading of the stanza, the poem, and other poems where the fertility of the sun is celebrated, to make the notion sure. The only bit of outside information that might help is the fact that in an earlier version this stanza concluded the poem.—In short, generally, you need only the dictionary and familiarity with the poem in question to clear up a good part of Mr. Stevens' obscurities.

The second example is taken from "The Man whose Pharynx was Bad" (page 128):

> Perhaps, if winter once could penetrate
> Through all its purples to the final slate.

Here, to obtain the full meaning, we have only to consult the sixth stanza of "Le Monocle de Mon Oncle" (page 18):

> If men at forty will be painting lakes
> The ephemeral blues must merge for them in one,
> The basic slate, the universal hue.
> There is a substance in us that prevails.

Mr. Stevens has a notion often intimated that the sky is the only permanent background for thought and knowledge; he would see things against the sky as a Christian would see them against the cross. The blue of the sky is the prevailing substance of the sky, and to Mr. Stevens it seems only necessary to look at the sky to share and be shared in its blueness.

If I have selected fairly types of obscurity from these poets, it should be clear that whereas the obscurities of Eliot and Pound are intrinsic difficulties of the poems, to which the reader must come well armed with specific sorts of external knowledge and belief, the obscurities of Mr. Stevens clarify themselves to the intelligence alone. Mode and value are different—not more or less valuable, but different. And all result from the concentrated language which is the medium of poetry. The three poets load their words with the maximum content; naturally, the poems remain obscure until the reader takes out what the poet puts in. What still remains will be the essential impenetrability of words, the bottomlessness of knowledge. To these the reader, like the poet, must submit.

Returning, this time without reference to Pound and Eliot, among the varieties of Mr. Stevens' tropes we find some worth notice which comparison will not help. In "Le Monocle de Mon Oncle," the ninth stanza (page 20), has nothing logically to do with the poem; it neither develops the subject nor limits it, but is rather a rhetorical interlude set in the poem's midst. Yet it is necessary to the poem, because its rhetoric, boldly announced as such, expresses the feeling of the poet toward his poem, and that feeling, once expressed, becomes incorporated in the poem.

> In verses wild with motion, full of din,
> Loudened by cries, by clashes, quick and sure
> As the deadly thought of men accomplishing
> Their curious fates in war, come, celebrate
> The faith of forty, ward of Cupido.
> Most venerable heart, the lustiest conceit
> Is not too lusty for your broadening.
> I quiz all sounds, all thoughts, all everything
> For the music and manner of the paladins
> To make oblation fit. Where shall I find
> Bravura adequate to this great hymn?

It is one of the advantages of a non-dramatic, meditative style, that pure rhetoric may be introduced into a poem without injuring its substance. The structure of the poem is, so to speak, a structure of loose ends, spliced only verbally, joined only by the sequence in which they appear. What might be fustian ornament in a dramatic poem, in a meditative poem casts a feeling far from fustian over the whole, and the slighter the relation of the rhetorical interlude to the substance of the whole, the more genuine is the feeling cast. The rhetoric does the same thing that the action does in a dramatic poem, or the events in a narrative poem; it produces an apparent medium in which the real substance may be borne.

Such rhetoric is not reserved to set interludes; it often occurs in lines not essentially rhetorical at all. Sometimes it gives life to a serious passage and cannot be separated without fatal injury to the poem. Then it is the trick without which the poem would fall flat entirely. Two poems occur where the rhetoric is the vital trope—"A High-Toned Old Christian Woman" (page 79), and "Bantams in Pine-Woods" (page 101), which I quote entire:

> Chieftain Iffucan of Azcan in caftan
> Of tan with henna hackles, halt!
>
> Damned universal cock, as if the sun
> Was blackamoor to bear your blazing tail.

> Fat! Fat! Fat! I am the personal.
> Your world is you. I am my world.
>
> You ten-foot poet among inchlings. Fat!
> Begone! An inchling bristles in these pines,
>
> Bristles, and points their Appalachian tangs,
> And fears not portly Azcan nor his hoos.

The first and last distichs are gauds of rhetoric; nevertheless they give not only the tone but the substance to the poem. If the reader is deceived by the rhetoric and believes the poem is no more than a verbal plaything, he ought not to read poetry except as a plaything. With a different object, Mr. Stevens' rhetoric is as ferociously comic as the rhetoric in Marlowe's *Jew of Malta*, and as serious. The ability to handle rhetoric so as to reach the same sort of intense condensation that is secured in bare, non-rhetorical language is very rare, and since what rhetoric can condense is very valuable it ought to receive the same degree of attention as any other use of language. Mr. Stevens' successful attempts in this direction are what make him technically most interesting. Simple language, dealing obviously with surds, draws emotion out of feelings; rhetorical language, dealing rather, or apparently, with inflections, employed with the same seriousness, creates a surface *equivalent* to an emotion by its approximately complete escape from the purely communicative function of language.[4]

We have seen in a number of examples that Mr. Stevens uses language in several different ways, either separately or in combination; and I have tried to imply that his success is due largely to his double adherence to words and experience as existing apart from his private sensibility. His

---

[4] There is a point at which rhetorical language resumes its communicative function. In the second of "Six Significant Landscapes" (page 98), we have this image:

> A pool shines
> Like a bracelet
> Shaken at a dance,

which is a result of the startling associations induced by an ornamental, social, rhetorical style in dealing with nature. The image perhaps needs its context to assure its quality.

great labor has been to allow the reality of what he felt personally to pass into the superior impersonal reality of words. Such a transformation amounts to an access of knowledge, as it raises to a condition where it may be rehearsed and understood in permanent form that body of emotional and sensational experience which in its natural condition makes life a torment and confusion.

With the technical data partly in hand, it ought now to be possible to fill out the picture, touch upon the knowledge itself, in Mr. Stevens' longest and most important poem, "The Comedian as the Letter C." Everywhere characteristic of Mr. Stevens' style and interests, it has the merit of difficulty—difficulty which when solved rewards the reader beyond his hopes of clarity.

Generally speaking the poem deals with the sensations and images, notions and emotions, ideas and meditations, sensual adventures and introspective journeyings of a protagonist called Crispin. More precisely, the poem expounds the shifting of a man's mind between sensual experience and its imaginative interpretation, the struggle, in that mind, of the imagination for sole supremacy and the final slump or ascent where the mind contents itself with interpreting pain and common things. In short, we have a meditation, with instances, of man's struggle with nature. The first line makes the theme explicit: "Nota: man is the intelligence of his soil, the sovereign ghost." Later, the theme is continued in reverse form: "His soil is man's intelligence." Later still, the soil is qualified as suzerain, which means sovereign over a semi-independent or internally autonomous state; and finally, at the end of the poem, the sovereignty is still further reduced when it turns out that the imagination can make nothing better of the world (here called a turnip), than the same insoluble lump it was in the beginning.

The poem is in six parts of about four pages each. A summary may replace pertinent discussion and at the same time preclude extraneous discussion. In Part I, called The World without Imagination, Crispin, who previously had cultivated a small garden with his intelligence, finds himself at sea, "a skinny sailor peering in the sea-glass." At first at loss and "washed away by magnitude," Crispin, "merest minuscule in the gales," at last finds the sea a vocable thing,

> But with a speech belched out of hoary darks
> Noway resembling his, a visible thing,
> And excepting negligible Triton, free
> From the unavoidable shadow of himself
> That elsewhere lay around him.

The sea "was no help before reality," only "one vast sub-jugating final tone," before which Crispin was made new. Concomitantly, with and because of his vision of the sea, "The drenching of stale lives no more fell down."

Part II is called Concerning the Thunder-Storms of Yucatan, and there, in Yucatan, Crispin, a man made vivid by the sea, found his apprehensions enlarged and felt the need to fill his senses. He sees and hears all there is before him, and writes fables for himself

> Of an aesthetic tough, diverse, untamed,
> Incredible to prudes, the mint of dirt,
> Green barbarism turning paradigm.

The sea had liberated his senses, and he discovers an earth like "A jostling festival of seeds grown fat, too juicily opulent," and a "new reality in parrot-squawks." His education is interrupted when a wind "more terrible than the revenge of music on bassoons," brings on a tropical thunder-storm. Crispin, "this connoisseur of elemental fate," identi-fies himself with the storm, finding himself free, which he was before, and "more than free, elate, intent, profound and studious" of a new self:

> the thunder, lapsing in its clap,
> Let down gigantic quavers of its voice,
> For Crispin to vociferate again.

With such freedom taken from the sea and such power found in the storm, Crispin is ready for the world of the imagination. Naturally, then, the third part of the poem, called Approaching Carolina, is a chapter in the book of moonlight, and Crispin "a faggot in the lunar fire." Moonlight is imagination, a reflection or interpretation of the sun, which is the source of life. It is also, curiously, this moonlight, North America, and specifically one of the Carolinas. And the Carolinas, to Crispin, seemed north; even the spring seemed arctic. He meditates on the poems he has denied himself because they gave less than "the relentless contact he desired." Perhaps the moon would establish the necessary liaison between himself and his environment. But perhaps not. It seemed

> Illusive, faint, more mist than moon, perverse,
> Wrong as a divagation to Peking. . . .
> Moonlight was an evasion, or, if not,
> A minor meeting, facile, delicate.

So he considers, and teeters back and forth, between the sun and moon. For the moment he decides against the moon and imagination in favor of the sun and his senses. The senses, instanced by the smell of things at the river wharf where his vessel docks, "round his rude aesthetic out" and teach him "how much of what he saw he never saw at all."

> He gripped more closely the essential prose
> As being, in a world so falsified,
> The one integrity for him, the one
> Discovery still possible to make,
> To which all poems were incident, unless
> That prose should wear a poem's guise at last.

In short, Crispin conceives that if the experience of the senses is but well enough known, the knowledge takes the form of imagination after all. So we find as the first line of the fourth part, called The Idea of a Colony, "Nota: his soil is man's intelligence," which reverses the original statement that man is the intelligence of his soil. With the new distinction illuminating his mind, Crispin plans a colony, and asks himself whether the purpose of his pilgrimage is not

> to drive away
> The shadow of his fellows from the skies,

> And, from their stale intelligence released,
> To make a new intelligence prevail?

The rest of the fourth part is a long series of synonymous tropes stating instances of the new intelligence. In a torment of fastidious thought, Crispin writes a prolegomena for his colony. Everything should be understood for what it is and should follow the urge of its given character. The spirit of things should remain spirit and play as it will.

> The man in Georgia waking among pines
> Should be pine-spokesman. The responsive man,
> Planting his pristine cores in Florida,
> Should prick thereof, not on the psaltery,
> But on the banjo's categorical gut.

And as for Crispin's attitude toward nature, "the melon should have apposite ritual" and the peach its incantation. These "commingled souvenirs and prophecies"—all images of freedom and the satisfaction of instinct—compose Crispin's idea of a colony. He banishes the masquerade of thought and expunges dreams; the ideal takes no form from these. Crispin will be content to "let the rabbit run, the cock declaim."

In Part V, which is A Nice Shady Home, Crispin dwells in the land, contented and a hermit, continuing his observations with diminished curiosity. His discovery that his colony has fallen short of his plan and that he is content to have it fall short, content to build a cabin,

> who once planned
> Loquacious columns by the ructive sea,

leads him to ask whether he should not become a philosopher instead of a colonizer.

> Should he lay by the personal and make
> Of his own fate an instance of all fate?

The question is rhetorical, but before it can answer itself, Crispin, sapped by the quotidian, sapped by the sun, has no energy for questions, and is content to realize, that for all the sun takes

> it gives a humped return
> Exchequering from piebald fiscs unkeyed.

Part VI, called And Daughters with Curls, explains the implications of the last quoted lines. The sun, and all the new intelligence which it enriched, mulcted the man Crispin, and in return gave him four daughters, four questioners and four sure answerers. He has been brought back to social nature, has gone to seed. The connoisseur of elemental fate has become himself an instance of all fate. He does not know whether the return was "Anabasis or slump, ascent or chute." His cabin—that is the existing symbol of his colony—seems now a phylactery, a sacred relic or amulet he might wear in memorial to his idea, in which his daughters shall grow up, bidders and biders for the ecstasies of the world, to repeat his pilgrimage, and come, no doubt, in their own cabins, to the same end.

Then Crispin invents his doctrine and clothes it in the fable about the turnip:

> The world, a turnip once so readily plucked,
> Sacked up and carried overseas, daubed out
> Of its ancient purple, pruned to the fertile main,
> And sown again by the stiffest realist,
> Came reproduced in purple, family font,
> The same insoluble lump. The fatalist
> Stepped in and dropped the chuckling down his craw,
> Without grace or grumble.

But suppose the anecdote was false, and Crispin a profitless philosopher,

> Glozing his life with after-shining flicks,
> Illuminating, from a fancy gorged
> By apparition, plain and common things,
> Sequestering the fluster from the year,
> Making gulped potions from obstreperous drops,
> And so distorting, proving what he proves
> Is nothing, what can all this matter since
> The relation comes, benignly, to its end.

So may the relation of each man be clipped.

The legend or subject of the poem and the mythology it develops are hardly new nor are the instances, intellectually considered, very striking. But both the clear depth of conception and the extraordinary luxuriance of rhetoric and image in which it is expressed, should be at least suggested in the summary here furnished. Mr. Stevens had a poem with an abstract subject—man as an instance of fate, and a concrete experience—the sensual confusion in which the man is waylaid; and to combine them he had to devise a form suitable to his own peculiar talent. The simple statement—of which he is a master—could not be prolonged to meet the dimensions of his subject. To the dramatic style his talents were unsuitable, and if by chance he used it, it would prevent both the meditative mood and the accent of intellectual wit which he needed to make the subject his own. The form he used is as much his own and as adequate, as the form of *Paradise Lost* is Milton's or the form of *The Waste Land* is Eliot's. And as Milton's form filled the sensibility of one aspect of his age, Mr. Stevens' form fits part of the sensibility—a part which Eliot or Pound or Yeats do little to touch—of our own age.

I do not know a name for the form. It is largely the form of rhetoric, language used for its own sake, persuasively to the extreme. But it has, for rhetoric, an extraordinary content of concrete experience. Mr. Stevens is a genuine poet in that he attempts constantly to transform what is felt with the senses and what is thought in the mind—if we can still distinguish the two—into that realm of being, which we call poetry, where what is thought is felt and what is felt has the strict point of thought. And I call his mode of achieving that transformation rhetorical because it is not lyric or dramatic or epic, because it does not transcend its substance, but is a reflection upon a hard surface, a shining mirror of rhetoric.

In its nature depending so much on tone and atmosphere, accenting precise management of ambiguities, and dealing with the subtler inflections of simple feelings, the elements of the form cannot be tracked down and put in order. Perhaps the title of the whole poem, "The Comedian as the

Letter C," is as good an example as any where several of the elements can be found together. The letter C is, of course, Crispin, and he is called a letter because he is small (he is referred to as "merest minuscule," which means small letter, in the first part of the poem) and because, though small, like a letter he stands for something—his colony, cabin, and children—as a comedian. He is a comedian because he deals finally with the quotidian (the old distinction of comedy and tragedy was between everyday and heroic subject matter), gorged with apparition, illuminating plain and common things. But what he deals with is not comic; the comedy, in that sense, is restricted to his perception and does not touch the things perceived or himself. The comedy is the accent, the play of the words. He is at various times a realist, a clown, a philosopher, a colonizer, a father, a faggot in the lunar fire, and so on. In sum, and any sum is hypothetical, he may be a comedian in both senses, but separately never. He is the hypothesis of comedy. He is a piece of rhetoric—a persona in words—exemplifying all these characters, and summing, or masking, in his persuasive style, the essential prose he read. He is the poem's guise that the prose wears at last.

Such is the title of the poem, and such is the poem itself. Mr. Stevens has created a surface, a texture, a rhetoric in which his feelings and thoughts are preserved in what amounts to a new sensibility. The contrast between his subjects—the apprehension of all the sensual aspects of nature as instances of fate,—and the form in which the subjects are expressed is what makes his poetry valuable. Nature becomes nothing but words and to a poet words are everything.

1931

# 9. Wallace Stevens: An Abstraction Blooded[1]

In one of Mr. Stevens' early poems he made the simple declaration that "Poetry is the supreme fiction," and in another there was a phrase about "the ultimate Plato, the tranquil jewel in this confusion." Now, in *Notes Toward a Supreme Fiction*, he shows us a combination of the two notions with a development into a third thing, which if it is not reached is approached from all round. The poem is like a pie marked for cutting in three pieces, with an imaginary center which is somehow limited, if you look long enough, only by the whole circumference. A triad makes a trinity, and a trinity, to a certain kind of poetic imagination, is the only tolerable form of unity. I think the deep skills of imagination, by which insights, ideas, and acts get into poetry, thrive best when some single, pressing theme or notion is triplicated. It is not a matter of understanding, but of movement and of identification and of access of being. The doublet is never enough, unless it breeds. War and peace need a third phase, as liquid and ice need vapor to fill out and judge the concept of water, as God the Father and God the Son need the Holy Ghost, or hell and heaven need purgatory, or act and place need time. The doublet *needs* what it makes. This is a habit of creative mind.

Mr. Stevens has acquired that habit. Wanting, as we all do, a supreme fiction, wanting, that is, to conceive, to imagine, to make a supreme being, wanting, in short, to discover and objectify a sense of such a being, he sets up three phases through which it must pass. It must be abstract; it

[1] *Notes Toward a Supreme Fiction,* by Wallace Stevens (The Cummington Press). *Parts of a World,* by Wallace Stevens (Knopf).

must change; it must give pleasure. Each phase is conceived as equal in dimension, each being given in ten sections of seven three-lined stanzas; and each phase is conceived as a version of the other two, that is, with a mutual and inextricable rather than with a successive relationship.

Let us see what the elements of the Fiction look like when taken separately. It must, the poet argues, be abstract, beyond, above, and at the beginning of our experience, and it must be an abstract idea of *being*, which when fleshed or blooded in nature or in thought, will absorb all the meanings we discover. That is to say, it must be archetypical and a source, an initiator of myth and sense, and also a reference or judgment for myth and sense; it tends to resemble a Platonic idea in character and operation, and its natural prototype, its easiest obvious symbol, will be the sun. But it must change in its abstractness, depending on the experience of it, as a seraph turns satyr "according to his thoughts"; for if it did not change it would tend to disappear or at least to become vestigial. You take character from what is not yourself and participate in what changes you. The process of change is the life of being, and like abstraction, requires constant iteration and constant experience. Most of all the Fiction must change because change is the condition of perception, vision, imagination. "A fictive covering/Weaves always glistening from the heart and mind." What changes is the general, the instances of the abstract, as they strike a fresh or freshened eye. That is why this fiction which changes, and is abstract, must give pleasure; it must be always open to discovery by a fresh eye, which is the eye of pleasure, the eye of feeling and imagination, envisaging the "irrational distortion."

> That's it: the more than rational distortion,
> The fiction that results from feeling.

In short, an abstract fiction can change and, if the abstraction was soundly conceived, the more it is the same the more it will seem to change, and by the feeling of change in identity, identity in change, give the great pleasure of access of being.

> The man-hero is not the exceptional monster,
> But he that of repetition is most master.

These are the bare bones of doctrine, and in another poet, most likely of another age, might exactly have been in control of the motion of the poem. In Stevens' poem the doctrine is not in control, nor does he pretend that it is; it is not a system, or even an organization, that he provides us with, but a set of notes brought together and graphed by the convention of his triad. If his notes are united, it is partly by the insight that saw the triad outside the poem, and partly by the sensibility—the clusters of perceptions, and the rotation of his rosary of minor symbols—into which he translates it. There is the great unity and the heroic vision in the offing, and they may indeed loom in the night of the poetry, but in the broad day of it there are only fragments, impressions, and merely associated individuations. Their maximum achieved unity is in their formal circumscription: that they are seen together in the same poem.

Whether a poet could in our time go much further—whether the speculative *imagination* is possible in our stage of belief—cannot be argued; there are no examples; yet it seems more a failure of will than of ability. Certainly Stevens has tackled Socrates' job: the definition of general terms. Certainly, too, he has seen one of the ways in which the poet in whom the philosopher has hibernated, muddled in sleep, can go on with the job: he has seen, in the sensibility, the relations between the abstract, the actual, and the imaginative. But he has been contented or been able only to make all his definitions out of fragments of the actual, seeing the fragments as transformations of the abstract: each one as good, as meaningful, as another, but bound not to each other in career but only to the center (the major idea) which includes them. That is why, I think, so many of the fragments are unavailable except in passing, and the comprehension of what is passing depends too often upon special knowledge of fashion and gibberish in vocabulary and idiom.

Mr. Stevens himself understands the problem, and has

expressed it characteristically in one of the segments of the decade requiring that the Fiction change. It is one of the segments, so common in so many poets of all ages, in which the poet assures himself of the nature and virtue of poetry: the protesting ritual of re-dedication.

> The poem goes from the poet's gibberish to
> The gibberish of the vulgate and back again . . .
> Is there a poem that never reaches words
> And one that chaffers the time away? . . .

> It is the gibberish of the vulgate that he seeks.
> He tries by a peculiar speech to speak

> The peculiar potency of the general,
> To compound the imagination's Latin with
> The lingua franca et jocundissima.

Granting the poet his own style, it could not be better expressed. Mr. Stevens, like the best of our modern poets, is free master of the fresh and rejoicing tongue of sensibility and fancy and the experience in flush and flux and flower; but he lacks, except for moments, and there, too, resembles his peers, the power of the "received," objective and authoritative imagination, whether of philosophy, religion, myth, or dramatic symbol, which is what he means by the imagination's Latin. The reader should perhaps be reminded that *gibberish* is not a frivolous word in the context; it is a word *manqué* more than a word mocking. One gibbers before a reality too great, when one is appalled with perception, when words fail though meaning persists: which is precisely, as Mr. Eliot suggested in a recent number of the *Partisan Review*, a proper domain of poetry.

One does what one can, and the limits of one's abilities are cut down by the privations of experience and habit, by the absence of what one has not thought of and by the presence of what is thought of too much, by the canalization and evaporation of the will. What is left is that which one touches again and again, establishing a piety of the imagination with the effrontery of repetition. Mr. Stevens has more left than most, and has handled it with more modulations of touch and more tenacious piety, so that it becomes itself exclusively, inexplicably, fully expressive of its own meaning. Of such things he says:

> These are not things transformed.
> Yet we are shaken by them as if they were.
> We reason about them with a later reason.

He knows, too,

> The fluctuations of certainty, the change
> Of degrees of perception in the scholar's dark,

which it is not hard to say that one knows, but which it is astonishing, always, to see exemplified in images of the seasons, of water-lights, the colors of flowers in the colors of air, or birdsong, for they make so "an abstraction blooded, as a man by thought."

It is all in the garden, perhaps, where the poet's gibberish returns to the gibberish of the vulgate, and where the intensity of the revelations of the single notion of redness dispenses, for a very considerable but by no means single occasion, with the imagination's Latin.

> A lasting visage in a lasting bush,
> A face of stone in an unending red,
> Red-emerald, red-slitted-blue, a face of slate,
>
> An ancient forehead hung with heavy hair,
> The channel slots of rain, the red-rose-red
> And weathered and the ruby-water-worn,
>
> The vines around the throat, the shapeless lips,
> The frown like serpents basking on the brow,
> The spent feeling leaving nothing of itself,
>
> Red-in-red repetitions never going
> Away, a little rusty, a little rouged
> A little roughened and ruder, a crown
>
> The eye could not escape, a red renown
> Blowing itself upon the tedious ear.
> An effulgence faded, dull cornelian
>
> Too venerably used.                    1943

# 10. On Herbert Read and Wallace Stevens [1]

*Poetry and Sensibility: Some Rules of Thumb*

Let us begin with a distinction which is also a description and which will set up a frame of mind which will do to make judgments from. Mr. Read's verse belongs more to the history of sensibility between the two wars than it does to the history of poetry. It is an example of that sensibility recording itself in verse: nothing is added, something is lost in the process. It is as if Mr. Read's sensibility only very rarely belonged in poetry at all, yet labored manfully, and nobly, to get there. We feel a full and noble pressure; a kind of magnanimity, *manqué* only because it is in verse. It is one of those necessary efforts beyond central ability which we would never do without, and which, having it, we will honor all the more if we distinguish it from actual achievement: for we see then that this body of a man's work *cries out* to be poems. As such, some of it will last next to verse truly alive.

Next, among others, to that quantity of work which is truly alive in the work of Wallace Stevens. Mr. Stevens has grown prolific, and sometimes prolix. There is therefore in *Transport to Summer* no great amount of work truly alive; but there is some, and it adds. Unlike Mr. Read's poems, it does not so much record sensibility, it creates it, adds to it; it is part of the regular everlasting job of making over again the absolute content of sensibility with which we get

[1] *Collected Poems*, by Herbert Read. Faber & Faber. *Transport to Summer*, by Wallace Stevens. Knopf.

on, or with which we acknowledge our failures to do so. If at a future time his work gets lost in some fire or fires, some *auto-da-fé*, it will have survived nevertheless in the work that followed it. His work is part of the history of poetry, which, like orthodoxy, exists whether anyone knows it or not.

This is not the place to judge either Mr. Read's magnanimity or Mr. Stevens' sensibility. Not at all the same elements enter into a judgment done in 1948 that entered into the judgment of 1930 or thereabouts, when each man had established his idiosyncrasy. The poems, and also the general body of poetry to which they belong or (for Mr. Read) which they illustrate, have changed the aspect which they show us. Either we have different needs, or we need these poems differently; in any case, it would seem that we have not caught up with what they have now to show us. Rather than judge, let us go about the tentative business of catching up. There should be the beginnings of judgment implied in the rules of thumb which it turns out possible to use; they show what can be measured.

Looking at the late poems of Wallace Stevens, and at the same time thinking of the state of poetry as a whole, the following observations seem plausible. They note something in Stevens and are useful elsewhere.

This is a poetry which ad libs with relation to a center, sometimes around it, sometimes to find it. If you ad lib having statement as your intention, you must have rhythm to begin with. If you ad lib having rhythm as your intention you must have statement to begin with.

Or put the whole thing the third way. This is a poetry which habitually moves by a mutual exchange of tokens or counters. If you have a set of counters to shove around they must have (and somehow deploy) whole sets of associations not your own, or your meanings will be merely assigned and will disappear with use.

This is a poetry of which an unusually high number of the words are recognizably a part of a special vocabulary. A specialized vocabulary, not charged and fixed by forces outside the vocabulary, will obliterate the perceptions it specializes. A live taxonomy must be idiomatic; it must survive its uses into another life—the life it taps.

This is a poetry which purports to wear a prose syntax. If you write your verse with a prose syntax, the statement itself must have a force of phrasing (in the musical sense) beyond the syntax. The line-structure must guide, and conform to, the movement of phrase. This is a particularly sound rule if it happens that your line averages the norm of blank verse. For blank verse to be as well-written as prose it must be very different from prose: precisely in the phrasing.

It is above all in thinking of phrasing that you see (to join two notions of Henry James) how "the platitude of statement" demands "the coercive charm of form."

It is when you have wholly given in to the temptation of your own habits of language that you will have lost capacity for the great temptation of language itself; no mere artifact will ever embrace your dreams.

What those with no eyes saw as the foibles of youth, missing your strength, may well become all you have left in age. Euphues may become Euphoria; the old dandy is nothing else.

This is a poetry of repetitions, within the poem and from poem to poem. Rebirth in the individual (poem or person) can be only a little repetition. It is the misery and the force not ourselves that is reborn; it is the music of these which is repeated everlastingly.

This is a poetry of hocus-pocus; there is a ritual who shall say how. You must not ever remove hocus-pocus that you feel; you must not ever add hocus-pocus to what you feel. Hocus-pocus has an ancestry not yours; nor can you father it.

> We say ourselves in syllables that rise
> From the floor, rising in speech we do not speak.

This is a poetry unusually high with the odor of "poets" and "poetry." Poems about poetry and poets, except when they are invocations or testaments of failure, hide or obliterate what the poet ought to see. Only exemplary invocations should leave the notebook, one for each volume. It is true that nearly one-tenth (62 out of 600 odd) of Rembrandt's paintings are self-portraits—let alone etchings and drawings; but they are all of a man—or all but one, the one you choose—not of the artist. Poetry wears the poet for a mask only on Shrove Tuesday; beginning Ash Wednesday, that party is over.

This is a poetry nevertheless. *The Dove in the Belly;* II, vi and III, iii of *Notes Toward a Supreme Fiction; Dutch Graves in Bucks County;* and part VII of *Esthétique du Mal* (beginning "How red the rose that is the soldier's wound")—all these, and no doubt others missed, go into that canon against which other poems merely beat; the canon of poems, no matter what their idiosyncrasy, which create sensibility in desperation.

What is the desperation? Ask a haunted man what is a haunt.—Holding in mind as much of Mr. Stevens' poetry —all thirty-five years of it—as possible, does it not seem that he has always been trying to put down tremendous statements; to put down those statements heard in dreams? His esthetic, so to speak, was unaware of those statements, and was in fact rather against making statements, and so got in the way. It is rather as if Lucretius had been compelled to write his invocation to Alma Venus in the esthetic of *The Rape of the Lock.* Thus the statements come out as lyric cries, all the more moving because we feel in them a craving for a fuller being than they can ever reach. Of such privations, in our place and time, is our actual drama made: "an ancient aspect touching a new mind." However inappropriate to its purpose, it was Mr. Stevens' own esthetic which gave his poems achievement. There is the desperation.

Thinking of that, if we look now at Herbert Read's *Collected Poems,* we see that his great privation lies not in working through an inappropriate esthetic but in being compelled to work without any esthetic at all, except in the theoretic sense. Put another way, Mr. Read has only that irreducible esthetic which goes with the making of statements at the communicative level. For all his experience of poetry, he has no way of putting the tremendousness of his own statements onto paper so that it can be picked up again—*through* the eye, *with* the ear—in the sensibility of his readers. That is why his epigraphs and mottoes are not only superior but strike the reader as of another kind to the poems that follow them.

The result is that Mr. Read gets as near poetry as is possible without being a poet. What is missing is no doubt what he might think of as got only by pulling at the bootstraps; perhaps it is; at any rate that is the right frame of mind, and that it works only rarely is nothing against it. Bootstraps are made of esthetic, of make-believe and *make-believe*, and of the struggle to shift your work from one status to the other.

In Mr. Read's poems you get rather a struggle between states, as for example (in many short poems) the struggle between the kind of psychology belonging to a novel and the kind of psychology belonging to incantation, the struggle between psychology and Psyche. You get the versification of thought, which, without the Psyche, gives always the effect of verse without thought: that is to say the trappings and harness of poetic form set upon a dummy. Put another way, you get (in the longer poems) the effort to create the metaphysical in verse on the model of those poets who created the poetry of their metaphysics: which is an example of the most fatal of all poetic mistakes. Poetry *thinks* by giving the actual experience—the *make-believe*—of thought; it does not convert thought into poetry, except at the expense of both. There are two consequences of Mr. Read's mistake in this direction, and each shows as a major privation of his work. First: his lines end only for reasons of the paradigm—whether metrical or intellectual—not for music, phrase, or gesture. Second: only the carrying part of the tradition of poetry survives in his verse, not what was carried. This is the double privation of having no make-believe—however merely esthetic, however much it hinders your original purpose—of your own. It adds up to the difference between what is part of the history of poetry and what is merely part of the history of sensibility.

1948

# 11. The Method of Marianne Moore

In making a formal approach to Marianne Moore, that is in deliberately drawing back and standing aside from the flux and fabric of long reading to see where the flux flowed and how the fabric was made, what at once predominates is the need for special terms and special adjustments to meet the texture and pattern of her poems. So only can the substance be reconciled and brought home to the general body of poetry; so only, that is, can the substance be made available and availing. The facts are clear enough and many of them even obvious to a wakened attention; the problem is to name them with names that both discriminate her work and relate it—if only in parallel—to other work with which it is cognate. Time and wear are the usual agents of this operation, whereby mutual interpenetration is effected between the new and old—always to be re-discriminated for closer contact—and the new becomes formally merely another resource of the art. Here we may assist and provisionally anticipate a little the processes of time and wear. What we make is a fiction to school the urgency of reading; no more; for actually we must return to the verse itself in its own language and to that felt appreciation of it to which criticism affords only overt clues.

In making up our own fiction let us turn first to some of those with which Miss Moore herself supplies us; which we may do all the more readily and with less wariness because she is so plainly responsible and deliberate in her least use of language—being wary only not to push illustrations past intention, insight, and method, into the dark. Substance is the dark, otherwise to be known.[1] And this is itself the nub of the first illustration. I quote complete "The Past is the Present."[2]

If external action is effete
  and rhyme is outmoded,
    I shall revert to you,
  Habakkuk, as on a recent occasion I was goaded
      into doing by XY, who was speaking of unrhymed
        verse.
This man said—I think that I repeat
  his identical words:
    Hebrew poetry is
  prose with a sort of heightened consciousness.' Ecstasy
    affords
      the occasion and expediency determines the form.

It is a delicate matter to say here only the guiding thing, both to avoid expatiation and to point the issue. I wish of course to enforce the last period, very possibly in a sense Miss Moore might not expect, yet in Miss Moore's terms too. A poem, so far as it is well-made for its own purpose, predicts much of which the author was not aware; as a saw cannot be designed for *all* its uses. Nor do the predictions emerge by deviling scripture, but rather by observation of the organic development of the words as they play

[1] As Matthew Arnold distinguished between descriptions of nature written in "the Greek way" and those written in "the faithful way," and made his distinction fruitful, we might, without being too solemn about it, distinguish between the content of verse taken on a rational, conventional plane, and the content, itself non-rational and unique, which can be reached only *through* the rational form and conventional scaffold.

[2] Text of all quotations from *Selected Poems*, with an Introduction by T. S. Eliot, New York, The Macmillan Co., 1935. This differs from the earlier *Observations* (New York, The Dial Press, 1925) by the addition of eight poems and the omission of fourteen. Most of the reprinted poems have been revised slightly, one or two considerably, and one is entirely rewritten and much expanded.

upon each other. A poem is an idiom and surpasses the sum of its uses.[3]

For ease of approach let us take the last and slightest fact first. In Miss Moore's work inverted commas are made to perform significantly and notably and with a fresh nicety which is part of her contribution to the language. Besides the normal uses to determine quotation or to indicate a special or ironic sense in the material enclosed or as a kind of minor italicization, they are used as boundaries for units of association which cannot be expressed by grammar and syntax. They are used sometimes to impale their contents for close examination, sometimes to take their contents as in a pair of tongs for gingerly or derisive inspection, some-times to gain the isolation of superiority or vice versa—in short for all the values of setting matter off, whether in eulogy or denigration. As these are none of them arbitrary but are all extensions and refinements of the common uses, the reader will find himself carried along, as by rhyme, to full appreciation. Which brings us with undue emphasis to the inverted commas in this poem. In earlier versions the last three lines were enclosed; here the second sentence, which is crucial to the poem, stands free, and thus gains a strength of isolation without being any further from its context, becoming in fact nearer and having a more direct relation to the *whole* poem: so much so that the earlier pointing must seem to have been an oversight. Once part of what the man said, part of his identical words, it is now Miss Moore's or the poem's comment on what the man said and the conclusion of the poem. So read, we have in this sentence not only a parallel statement to the statement about Hebrew poetry but also a clue to the earlier lines. It is what the rest of the poem builds to and explains; and

[3] Put the other way round we can borrow, for what it is worth, a mathematician's definition of number and apply it to poetry. A poem is, we can say, like any number, "the class of all classes having the properties of a given class"; it is ready for all its uses, but is itself "only" the class to which the uses belong. The analogue should not be pushed, as its virtue is in its incongruity and as afterthought.

it in its turn builds back and explains and situates the rest of the poem. And it is the pointing, or at any rate the comparison of the two pointings, which makes this clear. If it were a mere exercise of Miss Moore's and our own in punctuation, then as it depended on nothing it would have nothing to articulate. But Miss Moore's practice and our appreciation are analogous in scope and importance to the score in music. By a refinement of this notion Mr. Eliot observes in his Introduction that "many of the poems are in exact, and sometimes complicated formal patterns, and move with the elegance of a minuet." It is more than that and the very meat of the music, and one need not tire of repeating it because it *ought* to be obvious. The pattern establishes, situates, and organizes material which without it would have no life, and as it enlivens it becomes inextricably a part of the material; it participates as well as sets off. The only difficulty in apprehending this lies in our habit of naming only the conventional or abstract aspects of the elements of the pattern, naming never their enactment.[4]

So far we exemplify generally that ecstasy affords the occasion and expediency determines the form. We perceive the occasion and seize the nearest peg to hang the form on, which happened to be the very slight peg of inverted commas. Working backward, we come on Hebrew poetry and Habakkuk, one of its more rhetorical practitioners. Hebrew poetry (not to say the Bible) is used throughout Miss Moore's work as a background ideal and example of poetic language, an ideal, however, not directly to be served but rather kept in mind for impetus, reference, and comparison. A good part of the poem "Novices" is eulogy of Hebrew poetry. Here, in this poem, we have Habakkuk, who has a special as well as a representative business. As a poet Habakkuk was less than the Psalmist or Solomon or Job; nor had he the pith of the Proverbs or the serenity of Ecclesiastes. His service here is in the fact that he was a Prophet of the old school, a praiser of gone times, a man

---

[4] Whether this is a defect of language or of thinking I leave to I. A. Richards who alone has the equipment (among critics) and the will to determine.

goaded, as Miss Moore is, into crying out against the spiritual insufficience and formal decay of the times. The goading was the occasion of his ecstasy; anathema and prayer his most expedient—his most satisfactory—form. Miss Moore is speaking of matters no less serious; she couples external action and rhyme; and for her the expedient form is a pattern of elegant balances and compact understatement. It is part of the virtue of her attack upon the formless in life and art that the attack should show the courtesy and aloofness of formal grace. There is successful irony, too, in resorting through masterly rhymes to Habakkuk, who had none, and who would no doubt have thought them jingling and effete. (The rhymes have also the practical function of binding the particles of the poem. The notions which compound the poem mutually modify each other, as Coleridge and Mr. Richards would prescribe, and reach an equivalence; and the medium in which the modifications flow or circulate is emphasized and echoed in the rhymes.)

We note above that external action and rhyme are coupled, a juxtaposition which heightens the importance of each. If we conceive Habakkuk presiding upon it the import of the association should become clear. In the first line, "If external action is effete," the word *effete* is a good general pejorative, would have been suitable for Habakkuk in his capacity of goaded prophet. External action is the bodying forth of social life and when we call it effete we say the worst of it. Effete is a word much used of civilizations in decline—Roman, Byzantine, Persian—to represent that kind of sophistication which precedes the relapse into barbarism. What is effete may yet be bloody, stupid, and cruel, and its very refinements are of these. In the effete is the *flowering* of the vicious, a flowering essentially formless because without relation to the underlying substance. Thus, by Habakkuk, we find the morals implicit in the poem. Again, the poem may be taken declaratively (but only if it is tacitly held to include the implicit); if society and literature are in such shape that I cannot follow immediate traditions, well, I shall appeal to something still older. It is all the same. Ecstasy affords the occasion and expediency determines the form, whether I think of life or art.

I have, I think, laid out in terms of a lowered consciousness, a good deal of the material of this poem; but the reader need not think the poem has disappeared or its least fabric been injured. It is untouched. Analysis cannot touch but only translate for preliminary purposes the poem the return to which every sign demands. What we do is simply to set up clues which we can name and handle and exchange whereby we can make available all that territory of the poem which we cannot name or handle but only envisage. We emphasize the technique, as the artist did in fact, in order to come at the substance which the technique employed. Naturally, we do not emphasize all the aspects of the technique since that would involve discussion of more specific problems of language than there are words in the poem, and bring us, too, to all the problems of meaning which are *not* there.[5] We select, rather, those formal aspects which are most readily demonstrable: matters like rhyme and pattern and punctuation, which appear to control because they accompany a great deal else; and from these we reach necessarily, since the two cannot be detached except in the confusion of controversy, into the technical aspects, the conventional or general meanings of the words arranged by the form: as exemplified here by Habakkuk and the word effete. We show, by an analysis which always conveniently stops short, a selection of the ways in which the parts of a poem bear on each other; and we believe, by experience, that we thereby become familiar with what the various tensions produce: the poem itself.

[5] A perspective of just such a literally infinite labor is presented in I. A. Richards' *Mencius and the Mind,* which is fascinating but engulfing; as the opposite perspective is presented by the same author (with C. K. Ogden) in various works on Basic English, which combines the discipline of ascetic poverty with the expansiveness of, in a few hundred words, verbal omniscience. But I quote from Miss Moore's "Picking and Choosing," with I hope no more solemnity than the text affords: "We are not daft about the meaning but this familiarity with wrong meanings puzzles one."

This belief is of an arbitrary or miraculous character, and cannot be defended except by customary use. It should perhaps rather be put that as the poet requires his technique (which is not his knowledge) before he can put his poem on paper, so the reader requires a thorough awareness of technique (which again is not *his* knowledge) before he can read the poem. However that may be—and the best we can do is a doubtful scaffold of terms—the point here is that all that can ever actually be brought into the discussion of a poem is its technical aspects. Which happens in all but the best poetry to be very near the whole of it. Here, in Miss Moore's poem, "The Past is the Present," we might provisionally risk the assertion that the last line is the surd of the "poetry" in it. The rest both leads up to it and is suffused by it. The rest is nothing without it; and it would itself remain only a dislocated aphorism, lacking poetry, without the rest. "Ecstasy affords the occasion and expediency determines the form."

As it happens the line is actually pertinent as a maxim for Miss Moore's uncollected poetics; its dichotomy is at the intellectual base of all her work; and if we examine next the poem called "Poetry" we shall find Miss Moore backing us up in carefully measured understatement neatly placed among expedient ornament. But let us put off examination of the poem as such, and consider first what there is in it that may be translated to intellectual terms. The poem will outlast us and we shall come to it perhaps all the more sensitively for having libeled it; and it may indeed luckily turn out that our libel is the subject of the poem: that certainly will be the underlying set of argument. To translate is to cross a gap and the gap is always dark. Well then, whatever the injustice to the poem and to Miss Moore as an esthetician, the following notions may be abstracted from the text for purposes of discourse and amusement. Since these purposes are neither dramatic nor poetic the order in which the notions are here displayed is not that in which they appear in the poem.

Miss Moore's poem says, centrally, that we cannot have poetry until poets can be "literalists of the imagination."

The phrase is made from one in W. B. Yeats's essay, "William Blake and the Imagination." The cogent passage in Yeats reads: "The limitation of his [Blake's] view was from the very intensity of his vision; he was a too literal realist of the imagination, as others are of nature; and because he believed that the figures seen by the mind's eye, when exalted by inspiration, were 'eternal essences,' symbols or divine essences, he hated every grace of style that might obscure their lineaments." Yeats first printed his essay in 1897; had he written it when he wrote his postscript, in 1924, when he, too, had come to hate the graces which obscure, he would, I think, have adopted Miss Moore's shorter and wholly eulogistic phrase and called Blake simply a "literalist of the imagination,"[6] and found some other words to explain Blake's excessively arbitrary symbols. At any rate, in Miss Moore's version, the phrase has a bearing on the poem's only other overt reference, which is to Tolstoy's exclusion of "business documents and school books" from the field of poetry. Here her phrase leads to a profound and infinitely spreading distinction. Poets who can present, as she says they must, "imaginary gardens with real toads in them," ought also to be able to present, and indeed will if their interest lies that way, real school books and documents. The whole flux of experience and interpretation is appropriate subject matter to an imagination *literal* enough to see the poetry in it; an imagination, that is, as intent on the dramatic texture (on what is involved, is tacit, is immanent) of the quotidian, as the imagination of the painter is intent, in Velasquez, on the visual texture of lace. One is reminded here, too, of T. S. Eliot's dogma in reverse: "The spirit killeth; the letter giveth life"; and as with Eliot the result of his new trope is to refresh the original form by removing from it the *dead* part of its convention, so Miss Moore's object is to exalt the imagination at the expense of its conventional appearances. Her gardens are imaginary,

[6] My quotation is taken from the collected edition of Yeats's essays, New York, 1924, page 147; Miss Moore's reference, which I have not checked, was to the original *Ideas of Good and Evil*, printed some twenty years earlier by A. H. Bullen.

which makes possible the reality of her toads. Your commonplace mind would have put the matter the other way round—with the good intention of the same thing—and would have achieved nothing but the sterile assertion of the imagination as a portmanteau of stereotypes: which is the most part of what we are used to see carried, by all sorts of porters, as poetic baggage.

It is against them, the porters and their baggage, that Miss Moore rails when she begins her poem on poetry with the remark: "I, too, dislike it: there are things that are important beyond all this fiddle." But in the fiddle, she discovers, there is a place for the genuine. Among the conventions of expression there is the possibility of vivid, particularized instances:

> Hands that can grasp, eyes
> that can dilate, hair that can rise
> if it must,

and so on. Such hands, hair, and eyes are, we well know, props and crises of poetastry, and are commonly given in unusable, abstract form, mere derivative gestures we can no longer feel; as indeed their actual experience may also be. They remain, however, exemplars of the raw material of poetry. If you take them literally and make them genuine in the garden of imagination, then, as the poem says, "you are interested in poetry." You have seen them in ecstasy, which is only to say beside themselves, torn from their demeaning context; and if you are able to give them a new form or to refresh them with an old form—whichever is more expedient—then you will have accomplished a poem.

Perhaps I stretch Miss Moore's intentions a little beyond the pale; but the process of her poem itself I do not think I have stretched at all—have merely, rather, presented one of the many possible descriptions by analogue of the poetic process she actually employs. The process, like any process of deliberate ecstasy, involves for the reader as well as the writer the whole complex of wakened sensibility, which, once awakened, must be both constrained and driven along,

directed and freed, fed and tantalized, sustained by reason
to the very point of seeing, in every rational datum—I quote
from another poem, "Black Earth"—the "beautiful element
of unreason under it." The quotidian, having been shown
as genuine, must be shown no less as containing the strange,
as saying more than appears, and, even more, as containing
the print of much that cannot be said at all. Thus we find
Miss Moore constantly presenting images the most explicit
but of a kind containing inexhaustibly the inexplicable—
whether in gesture or sentiment. She gives what we know
and do not know; she gives in this poem, for example, "elephants pushing, a wild horse taking a roll, a tireless wolf
under a tree," and also "the baseball fan, the statistician."
We can say that such apposites are full of reminding, or
that they make her poem husky with unexhausted detail,
and we are on safe ground; but we have not said the important thing, we have not named the way in which we are
illuminated, nor shown any sign at all that we are aware of
the major operation performed—in this poem (elsewhere
by other agents)—by such appositions. They are as they
succeed the springboards—as when they fail they are the
obliterating quicksands—of ecstasy. In their variety and their
contrasts they force upon us two associated notions; first
we are led to see the elephant, the horse, the wolf, the baseball fan, and the statistician, as a group or as two groups
detached by their given idiosyncrasies from their practical
contexts, we see them beside themselves, for themselves
alone, like the lace in Velasquez or the water-lights in
Monet; and secondly, I think, we come to be aware,
whether consciously or not, that these animals and these
men are themselves, in their special activities, obsessed,
freed, and beside themselves. There is an exciting quality
which the pushing elephant and the baseball fan have in
common; and our excitement comes in feeling that quality,
so integral to the apprehension of life, as it were beside and
for itself, not in the elephant and the fan, but in terms of
the apposition in the poem.

Such matters are not credibly argued and excess of statement perhaps only confuses import and exaggerates value.

As it happens, which is why this poem is chosen rather than another, the reader can measure for himself exactly how valuable this quality is; he can read the "same" poem with the quality dominant and again with the quality hardly in evidence. On page 31 in *Observations* the poem appears in thirteen lines; in *Selected Poems* it has either twenty-nine or thirty, depending on how you count the third stanza. For myself, there is the difference between the poem and no poem at all, since the later version delivers—where the earlier only announces—the letter of imagination. But we may present the differences more concretely, by remarking that in the earlier poem half the ornament and all the point are lacking. What is now clearly the dominant emphasis—on poets as literalists of the imagination—which here germinates the poem and gives it career, is not even implied in the earlier version. The poem did not get that far, did not, indeed, become a poem at all. What is now a serious poem on the nature of esthetic reality remained then a half-shrewd, half-pointless conceit against the willfully obscure. But it is not, I think, this rise in level from the innocuous to the penetrating, due to any gain in the strength of Miss Moore's conception. The conception, the idea, now that we know what it is, may be as readily inferred in the earlier version as it is inescapably felt in the later, but it had not in the earlier version been articulated and composed, had no posture to speak of, had lacked both development and material to develop: an immature product. The imaginary garden was there but there were no real toads in it.

What we have been saying is that the earlier version shows a failure in the technique of making a thought, the very substantial failure to know when a thought is complete and when it merely adverts to itself and is literally insufficient. There is also—as perhaps there must always be in poetry that fails—an accompanying insufficience of verbal technique, in this instance an insufficience of pattern and music as compared to the later version. Not knowing, or for the moment not caring, what she had to do, Miss Moore had no way of choosing and no reason for using the tools of her trade. Miss Moore is to an extent a typographic poet, like Cummings or Hopkins; she employs the effects of the appearance and arrangement of printed words as well as their effects sounding in the ear: her words are in the end far more *printed* words than the words of Yeats, for example, can ever be. And this is made clear by the earlier version which lacks the *printed* effect rather than by the later version which exhibits it. When we have learned how, we often do not notice what we appreciate but rather what is not there to *be* appreciated.

But if we stop and are deliberate, by a stroke cut away our intimacy with the poem, and regard it all round for its physiognomy, an object with surfaces and signs, we see immediately that the later version looks better on the page, has architecture which springs and suggests deep interiors; we notice the rhymes and the stanza where they are missing and how they multiply heavily, *both to the ear and the eye,* in the last stanza; we notice how the phrasing is marked, how it is shaded, and how, in the nexus of the first and second stanzas, it is momentarily confused: we notice, in short, not how the poem was made—an operation intractable to any description—but what about it, now that it is made, will strike and be felt by the attentive examiner. Then turning back to the earlier version, knowing that it has pretty much the same heart, gave as much occasion for ecstasy, we see indefeasibly why it runs unpersuasively through the mind, and why the later, matured version most persuasively invades us. It is no use saying that Miss Moore has herself matured—as evidence the notion is inadmissible; the concept or idea or thought of the poem is not difficult, new or intense, but its presentation, in the later version, is all three. She found, as Yeats would say, the image to call out the whole idea; that was one half. The other half was finding how to dress out the image to its best advantage, so as to arouse, direct, sustain, and consolidate attention.

That is not, or hardly at all, a question of Miss Moore's personal maturity; as may be shown, I think, if we consult two poems, presumably more or less as early as the earlier version of "Poetry." One is a poem which Miss Moore omits from her *Selected Poems,* but which Mr. Eliot neatly reprints in his Introduction, called "The Talisman." In the light of what we have been saying, Miss Moore was right in omitting it (as she was mainly right in omitting thirteen other poems); it lacks the fundamental cohesiveness of a thing made complete: with a great air of implying everything, it implies almost nothing. Yet Mr. Eliot was right in quoting it, and for the reasons given; it shows a mastery of heavy rhyme which produces its fatal atmosphere, and it shows that authoritative manner of speech-English which is one device to achieve persuasion. But the omission is more justifiable than the quotation; the substantial immaturity of the poem diseases the maturity of the form and makes it specious, like the brightness of fevered eyes.

The other poem, "Silence," which I quote, Miss Moore reprints verbatim except for the addition of a single letter to perfect the grammar and the omission of double quotes in the next to last line.

My father used to say,
'Superior people never make long visits,
have to be shown Longfellow's grave
or the glass flowers at Harvard.
Self-reliant like the cat—
that takes its prey to privacy,
the mouse's limp tail hanging like a shoelace from its
     mouth—
they sometimes enjoy solitude,
and can be robbed of speech
by speech that has delighted them.
The deepest feeling always shows itself in silence;
not in silence, but restraint.
Nor was he insincere in saying, 'Make my house your inn.'
Inns are not residences.

There was no reason for change, only for scruples maintained and minute scrutiny; for the poem reaches that limit of being—both in the life of what it is about and in that other, musical life which is the play of a special joining of words—which we call maturity. It is important to emphasize here what commonly we observe last, namely the magnitude or scope of the poem; otherwise the sense of its maturity is lost. The magnitude is small but universal within the universe of those who distinguish cultivated human relations, which leaves us all the room we need to grow while reading the poem; and which signifies, too, that we should only diminish the value and injure the genuineness of the poem if we held its magnitude greater, its reach further. Thus the reader must contribute his sense of its maturity to the poem before it can be situated, before, as Wallace Stevens says, we can "let be be the finale of seem."

There is here the spirit of an old controversy which we need not re-enter, but which we ought to recognize in order to pass it by: the controversy about young men writing great poems and old men going to seed, about Wordsworth of the Lyrical Ballads and Wordsworth wordsworthian. It is a popular controversy in various senses of that adjective. A more pertinent phrasing of the seminal problem, by which we should escape the false controversy, is, I think, a phrasing in terms of the question of maturity; and the point is that there are various orders of maturity with complex mutually related conditions required to produce each. There are the broad and obvious classes of conditions which we list under the heads of technical competence and underlying import; but we do not, in actual poems, ever have import without competence or competence without import. Trouble rises from the confusion of import with intellectually demonstrable content, and technical competence with *mere* skill of execution. The music of words alone may lift common sentiment to great import, e.g., Take, O take those lips away; or at any rate we are faced with much great poetry which has only commonplace intellectual content and yet affects our fundamental convictions. Again— and I do not mean to leave the realm of poetry—we have, as an example of halfway house, such things as the best speeches in *The Way of the World,* where an effect like that of music and like that of thought, too, is had without full recourse to either, but rather through the perfection of the spoken word alone. And at the other end we have the great things in the great poets that do not *appear* to depend upon anything but their own barest bones. It is hard here to give an example beyond suspicion. There is Paolo's speech at the end of *Inferno* V, Blake's Time is the mercy of eternity, Shakespeare's Ripeness is all, perhaps the Epilogue to *The Poetaster*. The point is that a balance must be struck of complex conditions so that nothing is too much and nothing not enough; but most of all it must be remembered that the balance of conditions which produced maturity in one place will not necessarily produce it in another. Nor is it just to judge the maturity of one poem by standards brought from another order of poetry; nor, lastly, does the maturity of a poem alone determine its magnitude. Drayton's "The Parting," the ballad "Waly Waly," and *Antony and Cleopatra*, are all, and equally, mature poetry. *Hamlet*, we say, has a sick place in it, and for us the first part of the first act of *King Lear* is puerile; but we do not judge *Hamlet* and *Lear* in terms of Drayton or the balladist, although we may, for certain purposes, apply to them the special perfection of *Antony*. Maturity is the touchstone of achievement, not of magnitude.

Returning to Miss Moore's "Silence," let us see if we can what balance it is she has struck to bring it to a maturity which makes the question of magnitude for the moment irrelevant. The outer aids and props familiar in her best verse are either absent or negligible. The poem has no imposed, repetitive pattern, no rhyme for emphasis or sound, it calls particularly neither upon the eye nor the ear; it ignores everywhere the advantage of referring the reader, for strength, to any but the simplest elements of overt form—the rudiment of continuous iambic syllabification, which prevails in all but one line. Only one phrase—that about the mouse's limp tail—is specifically characteristic of Miss Moore; all the rest of the phrasing represents cultivated contemporary idiom, heightened, as we see at first glance, because set apart.

Here is one of the secrets—perhaps we ought to say one of the dominant fixed tropes—of Miss Moore's verse; and it is here what she has relied upon almost altogether. She resorts, or rises like a fish, continually to the said thing, captures it, sets it apart, points and polishes it to bring out just the special quality she heard in it. Much of her verse has the peculiar, unassignable, indestructible authority of speech overheard—which often means so much precisely because we do not know what was its limiting, and dulling, context. The quality in her verse that carries over the infinite possibilities of the overheard, is the source and agent of much of her power to give a sense of invading reality; and it does a good deal to explain what Mr. Eliot, in his Introduction, calls her authoritativeness of manner—which is a different thing from a sense of reality.

It does not matter that Miss Moore frequently works the other way round, abstracting her phrase from a guidebook, an advertisement, or a biography; what matters is that whatever her sources she treats her material as if it were quoted, isolated speech, and uses it, not as it was written or said—which cannot be known—but for the purpose which, taken beside itself, seems in it paramount and most appropriate. In "Silence" she takes phrases from Miss A. M. Homans and from Prior's life of Edmund Burke, and combines them in such a way that they declare themselves more fully, because isolated, emphasized, and lit by the incongruous image of the cat and the mouse, than either could have declared themselves in first context. The poet's labor in this respect is similar to that of a critical translation where, by selection, exclusion, and rearrangement a sense is emphasized which was found only on a lower level and diffusely in the original; only here there is no damage by infidelity but rather the reward of deep fidelity to what, as it turns out, was really there waiting for emphasis.

But besides the effect of heightened speech, Miss Moore relies also and as deeply upon the rhetorical device of understatement—by which she gains, as so many have before her, a compression of substance which amounts to the fact of form. Form is, after all, the way things are put, and it may be profitably though not finally argued that every device of saying is an element in the form of what is said, whether it be detachable and predictable like the stress of a syllable or inextricable and innate like the tone of a thought. Understatement is a misnomer in every successful instance, as it achieves exactly what it pretends not to do: the fullest possible order of statement consonant with the mode of language employed. In such classic examples as Shakespeare's "The rest is silence," or Wordsworth's "But oh, the difference to me!" who shall suggest that more could have been said another way? who rather will not believe that it is in phrases such as these that the radical failure of language (its inability ever explicitly to *say* what is in a full heart) is overcome? Never, surely, was there a poorer name for such a feat of imagination: what we call understatement is only secured when we have charged ordinary words with extraordinary content, content not naturally in words at all. But they must be the right words nonetheless. Did not Shakespeare and Wordsworth really state to the limit matters for which there are no large words, matters which must, to be apprehended at all, be invested in common words?

Such is the archetype, the seminal expectation of understatement, and Miss Moore's poem, on its special plane, subscribes to it. But we are here concerned more with its subordinate, its ancillary uses—with its composition with operative irony and with its use to avoid a *conventional form* while preserving the conventional intention in all freshness. These are the uses with which we are familiar in daily life—crassly in sarcasm and finely in shrewd or reasonable wit; and it is on the plane of daily life and what might be said there—only heightened and rounded off for inspection—that this poem is written. It is part of the understatement, in the sense here construed, that superior people should be compared not to the gods accredited to the great world but to the cat carrying a mouse into a corner. The advantage is double. By its very incongruity—its quaintness, if you will—the comparison forces into prominence the real nature of the following notion of chosen solitude. We cut away immediately all that does not belong to the business of the poem; and find ourselves possessed of a new point of view thrown up and "justified" by the contrast. By a proud irony, content barely to indicate itself, the conventional views of solitude and intimacy are both destroyed and re-animated. A smiliar effect is secured in the last two lines—perhaps most emphatically in the choice of the word *residences,* itself, in this context, an understatement for the emotional word *homes* that detonates far more than the word *homes* could have done.

Finally, it is perhaps worth noting that "Make my house your inn" is both an understatement and a different statement of Burke's intention. Burke did not have the glass flowers, nor cats proud with mice, preceding his invitation: "Throw yourself into a coach," said he. "Come down and make my house your inn." But Miss Moore heard the possibility and set it free with all it implied. That is the poem. As the reader agrees that it is successful without recourse to the traditional overt forms of the art, he ought perhaps to hold that its virtue rises from recourse to the mystery, the fount of implication, in the spoken word combined with a special use of understatement. It makes a sample of the paradigm in its purest order, but hardly its least complex. The ecstasy was of speech, the expediency the greatest economy of means—as it happened in this poem, understatement. Yet as it is genuine, the spirit of its imagination is seen through the letter of what the speech might say.

All this is meant to be accepted as a provisional statement of Miss Moore's practical esthetic—to denominate the ways her poems are made and to suggest the variety of purposes they serve. As it is acceptable, subject to modification and growth in any detail, it should be applicable elsewhere in her work, and if applied make intimacy easier. It may be profitable in that pursuit to examine lightly a selection of the more complex forms—both outward and inward—in which her work is bodied. Miss Moore is a poet bristling with notable facts—especially in the technical quarter—and it would be shameful in an essay at all pretentious not to make some indication of their seductiveness and their variety.

She is an expert in the visual field at compelling the incongruous association to deliver, almost startlingly to ejaculate, the congruous, completing image: e.g., in the poem about the pine tree called "The Monkey Puzzle,"— "It knows that if a nomad may have dignity, Gibraltar has had more"; "the lion's ferocious chrysanthemum head seeming kind in comparison"; and "This porcupine-quilled, complicated starkness." The same effect is seen with greater scope in the first stanza of "The Steeple-Jack."

> Dürer would have seen a reason for living
> in a town like this, with eight stranded whales
> to look at; with the sweet sea air coming into your house
> on a fine day, from water etched
> with waves as formal as the scales
> on a fish.

Here the incongruity works so well as perhaps to be imperceptible. The reader beholds the sea as it is for the poem, but also as it never was to a modern (or a sailor's) eye, with the strength and light of all he can remember of Dürer's water-etchings, formal and "right" as the scales on a fish. It is the same formal effect, the Dürer vision, that sets the continuing tone, as the moon sets the tide (with the sun's help), for the whole poem, bringing us in the end an emotion as clean, as ordered, as startling as the landscape which yields it.

> It could not be dangerous to be living
> in a town like this, of simple people,
> who have a steeple-jack placing danger signs by the church
> while he is gilding the solid-
> pointed star, which on a steeple
> stands for hope.

In "The Hero," which is complementary to "The Steeple-Jack" and with it makes "Part of a Novel, Part of a Poem, Part of a Play,"[7] we have another type of association, on the intellectual plane, which *apparently* incongruous,

[7] Something a hasty reader might miss is that (page 2, bottom) the Steeple-Jack, so orderly in his peril, might be part of a novel, and that the frock-coated Negro (page 5, top) might, with his sense of mystery, be part of a play. The text is "part of a poem." Miss Moore's titles are often the most elusive parts of her poems.

is at heart surprising mainly because it is so exact. Some men, says Miss Moore, have been "lenient, looking upon a fellow creature's error with the feelings of a mother—a woman or a cat." The "cat" refines, selects and—removing the sentimental excess otherwise associated with "mother" in similar contexts—establishes the gesture and defines, in the apposition, the emotion. It is a similar recognition of identic themes in the apparently incongruous—though here the example is more normal to poetic usage—that leads to her defining statement about the Hero.

> He's not out
> seeing a sight but the rock
> crystal thing to see—the startling El Greco
> brimming with inner light—that
> covets nothing that it has let go.

What Mr. Eliot puts into his Introduction about Miss Moore's exploitation of some of the less common uses of rhyme—besides stress-rhyme, rhyme against the metric, internal auditory rhyme, light rhyme—should excite the reader who has been oblivious to pursuit and the reader who has been aware to perusal. Here let us merely re-enforce Mr. Eliot with an example or so, and half an addition to his categories.

In the stanza from "The Hero" just quoted there is the paradigm for a rhyme-sound refrain which the well-memoried ear can catch. The first and last two lines of this and every other stanza rhyme on the sound of long "o," some light and some heavy. It is a question whether devices of this order integrally affect the poem in which they occur. If they do affect it, it must be in a manner that can neither be named nor understood, suffusing the texture unascertainably. But such devices do not need to be justified as integrating forces. It is enough for appreciation that this example should set up, as it does, a parallel music to the strict music of the poem which cannot be removed from it once it is there any more than it can be surely brought into it. It is part of the poem's weather. The Provençal poets worked largely in this order of rhyme, and in our own day Wallace Stevens has experimented with it.

Although many of the poems are made on intricate schemes of paired and delayed rhymes—there being perhaps no poem entirely faithful to the simple quatrain, heroic, or couplet structure—I think of no poem which for its rhymes is so admirable and so alluring as "Nine Nectarines and Other Porcelain." Granting that the reader employs a more analytical pronunciation in certain instances, there is in the last distich of each stanza a rhyme half concealed and half overt. These as they are first noticed perhaps annoy and seem, like the sudden variations, trills, mordents and turns in a Bach fugue, to distract from the theme, and so, later, to the collected ear, seem all the more to enhance it, when the pleasure that may be taken in them for themselves is all the greater. More precisely, if there be any ears too dull, Miss Moore rhymes the penultimate syllable of one line with the ultimate syllable of the next. The effect is of course cumulative; but the cumulus is of delicacy not mass; it is cumulative, I mean, in that in certain stanzas there would be no rhyme did not the precedent pattern make it audible. If we did not have

> a bat is winging. It
> is a moonlight scene, bringing . . .

we should probably not hear

> and sets of Precious Things
> dare to be conspicuous.

What must be remembered is that anyone can arrange syllables, the thing is to arrange syllables at the same time you write a poem, and to arrange them as Miss Moore does, on four or five different planes at once. Here we emphasize mastery on the plane of rhyme. But this mastery, this intricacy, would be worthless did the poem happen to be trash.

Leaving the technical plane—at least in the ordinary sense of that term—there is another order of facts no less beguiling, the facts of what Miss Moore writes about—an order which has of course been touched on obliquely all along. What we say now must be really as oblique as before,

no matter what the immediacy of approach; there is no
meeting Miss Moore face to face in the forest of her poems
and saying This is she, this is what she means and is: tautology is not the right snare for her or any part of her. The
business of her poetry (which for us is herself) is to set
things themselves delicately conceived in relations so fine
and so accurate that their qualities, mutually stirred, will
produce a new relation: an emotion. Her poems answer the
question, What will happen in poetry, what emotion will
transpire, when these things have been known or felt beside
each other? The things are words and have qualities that
may be called on apart from the qualities of the objects
they name or connect. Keats's odes are composed on the
same method, and Milton's *Lycidas*. But there are differences which must be mastered before the identity can be
seen.

For Keats the Nightingale was a touchstone and a liberating symbol; it let him pour himself forth and it gave
him a free symbol under which to subsume his images and
emotions; the nightingale was a good peg of metonymy,
almost, when he was done, a good synechdoche. For his
purposes, the fact that he had a nightingale to preside over
his poem gave the poem a suffusing order; and in the end
everything flows into the nightingale.

With Miss Moore, in such poems as "An Octopus,"
"England," "The Labours of Hercules," "The Monkeys,"
and "The Plumet Basilisk," there is less a freeing of emotions and images under the aegis of the title notion, than
there is a deliberate delineation of specific poetic emotions
with the title notion as a starting point or spur: a spur to
develop, compare, entangle, and put beside the title notion
a series of other notions, which may be seen partly for their
own sakes in passing, but more for what the juxtapositions
conspire to produce. Keats's emotions were expansive and
general but given a definite symbolic form; Miss Moore's
emotions are special and specific, producing something almost a contraction of the given material, and so are themselves their own symbols. The distinction is exaggerated, but
once seized the reader can bring it down to earth. Put an-

other way, it is comparatively easy to say what Keats's poem is about, or what it is about in different places: it is about death and love and nostalgia, and about them in ways which it is enough to mention to understand. It is not easy to say what one of Miss Moore's longer poems is about, either as a whole or in places. The difficulty is not because we do not know but precisely because we do know, far more perfectly and far more specifically than we know anything about Keats's poem. What it is about is what it does, and not at any one place but all along. The parts stir each other up (where Keats put stirring things in sequence) and the aura of agitation resulting, profound or light as it may be, is what it is about. Naturally, then, in attempting to explain one of these poems you find yourself reading it through several times, so as not to be lost in it and so that the parts will not only follow one another as they must, being words, but will also be beside one another as their purpose requires them to be. This perhaps is why Miss Moore could write of literature as a phase of life: "If one is afraid of it, the situation is irremediable; if one approaches it familiarly what one says of it is worthless."

It is a method not a formula; it can be emulated not imitated; for it is the consequence of a radical leaning, of more than a leaning an essential trope of the mind: the forward stress to proceed, at any point, to proceed from one thing to another, crossing all gaps regardless, but keeping them all in mind. The poem called "The Monkeys" (in earlier versions "My Apish Cousins") has monkeys in the first line only. We proceed at once to "zebras supreme in their abnormality," and "elephants with their fog-coloured skin"; proceed, that is, with an abstract attribution and a beautifully innervated visual image. But the monkeys were not there for nothing; they signify the zoo and they establish an air for the poem that blows through it taking up a burden, like seeds, as it passes. I cannot say how the monkeys perform their function. But if it could be told it would not help; no more than it helps to say that the poem is composed not only on a rhyme and a typographic but also on a rigidly syllabic pattern. The first line of each stanza has fifteen syllables and the second sixteen; the third lines have ten, and the last, with which they balance, ten; and the fifth lines, except in the third stanza with thirteen, have fifteen. The fact of syllabic pattern has a kind of tacit interest, but we cannot say whether we can appreciate it, because we do not know whether even the trained ear can catch the weight of variations of this order. The monkeys are in a different position, and even if we cannot say in blueprint words what it is, we know that the interest is functional because we can report the fact of its experience.

More could be said—and in description a poem merely difficult and complex enough to require deep and delicately adjusted attention might seem a labyrinth; but let us rather move to a different poem, "An Octopus," and there select for emphasis a different aspect of the same method. This is a poem, if you like, about the Rocky Mountain Parks, Peaks, Fauna, and Flora; it is also about the Greek mind and language, and a great deal else. It contains material drawn from illustrated magazines, travel books, Cardinal Newman, Trollope, Richard Baxter's *The Saint's Everlasting Rest* (a book used in a dozen poems), W. D. Hyde's *Five Great Philosophies,* the Department of the Interior Rules and Regulations, and a remark overheard at the circus. Composed in free rhythm, natural cadence, and lines terminated by the criteria of conversational or rhetorical sense, it has a resemblance in form and typical content to certain of the Cantos of Ezra Pound; a resemblance strong enough to suggest that Pound may have partly derived his method from Miss Moore. The dates do not make derivation impossible, and the changes in structure from the earlier to the later Cantos confirm the suggestion. The pity in that case is that Pound did not benefit more; for there is a wide difference in the level and value of the effects secured. The elements in Pound's Cantos, especially the later ones, remain as I have argued elsewhere essentially disjunct because the substance of them is insufficiently present in the text; whereas in Miss Moore's poems of a similar order, and especially in "An Octopus," although themselves disjunct and even inviolate, coming from different countries of the mind, the substances are yet sufficiently present in the poem to compel conspiracy and co-operation. You cannot look in the words of a poem and see two objects really side by side without seeing a third thing, which will be specific and unique. The test, if reference can again be made to "Poetry," is in the genuineness of the presentation of the elements:[8] there must be real toads in the imaginary garden. Miss Moore has a habit of installing her esthetics in her poems as she goes along, and in "An Octopus" she pleads for neatness of finish and relentless accuracy, both in mountains and in literature; and the mountain has also, what literature ought to have and Miss Moore does have, a capacity for fact. These notions only refine the notion of the letter of the imagination. The point here is that the notions about the treatment of detail explain why Pound's later Cantos seem diffuse in character and intangible in import and why Miss Moore's poem has a unity that grows with intimacy.

There are more aspects of Miss Moore's method as there are other lights in which to see it, but enough has been touched on here to show what the method is like, that it is not only pervasive but integral to her work. It is integral to the degree that, with her sensibility being what it is, it imposes limits more profoundly than it liberates poetic energy. And here is one reason—for those who like reasons—for the astonishing fact that none of Miss Moore's poems attempt to be major poetry, why she is content with smallness in fact so long as it suggests the great by implication. Major themes are not susceptible of expression through a method of which it is the virtue to produce the idiosyncratic in the fine and strict sense of that word. Major themes, by definition of general and predominant interest, require for expression a method which produces the general in terms not of the idiosyncratic but the specific, and require, too, a form which seems to *contain* even more than to *imply* the wholeness beneath. The first poem in the present collection, "Part

[8] Mr. Eliot in his Introduction and Mr. Kenneth Burke in a review agree in finding genuineness paramount in Miss Moore's work.

of a Novel, Part of a Poem, Part of a Play," comes as near to major expression as her method makes possible; and it is notable that here both the method and the content are more nearly "normal" than we are used to find. Elsewhere, though the successful poems achieve their established purposes, her method and her sensibility, combined, transform her themes from the normal to the idiosyncratic plane. The poem "Marriage," an excellent poem, is never concerned with either love or lust, but with something else, perhaps no less valuable, but certainly, in a profound sense, less complete.

Method and sensibility ought never, in the consideration of a poet, to be kept long separate, since the one is but the agent of growth and the recording instrument of the other. It is impossible to ascertain the stress of sensibility within the individual and it is an injustice to make the attempt; but it is possible to make at least indications of the sensibility informing that objective thing a body of poetry. Our last observation, that there is in the poem "Marriage" no element of sex or lust, is one indication. There is no sex anywhere in her poetry. No poet has been so chaste; but it is not the chastity that rises from an awareness—healthy or morbid—of the flesh, it is a special chastity aside from the flesh—a purity by birth and from the void. There is thus, by parallel, no contact by disgust in her work, but rather the expression of a cultivated distaste; and this is indeed appropriate, for within the context of purity disgust would be out of order. Following the same train, it may be observed that of all the hundreds of quotations and references in her poems none is in itself stirring, although some are about stirring things; and in this she is the opposite of Eliot, who as a rule quotes the thing in itself stirring; and here again her practice is correct. Since her effects are obtained partly by understatement, partly by ornament, and certainly largely by special emphasis on the quiet and the quotidian, it is clear that to use the thing obviously stirring would be to import a sore thumb, and the "great" line would merely put the poem off its track. Lastly, in this train, and to begin another, although she refers eulogistically many times to the dazzling color, vivid strength, and torrential flow of Hebrew poetry, the tone of her references is quiet and conversational.

By another approach we reach the same conclusion, not yet named. Miss Moore writes about animals, large and small, with an intense detached intimacy others might use in writing of the entanglements of people. She writes about animals as if they were people minus the soilure of over-weeningly human preoccupations, to find human qualities freed and uncommitted. Compare her animal poems with those of D. H. Lawrence. In Lawrence you feel you have touched the plasm; in Miss Moore you feel you have es-caped and come on the idea. The other life is there, but it is round the corner, not so much taken for granted as oblivi-ated, not allowed to transpire, or if so only in the light ease of conversation: as we talk about famine in the Orient in discounting words that know all the time that it *might* be met face to face. In Miss Moore life is remote (life as good *and* evil) and everything is done to keep it remote; it is reality removed, but it is nonetheless reality, because we *know* that it is removed. This is perhaps another way of put-ting Kenneth Burke's hypothesis: "if she were discussing the newest model of automobile, I think she could somehow contrive to suggest an antiquarian's interest." Let us say that everything she gives is minutely precise, immediately accu-rate to the witnessing eye, but that both the reality under her poems and the reality produced by them have a nostal-gic quality, a hauntedness, that cannot be reached, and per-haps could not be borne, by these poems, if it were.

Yet remembering that as I think her poems are expedient forms for ecstasies apprehended, and remembering, too, both the tradition of romantic reticence she observes and the fastidious thirst for detail, how could her poems be otherwise, or more? Her sensibility—the deeper it is the more persuaded it cannot give itself away—predicted her poetic method; and the defect of her method, in its turn, only represents the idiosyncrasy of her sensibility: that it, like its subject matter, constitutes the perfection of standing aside.

It is provisionally worth noting that Miss Moore is not alone but characteristic in American literature. Poe, Hawthorne, Melville (in *Pierre*), Emily Dickinson, and Henry James, all—like Miss Moore—shared an excessive sophistication of surfaces and a passionate predilection for the genuine—though Poe was perhaps not interested in too much of the genuine; and all contrived to present the conviction of reality best by making it, in most readers' eyes, remote.

1935

# 12. D. H. Lawrence and Expressive Form

As a poet, and only to a less degree as a novelist, Lawrence belongs to that great race of English writers whose work totters precisely where it towers, collapses exactly in its strength: work written out of a tortured Protestant sensibility and upon the foundation of an incomplete, uncomposed mind: a mind without defenses against the material with which it builds and therefore at every point of stress horribly succumbing to it. Webster, Swift, Blake, and Coleridge—perhaps Donne, Sterne, and Shelley, and on a lesser plane Marston, Thompson (of the Dreadful Night), and Beddoes—these exemplify, in their different ways, the deracinated, unsupported imagination, the mind for which, since it lacked rational structure sufficient to its burdens, experience was too much. Their magnitude was inviolate, and we must take account of it not only for its own sake but also to escape its fate; it is the magnitude of ruins—and the ruins for the most part of an intended life rather than an achieved art.

Such judgment—such prediction of the terms of appreciation—may seem heavy and the operation of willful prejudice (like that of our dying Humanism), but only if the reader refuses to keep in mind that of which he can say more. Criticism, the effort of appreciation, should be focused upon its particular objects, not limited to them. Shakespeare, Dante, and Milton, for example, remain monuments (not ruins) of the imagination precisely in what is here a relevant aspect. Their work, whatever the labors of exegesis,

remains approximately complete in itself. The work of
Shakespeare, even the Sonnets, is not for us an elongation
of the poet's self, but is independent of it because it has a
rational structure which controls, orders, and composes in
external or objective form the material of which it is made;
and for that effect it is dependent only upon the craft and
conventions of the art of poetry and upon the limits of language. We criticize adversely such work where it fails of
objective form or lacks unarticulated composition, as in the
Sonnets or *Hamlet*. We criticize *Lycidas* because the purpose of the digressions is not articulated and so there is injury to the composition—the growing together into an independent entity—of the poem. And this is the right meat for
criticism; this is the kind of complaint to which poetry is of
its own being subject; the original sin of which no major
work is entirely free.

This essay proposes to outline an attack upon Lawrence
as a poet on the grounds just laid out: that the strength of
his peculiar insight lacks the protection and support of a
rational imagination, and that it fails to its own disadvantage to employ the formal devices of the art in which it is
couched. Thus the attack will be technical. No objections
will be offered to the view of life involved—which is no more
confused than Dostoevski's, and no less a mirror than
Shakespeare's; only admiration for its vigor, regret that it
did not, and argument that in the technical circumstances
it could not, succeed. For it should be remembered that the
structure of the imagination no less than the sequence of
rhyme is in an important sense a technical matter.

Perhaps our whole charge may be laid on the pretension,
found in the Preface to the *Collected Poems*, that the radical imperfection of poetry is a fundamental virtue. That is
not how Lawrence frames it; he says merely that certain of
his early poems failed "because the poem started out to be
something it didn't quite achieve, because the young man
interfered with his demon"; which seems harmless enough
until we read that he regards many of his poems as a fragmentary biography, asks us to remember in reading them
the time and circumstance of his life, and expresses the wish

that in reading the Sonnets we knew more about Shakespeare's self and circumstance. After consideration, I take the young man in the quotation to be just what Lawrence thought he was not, the poet as craftsman, and the demon was exactly that outburst of personal feeling which needed the discipline of craft to become a poem. As for Shakespeare's Sonnets, if we did know more about Shakespeare's self, we should only know a little more clearly where he failed as a poet; the Sonnets themselves would be not a whit improved. A statement of which—since there is always a necessary baggage of historical and intellectual background—I wish to assert only the comparative or provisional truth.

However wrong Lawrence was about the young man, the demon, and Shakespeare's self, the point here is that his remarks explain why there is so little to say about his important poems as poetry, and they characterize the seed of personal strength, which, nourished exclusively, became his weakness, and ultimately brought about his disintegration and collapse as a poet. Lawrence was the extreme victim of the plague afflicting the poetry of the last hundred and fifty years—the plague of expressive form.

You cannot talk about the art of his poetry because it exists only at the minimum level of self-expression, as in the later, more important poems, or because, as in the earlier accentual rhymed pieces written while he was getting under way, its art is mostly attested by its badness. The ordering of words in component rhythms, the array of rhymes for prediction, contrast, transition and suspense, the delay of ornament, the anticipation of the exactly situated dramatic trope, the development of image and observation to an inevitable end—the devices which make a poem cohere, move, and shine apart—these are mostly not here, or are present badly and at fault. This absence of the advantages of craft is not particularly due to the inability to use them, but to a lack of interest. Lawrence hardly ever, after the first, saw the use of anything that did not immediately devour his interest, whether in life or in art. (Poetry, it may be remarked, is never an immediate art but always of implication.)

And he had besides, to control his interests, a special blinding light of his own, and it was only what this light struck or glared on that captured his interest, and compelled, by a kind of automatism, the writing hand. If a good deal else got in as well, it was not from concession or tactical motives, but by accident and willy-nilly, or because Lawrence was deceived and thought his demon illuminated him when not present at all. This is the presumptive explanation of the long reaches of dead-level writing. When you depend entirely upon the demon of inspiration, the inner voice, the inner light, you deprive yourself of any external criterion to show whether the demon is working or not. Because he is yours and you willfully depend on him, he will seem to be operating with equal intensity at every level of imagination. That is the fallacy of the faith in expressive form—the faith some aspects of which we have been discussing, that if a thing is only intensely enough felt its mere expression in words will give it satisfactory form, the dogma, in short, that once material becomes words it is its own best form. By this stultifying fallacy you cannot ever know whether your work succeeds or fails as integral poetry, can know only and always that what you have said symbolizes and substitutes for your experience to you, whatever it substitutes for in the minds of your readers. That Lawrence was aware of this fallacy, only thinking it a virtue, is I think evident; he would not otherwise have pled with his readers to put themselves in his place, to imagine themselves as suffering his experience, while reading the long section of his poems called "Look! We have come through!"; which is a plea, really, for the reader to do the work the poet failed to do, to complete the poems of which he gave only the expressive outlines.

There is a further vitiating influence of Lawrence's dogma as he seems to hold it, whether you take it as the demon of enthusiastic inspiration or the reliance on expressive form; it tends, on the least let-up of particularized intensity, to the lowest order of the very formalism which it was meant to escape: the formalism of empty verbiage, of rodomontade, masquerading as mystical or philosophical poetry. If you become content, even tormentedly, with self-expression, the process of education no less than that of taste ceases, and anything may come to stand, and interchangeably, for anything else. On the one hand the bare indicative statement of experience seems equivalent to insight into it, and on the other the use of such labels as Good or Evil, however accidentally come by, seems to have the force of the rooted concepts which they may, when achieved by long labor or genuine insight, actually possess. Thus a dog's dying howl may be made to express in itself the whole tragedy of life, which it indeed may or may not do, depending on the reach of the imagination, of represented experience, you bring to bear on it. In Lawrence's later poems, where he is most ambitious, there is more of this empty formalism, unknown to him, than in any poet of similar potential magnitude. Whatever happened in his own mind, what transpires in the poems is the statement without the insight, the label without the seizable implied presence of the imaginative reach. The pity is that had Lawrence matured an external form to anywhere near the degree that he intensified his private apprehension, that form would have persuaded us of the active presence of the insight and the imagination which we can now only take on trust or *ipse dixit*.

These radical defects in Lawrence's equipment and in his attitude toward his work, may be perhaps exhibited in certain of the early poems when he had not deliberately freed himself from those devices of form which, had he mastered them, might have saved him. He began writing in the ordinary way, using to express or discover his own impulses the contemporary models that most affected him. The freshness of his personal life, the process of personal awakening (since he had something to awaken) provided, by rule, a copious subject matter; and the freshness, to him, of other men's conventions amply supplied him and even, again by rule, sometimes overwhelmed him with forms. Occasionally, still in the natural course of a poet's progress, there was in his work a material as well as a formal influence, but rather less frequently than in most poets. For instance, "Lightning" and "Turned Down" are so strongly under the influence of the Hardy of *Time's Laughingstocks* and *Satires of Circumstances*, that there was very little room for Lawrence himself in the poems; Hardy's sensibility as well as Hardy's form crowded him out. By apparent paradox, the value of the poems to Lawrence was personal; as renderings of Hardy they add nothing. Where the influence was less apparent, it was more genuine because more digested, and far more successful, as, for example, in the two quatrains called "Gipsy." Hardy was the only then practicing poet who was in the hard-earned habit of composing so much implication in so brief a space and upon the nub of a special circumstance. It was from Hardy that Lawrence learned his lesson. (The nub of circumstance is of course the gypsy's traditional aversion to entering a house.)

I, the man with the red scarf,
    Will give thee what I have, this last week's earnings.
Take them and buy thee a silver ring
    And wed me, to ease my yearnings.

For the rest, when thou art wedded
    I'll wet my brow for thee
With sweat, I'll enter a house for thy sake,
    Thou shalt shut doors on me.

Thus houses and doors become "really" houses and doors. The poem is for that quality worth keeping in the early Lawrence canon; but its importance here is in the technical faults—by which I mean its radical and unnecessary variations from the norm of its model. It represents, I think (subject to correction), about as far as Lawrence ever went in the direction of strict accentual syllabic form; which is not very far. Hardy would have been ashamed of the uneven, lop-sided metrical architecture and would never have been guilty (whatever faults he had of his own) of the disturbing inner rhyme in the second quatrain. Lawrence was either ignorant or not interested in these matters; at any rate he failed to recognize the access of being which results from a perfected strict form. He preferred, in this poem, to depend on the best economical statement of his subject with the least imposition of external form, strict or not. This is an ex-

ample of the fallacy of expressive form; because, granted
that he used a set form at all, it is his substance, what he
had to say and was really interested in, that suffers through
his failure to complete the form. If the reader compares
this poem with say Blake's "To the Muses," which is not a
very strict poem in itself, the formal advantage will be plain.

A more important poem, a poem which measurably captured more of Lawrence's sensibility, and as it happens
more of ours, will illustrate the point, at least by cumulation,
more clearly. Take the first poem preserved in the collected
edition, "The Wild Common." We have here, for Lawrence
says that it was a good deal rewritten, the advantage of an
early and a late poem at once. It is, substantially, in its present form, one of the finest of all Lawrence's poems. It presents the pastoral scene suggested by the title, proceeds to
describe a naked man (the narrator) watching his white
shadow quivering in a sheep-dip; either actually or imaginatively the man enters the water and the shadow is resolved with the substance and is identified; the poem ends
with the affirmation, confirmed by singing larks and a lob-
bing rabbit, that "all that is good, all that is God takes
substance!" The feeling is deep and particularized and the
emotion is adequate to the material presented. The point
here is that in gaining his ends Lawrence used an extraordinary combination of inconsistent modes and means. I ask
only, for the sake of the argument, that the reader look at
the poem with the same attention to craft as is customary
(and is indeed the common proof of appreciation) in the
examination of a drawing or a fugue: that he look and read
*as if* he had a trained mind. Take the matter of rhymes.
Whether by weakness of sound, weakness of syntactical position, lack of metrical propulsion or, as the case is, restraint,
superfluity with regard to sense, or the use of mere homonym for true rhyme—the rhyme words not only fail as good
rhymes but because of the distortions they bring about injure the substance and disfigure the outline of the poem. (In
other poems such as "Discord in Childhood" the exigencies
of rhyme misunderstood dictate actually inconsistent images and tropes.) That is a formal defect; there are also

faults in the combinations of the modes of language. In this same poem, without dramatic change to warrant the variation, there are examples of fake "poetic" language, explicit direct presentation, the vague attribute and the precise attribute, colloquial language, and plain empty verbiage. It is as if in one drawing you found employed to the disadvantage of each the modes of outline and inner marking, chiaroscuro, and total visual effect.

Another poem, "Love on a Farm," has the special power of a dramatic fiction; it employs, dramatically, a violent but credible humanitarianism to force the feeling of death into the emotion of love. But it would have been better expanded and proved in prose. There is nothing in the poem to praise as poetry between the image of the intention and the shock of the result. Lawrence simply did not care in his verse—and, after *Sons and Lovers*, in many reaches of his more characteristic prose—for anything beyond the immediate blueprint expression of what he had in mind. The consequence is this. Since he willfully rejected as much as he could of the great mass of expressive devices which make up the craft of poetry, the success of his poems depends, not so much on his bare statements, as upon the constant function of communication which cannot be expunged from the language.

Only the articulate can be inarticulately expressed, even under the dogma of expressive form, and Lawrence was, within the limits of his obsessive interests, one of the most powerfully articulate minds of the last generation. Since he used language straightforwardly to the point of sloppiness, without ever willfully violating the communicative residue of his words, so much of his intention is available to the reader as is possible in work that has not been submitted to the completing persuasiveness of a genuine form. That much is a great deal; its capacity is the limit of greatness in the human personality. Being human, Lawrence could not escape in his least breath the burden of human experience, and, using language in which to express himself *for* himself, could not help often finding the existing, readily apprehensible word-forms the only suitable ones. That is a discipline by implication upon the soul of which the purest Protestant, as Lawrence was, cannot be free: the individual can contribute only infinitesimally even to his own idea of himself. In addressing even his most private thoughts he addresses a stranger and must needs find a common tongue between them. Thus Lawrence at his most personal, where he burrowed with most savage rapacity into himself, stood the best chance of terminating his passion in common experience. The language required, the objects of analogy and the tropes of identification, necessarily tended to the commonplace. This is at least negatively true of Lawrence's later, prophetic poems (as it is true on a level of greater magnitude in the prophetic poems of Blake); the fundamental declarations of insight, what Lawrence was after, in the Tortoise poems, could not help appearing in language commonplace for everything except its intensity. Here again it may be insisted, since such insistence is the object of this essay, that had Lawrence secured the same intensity in the process of his form as came naturally to him in seizing his subject, the poems would have escaped the inherent weakness of the commonplace (the loss of identity in the reader's mind) in the strength of separate being.

Before proceeding, as we have lastly to do, to measure and provisionally characterize the driving power in Lawrence's most important work, let us first examine, with a special object, one of the less important but uniquely successful poems. This is the poem called "Corot." It is written at the second remove from the experience involved. Not so much does it deal with a particular picture by Corot, or even with the general landscape vision of Corot, as it attempts a thinking back, by Lawrence, through Corot, into landscape itself as a major mode of insight. Corot—the accumulation of impressions, attitudes, and formal knowledge with which Corot furnishes the attentive mind—is the medium through which the poem transpires. It is perhaps the only poem of its kind Lawrence wrote; a poem with a deliberately apprehended external scaffolding. We know that most poems about pictures, and most illustrations of literature, stultify themselves by keeping to the terms of the art

they re-represent—or else come to mere minor acts of appreciation—come, in short, in either case, pretty much to nothing. Something very different took place here. By finding his
material at a second remove—the remove of Corot past the
remove of language—Lawrence provided himself, for once,
with a principle of objective form; which in the fact of this
poem composed his material better than he was ever able to
compose in terms of mere direct apprehension however intense. Despite the cloudy words—we have the word "dim"
used imprecisely three times in thirty-six lines—despite the
large words and phrases such as Life and Time, goal, purpose, and mighty direction—and despite the inconsistent
meters, Lawrence nevertheless was able to obtain merely
because of the constant presence of an external reference
("Corot"), a unity of effect and independence of being elsewhere absent in his work. That the poem may have been as
personal for Lawrence as anything he ever wrote makes no
difference; for the reader the terms of conception are objective, and the poem could thus not help standing by itself.

The poem is small, its value merely illustrative, and if it
is remembered at all it will be so only in the general context
of Lawrence; but I have emphasized the principle of its
compositional success because it is on similar principles that
most great poetry has been composed; or at least—a more
prudent statement—similar principles may be extracted from
most of the poetry we greatly value: the principle that the
reality of language, which is a formal medium of knowledge, is superior and anterior to the reality of the uses to
which it is put, and the operative principle, that the chaos
of private experience cannot be known or understood until
it is projected and ordered in a form external to the consciousness that entertained it in flux. Of the many ways in
which these principles may be embodied, Lawrence's poetry
enjoys the advantage of but few, and those few by accident,
as in "Corot," or because he could not help it, as in the constant reliance on the communicative function of language
mentioned above. But he worked in the poverty of apparent riches and felt no need. There was a quality in his apprehension of the experience that obsessed him that in itself

sufficed to carry over the reality of his experience in the words of his report—always for him and sometimes for the reader. This I think, for lack of a better word, may be called the quality of hysteria.

Hysteria comes from the Greek word for womb, and, formerly limited to women, was the name given to extraordinary, disproportionate reactions to the shock of experience. In hysteria the sense of reality is not annulled, resort is not to fancy or unrelated illusion; the sense of reality is rather heightened and distorted to a terrifying and discomposing intensity. The derangement of the patient is merely the expression, through a shocked nervous system, of the afflicting reality. But hysteria is not limited in its expressive modes to convulsions and shrieking. We have hysterias which express themselves in blindness, deafness, paralysis, and even secondary syphilis (lacking of course the appropriate bacteria). Some forms of romantic love may be called habit-hysterias of a comparatively benign character. In all these modes what is expressed has an apparent overwhelming reality. The blind man is really blind, the deaf deaf, and the paralytic cannot move—while hysteria lasts.

Now I do not wish to introduce Lawrence as a clinical example of hysteria; it would be inappropriate and unnecessary to any purpose of literary criticism; but I think it can be provisionally put that the reality in his verse, and in his later prose (from *The Rainbow* to *Mornings in Mexico* if not in *Lady Chatterley's Lover*) is predominantly of the hysterical order. Hysteria is certainly one of the resources of art—as it represents an extreme of consciousness; and it is arguable that much art is hysteria controlled—that is, restored to proportion by seizure in objective form. And the reader should remember that in a life so difficult to keep balanced, plastic, and rational, the leaning toward the expressive freedom of hysteria may often be intractable. The pretense or fact of hysteria is an ordinary mode of emotional expression. The reality of what is expressed is intense and undeniable, and is the surest approach to the absolute. But what is expressed in hysteria can never be wholly understood until the original reality is regained either by analysis or the imposition of limits. Otherwise, and in art, the hysteria is heresy and escapes the object which created it. That is how I think Lawrence worked; he submitted the obsessions of his experience to the heightening fire of hysteria and put down the annealed product just as it came. His special habit of hysteria is only a better name for the demon, the divinity, referred to in the Preface to the *Collected Poems;* and there is no reason to suppose that Lawrence would himself reject the identification. The reality persists, and is persuasive to those who catch the clue and accept the invitation by its very enormity.

Certainly it is in terms of some such notion that we must explain Lawrence's increasing disregard of the control of rationally conceived form and his incipient indifference, in the very last poems, to the denotative functions of language. So also we may explain the extraordinary but occasional and fragmentary success of his poetry as expression: by the enormity of the reality exposed. As it happens, Lawrence's obsessions ran to sex, death, the isolation of the personality, and the attempt at mystical fusion. Had he run rather to claustrophobia, fetish-worship, or some of the more obscure forms of human cowardice, his method of expression would have been less satisfactory: since it would not have commanded the incipient hysteria of sympathy. The normal subject matter, in the sense of a sturdy preoccupation with ordinary interests, kept his enormity of expression essentially accessible in most of his poems, although there are some places, for example in "The Ship of Death" or "Sicilian Cyclamens," where the hysteric mode carries the pathetic fallacy and the confusion of symbols beyond any resolution.

But normal subject matter was not the only saving qualification; there is in the best poems a kind of furious underlying honesty of observation—the very irreducible surd that makes the hysteria an affair of genius not of insanity. One aspect of this honesty is perhaps most clearly seen in the poem called "She Said as Well to Me," which I think marks the climax of the long series called "Look! We Have Come Through!" There Lawrence manages to present, for all the faults of the work he did not do, and merely by the intensified honesty of the observation, the utter dignity of the singleness and isolation of the individual. Later in "Medlars and Sorb Apples," the hysteria is increased and the observation becomes vision, and leaves, perhaps, the confines of poetry.

> Orphic farewell, and farewell, and farewell
> And the *ego sum* of Dionysos
> The *sono io* of perfect drunkenness
> Intoxication of final loneliness.

It became, in fact, ritual frenzy; a matter to which we shall return. But first let us examine the eighteen pages of the poems about tortoises. Here we have the honesty working the other way round. In "She Said as Well to Me" and in all the poems of "Look! We Have Come Through!" which make up Lawrence's testament of personal love, the movement is from the individual outward: it is the report or declaration, made unequivocally, of an enormously heightened sense of self. The self, the individual, is the radial point of sensibility. The six tortoise poems (which I take as the type of all the later poems) have as their motive the effort to seize on the plane of self-intoxication the sense of the outer world. The exhilarated knowledge of the self is still the aim, but here the self is the focal, not the radial, point of sensibility. The bias, the predicting twist of the mind, is no longer individual love, but the sexual, emergent character of all life; and in terms of that bias, which is the controlling principle, the seed of reality, in the hysteria of expression, Lawrence brings every notation and association, every symbolic suggestion he can find, to bear upon the shrieking plasm of the self. I quote the concluding lines of "Tortoise Shout."

> The cross,
> The wheel on which our silence first is broken,
> Sex, which breaks up our integrity, our single inviolability, our deep silence,
> Tearing a cry from us.
>
> Sex, which breaks us into voice, sets us calling across the deeps, calling, calling for the complement,

Singing and calling, and singing again, being answered, having found.

Torn, to become whole again, after long seeking what is lost,

The same cry from the tortoise as from Christ, the Osiris-cry of abandonment,

That which is whole, torn asunder,

That which is in part, finding its whole again throughout the universe.[1]

Here again the burden of honesty is translated or lost in the condition of ritual, of formal or declarative prayer and mystical identification; which is indeed a natural end for emotions of which the sustaining medium is hysteria. To enforce the point, let us take "Fish" (the poems of the four Evangelistic Beasts would do as well), which represented for Lawrence, in the different fish he observes, the absolute, untouchable, unknowable life, "born before God was love, or life knew loving," "who lies with the waters of his silent passion, womb-element," and of whom he can write, finally:

> In the beginning
> Jesus was called The Fish . . .
> And in the end.

*Per omnia saecula saeculorum.* The Fish and likewise the Tortoise are acts of ceremonial adoration, in which the reader, if he is sympathetic, because of the intensity of the

---

[1] May I suggest that the reader compare this passage from Lawrence with the following lines from T. S. Eliot's *Ash Wednesday* as a restorative to the sense of *controlled* hysteria. The two poems have nearly the same theme.

| | |
|---|---|
| Lady of silences | The greater torment |
| Calm and distressed | Of love satisfied |
| Torn and most whole | End of the endless |
| Rose of memory | Journey to no end |
| Rose of forgetfulness | Conclusion of all that |
| Exhausted and life-giving | Is inconclusible |
| Worried reposeful | Speech without word and |
| The single Rose | Word of no speech |
| Is now the Garden | Grace to the Mother |
| Where all loves end | For the Garden |
| Terminate torment | Where all love ends. |
| Of love unsatisfied | |

act, cannot help sharing. Lawrence was by consequence of the type of his insight and the kind of experience that excited him, a religious poet. His poetry is an attempt to declare and rehearse symbolically his pious recognition of the substance of life. The love of God for him was in the declaration of life in the flux of sex. Only with Lawrence the piety was tortured—the torture of incomplete affirmation. The great mystics saw no more profoundly than Lawrence through the disorder of life to their ultimate vision, but they saw within the terms of an orderly insight. In them, reason was stretched to include disorder and achieved mystery. In Lawrence, the reader is left to supply the reason and the form; for Lawrence only expresses the substance.

The affirmation to which the more important poems of Lawrence mount suffers from incompleteness for the same reasons that the lesser poems examined in the first part of this essay suffered. On the one hand he rejected the advantage of objective form for the immediate freedom of expressive form, and on the other hand he preferred the inspiration of immediate experience to the discipline of a rationally constructed imagination. He had a powerful sensibility and a profound experience, and he had the genius of insight and unequivocal honesty: he was in contact with the disorder of life. In his novels and tales the labor of creating and opposing characters, the exigencies of narrative, all the detail of execution, combined to make his works independent, controlled entities to a great extent. But in his poetry, the very intensity of his self-expression overwhelmed all other considerations, and the disorder alone prevailed.

The point at issue, and the pity of it, can be put briefly. Lawrence the poet was no more hysterical in his expressive mode than the painter Van Gogh. But where Van Gogh developed enough art to control his expression objectively, and so left us great paintings, Lawrence developed as little art as possible, and left us the ruins of great intentions; ruins which we may admire and contemplate, but as they are ruins of a life merely, cannot restore as poetry. Art was too long for Lawrence; life too close.

1935

# 13. New Thresholds, New Anatomies

*Notes on a Text of Hart Crane*

I

It is a striking and disheartening fact that the three most ambitious poems of our time should all have failed in similar ways: in composition, in independent objective existence, and in intelligibility of language. *The Waste Land,* the *Cantos,* and *The Bridge* all fail to hang together structurally in the sense that "Prufrock," "Envoi," and "Praise for an Urn"—lesser works in every other respect—do hang together. Each of the three poems requires of the reader that he supply from outside the poem, and with the help of clues only, the important, *controlling* part of what we may loosely call the meaning. And each again deliberately presents passages, lines, phrases, and single words which no amount of outside work can illumine. The fact is striking because, aside from other considerations of magnitude, relevance, and scope, these are not the faults we lay up typically against the great dead. The typical great poet is profoundly rational, integrating, and, excepting minor accidents of incapacity, a master of ultimate verbal clarity. Light, radiance, and wholeness remain the attributes of serious art. And the fact is disheartening because no time could have greater need than our own for rational art. No time certainly could surrender more than ours does daily, with drums beating, to fanatic politics and despotically construed emotions.

But let us desert the disheartening for the merely striking aspect, and handle the matter, as we can, within the realm of poetry, taking up other matters only tacitly and by implication. Let us say provisionally that in their more important works Eliot, Pound, and Crane lack the ultimate, if mythical, quality of aseity, that quality of completeness, of independence, so great that it seems underived and an effect of pure creation. The absence of aseity may be approached variously in a given poet; but every approach to be instructive, even to find the target at all, must employ a rational mode and the right weapon. These notes intend to examine certain characteristic passages of Hart Crane's poems as modes of language and to determine how and to what degree the effects intended were attained. The rationale is that of poetic language; the weapons are analysis and comparison. But there are other matters which must be taken up first before the language itself can be approached at all familiarly.

Almost everyone who has written on Crane has found in him a central defect, either of imagination or execution, or both. Long ago, in his Preface to *White Buildings,* Allen Tate complained that for all his talent Crane had not found a suitable theme. Later, in his admirable review of *The Bridge,* Yvor Winters brought and substantiated the charge (by demonstrating the exceptions) that even when he had found a theme Crane could not entirely digest it and at crucial points simply was unable to express it in objective form. These charges hold; and all that is here said is only in explication of them from a third point of view.

Waldo Frank, in his Introduction to the *Collected Poems,* acting more as an apologist than a critic, proffers two explanations of Crane's incompleteness as a poet, to neither of which can I assent, but of which I think both should be borne in mind. Mr. Frank believes that Crane will be understood and found whole when our culture has been restored from revolutionary collectivism to a predominant interest in the person; when the value of expressing the personal in the terms of the cosmic shall again seem supreme. This hypothesis would seem untenable unless it is construed as relevant to the present examination; when it runs immediately into the hands of the obvious but useful statement that Crane was interested in persons rather than the class struggle. Mr.

Frank's other explanation is that Crane's poetry was based upon the mystical perception of the "organic continuity between the self and a seemingly chaotic world." Crane "was too virile to deny the experience of continuity; he let the world pour in; and since his nuclear self was not disciplined to detachment from his nerves and passions, he lived exacerbated in a constant swing between ecstasy and exhaustion." I confess I do not understand "organic continuity" in this context, and all my efforts to do so are defeated by the subsequent word "detachment." Nor can I see how this particular concept of continuity can be very useful without the addition and control of a thorough supernaturalism. The control for mystic psychology is theology, and what is thereby controlled is the idiosyncrasy of insight, not the technique of poetry.

What Mr. Frank says not-rationally can be usefully retranslated to that plane on which skilled readers ordinarily read good poetry; which is a rational plane; which is, on analysis, the plane of competent technical appreciation. Such a translation, while committing grave injustice on Mr. Frank, comes nearer doing justice to Crane. It restores and brings home the strictures of Tate and Winters, and it brings judgment comparatively back to the minute particulars (Blake's phrase) which are alone apprehensible. To compose the nuclear self and the seemingly chaotic world is to find a suitable theme, and the inability so to compose rises as much from immaturity and indiscipline of the major poetic uses of language as from personal immaturity and indiscipline. Baudelaire only rarely reached the point of self-discipline and Whitman never; but Baudelaire's language is both disciplined and mature, and Whitman's sometimes so. *Les Fleurs du Mal* are a profound poetic ordering of a life disorderly, distraught, and deracinated, a life excruciated, in the semantic sense of that word, to the extreme. And Whitman, on his side, by a very different use of language, gave torrential expression to the romantic disorder of life in flux, whereas his private sensibility seems either to have been suitably well-ordered or to have felt no need of order.

Whitman and Baudelaire are not chosen with reference

to Crane by accident but because they are suggestively apposite. The suggestion may be made, not as blank truth but for the light there is in it, that Crane had the sensibility typical of Baudelaire and so misunderstood himself that he attempted to write *The Bridge* as if he had the sensibility typical of Whitman. Whitman characteristically let himself go in words, in any words and by all means the handiest, until his impulse was used up. Baudelaire no less characteristically caught himself up in his words, recording, ordering, and binding together the implications and tacit meanings of his impulse until in his best poems the words he used are, as I. A. Richards would say, inexhaustible objects of meditation. Baudelaire aimed at control, Whitman at release. It is for these reasons that the influence of Whitman is an impediment to the *practice* (to be distinguished from the reading) of poetry, and that the influence of Baudelaire is re-animation itself. (It may be noted that Baudelaire had at his back a well-articulated version of the Catholic Church to control the moral aspect of his meanings, where Whitman had merely an inarticulate pantheism.)

To apply this dichotomy to Crane is not difficult if it is done tentatively, without requiring that it be too fruitful, and without requiring that it be final at all. The clue or nexus is found, aside from the poems themselves, in certain prose statements. Letters are suspect and especially letters addressed to a patron, since the aim is less conviction by argument than the persuasive dramatization of an attitude. It is therefore necessary in the following extract from a letter to Otto Kahn that the reader accomplish a reduction in the magnitude of terms.

Of the section of *The Bridge* called "The Dance" Crane wrote: "Here one is on the pure mythical and smoky soil at last! Not only do I describe the conflict between the two races in this dance—I also became identified with the Indian and his world before it is over, which is the only method possible of ever really possessing the Indian and his world as a cultural factor." Etc. I suggest that, confronted with the tight, tense, intensely personal lyric quatrains of the verse itself, verse compact with the deliberately inarticulate interfusion of the senses, Crane's statement of intention has only an *ipse dixit* pertinence; that taken otherwise, taken as a living index of substance, it only multiplies the actual confusion of the verse and impoverishes its achieved scope. Taken seriously, it puts an impossible burden on the reader: the burden of reading two poems at once, the one that appears and the "real" poem which does not appear except by an act of faith. This would be reading by legerdemain, which at the moment of achievement must always collapse, self-obfuscated.

Again, in the same letter, Crane wrote that, "The range of *The Bridge* has been called colossal by more than one critic who has seen the ms., and though I have found the subject to be vaster than I had at first realized, I am still highly confident of its final articulation into a continuous and eloquent span. . . . *The Aeneid* was not written in two years—nor in four, and in more than one sense I feel justified in comparing the historical and cultural scope of *The Bridge* to that great work. It is at least a symphony with an epic theme, and a work of considerable profundity and inspiration."

The question is whether this was wishful thinking of the vague order commonest in revery, convinced and sincere statement of intention, or an effect of the profound duplicity —a deception in the very will of things—in Crane's fundamental attitudes toward his work; or whether Crane merely misunderstood the logical import of the words he used. I incline to the notion of duplicity, since it is beneath and sanctions the other notions as well; the very duplicity by which the talents of a Baudelaire appear to their possessor disguised and disfigured in the themes of a Whitman, the same fundamental duplicity of human knowledge whereby an accustomed disorder seems the order most to be cherished, or whereby a religion which at its heart denies life enriches living. In the particular reference, if I am right, it is possible to believe that Crane labored to perfect both the strategy and the tactics of language so as to animate and maneuver his perceptions—and then fought the wrong war and against an enemy that displayed, to his weapons, no vulnerable target. He wrote in a language of which it was the virtue to accrete, modify, and interrelate moments of emotional vision—moments at which the sense of being gains its greatest access—moments at which, by the felt nature of knowledge, the revealed thing is its own meaning; and he attempted to apply his language, in his major effort, to a theme that required a sweeping, discrete, indicative, anecdotal language, a language in which, by force of movement, mere cataloguing can replace and often surpass representation. He used the private lyric to write the cultural epic; used the mode of intensive contemplation, which secures ends, to present the mind's actions, which have no ends. The confusion of tool and purpose not only led him astray in conceiving his themes; it obscured at crucial moments the exact character of the work he was actually doing. At any rate we find most impenetrable and ineluctable, in certain places, the very matters he had the genius to see and the technique to clarify: the matters which are the substance of rare and valid emotion. The confusion, that is, led him to content himself at times with the mere cataloguing statement, enough for him because he knew the rest, of what required completely objective embodiment.

Another, if ancillary, method of enforcing the same suggestion (of radical confusion) is to observe the disparity between Crane's announced purpose and the masters he studied. Poets commonly profit most where they can borrow most, from the poets with whom by instinct, education, and accident of contact, they are most nearly unanimous. Thus poetic character is early predicted. In Crane's case, the nature of the influences to which he submitted himself remained similar from the beginning to the end and were the dominant ones of his generation. It was the influence of what we may call, with little exaggeration, the school of tortured sensibility—a school of which we perhaps first became aware in Baudelaire's misapprehension of Poe, and later, in the hardly less misapprehending resurrection of Donne. Crane benefited, and was deformed by, this influence both directly and by an assortment of indirection; but he never surmounted it. He read the modern French poets who are the result of Baudelaire, but he did not read Racine of whom Baudelaire was himself a product. He read Wallace Stevens, whose strength and serenity may in some sense be assigned to the combined influence of the French moderns and, say, Plato; but he did not, at least affectively, read Plato. He read Eliot, and through and in terms of him, the chosen Elizabethans—though more in Donne and Webster than in Jonson and Middleton; but he did not, so to speak, read the Christianity from which Eliot derives his ultimate strength, and by which he is presently transforming himself. I use the word *read* in a strong sense; there is textual evidence of reading throughout the poems. The last influence Crane exhibited is no different in character and in the use to which he put it than the earliest: the poem called "The Hurricane" derives immediately from the metric of Hopkins but not ultimately from Hopkins' integrating sensibility. Thus Crane fitted himself for the exploitation of the peculiar, the unique, the agonized and the tortured perception, and he developed language-patterns for the essentially incoherent aspects of experience: the aspects in which experience assaults rather than informs the sensibility. Yet, granting his sensibility, with his avowed epic purpose he had done better had he gone to school to Milton and Racine, and, in modern times, to Hardy and Bridges—or even Masefield—for narrative sweep.

Crane had, in short, the wrong masters for his chosen fulfillment, or he used some of the right masters in the wrong way: leeching upon them, as a poet must, but taking the wrong nourishment, taking from them not what was hardest and most substantial—what made them great poets—but taking rather what was easiest, taking what was peculiar and idiosyncratic. That is what kills so many of Crane's poems, what must have made them impervious, once they were discharged, even to himself. It is perhaps, too, what killed Crane the man—because in a profound sense, to those who use it, poetry is the only means of putting a tolerable order upon the emotions. Crane's predicament—that his means defeated his ends—was not unusual, but his case was extreme. In more normal form it is the predicament of immaturity. Crane's mind was slow and massive, a cumulus of substance; it had, to use a word of his own, the synergical quality, and with time it might have worked together, clarified, and become its own meaning. But he hastened the process and did not survive to maturity.

Certainly there is a hasty immaturity in the short essay on Modern Poetry, reprinted as an appendix to the *Collected Poems,* an immaturity both in the intellectual terms employed and in the stress with which the attitude they rehearse is held. Most of the paper tilts at windmills, and the lance is too heavy for the wielding hand. In less than five pages there is deployed more confused thinking than is to be found in all his poems put together. Poetry is not, as Crane says it is, an architectural art—or not without a good deal of qualification; it is a linear art, an art of succession, and the only art it resembles formally is plain song. Nor can Stravinsky and the cubists be compared, as Crane compares them, in the quality of their abstractions with the abstractions of mathematical physics: the aims are disparate; expression and theoretic manipulation can never exist on the same plane. Nor can psychological analyses, in literature, be distinguished in motive and quality from dramatic analyses. Again, and finally, the use of the term *psychosis* as a laudatory epithet for the substance of Whitman, represents to me the uttermost misconstruction of the nature of poetry: a psychosis is a mental derangement not due to an organic lesion or neurosis. A theory of neurosis (as, say, Aiken has held it in *Blue Voyage*) is more tenable scientifically; but neither it seems to me has other than a stultifying critical use. Yet, despite the confusion and positive irrationality of Crane's language the general tendency is sound, the aspiration sane. He wanted to write good poetry and his archetype was Dante; that is enough. But in his prose thinking he had the wrong words for his thoughts, as in his poetry he had often the wrong themes for his words.

II

So far, if the points have been maintained at all, what I have written adds up to the suggestion that in reading Hart

Crane we must make allowances for him—not historical allowances as we do for Shakespeare, religious allowances as for Dante and Milton, or philosophical as for Goethe and Lucretius—but fundamental allowances whereby we agree to supply or overlook what does not appear in the poems, and whereby we agree to forgive or guess blindly at those parts of the poems which are unintelligible. In this Crane is not an uncommon case, though the particular allowances may perhaps be unique. There are some poets where everything is allowed for the sake of isolated effects. Sedley is perhaps the supreme example in English; there is nothing in him but two lines, but these are famous and will always be worth saving. Waller is the more normal example, or King, where two or three poems are the whole gist. Crane has both poems and passages; and in fact there is hardly a poem of his which has not something in it, and a very definite something, worth saving.

The nature of that saving quality, for it saves him no less than ourselves, Crane has himself most clearly expressed in a stanza from the poem called "Wine Menagerie."

> New thresholds, new anatomies! Wine talons
> Build freedom up about me and distill
> This competence—to travel in a tear
> Sparkling alone, within another's will.

I hope to show that this stanza illustrates almost inexhaustibly, to minds at all aware, both the substance and the aspiration of Crane's poetry, the character and value of his perceptions, and his method of handling words to control them. If we accept the stanza as a sort of declaration of policy and apply it as our own provisional policy to the sum of his work, although we limit its scope we shall deepen and articulate our appreciation—a process, that of appreciation, which amounts not to wringing a few figs from thistles but to expressing the wine itself.

Paraphrase does not greatly help. We can, for the meat of it, no more be concerned with the prose sense of the words than Crane evidently was. Crane habitually re-created his words from within, developing meaning to the point of idiom; and that habit is the constant and indubitable sign of talent. The meanings themselves are the idioms and have a twist and life of their own. It is only by ourselves meditating on and *using* these idioms—it is only by emulation—that we can master them and accede to their life.

Analysis, however, does help, and in two directions. It will by itself increase our intimacy with the words as they appear; and it will as the nexus among comparisons disclose that standard of achievement, inherent in this special use of poetic language, by which alone the value of the work may be judged. (Analysis, in these uses, does not cut deep, it does not cut at all: it merely distinguishes particulars; and the particulars must be re-seen in their proper focus before the labor benefits.)

Moving in the first direction, toward intimacy, we can say that Crane employed an extreme mode of free association; that operation among words where it is the product rather than the addition that counts. There was, for example, no logical or emotional connection between thresholds and anatomies until Crane verbally juxtaposed them and tied them together with the cohesive of his meter. Yet, so associated, they modify and act upon each other mutually and produce a fresh meaning of which the parts cannot be segregated. Some latent, unsuspected part of the cumulus of meaning in each word has excited, so to speak, and affected a corresponding part in the others. It is the juxtaposition which is the agent of selection, and it is a combination of meter and the carried-over influence of the rest of the poem, plus the as yet undetermined expectations aroused, which is the agent of emphasis and identification. It should be noted that, so far as the poem is concerned, the words themselves contain and do not merely indicate the feelings which compose the meaning; the poet's job was to put the words together like bricks in a wall. In lesser poetry of the same order, and in poetry of different orders, words may only indicate or refer to or substitute for the feelings; then we have the poetry of vicarious statement, which takes the place of, often to the highest purpose, the actual complete presentation, such as we have here. Here there is nothing for the words to take the place of; they are their own life, and have an organic continuity, not with the poet's mind nor with the experience they represent, but with themselves. We see that thresholds open upon anatomies: upon things to be explored and understood and felt freshly as an adventure; and we see that the anatomies, what is to be explored, are known from a new vantage, and that the vantage is part of the anatomy. The separate meanings of the words fairly rush at each other; the right ones join and those irrelevant to the juncture are for the moment—the whole time of the poem—lost in limbo. Thus the association "New thresholds, new anatomies!" which at first inspection might seem specious or arbitrary (were we not used to reading poetry) not only does not produce a distortion but, the stress and strain being equal, turns out wholly natural and independently alive.

In the next phrase the association of the word "talons" with the context seems less significantly performed. So far as it refers back and expresses a seizing together, a clutching by a bird of prey, it is an excellent word well chosen and spliced in. The further notion, suggested by the word "wine," of release, would also seem relevant. There is, too, an unidentifiable possibility—for Crane used words in very special senses indeed—of "talons" in the sense of cards left after the deal; and there is even, to push matters to the limit, a bare chance that some element of the etymon—ankle, heel —has been pressed into service. But the possibilities have among them none specially discriminated, and whichever you choose for use, the dead weight of the others must be provisionally carried along, which is what makes the phrase slightly fuzzy. And however you construe "wine talons" you cannot, without distorting what you have and allowing for the gap or lacuna of what you have not, make your construction fit either or both of the verbs which it governs. Talons neither build nor distill even when salvation by rhyme is in question. If Crane meant—as indeed he may have—that wines are distilled and become brandies or spirits, then he showed a poverty of technique in using the transitive instead of the intransitive form. Objection can be carried too far, when it renders itself nugatory. These re-marks are meant as a kind of exploration; and if we now make the allowance for the unidentified distortion and sup-ply with good will the lacuna in the very heart of the middle phrases, the rest of the stanza becomes as plain and vivid as poetry of this order need ever be. To complete the whole association, the reader need only remember that Crane probably had in mind, and made new use of Blake's lines:

> For a Tear is an Intellectual Thing,
> And a Sigh is the Sword of an Angel King.

It is interesting to observe that Blake was talking against war and that his primary meaning was much the same as that expressed negatively in "Auguries of Innocence" by the following couplet:

> He who shall train the Horse to War
> Shall never pass the Polar Bar.

Crane ignored the primary meaning, and extracted and em-phasized what was in Blake's image a latent or secondary meaning. Or possibly he combined—made a free association of—the intellectual tear with

> Every Tear from Every Eye
> Becomes a Babe in Eternity;

only substituting the more dramatic notion of will for intel-lect. What is important to note is that, whatever its origin, the meaning as Crane presents it is completely transformed and subjugated to the control of the "new thresholds, new anatomies!"

The stanza we have been considering is only arbitrarily separated from the whole poem—just as the poem itself ought to be read in the context of the whole *White Buildings* section. The point is, that for appreciation—and for denigration—all of Crane should be read thoroughly, at least once, with similar attention to detail. That is the way in which Crane worked. Later readings may be more liberated and more irresponsible—as some people read the Bible for what they call its poetry or a case history for its thrill; but they never get either the poetry or the thrill without a preliminary fundamental intimacy with the rational technique involved. Here it is a question of achieving some notion of a special poetic process. The principle of association which controls this stanza resembles the notion of wine as escape, release, father of insight and seed of metamorphosis, which controls the poem; and, in its turn, the notion of extra-logical, intoxicated metamorphosis of the senses controls and innervates Crane's whole sensibility.

To illustrate the uniformity of approach, a few examples are presented, some that succeed and some that fail. In "Lachrymae Christi" consider the line

> Thy Nazarene and tinder eyes.

(Note, from the title, that we are here again concerned with tears as the vehicle-image of insight, and that, in the end, Christ is identified with Dionysus.) Nazarene, the epithet for Christ, is here used as an adjective of quality in conjunction with the noun tinder also used as an adjective; an arrangement which will seem baffling only to those who underestimate the seriousness with which Crane remodeled words. The first three lines of the poem read:

> Whitely, while benzine
> Rinsings from the moon
> Dissolve all but the windows of the mills.

Benzine is a fluid, cleansing and solvent, has a characteristic tang and smart to it, and is here associated with the light of the moon, which, through the word "rinsings," is itself modified by it. It is, I think, the carried-over influence of benzine which gives startling aptness to Nazarene. It is, if I am correct for any reader but myself, an example of suspended association, or telekinesis; and it is, too, an example of syllabic interpenetration or internal punning as habitually practiced in the later prose of Joyce. The influence of one word on the other reminds us that Christ the Saviour cleanses and solves and has, too, the quality of light. "Tinder" is a simpler instance of how Crane could at once isolate a word and bind it in, impregnating it with new meaning. Tinder is used to kindle fire, powder, and light;

a word incipient and bristling with the action proper to its being. The association is completed when it is remembered that tinder is very nearly a homonym for tender and, *in this setting*, puns upon it.

Immediately following, in the same poem, there is a parenthesis which I have not been able to penetrate with any certainty, though the possibilities are both fascinating and exciting. The important words in it do not possess the excluding, limiting power over themselves and their relations by which alone the precise, vital element in an ambiguity is secured. What Crane may have meant privately cannot be in question—his words may have represented for him a perfect tautology; we are concerned only with how the words act upon each other—or fail to act—so as to commit an appreciable meaning. I quote the first clause of the parenthesis.

> Let sphinxes from the ripe
> Borage of death have cleared my tongue
> Once and again . . .

It is syntax rather than grammar that is obscure. I take it that "let" is here a somewhat homemade adjective and that Crane is making a direct statement, so that the problem is to construe the right meanings of the right words in the right references; which will be an admirable exercise in exegesis, but an exercise only. The applicable senses of "let" are these: neglected or weary, permitted or prevented, hired, and let in the sense that blood is let. Sphinxes are inscrutable, have secrets, propound riddles to travelers and strangle those who cannot answer. "Borage" has at least three senses: something rough (sonantly suggestive of barrage and barrier), a blue-flowered, hairy-leaved plant, and a cordial made from the plant. The Shorter Oxford Dictionary quotes this jingle from Hooker: "I Borage always bring courage." One guess is that Crane meant something to the effect that if you meditate enough on death it has the same bracing and warming effect as drinking a cordial, so that the riddles of life (or death) are answered. But something very near the contrary may have been intended; or both. In any case a guess is ultimately worthless because, with the defective syntax, the words do not verify it. Crane had a profound feeling for the hearts of words, and how they beat and cohabited, but here they overtopped him; the meanings in the words themselves are superior to the use to which he put them. The operation of selective cross-pollination not only failed but was not even rightly attempted. The language remains in the condition of that which it was intended to express: in the flux of intoxicated sense; whereas the language of the other lines of this poem here examined—the language, not the sense—is disintoxicated and candid. The point is that the quality of Crane's success is also the quality of his failure, and the distinction is perhaps by the hair of accident.

In the part of *The Bridge* called "Virginia," and in scores of places elsewhere, there is a single vivid image, of no structural importance, but of great delight as ornament: it both fits the poem and has a startling separate beauty of its own, the phrase: "Peonies with pony manes."[1] The freshness has nothing to do with accurate observation, of which it is devoid, but has its source in the arbitrary character of the association: it is created observation. Another example is contained in

> Down Wall, from girder into street noon leaks,
> A rip-tooth of the sky's acetylene;

which is no more forced than many of Crashaw's best images. It is, of course, the pyramiding associations of the word acetylene that create the observation: representing as it does an intolerable quality of light and a torch for cutting metal, and so on.

Similarly, again and again, both in important and in ornamental phrases, there are effects only half secured, words which are not the right words but only the nearest words. E.g.: "What eats the pattern with *ubiquity*. . . . Take this *sheaf* of dust upon your tongue . . . Preparing *penguin* flexions of the arms . . . [A tugboat] with one

---

[1] Compare Marianne Moore's "the lion's ferocious chrysanthemum head."

*galvanic* blare . . . I heard the *hush of lava wrestling* your arms." Etc. Not that the italicized words are wrong but that they fall short of the control and precision of impact necessary to vitalize them permanently.

There remains to consider the second help of analysis (the first was to promote intimacy with particulars), namely, to disclose the standard of Crane's achievement in terms of what he actually accomplished; an effort which at once involves comparison of Crane with rendered possibilities in the same realm of language taken from other poets. For Crane was not alone; style, like knowledge, of which it is the expressive grace, is a product of collaboration; and his standard, whether consciously or not, was outside himself, in verse written in accord with his own bent: which the following, if looked at with the right eye, will exemplify.

Sunt lacrimae rerum et mentem mortalia tangunt.—Vergil.

Lo giorno se n'andava, e l'aer bruno
    toglieva gli animai, che sono in terra,
    dalle fatiche loro.—Dante.

A brittle glory shineth in his face;
As brittle as the glory is the face.—Shakespeare.

Adieu donc, chants du cuivre et soupirs de la flûte!
Plaisirs, ne tentez plus un coeur sombre et boudeur!
Le Printemps adorable a perdu son odeur!—Baudelaire.

But Love has pitched his mansion in
The place of excrement;
For nothing can be sole or whole
That has not been rent.—Yeats.

She dreams a little, and she feels the dark
Encroachment of that old catastrophe,
As a calm darkens among water-lights.—Stevens.

The relevant context is assumed to be present, as we have been assuming it all along with Crane. Every quotation, except that from Yeats which is recent, should be well known. They bring to mind at once, on one side, the sustaining, glory-breeding power of magnificent form joined to great intellect. Before that impact Crane's magnitude shrinks. On the other side, the side of the particulars, he shrinks no less. The significant words in each selection, and so in the lines themselves, will bear and require understanding to the limit of analysis and limitless meditation. Here, as in Crane, words are associated by the poetic process so as to produce a new and living, an idiomatic, meaning, differing from and surpassing the separate factors involved. The difference—which is where Crane falls short of his standard—is this. Crane's effects remain tricks which can only be resorted to arbitrarily. The effects in the other poets—secured by more craft rather than less—become, immediately they are understood, permanent idioms which enrich the resources of language for all who have the talent to use them. It is perhaps the difference between the immediate unbalance of the assaulted, intoxicated sensibility and the final, no less exciting, clarity of the sane, mirroring sensibility.

It is said that Crane's inchoate heart and distorted intellect only witness the disease of his generation; but I have cited two poets, if not of his generation still his contemporaries, who escaped the contagion. It is the stigma of the first order of poets (a class which includes many minor names and deletes some of the best known) that they master so much of life as they represent. In Crane the poet succumbed with the man.

What judgment flows from these strictures need not impede the appreciation of Crane's insight, observation, and intense, if confused, vision, but ought rather to help determine it. Merely because Crane is imperfect in his kind is no reason to give him up; there is no plethora of perfection, and the imperfect beauty, like life, retains its fascination. And there is about him, too—such were his gifts for the hearts of words, such the vitality of his intelligence—the distraught but exciting splendor of a great failure.

1935

# 14. Notes on E. E. Cummings' Language

In his four books of verse, his play, and the autobiographical *Enormous Room*,[1] Mr. Cummings has amassed a special vocabulary and has developed from it a special use of language which these notes are intended to analyze and make explicit. Critics have commonly said, when they understood Mr. Cummings' vocabulary at all, that he has enriched the language with a new idiom; had they been further interested in the uses of language, they would no doubt have said that he had added to the general sensibility of his time. Certainly his work has had many imitators. Young poets have found it easy to adopt the attitudes from which Mr. Cummings has written, just as they often adopt the superficial attitudes of Swinburne and Keats. The curious thing about Mr. Cummings' influence is that his imitators have been able to emulate as well as ape him; which is not so frequently the case with the influence of Swinburne and Keats. Mr. Cummings is a school of writing in himself; so that it is necessary to state the underlying assumptions of his mind, and of the school which he teaches, before dealing with the specific results in poetry of those assumptions.

It is possible to say that Mr. Cummings belongs to the anti-culture group; what has been called at various times vorticism, futurism, dadaism, surrealism, and so on.[2] Part

[1] As of 1930. There would seem little modification of these notes necessary because of *Eimi* or the subsequent volumes of verse.

[2] The reader is referred to the late numbers of *transition* for a serial and collaborative expression of the latest form which this group has assumed: the Battle of the Word. [As of 1930.]

of the general dogma of this group is a sentimental denial of the intelligence and the deliberate assertion that the unintelligible is the only object of significant experience. These dogmas have been defended with considerable dialectical skill, on the very practical premise that only by presenting the unintelligible as viable and actual *per se* can the culture of the *dead intelligence* (Brattle Street, the Colleges, and the Reviews) be shocked into sentience. It is argued that only by denying to the intelligence its function of discerning quality and order, can the failures of the intelligence be overcome; that if we take things as they come without remembering what has gone before or guessing what may come next, and if we accept these things at their face value, we shall know life, as least in the arts, as it really is. Nothing could be more arrogant, and more deceptively persuasive to the childish spirit, than such an attitude when held as fundamental. It appeals to the intellect which wishes to work swiftly and is in love with immediate certainty. A mind based on it accepts every fragment of experience as final and every notion as definite, yet never suffers from the delusion that it has learned anything. By an astonishing accident, enough unanimity exists among these people to permit them to agree among themselves; to permit them, even, to seem spiritually indistinguishable as they appear in public.

The central attitude of this group has developed, in its sectaries, a logical and thoroughgoing set of principles and habits. In America, for example, the cause of the lively arts has been advanced against the ancient seven; because the lively arts are necessarily immediate in appeal and utterly transitory. Thus we find in Mr. Cummings' recent verse and in his play *Him* the side show and the cabaret set up as "inevitable" frames for experience. Jazz effects, tough dialects, tough guys, slim hot queens, barkers, fairies, and so on, are made into the media and symbols of poetry. Which is proper enough in Shakespeare where such effects are used ornamentally or for pure play. But in Cummings such effects are employed as substance, as the very mainstay of the poetry. There is a continuous effort to escape the realism of the intelligence in favor of the realism of the obvious. What might be stodgy or dull because not properly worked up into poetry is replaced by the tawdry and by the fiction of the immediate.

It is no great advantage to get rid of one set of flabby generalities if the result is merely the immersion of the sensibility in another set only superficially less flabby. The hardness of the tough guy is mostly in the novelty of the language. There is no hardness in the emotion. The poet is as far from the concrete as before. By denying the dead intelligence and putting on the heresy of unintelligence, the poet only succeeds in substituting one set of unnourished conventions for another. What survives, with a deceptive air of reality, is a surface. That the deception is often intentional hardly excuses it. The surface is meant to clothe and illuminate a real substance, but in fact it is impenetrable. We are left, after experiencing this sort of art, with the certainty that there was nothing to penetrate. The surface was perfect; the deceit was childish; and the conception was incorrigibly sentimental: all because of the dogma which made them possible.

If Mr. Cummings' tough-guy poems are excellent examples of this sentimentality, it is only natural that his other poems—those clothed in the more familiar language of the lyric—should betray even more obviously, even more perfectly, the same fault. There, in the lyric, there is no pretense at hardness of surface. We are admitted at once to the bare emotion. What is most striking, in every instance, about this emotion is the fact that, in so far as it exists at all, it is Mr. Cummings' emotion, so that our best knowledge of it must be, finally, our best guess. It is not an emotion resulting from the poem; it existed before the poem began and is a result of the poet's private life. Besides its inspiration, every element in the poem, and its final meaning as well, must be taken at face value or not at all. This is the extreme form, in poetry, of romantic egoism: whatever I experience is real and final, and whatever I say represents what I experience. Such a dogma is the natural counterpart of the denial of the intelligence.

Our interest is not in the abstract principle, but in the results of its application in poetry. Assuming that a poem should in some sense be understood, should have a meaning apart from the poet's private life, either one of two things will be true about any poem written from such an attitude as we have ascribed to Mr. Cummings. Either the poem will appear in terms so conventional that everybody will understand it—when it will be flat and no poem at all; or it will appear in language so far distorted from convention as to be inapprehensible except by lucky guess. In neither instance will the poem be genuinely complete. It will be the notes for a poem, from which might flow an infinite number of possible poems, but from which no particular poem can be certainly deduced. It is the purpose of this paper to examine a few of the more obvious types of distortion which Mr. Cummings has practiced upon language.

The question central to such a discussion will be what kind of meaning does Mr. Cummings' poetry have; what is the kind of equivalence between the language and its object. The pursuit of such a question involves us immediately in the relations between words and feelings, and the relations between the intelligence and its field in experience —all relations which are precise only in terms themselves essentially poetic—in the feeling for an image, the sense of an idiom. Such relations may only be asserted, may be judged only tentatively, only instinctively, by what seems to be the disciplined experience, but what amounts, perhaps, only to the formed taste. Here criticism is appreciation. But appreciation, even, can take measures to be certain of its grounds, and to be full should betray the constant apprehension of an end which is the necessary consequence, the proper rounding off, of just those grounds. In the examination of Mr. Cummings' writings the grounds will be the facts about the words he uses, and the end will be apprehended in the quality of the meaning his use of these words permits.

There is one attitude toward Mr. Cummings' language which has deceived those who hold it. The typographical peculiarities of his verse have caught and irritated public attention. Excessive hyphenation of single words, the use of lower case "i," the breaking of lines, the insertion of punctuation between the letters of a word, and so on, will have a possible critical importance to the textual scholarship of the future; but extensive consideration of these peculiarities today has very little importance, carries almost no reference to the *meaning* of the poems. Mr. Cummings' experiments in typography merely extend the theory of notation by adding to the number, *not* to the *kind*, of conventions the reader must bear in mind, and are dangerous only because since their uses cannot readily be defined, they often obscure rather than clarify the exact meaning. No doubt the continued practice of such notation would produce a set of well-ordered conventions susceptible of general use. At present the practice can only be "allowed for," recognized in the particular instance, felt, and forgotten: as the diacritical marks in the dictionary are forgotten once the sound of the word has been learned. The poem, after all, only takes wing on the page, it persists in the ear.[3]

Considering typographical peculiarities for our present purposes as either irrelevant or unaccountable, there remain the much more important peculiarities of Mr. Cummings' vocabulary itself; of the poem *after* it has been read, as it is in the mind's ear, as it is on the page only for reassurance and correction.

If a reader, sufficiently familiar with these poems not to be caught on the snag of novelty, inspects carefully any score of them, no matter how widely scattered, he will

---

[3] It is not meant to disparage Mr. Cummings' inventions, which are often excellent, but to minimize an exaggerated contemporary interest. A full discussion of the virtues of notation may be found in *A Survey of Modernist Poetry* by Laura Riding and Robert Graves (London, Heinemann, 1927), especially in Chapter III which is labeled: "William Shakespeare and E. E. Cummings: A study in original punctuation and spelling." Their point is made by printing sonnet 129 in its original notation beside a modern version; the point being that Shakespeare knew what he was doing and that his editors did not.

especially be struck by a sameness among them. This sameness will be in two sorts—a vagueness of image and a constant recurrence of words. Since the one depends considerably upon the other, a short list of some of Mr. Cummings' favorite words will be a good preliminary to the examination of his images. In *Tulips and Chimneys* words such as these occur frequently—thrilling, flowers, serious, absolute, sweet, unspeaking, utter, gradual, ultimate, final, serene, frail, grave, tremendous, slender, fragile, skillful, carefully, intent, young, gay, untimid, incorrigible, groping, dim, slow, certain, deliberate, strong, chiseled, subtle, tremulous, perpetual, crisp, perfect, sudden, faint, strenuous, minute, superlative, keen, ecstatic, actual, fleet, delicious, stars, enthusiastic, capable, dull, bright. In listing these as favorite words, it is meant that these words do the greater part of the work in the poems where they occur; these are the words which qualify the subject matter of the poems, and are sometimes even the subjects themselves. Observe that none of them, taken alone, are very *concrete* words; and observe that many of them are the rather *abstract,* which is to say typical, *names* for precise qualities, but are not, and cannot be, as *originally important* words in a poem, very precise or very concrete or very abstract: they are middling words, not in themselves very much one thing or the other, and should be useful only with respect to something concrete in itself.

If we take Mr. Cummings' most favored word "flower" and inspect the uses to which he puts it, we should have some sort of key to the kind of poetry he writes. In *Tulips and Chimneys* the word "flower" turns up, to a casual count, forty-eight times, and in *&*, a much smaller volume, twenty-one times. We have among others the following: smile like a flower; riverly as a flower; steeped in burning flowers; last flower; lipping flowers; more silently than a flower; snow flower; world flower; softer than flowers; forehead a flight of flowers; feet are flowers in vases; air is deep with flowers; slow supple flower of beauty; flower-terrible; flower of thy mouth; stars and flowers; mouth a new flower; flower of silence; god's flowers; flowers of reminding; dissonant flowers; flower-stricken air; Sunday flower; tremendous flower; speaking flower; flowers of kiss; futile flowers, etc., etc. Besides the general term there is a quantity of lilies and roses, and a good assortment of daisies, pansies, buttercups, violets, and chrysanthemums. There are also many examples of such associated words as "petals" and "blooms" and "blossoms," which, since they are similarly used, may be taken as alternative to flowers.

Now it is evident that this word must attract Mr. Cummings' mind very much; it must contain for him an almost unlimited variety and extent of meaning; as the mystic says god, or at least as the incomplete mystic repeats the name of god to every occasion of his soul, Mr. Cummings in some of his poems says flower. The question is, whether or not the reader can possibly have shared the experience which Mr. Cummings has had of the word; whether or not it is possible to discern, after any amount of effort, the precise impact which Mr. Cummings undoubtedly feels upon his whole experience when he uses the word. "Flower," like every other word not specifically the expression of a logical relation, began life as a metaphor, as a leap from feeling to feeling, as a bridge in the imagination to give meaning to both those feelings. Presumably, the amount of meaning possible to the word is increased with each use, but only the meaning *possible*. Actually, in practice, a very different process goes on. Since people are occupied mostly with communication and argument and conversation, with the erection of discursive relationships, words are commonly spoken and written with the *least* possible meaning preserved, instead of the most. History is taken for granted, ignored, or denied. Only the outsides of words, so to speak, are used; and doubtless the outsides of words are all that the discursive intellect needs. But when a word is used in a poem it should be the sum of all its appropriate history made concrete and particular in the individual context; and in poetry all words act *as if* they were so used, because the only kind of meaning poetry can have requires that all its words resume their full life: the full life being modified and made unique by the *qualifica-*

*tions* the words perform one upon the other in the poem. Thus even a very bad poem may seem good to its author, when the author is not an acute critic and believes that there is life in his words merely because there was life (and a very different sort of life, truly) in the feelings which they represent. An author should remember, with the Indians, that the reality of a word is anterior to, and greater than, his use of it can ever be; that there is a perfection to the feelings in words to which his mind cannot hope to attain, but that his chief labor will be toward the approximation of that perfection.

We sometimes speak of a poet as a master of his words, and we sometimes say that a man's poetry has been run away with by words—meaning that he has not mastered his words but has been overpowered by his peculiar experience of certain among them. Both these notions are commonly improper, because they represent misconceptions of the nature of poetry in so far as they lay any stress upon originality, or the lack of it, in the poet's use of words. The only mastery possible to the poet consists in that entire submission to his words which is perfect knowledge. The only originality of which the poet is properly capable will be in the choice of order, and even this choice is largely a process of discovery rather than of origination. As for words running away with a poet or a poem, it would be more accurate to say that the poet's *ideas* had run away with him than his words.

This is precisely what has occurred with Mr. Cummings in his use of the word "flower" as a maid of all work. The word has become an idea, and in the process has been deprived of its history, its qualities, and its meaning. An idea, the intellectual pin upon which a thought is hung, is not transmissible in poetry as an important element in the poem and ought only to be employed to pass over, with the greatest possible velocity, the area of the uninteresting (what the poet was not interested in). That is, in a poem whose chief intent was the notation of character and yet required a descriptive setting, the poet might well use for the description such vague words as space and time, but could not use such words as goodness or nobleness without the risk of flatness. In Mr. Cummings' poetry we find the contrary; the word "flower," because of the originality with which he conceives it, becomes an idea and is used to represent the most interesting and most important aspect of his poem. Hence the center of the poem is permanently abstract and unknowable for the reader, and remains altogether without qualifications and concreteness. It is not the mere frequency of use that deadens the word flower into an idea; it is the kind of thought which each use illustrates in common. By seldom saying *what* flower, by seldom relating immitigably the abstract word to a specific experience, the content of the word vanishes; it has no inner mystery, only an impenetrable surface.

This is the defect, the essential deceit, we were trying to define. Without questioning Mr. Cummings, or any poet, as to sincerity (which is a personal attitude, irrelevant to the poetry considered) it is possible to say that when in any poem the important words are forced by their use to remain impenetrable, when they can be made to surrender nothing actually to the senses—then the poem is defective and the poet's words have so far deceived him as to become ideas merely.[4] Mr. Cummings is not so much writing poetry, as he is dreaming, idly ringing the changes of his reveries.

Perhaps a small divagation may make clearer the relation of these remarks to Mr. Cummings' poems. Any poetry which does not consider itself as much of an art and having the same responsibilities to the consumer as the arts of

[4] It should be confessed that for all those persons who regard poetry only as a medium of communication, these remarks are quite vitiated. What is communicated had best remain as abstract as possible, dealing with the concrete as typical only; then "meaning" will be found to reside most clearly in the realm of ideas, and everything will be given as of equal import. But here poetry is regarded not at all as communication but as expression, as statement, as presentation of experience, and the emphasis will be on what is made known concretely. The question is not what one shares with the poet, but what one knows in the poem.

silversmithing or cobbling shoes—any such poetry is likely
to do little more than rehearse a waking dream. Dreams
are everywhere ominous and full of meaning; and why
should they not be? They hold the images of the secret
self, and to the initiate dreamer betray the nerve of life at
every turn, not through any effort to do so, or because of
any inherited regimen, but simply because they cannot help
it. Dreams are like that—to the dreamer the maximal limit
of experience. As it happens, dreams employ words and
pictorial images to fill out their flux with a veil of substance.
Pictures are natural to everyone, and words, because they
are prevalent, seem common and inherently sensible. Hence,
both picture and word, and then with a little stretching of
the fancy the substance of the dream itself, seem express-
ible just as they occur—as things created, as the very flux
of life. Mr. Cummings' poems are often nothing more than
the report of just such dreams. He believes he knows what
he knows, and no doubt he does. But he also believes,
apparently, that the words which he encourages most
vividly to mind are those most precisely fitted to put his
poem on paper. He transfers the indubitable magic of his
private musings from the cell of his mind, where it is honest
incantation, to the realm of poetry. Here he forgets that
poetry, so far as it takes a permanent form, is written and
is meant to be read, and that it cannot be a mere private
musing. Merely because his private fancy furnishes his
liveliest images, is the worst reason for assuming that this
private fancy will be approximately experienced by the
reader or even indicated on the printed page.

But it is unfair to limit this description to Mr. Cummings;
indeed, so limited, it is not even a description of Mr.
Cummings. Take the Oxford Book of English Verse, or any
anthology of poems equally well known, and turn from the
poems printed therein of such widely separated poets as
Surrey, Crashaw, Marvell, Burns, Wordsworth, Shelley, and
Swinburne, to the collected works of these poets respectively. Does not the description of Mr. Cummings' mind at
work given above apply nearly as well to the bulk of this
poetry as to that of Mr. Cummings, at least on the senses'

first immersion? The anthology poems being well known are conceived to be understood, to be definitely intelligible, and to have, without inspection, a precise meaning. The descent upon the collected poems of all or of any one of these authors is by and large a descent into tenuity. Most of their work, most of any poet's work, with half a dozen exceptions, is tenuous and vague, private exercises or public playthings of a soul in verse. So far as he is able, the reader struggles to reach the concrete, the solid, the definite; he must have these qualities, or their counterparts among the realm of the spirit, before he can understand what he reads. To translate such qualities from the realm of his private experience to the conventional forms of poetry is the problem of the poet; and the problem of the reader, likewise, is to come well equipped with the talent and the taste for discerning the meaning of those conventions as they particularly occur. Neither the poet's casual language nor the reader's casual interlocution is likely to be much help. There must be a ground common but exterior to each: that is the poem. The best poems take the best but not always the hardest reading; and no doubt it is so with the writing. Certainly, in neither case are dreams or simple reveries enough. Dreams are natural and are minatory or portentous; but except when by accident they fall into forms that fit the intelligence, they never negotiate the miracle of meaning between the poet and the poem, the poem and the reader.

Most poetry fails of this negotiation, and it is sometimes assumed that the negotiation was never meant, by the poet, to be made. For the poet, private expression is said to be enough; for the reader, the agitation of the senses, the perception of verbal beauty, the mere sense of stirring life in the words, are supposed sufficient. If this defense had a true premise—if the poet did express himself to his private satisfaction—it would be unanswerable; and to many it is so. But I think the case is different, and this is the real charge against Mr. Cummings: the poet does not ever express himself privately. The mind cannot understand, cannot properly know its own musings until those musings take some sort of conventional form. Properly speaking a poet, or any man, cannot be adequate to himself in terms of himself. True consciousness and true expression of consciousness must be external to the blind seat of consciousness—man as a sensorium. Even a simple image must be fitted among other images, and conned with them, before it is understood. That is, it must take a form in language which is highly traditional and conventional. The genius of the poet is to make the convention apparently disappear into the use to which he puts it.

Mr. Cummings and the group with which he is here roughly associated, the anti-culture or anti-intelligence group, persists to the contrary. Because experience is fragmentary as it strikes the consciousness it is thought to be essentially discontinuous and therefore essentially unintelligible except in the fragmentary form in which it occurred. They credit the words they use with immaculate conception and there hold them unquestionable. A poem, because it happens, must mean something and mean it without relation to anything but the private experience which inspired it. Certainly it means something, but not a poem; it means that something exciting happened to the writer and that a mystery is happening to the reader. The fallacy is double: they believe in the inexorable significance of the unique experience; and they have discarded the only method of making the unique experience into a poem—the conventions of the intelligence. As a matter of fact they do not write without conventions, but being ignorant of what they use, they resort most commonly to their own inefficient or superficial conventions—such as Mr. Cummings' flower and doll. The effect is convention without substance; the unique experience becomes a rhetorical assurance.

If we examine next, for the sake of the greatest possible contrast, one of the "tough" poems in *Is 5*, we will find a similar breach with the concrete. The use of vague words like "flower" in the lyrical poems as unexpanded similes, is no more an example of sentimental egoism than the use of vague conventions about villains. The distortion differs in terms but is essentially identical.

Sometimes the surface of the poem is so well constructed that the distortion is hard to discover. Intensity of process occasionally triumphs over the subject. Less frequently the subject itself is conceived directly and takes naturally the terms which the language supplies. The poem numbered One-XII in *Is 5* is an example in so far as the sentimental frame does not obscure the process.

now dis "daughter" uv eve (who aint precisely slim) sim

ply don't know duh meanin uv duh woid sin in
not disagreeable contras tuh dat not exacly fat

"father" (adjustin his robe) who now puts on his flat hat.

It is to be noted in this epigram, that there is no inexorable reason for either the dialect or the lapses from it into straight English. No one in particular is speaking, unless it be Mr. Cummings slumming in morals along with he-men and lady social workers, and taking it for granted that the dialect and the really refined language which the dialect exercises together give a setting. There are many other poems in *Is 5*, more sentimental and less successful, where the realism is of a more obvious sort; not having reference to an ideal so much as to a kind of scientific reality. That is, there is an effort to ground an emotion, or the facts which make the emotion, in the style of the character to whom the emotion happens. It is the reporter, the man with the good ear for spoken rhythms, who writes out of memory. The war poems and the poem about Bill and his chip (One-XVI) are examples. Style in this sense (something laid on) is only an attribute; is not the man; is not the character. And when it is substituted for character, it is likely to be sentimental and melodramatic. That is, the emotion which is named in the poem (by one of its attributes) is in excess of its established source (that same attribute). There is a certain immediate protection afforded to this insufficiency by the surface toughness, by the convention of burlesque; as if by mocking oneself one made sure there was something to mock. It is a kind of trickery resulting from eager but lazy senses; where the sensation itself is an excess, and appears to have done all the work of intuition and intelligence; where sensation seems expert without incorporation into experience. As if sensation could be anything more than the idea of sensation, so far as poetry goes, without being attached to some central body of experience, genuinely understood and *formed* in the mind.

The intrusion of science into art always results in a sentimental realism and always obfuscates form when that science is not kept subordinate to the qualitative experience of the senses—as witness the run of sociological novels. The analogues of science, where conventions are made to do the work of feeling instead of crowning it, are even more dangerous. Mr. Cummings' tough guy and his hard-boiled dialects are such analogues.

Mr. Cummings has a fine talent for using familiar, even almost dead words, in such a context as to make them suddenly impervious to every ordinary sense; they become unable to speak, but with a great air of being bursting with something very important and precise to say. "The bigness of cannon is *skillful* . . . enormous rhythm of *absurdity* . . . *slimness* of *evenslicing* eyes are chisels . . . electric Distinct face haughtily vital *clinched* in a swoon of *synopsis* . . . my friend's being continually whittles *keen* careful futile *flowers*," etc. With the possible exception of the compound *evenslicing* the italicized words are all ordinary words; all in normal contexts have a variety of meanings both connotative and denotative; the particular context being such as to indicate a particular meaning, to establish precisely a feeling, a sensation or a relation.

Mr. Cummings' contexts are employed to an opposite purpose in so far as they wipe out altogether the history of the word, its past associations and general character. To seize Mr. Cummings' meaning there is only the free and *uninstructed* intuition. Something precise is no doubt intended; the warrant for the belief is in the almost violent isolation into which the words are thrown; but that precision can seldom, by this method, become any more than just that "something precise." The reality, the event, the feeling, which we will allow Mr. Cummings has in mind, is not sensibly in the word. It is one thing for meaning to be difficult, or abstruse—hidden in its heart, that is. "Absent thee from *felicity* a while," Blake's "Time is the *mercy* of eternity" are reasonable examples; there the mystery is inside the words. In Mr. Cummings' words the mystery flies in the face, is on the surface; because there is no inside, no realm of possibility, of essence.

The general movement of Mr. Cummings' language is away from communicable precision. If it be argued that the particular use of one of the italicized words above merely makes that word unique, the retort is that such uniqueness is too perfect, is sterile. If by removing the general sense of a word the special sense is apotheosized, it is only so at the expense of the general sense itself. The destruction of the general sense of a word results in the loss of that word's individuality; for in practice the character of a word (which is its sense) is manifest only in good society, and meaning is distinguished only by conventional association. Mr. Cummings' use of words results in a large number of conventions, but these conventions do not permeate the words themselves, do not modify their souls or change their fates; they cannot be adopted by the reader because they cannot be essentially understood. They should rather be called inventions.

If we take a paragraph from the poem beginning on page thirty in *Is 5*, we will discover another terminus of the emotional habit of mind which produced the emphasis on the word "flower" in *Tulips and Chimneys*.

the Bar. tinking luscious jugs dint of ripe silver with warmlyish wetflat splurging smells waltz the glush of squirting taps plus slush of foam knocked off and a faint piddle-of-drops she says I ploc spittle what the lands thaz me kid in no sir hopping sawdust you kiddo he's a palping wreaths of badly Yep cigars who jim him why gluey grins topple together eyes pout gestures stickily point made glints squinting who's a wink bum-nothing and money fuzzily mouths take big wobbly footsteps every goggle cent of it get out ears dribbles soft right old feller belch the chap hic summore eh chuckles skulch. . . .

Now the point is that the effect of this whole paragraph has much in common with the effect of the word "flower." It is a flower disintegrated, and the parts are not component; so that by presenting an analysis of his image Mr. Cummings has not let us into its secret: the analysis is not a true analysis, because it exhibits, finally, what are still only the results, not the grounds, of his private conventions, his personal emotions. It is indubitable that the words are alive; they jostle, even overturn, the reader in the assurance of their vitality; but the notion of what their true vitality is remains Mr. Cummings' very own. The words remain emotive. They have a gusty air of being something, but they defeat themselves in the effort to say what, and come at last to a bad end, all fallen in a heap.

The easiest *explanation* of the passage would be to say that each separate little collection of words in it is a note for an image; an abstraction, very keen and lively in Mr. Cummings' mind, of something very precise and concrete. Some of the words seem like a painter's notes, some a philologist's. But they are all, as they are presented, notes, abstractions, ideas—with their concrete objects unknown—except to the most arbitrary guess. The guess must be arbitrary because of the quantity, not the quality, of the words employed. Mr. Cummings is not here overworking the individual words, but by heaping so many of them together he destroys their individuality. Meaning really residual in the word is not exhausted, is not even touched; it must remain abstract and only an emotional substitute for it can be caught. The interesting fact about emotional substitutes in poetry, as elsewhere, is their thinness, and the inadequacy resulting from the thinness. The thinness is compulsory because they can, so far as the poem is concerned, exist only as a surface; they cannot possess tentacular roots reaching into, and feeding on, feelings, because the feelings do not exist, are only present by legerdemain. Genuine emotion in poetry perhaps does not *exist* at all; though it is none the less real for that, because a genuine emotion does not need the warrant of existence: it is the necessary result, in the mind, of a convention of feelings: like the notion of divine grace.

In *Tulips and Chimneys* (p. 109) there is a poem whose first and last lines supply an excellent opposition of proper and improper distortion of language.

> the Cambridge ladies who live in furnished souls . . .
>> the
> moon rattles like a fragment of angry candy.

In the context the word "soul" has the element of surprise which is surprise at *justness;* at *aptness;* it fits in and finishes off the notion of the line. "Furnished souls" is a good, if slight, conceit; and there is no trouble for the reader who wishes to know what the line means: he has merely to *extend* his knowledge slightly, just as Mr. Cummings merely extended the sense of his language slightly by releasing his particular words in this particular order. The whole work that the poet here demands of his reader is pretty well defined. The reader does not have to *guess;* he is enabled to *know.* The reader is not collecting data, he is aware of a meaning.

It would be unfair not to quote the context of the second line.

> . . . the Cambridge ladies do not care, above
> Cambridge if sometimes in its box of
> sky lavender and cornerless, the
> moon rattles like a fragment of angry candy.

We can say that Mr. Cummings is putting beauty next to the tawdry; juxtaposing the dead with the live; or that he is being sentimentally philosophical in verse—that is, releasing from inadequate sources something intended to be an emotion.[5]

We can go on illustrating Mr. Cummings' probable in-

[5] That is, as the most common form of sentimentality is the use of emotion in *excess* of its impetus in the feelings, here we have an example of emotion which fails by a great deal to *come up* to its impetus. It is a very different thing from understatement, where the implications are always definite and where successful disarming.

tentions almost infinitely. What Mr. Cummings likes or admires, what he holds dear in life, he very commonly calls flowers, or dolls, or candy—terms with which he is astonishingly generous; as if he thought by making his terms general enough their vagueness could not matter, and never noticed that the words so used enervate themselves in a kind of hardened instinct. We can understand what Mr. Cummings intended by "moon" and "candy" but in the process of understanding, the meaning of the words themselves disappears. The thrill of the association of "rattles" with "moon" and "angry" with "candy" becomes useless as a guide. "Rattles" and "angry" can only be continued in the meaning of the line if the reader supplies them with a force, a definiteness of suggestion, with which Mr. Cummings has not endowed them.

The distortion is here not a release of observation so keen that commonplace language would not hold it; it is not the presentation of a vision so complete that words must lose their normal meanings in order to suggest it. It is, on the contrary, the distortion of the commonplace itself; and the difficulty about a commonplace is that it cannot be known, it has no character, no fate, and no essence. It is a substitute for these.

True meaning (which is here to say knowledge) can only exist where some contact, however remote, is preserved between the language, forms, or symbols in which it is given and something concrete, individual, or sensual which inspired it; and the degree in which the meaning is seized will depend on the degree in which the particular concreteness is realized. Thus the technique of "meaning" will employ distortion only in so far as the sense of this concreteness is promoted by it. When contrast and contradiction disturb the ultimate precision of the senses the distortion involved is inappropriate and destructive. Mr. Cummings' line about the moon and candy does not weld a contradiction, does not identify a substance by a thrill of novel association. It leaves the reader at a loss; where it is impossible to *know*, after any amount of effort and good will, what the words mean. If it be argued that Mr. Cummings was not interested in meaning then Mr. Cummings is not a serious poet, is a mere collector of sensations, and can be of very little value to us. And to defend Mr. Cummings on the ground that he is in the pretty good company of Swinburne, Crashaw, and Victor Hugo, is partly to ignore the fact that by the same argument all four also enjoy the companionship of Mr. Guest. Such defense would show a very poor knowledge of the verses of Mr. Cummings, who is nothing if not serious in the attempt to exhibit precise knowledge. His interest in words and in their real meaning is probably greater than that of most poets of similar dimensions. He has consciously stretched syntax, word order, and meaning in just the effort to expand knowledge in poetry; and his failure is because he has gone too far, has lost sight of meaning altogether—and because, perhaps, the experience which he attempts to translate into poetry remained always personal to him and was never known objectively as itself. By his eagerness Mr. Cummings' relation to language has become confused; he has put down what has meant much to him and can mean little to us, because for us it is not put down—is only indicated, only possibly there. The freshness and depth of his private experience is not denied; but it is certain that, so far as its meaning goes, in the poetry into which he translated it, sentimentality, empty convention, and commonplace rule. In short, Mr. Cummings' poetry ends in ideas *about* things.

When Mr. Cummings resorts to language for the *thrill* that words may be made to give, when he allows his thrill to appear as an equivalent for concrete meaning, he is often more successful than when he is engaged more ambitiously. This is true of poets like Swinburne and Poe, Shelley and the early Marlowe: where the first pair depended almost as much upon *thrill* as Mr. Cummings in those poems where they made use of it at all, and where the second pair, particularly Marlowe, used their thrills more appropriately as ornament: where all four were most successful in their less ambitious works, though perhaps not as interesting. Likewise, today, there is the example of Archibald MacLeish, whose best lines are those that thrill and do nothing more.

So that at least in general opinion Mr. Cummings is in this respect not in bad company. But if an examination of thrill be made, whether in Mr. Cummings' verse or in that of others, it will be shown that the use of thrill has at heart the same sentimental impenetrability that defeats the possibility of meaning elsewhere. Only here, in the realm of thrill, the practice is comparatively less illegitimate. Thrill, by itself, or in its proper place, is an exceedingly important element in any poem: it is the circulation of its blood, the *quickness* of life, by which we know it, when there is anything in it to know, most intimately. To use a word for its thrill, is to resurrect it from the dead; it is the incarnation of life in consciousness; it is movement.[6]

But what Mr. Cummings does, when he is using language as thrill, is not to resurrect a word from the dead: he more often produces an apparition, in itself startling and even ominous, but still only a ghost: it is all a thrill, and what it is that thrilled us cannot be determined. For example in *XLI Poems,* the following phrases depend considerably for their effect upon the thrill that is in them: "Prisms of sharp *mind;* where strange birds *purr;* into the *smiling* sky *tense* with *blending;* ways cloaked with *renewal;* sinuous riot; *steeped* with burning flowers; little kittens who are called *spring;* electric Distinct face haughtily vital clinched in a *swoon* of synopsis; unreal *precise* intrinsic fragment of actuality; an orchid whose *velocity* is *sculptural;* scythe

---

[6] Cf. Owen Barfield's *Poetic Diction* (London, Faber and Gwyer, 1928), page 202. "For what is absolutely necessary to the present existence of poetry? Movement. The wisdom which she has imparted may remain for a time at rest, but she herself will always be found to have gone forward to where there is life, and therefore movement, *now.* And we have seen that the experience of esthetic pleasure betrays the real presence of movement. . . . But without the continued existence of poetry, without a steady influx of new meaning into language, even the knowledge and wisdom which poetry herself has given in the past must wither away into a species of mechanical calculation. Great poetry is the progressive incarnation of life in consciousness." That is, we must know what thrills us; else being merely thrilled we are left gasping and aghast, like the little girl on the roller coaster.

takes *crisply* the *whim* of thy *smoothness;* perpendicular *taste;* wet stars, etc., etc. (The italics are mine.)

Take especially the phrase, "scythe takes *crisply* the *whim* of thy *smoothness.*" We know in the poem that it is the scythe of death and that it is youth and beauty (in connection with love) that is to be cut off. So much is familiar, is very conventional; and so the conventional or dead emotion is placed before us; the educated reader receives it and reacts to it without a whimper. But Mr. Cummings must not have been content with presenting the conventional emotion in its conventional form; he felt bound to enliven it with metaphor, with overtones of the senses and the spirit: so that he substituted for the direct statement a rather indirect image combining three unusually sensed words for the sake of the *thrill* the special combination might afford. As the phrase stands there is no precision in it. There is a great suggestion of precision about it—like men going off to war; but precisely *what* is left for the reader to guess, to supply from his own heart. By themselves *whim* and *smoothness* are abstract quality words; and in order for them to escape the tensity, the dislocated strain, of abstractness and gain the intensity, the firm disposition, of concrete meaning, they should demand a particular reference.

*Smoothness* is probably the smoothness of the body and is used here as a kind of metonymy; but it may be pure metaphor and represent what is really to die—the spirit—taken in its physical terms; or it may be that all that is to be understood is a pure tautology. And so on. Even with this possible variety of reference, *smoothness* would not be very objectionable, were it the only word in the phrase used in this way, or were the other words used to clarify the *smoothness.* But we have also the noun *whim* bearing directly on *smoothness* and the adverb *crisply* which while it directly modifies *takes,* really controls the entire phrase. Taken seriously *whim,* with reference to the smoothness of either the body or the spirit or the love it inspires, is to say the least a light word; one might almost say a "metrical" word, introduced to stretch the measure, or because the author liked the sound of it, or enjoyed whimsy. It diminishes without limiting the possibilities of *smoothness*. Because it is here, in the phrase, it is inseparable from the phrase's notion of smoothness; yet instead of assisting, tends to prevent what that notion of smoothness is from being divulged.

*Crisply* is even more difficult to account for; associated with a scythe it perhaps brings to mind the sound of a scythe in a hayfield, which is surely not the reference here intended; it would be very difficult for such a crispness to associate itself with death, which the scythe represents, or *whim*, or *smoothness* in either the spiritual or fleshly sense. If it implies merely a cleanness, a swiftness of motion in the apparition of death, some other word would have seemed better chosen. If this analysis be correct, the three words are unalterably combined by the force of *crisply* in such a way as to defeat the only possible sense their *thrilling* use would have had. They are, so to speak, only the notions of themselves and those selves must remain forever unknown. All we are left with in such a phrase as this is the strangeness which struck us on our first encounter; and the only difference is that the strangeness is the more intensified the more we prolong the examination. This is another test of poetry: whether we understand the *strangeness* of a poem or not.[7]

As it happens there is an exquisite example of the proper use of this strangeness, this thrill, in another poem of Mr. Cummings: where he speaks of a cathedral before whose face "the streets turn *young* with rain." While there might be some question as to whether the use of *young* presents the only adequate image, there is certainly no question at

---

[7] *Poetic Diction, op. cit.*, pp. 197-8: "It (strangeness) is not synonymous with wonder; for wonder is our reaction to things which we are conscious of not quite understanding, or at any rate of understanding less than we had thought. The element of strangeness in beauty has the contrary effect. It arises from contact with a different kind of *consciousness* from our own, different, yet not so remote that we cannot partly share it, as indeed, in such a connexion, the mere word 'contact' implies. Strangeness, in fact, arouses wonder when we do not understand; esthetic imagination when we do."

all that the phrase is entirely successful: that is, the suggestive feeling in *young* makes the juncture, the emotional conjugation, of streets and rain transparent and perfect. This may be so because there is no element of essential contradiction, in the terms of feeling, between the emotional word *young* and the factual word *streets* and *rain;* or because, positively, what happens to the context by the insertion of *young* is, by a necessary leap of the imagination, something qualified. *Young* may be as abstract a word by itself, as purely relative and notional a word, as any other; but here it is brought into the concrete, is fixed there in a proper habitation. Just because reference is not commonly made either to young streets or young rain, the combination here effected is the more appropriate. The surprise, the contrast, which lend force to the phrase, do not exist in the poem; but exist, if at all, rather in the mind of the reader who did not foresee the slight stretch of his sensibility that the phrase requires—which the phrase not only requires, but necessitates. This, then, is a *strangeness* understood by its own viableness. No preliminary agreement of taste, or contract of symbols, was necessary.

The point is that Mr. Cummings did not here attempt the impossible, he merely stretched the probable. The business of the poet who deals largely with tactual and visual images, as Mr. Cummings does, for the meat of his work, is to escape the prison of his private mind; to use in his poem as little as possible of the experience that happened to him personally, and on the other hand to employ as much as possible of that experience as it is data.

It is idle for a critic to make the familiar statement that the mind of the writer is his work, or that "the style is the man," when by mind and man is meant the private experience of the author. So far as, in this sense, the mind *is* the work, or the style *is* the man, we can understand the work or the style only through an accidental unanimity; and what we understand is likely to be very thin—perhaps only the terms of understanding. For the author himself, in such circumstances, can have understood very little more. He has been pursuing the impossible, when the probable was right at hand; he has been transcending his experience instead of submitting to it. And this is just what Mr. Cummings does in the phrases quoted above.

It would be ungracious to suppose that as a poet "a swoon of synopsis" did not represent to Mr. Cummings a very definite and very suggestive image. But to assent to that image would be a kind of *tour de force;* the application of such assent would imply that because the words appear, and being words contain notions, they must in this particular instance exhibit the undeniable sign of interior feeling. The proper process of poetry designs exactly what the reader will perceive; that is what is meant when a word is said to be inevitable or *juste*. But this exactness of perception can only come about when there is an extreme fidelity on the part of the poet to his words as living things; which he can discover and control—which he must learn, and nourish, and stretch; but which he cannot invent. This unanimity in our possible experience of words implies that the only unanimity which the reader can feel in what the poet represents must be likewise exterior to the poet; must be somehow both anterior and posterior to the poet's own experience. The poet's mind, perhaps, is what he is outside himself with; is what he has learned; is what he knows: it is also what the reader knows. So long as he is content to remain in his private mind, he is unknowable, impenetrable, and sentimental. All his words perhaps must thrill us, because we cannot know them in the very degree that we sympathize with them. But the best thrills are those we have without knowing it.

This essay has proceeded so far on the explicit assumption that the poems of Mr. Cummings are unintelligible, and that no amount of effort on the part of the reader can make them less so. We began by connecting Mr. Cummings to two schools, or groups, which are much the same essentially —the anti-culture group which denies the intelligence, and the group, not limited to writers, of which the essential attitude is most easily defined as sentimental egoism or romantic idealism. Where these schools are most obviously identical is in the poetry they nourish: the avowed interest is the relentless pursuit of the actual in terms of the immediate as the immediate is given, without overt criticism, to the ego. Unintelligibility is a necessary consequence of such a pursuit, if by the intelligible we mean something concrete, qualified, permanent, and public. Poetry, if we understand it, is not in immediacy at all. It is not given to the senses or to the free intuition. Thus, when poetry is written as if its substance were immediate and given, we have as a result a distorted sensibility and a violent inner confusion. We have, if the poet follows his principles, something abstract, vague, impermanent, and essentially private. When every sensation and every word is taken as final and perfect, the substance which sensations report and for which words must stand remains inexplicable. We can understand only by accident.

Of course there is another side to the matter. In a sense anyone can understand Mr. Cummings and his kind by the mere assertion that he does understand. Nothing else is needed but a little natural sympathy and a certain aptness for the resumption of a childish sensibility. In much the same way we understand a stranger's grief—by setting up a private and less painful simulacrum. If we take the most sentimental and romantic writers as they come, there will be always about their works an excited freshness, the rush of sensation and intuition, all the ominous glow of immediacy. They will be eagerly at home in the mystery of life. Adroitness, expertness, readiness for any experience, will enlighten their activities even where they most miserably fail. They are all actors, ready to take any part, for they put themselves, and nothing else, into every part they play. Commonly their real success will depend on the familiarity of the moments into which they sink themselves; they will depend on convention more than others, because they have nothing else to depend on.

So with the poetry of Mr. Cummings we might be altogether contented and pleased, were he himself content with the measure of his actual performance. But no poetry is so pretentious. No poetry ever claimed to mean more; and in making this claim it cannot avoid submitting itself, disastrously, to the criticism of the intelligence. So soon as we take it seriously, trying to discover what it really says about human destiny and the terms of love and death, we see how little material there is in this poetry except the assurance, made with continuous gusto, that the material exists. We look at the poetry. Sometimes one word, in itself vague and cloudy, is made to take on the work of an entire philosophy—like flower. Sometimes words pile themselves up blindly, each defeating the purport of the others. No feeling is ever defined. No emotion betrays a structure. Experience is its own phantoms, and flows willy-nilly. With the reality of experience the reality of language is lost. No metaphor crosses the bridge of tautology, and every simile is unexpanded. All the "thought" is metonymy, yet the substance is never assigned; so in the end we have only the thrill of substance.

Such an art when it pretends to measure life is essentially vicarious; it is a substitute for something that never was—like a tin soldier, or Peter Pan. It has all the flourish of life and every sentimental sincerity. Taken for what it is, it is charming and even instructive. Taken solemnly, as it is meant to be, the distortion by which it exists is too much for it, and it seems a kind of baby-talk.

1930

# 15. And Others

## A. THE EXPERIENCE OF IDEAS[1]

Mr. Tate has a powerful, because an unusually integrated sensibility, and in approaching the experience of it there is an advantage in setting up as a foil of comparison another sensibility, no less powerful perhaps, but less integrated than idiosyncratic, namely that of Mr. Hemingway. All minds may be made to agree upon a greater or less reduction of the terms in which they are enacted; here it is the terms that count, and we want a deliberate emphasis on incongruity. One common feature is enough. Mr. Tate is one of the few men of our time who find in writing both an absorbing *métier* and a responsible allegiance. Mr. Hemingway is equally absorbed in his *métier;* which is our common feature, and in both men it has at least the importance of rarity. It would be hard to think even of the wildest of Mr. Hemingway's adventures and not think of them as fodder for his writing; but, and here the incongruity begins, Mr. Hemingway's writings themselves tend to fly apart at the center, and, such is the mutual irrelevance of elements, to escape at any tangent. Mr. Hemingway lacks, in his writing, a central allegiance, a magnet, the momentum of the organic; he writes to get rid of the weight of experience by recording it, by expressing it like a juice; and he is read largely for similar purposes. Mr. Tate moves in the opposite direction—and this is precisely the agency of a central allegiance, and what the feeling of it provides; he writes to achieve the possession of experience in objective form. Hence the conventions of form are vital to his work and

[1] *Reactionary Essays on Poetry and Ideas,* by Allen Tate. Scribner's.

are its intimate animation, where in Mr. Hemingway's work they are merely incidental to its substantially random progress. Both use forms, but Mr. Hemingway's forms are like molds or scaffolds and Mr. Tate's forms are mediums, the architecture itself; the distinction is our emphasis.

The matter of comparable value is only incidentally in discussion. We want here only a notion of difference in kind. What we value most in Mr. Hemingway is the process of expression, and what we value most in Mr. Tate is the experience of the thing possessed. Process of expression may or may not be form; it may be only a squeezing, a relief, a waste-process, a cursory practical ejaculation. A thing expressed so as to be experienced is everywhere self-critical of its form, as without form it could not be completely experienced but only more or less sentimentally construed. Mr. Leo Stein makes somewhere an analogous distinction that if you look at the sea and are sentimental you will feel *yourself* infinite, but that if you are concerned with the object experienced you may or may not feel that the *sea* is infinite, a much harder thing to feel, and, incidentally, a much more difficult exercise in mystical intuition. Mr. Hemingway draws on the infinite reservoir of sentimental construction, which is why more than any distinguished writer of our time he resents criticism much as a private man resents criticism of his private feelings. Mr. Tate, in his writing, draws on that reservoir for only so much as he can effectively enact in external form, only so much as he can transform into an objective experience, conventionally complete on its own account, like the visual image of the sea; and that is why I assume he compels his work to the maximum point of self-critical scrutiny. Certainly that is why his critical essays, his biographies and his political excursions, are obsessed, no more than his poems but more conspicuously, with the problem of the modes of credible form and with the cognate ulterior problem of the insights which reveal credible forms.

Let us put the distinction between the sensibilities of Mr. Tate and Mr. Hemingway once more, on a slightly different plane, and be done with it. To Mr. Hemingway experi-

ence is unique and his own and self-created. To Mr. Tate
events do not become experience until the imagination creates them in objective form. The act of experience, in the
arts, transpires only in form. What does not transpire cannot
be said to have been experienced, though one is affected
by it and may suffer from it and though it is available to
every sentimental construction and every desperation of
what is usually called the life of action—the life where we
mostly live of action without experience. In Mr. Hemingway, finally, you escape experience in sentimental action;
and a very good escape. In Mr. Tate, where he is successful,
you achieve experience and escape, for the moment, the
burden of action in reaction. Hence Mr. Tate's title and
hence his value, which is the highest or the most fundamental of which the imagination is capable.

Now let us forget Mr. Hemingway and witness the operation of Mr. Tate's sensibility without, so far as possible, the
foil of any comparison at all except the inner foils he himself provides. We are brought back at once and everywhere
to the problems of credible form and the insights that make
them available. Credible form is effective form, the effect
is of persuasion, and the persuasion is of the only absolute
we can ever justly assert—the absolute actuality of a given
experience. Form rises from two sources which are inseparable in the event but which may be distinguished in emphatic discourse. There is the form won from the pursuit of
craft; and there is the form which is not won but is possessed in a body of belief or myth or religion—the body of
fundamental conventional insight. Both elements of form
represent the capacity and the means of experience in the
sense distinguished above. Mr. Tate's emphasis in these essays is upon the relation between form and insight; but
such is the vitality of his own insight that he makes his emphasis in terms which might everywhere be translated to
the terms of craft. Insight is the source of craft in imagination as statistics are the source of craft in physics. If you
like, an effective insight is more a technical dodge than the
effective rhyme which clinches it; neither is come by off-
hand, though either may be sudden, and neither may be

separated from the object which they bring to experience, which is the poem. Neither merely participates in the experience, they *are* the experience in symbolic form; and if you distinguish one you have caused the other, if obliviously, to transpire.

In choosing to deal largely with the conditioning insights rather than the perfecting technique of poetry, Mr. Tate exposes himself to two difficulties which cannot be entirely overcome. There is the difficulty about the audience. Most minds cannot accept either the familiar insights they abuse or those of an alien sensibility as fundamentally conventional in character and necessarily imaginative in application; which means they will not think of an insight in a particular instance. A poem is a particular instance. And if by chance the critic does demonstrate the conventional and imaginative aspect the audience will be convinced that you have reduced the insight to an empty formula where actually you have raised it, in the instance, to experienced form. In short, most minds are bound to use as literal forms of action or not at all whatever insights they can muster. The insuperable difficulty is that all of us employ most of our insights literally most of the time, that is without attending to them.

The second difficulty is in the critic, not the subject. The critic here happens to be Mr. Tate but might as well be Mr. Eliot or Mr. Richards. Insights are not amenable to any form but that of experience. Unable to depend upon his reader possessing the appropriate experience, and equally unable to *present* the whole experience in the context of his criticism, the critic is compelled to resort to the substitute or blueprint form of dogmatic statement; which is to say he is compelled to use absolute form to make a provisional statement. There is no way out. Good dogma telescopes its material by concentrating a focus; weak dogma telescopes its material to the vanishing point, leaving only the telescope and the willed notion of vision. In order to know what dogma is good and what weak there must be somewhere a resort to fresh experience, and in the intellectual discourse which comprises the most of criticism there is no sure principle of resort. That is the advantage, which Mr. Tate seldom takes, of pinning the form of insight invariably upon the rhyme that clinches it, when the technical elucidation may be made to cast an implied light or shadow upon the insight.—It is a neat question, however, whether the discussion (not the experience) of technical problems does not lead to rasher dogmatic statements than any Mr. Tate has found necessary in his own mode. A dogma is a conviction, and no conviction, looked at, fails to show a double face, one or the other overdrawn.

The two difficulties naturally involve each other, but if they are together the source of Mr. Tate's weakness—if some of his statements do not seem to apply and others seem only to apply *faute de mieux*—they are, in the consistent attempt to overcome them, also the occasion of his strength. Intensity of effort forces his thinking to the condition of insight and makes his convictions ring imaginatively true. The *conception* of necessity seems provisionally equivalent to the actuality, which is only another way of putting Spinoza's remark that if you recognize a necessity you are free of it. Here I refer particularly to two dominant insights in Mr. Tate's thought as illustrated in the essays "Humanism and Naturalism," "The Profession of Letters in the South," and "Religion in the Old South." One is the insight which reveals that an objective body of religion or myth is prerequisite to a complete culture, and the other is relative to the first, that with the religious there must be composed a political body of myth. Mr. Tate feels the necessity of such bodies so intensely that he is able to write as if they actually existed in the social forms of our day. He "knows" they do not exist; it is them he works for, and he may do himself practical harm; but they have the force of virtual existence because he has experienced their need. Which is perhaps the most lucid possible type of demonstration of the conventional character and imaginative application of major human insights.

It is on the basis of these insights that he criticizes the poetry of Hart Crane, Pound, Bishop, MacLeish, Cummings, and Eliot. The actuality of his insights gives a central allegiance to his own work and directs him to the center of the works of others. And this is all the more plainly seen —which is what I have been leading up to—in the two most important essays in the book, "Emily Dickinson" and "Three Types of Poetry." The connection between the two is that the second completes the first on another level.

Emily Dickinson is made to represent, with an example of performance, the right literary situation, the situation every artist hopes for, when one's greatest work is also the best and most natural work to do. Few writers have been presented with such a situation, and fewer still have been able to take advantage of one. The decay of the New England Theocracy to the point where it provisioned sensibility without riding it, to the point where the literal aspect of authority had been lost in the conventional aspect and where the imaginative application had become the only possible application—this process at this point provided the right literary situation for Emily Dickinson and she became a great poet. Her best poems were composed in insight before she wrote them. Mr. Tate shows us, in short, the experience of Emily Dickinson of the insights that concern him. His argument may be dubious if applied elsewhere; his casual application of it to Henry James does not seem to me to fit; but his experience of it in Emily Dickinson is indubitable.

The "Three Types of Poetry" completes the argument and gives it universal dogmatic form, by which the exceptions seem immediately only apparent. The three types are these: the poetry of the practical will which leans either upon allegory or abstract ideas; the poetry of romantic irony or sentimental self-dramatization; and a third type which is great poetry and subject, as a type, to experience not definition. In the first and second types the will is made to do the work of imagination: Spenser, Shelley, and Tennyson are prototypes, and we are reminded of Mr. Hemingway. In the third type imagination does the work which the will, for all that it is always with us, has never done and never can do, whether in poetry or politics: the work of rendering experience in objective form. I truncate Mr.

Tate's argument because I approve it, and hasten to his conclusion to which I assent.

Poetry finds its true usefulness in its perfect inutility, a focus of repose for the will-driven intellect that constantly shakes the equilibrium of persons and societies with its unrelieved imposition of partial formulas upon the world. When the will and its formulas are put back into an implicit relation with the whole of our experience, we get the true knowledge which is poetry.

That his essays variously "prove" his conclusion is due to Mr. Tate's use of a faculty which has no formula and cannot be willed but which has a craft to master, the faculty whereby dogma remains intimately related to the experience of which it is the convinced form. Poetry, says Mr. Tate, "is ideas tested by experience, by the act of direct apprehension." The best of this criticism is the experience of that test.

1936

## B. JOHN WHEELWRIGHT AND DR. WILLIAMS

With Mr. Wheelwright's *Mirrors of Venus* and Dr. Williams' *Collected Poems* we come upon one man who insists upon his inheritance and attempts to make the most of it and another man who, looking at the botch of the half-inherited, denies that there is anything to inherit. The difference is clear. In Mr. Wheelwright you get the sense of perceptions powerfully backed, fed, and formed; shaped otherwise, celebrated here; a pattern not repeated but rediscovered. In Dr. Williams at his best you get perceptions powerful beyond the possibility of backing; the quotidian burgeoning without trace of yesterday; the commonplace made unique because violently felt. Dr. Williams of course inherits more than he thinks and Mr. Wheelwright not unnaturally suffers from what he inherits. *The Mirrors of Venus* lack richness, the *Collected Poems* lack culmination. Dr. Williams is full of tags that he knows nothing about;

Mr. Wheelwright knows too much about his tags and by over-deliberation occasionally uncovers a void. Mr. Wheelwright moves toward the kinky, the special, the willful, the sport of thought and spirit and form because he is so much aware of the general; Dr. Williams moves toward the flatness of the general because he takes every object, uninspected, as fresh. Mr. Wheelwright deals with moral and spiritual struggle; Dr. Williams deals with the same struggle before it has reached the level of morals and touches on the spirit only by accident. Mr. Wheelwright reaches the explicit through abstraction, by celebrating the fulfillment of pattern:

> Habit is evil,—all habit, even speech;
> and promises prefigure their own breach.

Dr. Williams reaches the implicit through the concrete, by acknowledging what he sees:

> It's a strange courage
> you give me ancient star:
>
> Shine alone in the sunrise
> toward which you lend no part!

There are facts about these two poets which implement our respect for their poetry and put iron in the bias of our general regard for them as figures in the world of our present sensibility. The facts have nothing to do with magnitude, which is a gift of heaven, and of which our appreciation depends as much on distance as on use. We are concerned here merely with the facts of poetic character. There is, to begin with, the fact that Dr. Williams writes exclusively in free verse of an extraordinarily solid and flexible species. Further he despises traditional English meters; the sonnet he thinks good only for doggerel, subverts most intelligences, and has as a word a definitely fascistic meaning. I do not doubt that he may be right for himself; which goes to show only that his intellect is in him so badly proportioned that it interferes with the operation of his sensibility. He needs to work, as it were, under cover; needs to find his work seemingly already done for him when he takes it up. The depth and rightness of his instinct for himself is shown by the mastery in at least twenty poems of varying length of a form adequate in every respect to his poetic purpose. Yvor Winters says that this is the form of free verse, and that it scans, has outer rules and an inner scheme. I refer the reader to Winters' *Primitivism and Decadence* where the technique of Dr. Williams' free verse is fully discussed; I cannot follow the discussion myself, preferring to believe (until I can follow it) that Dr. Williams' astonishing success comes from the combination of a good ear for speech cadence and for the balance of meaning and sound, plus a facility for the double effect of weight and speed. When Mr. Winters (in the *Kenyon Review*, January 1939) compares Dr. Williams to Herrick as equally indestructible, the justice of his comparison, if there be any, must lie in the comparison of incongruities; for the older poet spent his life refining his sensibility in terms of his medium, precisely as the younger has evidently insisted on his sensibility at the *expense* of his medium.

However that may be, what remains of Dr. Williams' medium has been so successful for himself, that many have thought it would be successful for anybody. We are accustomed to think of him as a fertile poet—as fruitful in poems for other poets to read. The pages of the poetry journals every now and then show the results; curiously, the imitation is almost always of the poorer or more crotchety poems. The fact is, it seems to me, that Dr. Williams is a product of fertility. All the signs and recognitions of fertility in his work point backward. He is almost a reduction not a product, a reduction to a highly personalized style to express personal matters—a remarkable, but sterile, sport. You can imitate him, as you can imitate anything; but you cannot incorporate him. In short, his work adds to the sentiments but not to the sensibility.

One reason is that almost everything in Dr. Williams' poetry, including the rendering, is unexpanded notation. He isolates and calls attention to what we are already presently in possession of. Observation of which any good novelist must be constantly capable, here makes a solo appearance:

the advantage is the strength of isolation as an attention-caller to the terrible persistence of the obvious, the unrelenting significance of the banal. Dr. Williams perhaps tries to write as the average man—that man who even less than the normal man hardly exists but is immanent. The conviction which attaches to such fine poems as "The Widow's Lament in Springtime," "Youth and Beauty," or the first section of "Spring and All," perhaps has its source, its rationale, in our instinctive willingness to find ourselves immanently average; just as, perhaps, the conviction attaching to tragic poetry is connected with our fascinated dread of seeing ourselves as normal. Dr. Williams has no perception of the normal; no perspective, no finality—for these involve, for imaginative expression, both the intellect which he distrusts and the imposed form which he cannot understand. What he does provide is a constant freshness and purity of language which infects with its own qualities an otherwise gratuitous exhibition of the sense and sentiment of humanity run-down—averaged—without a trace of significance or a vestige of fate in the fresh familiar face.

The facts about Mr. Wheelwright are very much on the level of significance and fate; they make the matter of his preoccupation; and as they are delivered or aborted they make the failure or the success of his poems. The subject is the significance of friendship and the fate of friends: "the mirror of Venus reflects loved ones as each would be seen." The emphasis—the feeling for pattern—is protestant-christian; divine but apprehended by the individual. The form is that of the sonnet, varied, twisted, transformed, restored: some inverted, some in couplets, some Shakespearean, some in free verse, some in blank verse; for Mr. Wheelwright feels that a sequence of "perfect" sonnets would produce hypnosis in the reader instead of demanding and controlling full attention. That may be so; but I observe that all the nine sonnets that seem to me almost wholly successful depart least from one or other of the stricter sonnet forms, and that those which seem to me to abort their subject matter are in free or metrically unequal verse. (Those which seem to me successful—nine out of thirty-five—are "Abel," "Sanct,"

"Father," "Holy Saturday," "Lens," "Plus," "Phallus," "Mirror," and "Keeper." The worst failures, "Kin," "Parting in Harlem," and "Village Hangover," seem to have been put in for structural reasons without becoming part of the architecture.) Whether the imposition of external form is responsible for the emergence of a whole pattern in these poems, I do not know. The interesting thing is that we have the form and we have the pattern.

It is at least suggestive, that had Mr. Wheelwright everywhere mastered his form, then his pattern would everywhere have been clear. But diagnosis is not cure; and it may be the other way round. None of us today, none even with the full strength of Christian or Marxist belief, can take full advantage—full nourishment—of our heritage, whether of enlivening form or enduring pattern, without extraordinary and almost impossible luck—like that of Thomas Mann in his novels. Without such luck, without that gift, the struggle is too much to the individual and against the society in which he lives. Success seems to involve concession to oneself as well as to society. One is the product as well as the victim of the damage of one's lifetime. We are in the predicament of the protagonist in Mr. Wheelwright's sonnet "Sanct"; protestant to the last drop.

> We know the Love the Father bears the Son
> is a third Mask and that the Three form One.
> We also know, machines and dynamos
> —Preservers in motion; Destroyers in repose—
> like visions of wheeled eyes the addict sees
> are gods, not fashioned in our images.
>
> Then let us state the unknown in the known:
> The mechanism of our friendship, grown
> transcendent over us, maintains a being
> by seeing us when we grow lax in seeing,
> although without our sight it could not be.
> (One states, one does not solve, a mystery.)
> This human Trinity is comprehended
> when doubt of its divinity is ended.

Not only protestant, but also heretical.

> Turn by an inward act upon the world!
> An innocence like our Creator's faith
> is younger than my doubt. You give it birth
> who, seeing evil less veiling than clear rain,
> see truth in thought as through a lens of air.

That is, both inimical and foreign; trying for the scope of the normal rather than the closeness of the average. I fear that the readers of this review may have difficulty with Mr. Wheelwright and none with Dr. Williams; yet I am certain that when he finds that he has understood Mr. Wheelwright, and enjoyed him, he will understand much better what he misses as well as what he enjoys in Dr. Williams. There is room for both poets.

1939

### C. NOTES ON SEVEN POETS[2]

One of these poets—H. D.—has been publishing for some thirty years in a mode which she helped originate, which has not yet entirely broken up, and which she has never been quite able to get ahead of. Her special form of the mode of Imagism—cold, "Greek," fast, and enclosed—has become one of the ordinary resources of the poetic language; it is a regular means of putting down words so that they will keep; and readers are mistaken who confuse its familiarity with flatness or who think facile imitation of the form emulates the perception that goes with the mode. She has herself made sharply varied use of her mode, but she has not exhausted it; she has only—for present changing purposes of a changing mind—partly broken it down into the older, perhaps primary mode of the distich. The relatively long uncoiling of a single spring of image, unpredictable in its completeness, now receives a regular series of impulses

[2] *Land of Unlikeness*, by Robert Lowell; *The Walls Do Not Fall*, by H. D.; *Beast in View*, by Muriel Rukeyser; *The Summer Landscape*, by Rolfe Humphries; *The Wedge*, by William Carlos Williams; *The Winter Sea*, by Allen Tate; *Nevertheless*, by Marianne Moore.

and arrests of alternations and couplings. Those who have a care for such things may try to discover whether it is not the stress between the two modes—as they balance or fail to balance—that gives or collapses the gift of life to these poems. This suggests of course that H. D.'s mode of writing cannot bear very much direct burden of reality and can handle it only by keeping it at a remove; the mode *is* the re-move, a lever, a long pry; but if there is a general loss there is a special gain—a sense of movement a long way off, but pressing in. Consider, for this sense the eighteenth set of distichs from *The Walls Do Not Fall:*

> The Christos-image
> is most difficult to disentangle
>
> from its art-craft junk-shop
> paint-and-plaster medieval jumble
>
> of pain-worship and death-symbol,
> that is why, I suppose, the Dream
>
> deftly stage-managed the bare, clean
> early colonial interior,
>
> without stained-glass, picture,
> image or colour,
>
> for now it appears obvious
> that *Amen* is our Christos.

William Carlos Williams has been publishing almost as long as H. D., and has been writing perhaps longer; his work represents another course, just as limited but differently, of the Imagism that started H. D. off. Where H. D. is, to repeat, cold, "Greek," fast, and enclosed, Williams is warm, "primitive," of varying speed, and open to every wind. He is so excited with actuality at the minimum remove possible to the machine of language that it does not occur to him that reality is other than immediately contingent and equal to the actuality. Sometimes, by grace of insight, it is; more often, by the fouler accident of mere observation, it is not. In the sense that H. D. depends on a mode of poetry—that the description of her formal verbal means assigns the area of significance to her work—Williams does not employ modes; out of the private abundance of his perceptions his poems take each their forms for, almost, the mere sake of print. This is only to say that Williams takes a great, but unredeemed, care for the underlying modes that inhabit the language itself: the modes that give magnanimous reality to the *report* of a conversation; but it is a spoiling care, it lets the modes do as far as possible all the work; and what it spoils is the chance of that high level of performance which is possible, apparently, only to purposive and convicted minds, with just so much of a felt need of order as makes anarchy actual. Williams ignores the sense of order that goes with the long history of the craft of verse by transposing it to the belief that each poem has an intimate order of its own, which it is the business of the poet to make out of the ardor of his direct perceptions. There is no reason why he should not be right for himself, in his own relation to his verse; he can, as he does, find the sonnet as dead as dead; but he is wrong for his readers in their relations to his poems, because his readers, finding the relations (not the substance) of the verses uncontrolled, cannot tell whether or not they are in intelligent contact with the intimate form of the verse. To the reader it seems no more likely that a piece of verse has an intimate form *de novo* than a woman has, and if either did it would not excite him. The most intimate form underlies common flesh. Some of Williams' poems know this for themselves even if their maker did not. Here is one:

> Liquor and love
> when the mind is dull
> focus the wit
> on a world of form
>
> The eye awakes
> perfumes are defined
> inflections
> ride the quick ear
>
> Liquor and love
> rescue the cloudy sense

> banish its despair
> give it a home.

Here, as you might say, intimate form and common form are identical, and are so because of the uniting force, the warming relish, of an old convention about love and drunkenness. There is something a little more in the third quatrain of "The A, B and C of It." The first quatrain says "Love's very fleas are mine," and the second says the fleas recoiled from the odors of the lover.

> Take me then, Spirit of Loneliness
> insatiable Spirit of Love
> and let be—for Time without
> odor is Time without me.

The little more is in certain musical and rhetorical conventions like those in the dead sonnet; that is to say, conventions or habits of perception itself. Form is a way of thinking. It may be observed, too, for what it is worth, that to the accustomed ear Williams' four lines tend to rearrange themselves as three iambic pentameters, with the second and third rhyming. What it suggests is that the poetic mind gets ahead somewhat by counting.

Marianne Moore knows that very well, and has long since mastered an intricately patterned and divided system of syllabic counting upon which both the superficial form and the inward strategy of her poems depend. Like a strange code of manners, you have to get used to her system of counting before you can understand it or feel it at work. It seems arbitrary, capricious, and offish; it stands for more than it shows, and shows, when you are on to it, more than it can possibly stand for; but it keeps a great deal of small perception in large motion and brings a certain amount of deep perception into minute, almost visible focus, and furthermore it is beautifully suited to set off and counterpoint the rhythm of the flashing, dancing everyday idiom in which she so much finds the burden—the made thing— of her poems. Who but Marianne Moore would have thought of counting the syllables in "It's a promise," say, or "Made in Sweden; carts are my trade"? but who could have rendered so close an appreciation of the unaccountable, in her special version of it, except by such counting? Counting is a means of putting up with, of displaying for view, and sometimes of absorbing into the sensibility the unaccountables of perception; and it is all these because it does not touch the perceptions but only manages one aspect of their external relations. Such a system has the advantage that it permits uncontrollable affinities to assert or discover themselves, and the disadvantage that it sometimes lets merely random or casual attractions look as if they were inevitable. And again—as with H. D.'s distichs and Williams' structure by anecdote or observation—the standard meters and conventions find room, whether as ballast or fuel, and right in the system, by self-invocation from the language itself. In *Nevertheless,* for example, the title poem operates both by the Moore system of counting and by the three-beat rhyming iambics; and no one could say that either system did the major work of motion. One can only risk, rather, that no individual metrical system— whether H. D., Williams, or Moore—is sufficient to the needs even of the most individual poet unless the poet is willing to deprive needs for the sake of the system.

It is at this point that the best practice of Marianne Moore differs most from the best practice of H. D. and Williams; as her practice is far more conscious—has far more ascertainable and predictable steps as a learned craft—so it is far more flexible, suggestible, and amenable. As her old poem about Habakkuk says: "Ecstasy affords the occasion, and expediency determines the form"; it is a combined principle which none of her best work has ever forgotten. In the present volume, "A Carriage from Sweden" and "In Distrust of Merits" show the polar opposites of the principle at work, where in the first minute particulars of relish in taste, manners, and craft are worked up into major moral perception, and in the second the obsessively personal moral perception is worked up, or through, a series of large images of war and death. The first called for great pains of expedience within the individual system; in the second, skill consisted more in assent, so to speak, to the tremendous expedience of the institutions of the Christian tradition—of which last it may be remarked that it is not only her war poems that come from assent to that expedience but also the principal poems in each of her volumes. It is thus, to paraphrase another of her old poems, that she is able to see real toads in her imaginary gardens. By cultivating the minute, the particular, the well-turned—by developing taste and skill and pattern—she is able when the occasions fall to perceive the general with all the self-evident force of the particular. "When what we hoped for came to nothing, we revived."

Coming now to Allen Tate's *The Winter Sea*, we find late samples of a body of verse which has worked along very different lines from either H. D. or Williams and which shares with Marianne Moore chiefly a care for craft. The attitudes of conscious sensibility which we mean by the names of Pope, Vergil, Dante, and perhaps Horace, have a good deal to do with the attitudes by which he frames and patterns the material that gets into his poems. All of these poets deliberately apply a received order to the disorder of their own times and their own sensibilities. This is said not to push Tate away but to show in what way he is close to us, and to suggest why he can fight his lost cause as if there was money in it and fight for immediate values with the tenacity and rage that usually go with the lost cause. His order is not archaic; he—his poetry—is the living end to the order which he asserts; his lost cause is the dignity of man, and the rage and tenacity with which he supports the insights that constitute his version of that dignity are utopian and individual, and neither partisan nor inchoate. The revolt of the masses is not for him, except as a target. He knows two things, which are complementary, that order is imposed on chaos and that chaos is the substance of order; the order is real and the chaos is actual; poetry is the means to knowledge of the complementary relation between the two; and Tate would be the first to admit that the poetry often outruns the knowledge just as he would be the first to insist that his poetry is troubled by knowledge that has not quite got into it—or has gotten into the rhythm without having transpired into the words. That is why, perhaps, so many of Tate's poems have in them a commotion that agitates in obscurity without ever quite articulating through the surface. That is why the words play on each other in the seventeenth-century sense. And that is why, above all, Tate resorts to the traditional meters, forms, and allusions and why, having resorted, he is compelled a little to break them down. He is dealing with material that is tractable only to the force of superior form and that is poetically viable only if it transgresses that form. No wonder he has been so much concerned with tension in poetry. The tension is the riches that we feel in his obscurity, and the tension is secured by the tradition of form against which it struggles. If Dr. Johnson's language may be reversed, in Tate's poetry we have images of violence yoked together by form.

No distinction has been made between the problem of order and the chaos in Tate's mind and in his principles of form because, in the poems here printed, the distinction would seem arbitrary; so far as one can see the problem in his poems is one and the same; in each poem there is an assertion of order in the attitude and in the form accompanied by fresh disorder in the substance to which the order both of form and attitude somewhat give in. To experience the giving in is to experience tension and, to repeat, the tension is the poem: the struck sound and resilient echo of the conflict as Tate has actually felt it. The most easily demonstrable example of this sort of tension in this volume is "False Nightmare" which purports to be a willed dream about Walt Whitman and America. It is written—and Whitman is made to speak—in *terza rima;* it has biblical and classical allusions; and it has a series of furious, not quite eluctable images about life in America, capitalism in America, what these two have done to tradition in America, and in conclusion a strange underwater landscape image. (It is curious to reflect that the classical mode in the arts should so often only prove its restraint when it engages itself with the violence and strangeness of the actual: as if order *required* distress.) The *terza rima*—both its strictness as metric and its implied value as a complete structural ordering of emotion—seems to have two functions: to criticize Whitman and to carry and render shapely the fury of the images. It comes off very well in relation to Whitman, as it were unscathed; but it is compelled to give in at some five places to the force of the images, and in giving in takes on some of the force: which is the tension of the poem. Since almost entire quotation would be required of these tercets, a sample is given, rather, from the "Ode to our Young Proconsuls of the Air." It is the last stanza, in which American airmen flying over Everest are asked to spy

> Upon the Tibetan plain
> A limping caravan,
>     Dive, and exterminate
>     The Lama, late
> Survival of old pain.
> Go kill the dying swan.

The attitude is, to say the least of it, difficult, ironic, and has internal echoes that can be understood as one understands gesture, as at once formal, close with old meaning, and untoward, full of the unaccountable. Not so with Rolfe Humphries, whose forms and attitudes in *The Summer Landscape* are on an easy level, full of good sense, charm, coherence, and clear skill: a pleasure unmitigated by difficulty to read, the very kind of verse which there is the greatest tendency to underestimate, and perhaps because of its surest virtue, its fastidiousness of perception which is like that of an animal, in itself, not like that of a man, which may be only in costume. Not that Humphries has no tradition. On the contrary he writes from a very old tradition which is only difficult when you have to speak about it, the tradition of generalized human orthodoxy: this is how you think and feel and act for the most part of your best time, only heightened a little in perception and speeded up a little in meter so that you may the better recognize it, that is to say a little idealized but not at all transcended. In such orthodoxy judgment is by agreement and disagreement, assent and rejection, not by penetration or new creation. It produces not a poetry of causes; there is no *hubris* in it; but there is sweetness and affection and the sense of deep adjustment in the process of being achieved—as, for example, in the poem about refugees which brings up on the image that exile is the role of the universal fellow within. Adjustment, in this orthodoxy, is justness: charity of perception. The exemplar in English verse of Humphries' order of things is perhaps in the earlier work (*Collected Poems*) of Ford Madox Hueffer; but there is a better prose exemplar in the Smollett of *Humphrey Clinker;* by which I wish to remind the reader of the values of what Ezra Pound called the Prose Tradition in Verse, and also to prepare for a quotation:

> Dwell fondly, darling, on delightful things,
> In art, in music, in the way we write:
> On the grave and lovely, on the gay and bright,
> Dwell fondly, darling.
>
> Leave to their sorrow all the septic people,
> Those who, mismanaging their need, create
> Fatigue and failure out of fear and hate
>
> And those for whom inverted guilt revives
> The dwindling interest in the dwindling lives,
> Oh leave these unbecoming to their sorrow!
>
> All visible objects, all invisible angels
> Wait for the happy first and second sight,
> Stable and changeful, graced with love and light,
> Dwell fondly, darling.

On which the best present comment must be the last four lines of another poem:

> Ah, what stubborn stuff
> I waken to find
> In the cells of the mind
> On the sills of the morning.

For Humphries' verse is precisely such stubborn stuff. No doubt in some other way, perhaps at some future stage of itself, so is Muriel Rukeyser's verse. But it seems to me it is the beast not yet in view, or not much in view. *The Beast in View* offers hardly more than its title (from Dryden) as representative of the tradition of craft in English poetry. It is true that she writes a good deal of rough blank verse and a good deal of rough rhyme, half rhyme, and assonance; but her meters remain substantially amorphous: they are either inadvertent or an afterthought, have nothing to do with the speed and little to do with the shape of the poetry. For all the work they do, they had as well not be there: they neither demand nor command attention; and it may be risked that this is because they have never been learned as ways of feeling and attitudes of control for both feeling and emotion, but operate rather as a vehicle of spontaneity. This may be deliberate, but it is wrong just the same. It is a way of writing which can be defended only in the sense that each of us can defend *himself*—and in Miss Rukeyser's book the one poem which shows both cumulus and reserve of strength in its form is a fragment of translation from the German. Thus, in the act of writing, Miss Rukeyser has to depend as much on herself as Williams. Her strength must therefore come from direct perception, reportage, anecdotage, and the forces to which she gives in, whether by accident or on purpose makes little difference. Now there is a great deal of strength to be derived from such sources, but it can only, so to speak, *escape* into verse, and in effect it usually takes over the verse; and it never communicates such strength as is to be found, for example, in the *form* of the following eight lines of John Fletcher.

> Lay a garland on my herse
>   Of the dismal yew;
> Maidens, willow branches bear;
>   Say, I died true.
>
> My love was false, but I was firm
>   From my hour of birth.
> Upon my buried body lie
>   Lightly, gentle earth!

Here the strength of the form—the meter, the musical phrase, the attitude, the whole weight of previous use—

pulls the poem into such a state of autonomous being as
carries a kind of meaning of which the words as mere
bearers of perception would have been incapable; perception goes beyond the words because of the form. The nearest Miss Rukeyser comes to the strength of this sort of form is
in her eight lines called "Song." It is an invidious comparison.

> The world is full of loss; bring, wind, my love,
>    My home is where we make our meeting-place,
>    And love whatever I shall touch and read
>    Within that face.
>
> Lift, wind, my exile from my eyes;
>    Peace to look, life to listen and confess,
>    Freedom to find to find to find
>    That nakedness.

The comparison is invidious because what Miss Rukeyser
has done becomes, confronted with Fletcher's lines, only
the sign of what she ought to have done and could do. If
a comparison is wanted between examples of more "serious" or less "artificial" verse, the title poem may be compared with the passage from Dryden from which it is
drawn; but the reader, lest invidiousness grow wholly ma-
licious, had better do that for himself; with a comparable
depth of intent, the degree of high organization in Dryden's
verse and the degree of looseness in Miss Rukeyser's are not
comparable at all. It may be thrown out for what it is worth
that sex seems to be the source of what organization there
is in Miss Rukeyser's poems, but that until she decides
whether sex is predominantly a force or a sentiment, her
poems and her readers' response to them will be left at a
loss.

Robert Lowell's *Land of Unlikeness* makes a fairer foil
for Miss Rukeyser than either Dryden or Fletcher, because
it shows, not examples of high formal organization achieved,
but poems that are deliberately moving in that direction
and that have things put in to give the appearance of the
movement of form when the movement itself was not
secured. In fact, Lowell's verse is a beautiful case of citation
in any argument in support of the belief in the formal in-

extricability of the various elements of poetry: meter is not meter by itself, any more than attitude or anecdote or perception, though any one of them can be practiced by itself at the expense of the others, when the tensions become mere fanaticism of spirit and of form: conditions, one would suppose, mutually mutilating. Something of that sort seems to be happening in Lowell's verse. It is as if he demanded to *know* (to judge, to master) both the substance apart from the form with which he handles it and the form apart from the substance handled in order to set them fighting. Much as Miss Rukeyser is confused about sex, Lowell is distraught about religion; he does not seem to have decided whether his Roman Catholic belief is the form of a force or the sentiment of a form. The result seems to be that in dealing with men his faith compels him to be fractiously vindictive, and in dealing with faith his experience of men compels him to be nearly blasphemous. By contrast, Dante loved his living Florence and the Florence to come and loved much that he was compelled to envisage in hell, and he wrote throughout in loving meters. In Lowell's *Land of Unlikeness* there is nothing loved unless it be its repellence; and there is not a loving meter in the book. What is thought of as Boston in him fights with what is thought of as Catholic; and the fight produces not a tension but a gritting. It is not the violence, the rage, the denial of this world that grits, but the failure of these to find *in verse* a tension of necessity; necessity has, when recognized, the quality of conflict accepted, not hated. To put a thing, or a quality, or an intimation, *in verse* is for the poet the same job as for the man not a poet the job of putting or holding a thing *in mind*. Mind and verse are mediums of response. If Lowell, like St. Bernard whom he quotes on his title page, conceives the world only as a place of banishment, and poetry (or theology) only as a means of calling up memories of life before banishment, he has the special problem of maturing a medium, both of mind and verse, in which vision and logic combine; and it is no wonder he has gone no further. *Inde anima dissimilis deo inde dissimilis est et sibi.* His title and his motto suggest that the

problem is actual to him; the poems themselves suggest, at
least to an alien mind, that he has so far been able to express
only the violence of its difficulty. As it is now, logic lac-
erates the vision and vision turns logic to zealotry. I quote
the last section of "The Drunken Fisherman" which seems
to me the best-managed poem in the book.

> Is there no way to cast my hook
> Out of this dynamited brook?
> The Fisher's sons must cast about
> When shallow waters peter out.
> I will catch Christ with a greased worm,
> And when the Prince of Darkness stalks
> My bloodstream to its Stygian term . . .
> On water the Man-Fisher walks.

1945

D. THREE NOTES

1. *Plot in Poetry.* Perhaps what is needed is a notion which
reduced to prose—that is to the statement of the logical
structure of the poem—is not silly, but a notion, rather, that
would bear complete working out. In saying this I have no
ax to grind for the logic of the textbooks. Many of the most
suitable structures for poetry are not logical in that sense
at all, and may be self-contradictory in their related parts
under merely logical inspection. Every artist carries various
shades of contradiction along the stream of expression with
no feeling of bafflement. As opposites, as contradictions,
they make a third thing, which is the logic of art: the plot,
the intention and the intension—the things put into tension
—of the work. Aristotle was everlastingly right when he
observed that evidently the plot was the hardest thing to
master, that details were much easier. The reason is simple:
plot, the structure or frame of it, is the greatest non-poetic
agent in poetry; and it must be welded (not riveted) into
the poem. The bad or riveted plot, like your weak allegory
which is an example of the worst kind of willed plot, is
merely overt, exists merely in parallel. What happens in

young poets, in poets short of mastery of plot, is that they use the plots of elder poets as if they were, what they appeared to be when seen, actually integral to the poems instead of the mere integrating agent. In short, your young poet treats plot like a detail, as if it were one more tension in his substance. Plot on the contrary is the very soul of action.

1941

2. *Vocabulary as Poetry.* Poetry is to be regarded as the use of one vocabulary of the language. I have heard a medical man high in his profession assert that all medicine lay in an up-to-date medical dictionary; by which he meant that if he knew his vocabulary he could objectify his knowledge. It is the same thing with poetry, and with as much responsibility for life and death.

1939

3. *Art and Manufacture.* The art of poetry is amply distinguished from the manufacture of verse by the animating presence in the poetry of a fresh idiom: language so twisted and posed in a form that it not only expresses the matter in hand but adds to the stock of available reality.

1935

# 16. A Critic's Job of Work

## I

Criticism, I take it, is the formal discourse of an amateur. When there is enough love and enough knowledge represented in the discourse it is a self-sufficient but by no means an isolated art. It witnesses constantly in its own life its interdependence with the other arts. It lays out the terms and parallels of appreciation from the outside in order to convict itself of internal intimacy; it names and arranges what it knows and loves, and searches endlessly with every fresh impulse or impression for better names and more orderly arrangements. It is only in this sense that poetry (or some other art) is a criticism of life; poetry names and arranges, and thus arrests and transfixes its subject in a form which has a life of its own forever separate but springing from the life which confronts it. Poetry is life at the remove of form and meaning; not life lived but life framed and identified. So the criticism of poetry is bound to be occupied at once with the terms and modes by which the remove was made and with the relation between—in the ambiguous stock phrase—content and form; which is to say with the establishment and appreciation of human or moral value. It will be the underlying effort of this essay to indicate approaches to criticism wherein these two problems —of form and value—will appear inextricable but not confused—like the stones in an arch or the timbers in a building.

These approaches—these we wish to eulogize—are not the only ones, nor the only good ones, nor are they complete. No approach opens on anything except from its own point of view and in terms of its own prepossessions. Let us set against each other for a time the facts of various approaches to see whether there is a residue, not of fact but of principle.

The approaches to—or the escapes from—the central work of criticism are as various as the heresies of the Christian church, and like them testify to occasional needs, fanatic emphasis, special interest, or intellectual pride, all flowing from and even the worst of them enlightening the same body of insight. Every critic like every theologian and every philosopher is a casuist in spite of himself. To escape or surmount the discontinuity of knowledge, each resorts to a particular heresy and makes it predominant and even omnivorous.[1]

For most minds, once doctrine is sighted and is held to be the completion of insight, the doctrinal mode of thinking seems the only one possible. When doctrine totters it seems it can fall only into the gulf of bewilderment; few minds risk the fall; most seize the remnants and swear the edifice remains, when doctrine becomes intolerable dogma.[2] All fall notwithstanding; for as knowledge itself is a fall from the paradise of undifferentiated sensation, so equally every formula of knowledge must fall the moment too much weight is laid upon it—the moment it becomes omnivorous and pretends to be omnipotent—the moment, in short, it is taken literally. Literal knowledge is dead knowledge; and the worst bewilderment—which is always only comparative —is better than death. Yet no form, no formula, of knowledge ought to be surrendered merely because it runs the risk in bad or desperate hands of being used literally; and similarly, in our own thinking, whether it is carried to the point of formal discourse or not, we cannot only afford, we ought scrupulously to risk the use of any concept that seems

[1] The rashest heresy of our day and climate is that exemplified by T. S. Eliot when he postulates an orthodoxy which exists whether anyone knows it or not.

[2] Baudelaire's sonnet *"Le Gouffre"* dramatizes this sentiment at once as he saw it surmounted in Pascal and as it occurred insurmountably in himself.

propitious or helpful in getting over gaps. Only the use should be consciously provisional, speculative, and dramatic. The end-virtue of humility comes only after a long train of humiliations; and the chief labor of humbling is the constant, resourceful restoration of ignorance.

The classic contemporary example of use and misuse is attached to the name of Freud. Freud himself has constantly emphasized the provisional, dramatic character of his speculations: they are employed as imaginative illumination, to be relied on no more and no less than the sailor relies upon his buoys and beacons.[3] But the impetus of Freud was so great that a school of literalists arose with all the mad consequence of schism and heresy and fundamentalism which have no more honorable place in the scientific than the artistic imagination. Elsewhere, from one point of view, Caesarism in Rome and Berlin is only the literalist conception of the need for a positive state. So, too, the economic insights of Marxism, merely by being taken literally in their own field, are held to affect the subject and value of the arts, where actually they offer only a limited field of interest and enliven an irrelevant purpose. It is an amusing exercise—as it refreshes the terms of bewilderment and provides a common clue to the secrets of all the modes of thinking—to restore the insights of Freud and Fascism and Marxism to the terms of the Church; when the sexual drama in Freud becomes the drama of original sin, and the politics of Hitler and Lenin becomes the politics of the City of God in the sense that theology provides both the sanctions of economics and the values of culture. Controversy is in terms absolutely held, when the problems argued are falsely conceived because necessarily abstracted from "real" experience. The vital or fatal nexus is in interest and emotion and is established when the terms can be represented dramatically, almost, as it were, for their own sakes

[3] Santayana's essay "A Long Way Round to Nirvana" (in *Some Turns of Thought in Modern Philosophy*) illustrates the poetic-philosophic character of Freud's insight into death by setting up its analogue in Indian philosophy; and by his comparison only adds to the stimulus of Freud.

alone and with only a pious or ritualistic regard for the doctrines in which they are clothed. The simple, and fatal, example is in the glory men attach to war; the vital, but
precarious example, is in the intermittent conception of free
institutions and the persistent re-formulation of the myth of
reason. Then the doctrines do not matter, since they are
taken only for what they are worth (whatever rhetorical
pretensions to the contrary) as guides and props, as aids to
navigation. What does matter is the experience, the life represented and the value discovered, and both dramatized or
enacted under the banner of doctrine. All banners are
wrong-headed, but they make rallying points, free the impulse to cry out, and give meaning to the cry itself simply
by making it seem appropriate.

It is on some analogue or parallel to these remarks alone
that we understand and use the thought and art of those
whose doctrines differ from our own. We either discount,
absorb, or dominate the doctrine for the sake of the life
that goes with it, for the sake of what is *formed* in the progressive act of thinking. When we do more—when we refine
or elaborate the abstracted notion of form—we play a different game, which has merit of its own like chess, but which
applied to the world we live in produces false dilemmas like
solipsism and infant damnation. There is, taking solipsism
for example, a fundamental distinction. Because of the logical doctrine prepared to support it, technical philosophers
employ years[4] to get around the impasse in which it leaves
them; whereas men of poetic imagination merely use it for
the dramatic insight it contains—as Eliot uses it in the last
section of *The Waste Land;* or as, say, everyone uses the
residual mythology of the Greek religion—which its priests
nevertheless used as literal sanctions for blood and power.

Fortunately, there exist archetypes of unindoctrinated
thinking. Let us incline our minds like reflectors to catch
the light of the early Plato and the whole Montaigne. Is

---

[4] Santayana found it necessary to resort to his only sustained
labor of dialectic, *Scepticism and Animal Faith,* which, though
a beautiful monument of intellectual play, is ultimately valuable for its *incidental* moral wisdom.

not the inexhaustible stimulus and fertility of the Dialogues
and the Essays due as much as anything to the absence of
positive doctrine? Is it not that the early Plato always holds
conflicting ideas in shifting balance, presenting them in con-
test and evolution, with victory only the last shift? Is it not
that Montaigne is always making room for another idea,
and implying always a third for provisional, adjudicating
irony? Are not the forms of both men themselves ironic,
betraying in their most intimate recesses the duplicity of
every thought, pointing it out, so to speak, in the act of
self-incrimination, and showing it not paled on a pin but in
the buff life? . . . Such an approach, such an attempt at
vivid questing, borrowed and no doubt adulterated by our
own needs, is the only rational approach to the multiplication of doctrine and arrogant technologies which fills out
the body of critical thinking. Anything else is a succumbing, not an approach; and it is surely the commonest of
ironies to observe a man altogether out of his depth do his
cause fatal harm merely because, having once succumbed to
an idea, he thinks it necessary to stick to it. Thought is a
beacon not a life-raft, and to confuse the functions is tragic.
The tragic character of thought—as any perspective will
show—is that it takes a rigid mold too soon; chooses destiny
like a Calvinist, in infancy, instead of waiting slowly for
old age, and hence for the most part works against the
world, good sense, and its own object: as anyone may see
by taking a perspective of any given idea of democracy,
of justice, or the nature of the creative act.

Imaginative skepticism and dramatic irony—the modes of
Montaigne and Plato—keep the mind athletic and the spirit
on the stretch. Hence the juvenescence of *The Tempest*,
and hence, too, perhaps, the air almost of precocity in *Back
to Methuselah*. Hence, at any rate, the sustaining power
of such varied works as *The Brothers Karamazov*, *Cousine
Bette*, and *The Magic Mountain*. Dante, whom the faithful
might take to the contrary, is yet "the chief imagination of
Christendom"; he took his doctrine once and for all from
the Church and from St. Thomas and used it as a foil (in
the painter's sense) to give recessiveness, background, and

contrast. Vergil and Aristotle, Beatrice and Bertrans de Born, have in their way as much importance as St. Thomas and the Church. It was this security of reference that made Dante so much more a free spirit than were, say, Swift and Laurence Sterne. Dante had a habit (not a theory) of imagination which enabled him to dramatize with equal ardor and effect what his doctrine blessed, what it assailed, and what, at heart, it was indifferent to. Doctrine was the seed and structure of vision, and for his poems (at least to us) never more. The Divine Comedy no less than the Dialogues and the Essays is a true Speculum Mentis.

With lesser thinkers and lesser artists—and in the defective works of the greater—we have in reading, in criticizing, to supply the skepticism and the irony, or, as may be, the imagination and the drama, to the degree, which cannot be complete since then we should have had no prompts, that they are lacking. We have to rub the looking-glass clear. With *Hamlet,* for example, we have to struggle and guess to bring the motive out of obscurity: a struggle which, aiming at the wrong end, the psychoanalysts have darkened with counsel. With Shelley we have to flesh out the Platonic Ideas, as with Blake we have to cut away, since it cannot be dramatized, all the excrescence of doctrine. With Baudelaire we have sometimes to struggle with and sometimes to suppress the problem of belief, working out the irony implicit in either attitude. Similarly, with a writer like Pascal, in order to get the most out of him, in order to compose an artistic judgment, we must consider such an idea as that of the necessity of the wager, not solemnly as Pascal took it, but as a dramatized possibility, a savage, but provisional irony; and we need to show that the skepticisms of Montaigne and Pascal are not at all the same thing—that where one produced serenity the other produced excruciation.

Again, speaking of André Gide, we should remind ourselves not that he has been the apologist of homosexuality, not that he has become a Communist, but that he is par excellence the French puritan chastened by the wisdom of the body, and that he has thus an acutely scrupulous ethical sensibility. It is by acknowledging the sensibility that we feel the impact of the apologetics and the political conversion. Another necessity in the apprehension of Gide might be put as the recognition of similarity in difference of the precocious small boys in Dostoevski and Gide, e.g. Kolya in *Karamazov* and young George in *The Counterfeiters:* they are small, cruel engines, all naked sensibility and no scruple, demoniacally possessed, and used to keep things going. And these in turn may remind us of another writer who had a predilection for presenting the *terrible* quality of the young intelligence: of Henry James, of the children in *The Turn of the Screw,* of Maisie, and all the rest, all beautifully efficient agents of dramatic judgment and action, in that they take all things seriously for themselves, with the least prejudice of preparation, candidly, with an intelligence life has not yet violated.

Such feats of agility and attention as these remarks illustrate seem facile and even commonplace, and from facile points of view there is no need to take them otherwise. Taken superficially they provide escape from the whole labor of specific understanding; or, worse, they provide an easy vault from casual interpretation to an omnivorous world-view. We might take solemnly and as of universal application the two notions of demonic possession and inviolate intelligence in the children of Gide, Dostoevski, and James, and on that frail nexus build an unassailable theory of the sources of art, wisdom, and value; unassailable because affording only a stereotyped vision, like that of conservative capitalism, without reference in the real world. The maturity of Shakespeare and of Gertrude Stein would then be found on the same childish level.

But we need not go so far in order to draw back. The modes of Montaigne and Plato contain their own safety. Any single insight is good only at and up to a certain point of development and not beyond, which is to say that it is a provisional and tentative and highly selective approach to its field. Furthermore, no observation, no collection of observations, ever tells the whole story; there is always room for more, and at the hypothetical limit of attention and interest there will always remain, quite untouched, the thing itself. Thus the complex character—I say nothing of the value—of the remarks above reveals itself. They flow from a dramatic combination of all the skills and conventions of the thinking mind. They are commonplace only as criticism—as an end-product or function. Like walking, criticism is a pretty nearly universal art; both require a constant intricate shifting and catching of balance; neither can be questioned much in process; and few perform either really well. For either a new terrain is fatiguing and awkward, and in our day most men prefer paved walks or some form of rapid transit—some easy theory or outmastering dogma. A good critic keeps his criticism from becoming either instinctive or vicarious, and the labor of his understanding is always specific, like the art which he examines; and he knows that the sum of his best work comes only to the pedagogy of elucidation and appreciation. He observes facts and he delights in discriminations. The object remains, and should remain, itself, only made more available and seen in a clearer light. The imagination of Dante is for us only equal to what we can know of it at a given time.

Which brings us to what, as T. S. Eliot would say,[5] I have been leading up to all the time, and what has indeed been said several times by the way. Any rational approach is valid to literature and may be properly called critical which fastens at any point upon the work itself. The utility of a given approach depends partly upon the strength of the mind making it and partly upon the recognition of the limits appropriate to it. Limits may be of scope, degree, or relevance, and may be either plainly laid out by the critic himself, or may be determined by his readers; and it is, by

[5] . . . that when "morals cease to be a matter of tradition and orthodoxy—that is, of the habits of the community formulated, corrected, and elevated by the continuous thought and direction of the Church—and when each man is to elaborate his own, then *personality* becomes a thing of alarming importance" (*After Strange Gods*). Thus Mr. Eliot becomes one of those viewers-with-alarm whose next step forward is the very hysteria of disorder they wish to escape. The hysteria of institutions is more dreadful than that of individuals.

our argument, the latter case that commonly falls, since an active mind tends to overestimate the scope of its tools and to take as necessary those doctrinal considerations which habit has made seem instinctive. No critic is required to limit himself to a single approach, nor is he likely to be able to do so; facts cannot be exhibited without comment, and comment involves the generality of the mind. Furthermore, a consciously complex approach like that of Kenneth Burke or T. S. Eliot, by setting up parallels of reference, affords a more flexible, more available, more stimulating standard of judgment—though of course at a greater risk of prejudice—than a single approach. What produces the evil of stultification and the malice of controversy is the confused approach, when the limits are not seen because they tend to cancel each other out, and the driving power becomes emotional.

The worse evil of fanatic falsification—of arrogant irrationality and barbarism in all its forms—arises when a body of criticism is governed by an *idée fixe*, a really exaggerated heresy, when a notion of genuine but small scope is taken literally as of universal application. This is the body of tendentious criticism where, since something is assumed proved before the evidence is in, distortion, vitiation, and absolute assertion become supreme virtues. I cannot help feeling that such writers as Maritain and Massis—no less than Nordau before them—are tendentious in this sense. But even here, in this worst order of criticism, there is a taint of legitimacy. Once we reduce, in a man like Irving Babbitt, the magnitude of application of such notions as the inner check and the higher will, which were for Babbitt paramount—that is, when we determine the limits within which he really worked—, then the massive erudition and acute observation with which his work is packed become permanently available.

And there is no good to be got in objecting to and disallowing those orders of criticism which have an ulterior purpose. Ulterior is not in itself a pejorative, but only so when applied to an enemy. Since criticism is not autonomous—not a light but a process of elucidation—it cannot avoid discovering constantly within itself a purpose or purposes ulterior in the good sense. The danger is in not knowing what is ulterior and what is not, which is much the same as the cognate danger in the arts themselves. The arts serve purposes beyond themselves; the purposes of what they dramatize or represent at that remove from the flux which gives them order and meaning and value; and to deny those purposes is like asserting that the function of a handsaw is to hang above a bench and that to cut wood is to belittle it. But the purposes are varied and so bound in his subject that the artist cannot always design for them. The critic, if that is his bent, may concern himself with those purposes or with some one among them which obsess him; but he must be certain to distinguish between what is genuinely ulterior to the works he examines and what is merely irrelevant; and he must further not assume except within the realm of his special argument that other purposes either do not exist or are negligible or that the works may not be profitably discussed apart from ulterior purposes and as examples of dramatic possibility alone.

## II

Three examples of contemporary criticism primarily concerned with the ulterior purposes of literature should, set side by side, exhibit both the defects and the unchastened virtues of that approach; though they must do so only tentatively and somewhat invidiously—with an exaggeration for effect. Each work is assumed to be a representative ornament of its kind, carrying within it the seeds of its own death and multiplication. Let us take then, with an eye sharpened by the dangers involved, Santayana's essay on Lucretius (in *Three Philosophical Poets*), Van Wyck Brooks's *Pilgrimage of Henry James,* and Granville Hicks's *The Great Tradition*. Though that of the third is more obvious in our predicament, the urgency in the approach is equal in all three.

Santayana's essay represents a conversion or transvalu-

ation of an actually poetic ordering of nature to the terms
of a moral philosophy which, whatever its own responsibilities, is free of the special responsibility of poetry. So ably
and so persuasively is it composed, his picture seems complete and to contain so much of what was important in
Lucretius that *De Rerum Natura* itself can be left behind.
The philosophical nature of the insight, its moral scope and
defect, the influence upon it of the Democritan atom, once
grasped intellectually as Santayana shows us how to grasp
them, seem a good substitute for the poem and far more
available. But—what Santayana remembers but does not
here emphasize since it was beyond his immediate interest
—there is no vicar for poetry on earth. Poetry is idiom, a
special and fresh saying, and cannot for its life be said
otherwise; and there is, finally, as much difference between
words used about a poem and the poem as there is between
words used about a painting and the painting. The gap
is absolute. Yet I do not mean to suggest that Santayana's essay—that any philosophical criticism—is beside the
point. It is true that the essay may be taken as a venture
in philosophy for its own sake, but it is also true that it
reveals a body of facts about an ulterior purpose in Lucretius' poem—doubtless the very purpose Lucretius himself
would have chosen to see enhanced. If we return to the
poem it will be warmer as the facts come alive in the verse.
The re-conversion comes naturally in this instance in that,
through idioms differently construed but equally imaginative, philosophy and poetry both buttress and express
moral value. The one enacts or represents in the flesh what
the other reduces to principle or raises to the ideal. The
only precaution the critic of poetry need take is negative:
that neither poetry nor philosophy can ever fully satisfy
the other's purposes, though each may seem to do so if
taken in an ulterior fashion. The relationship is mutual but
not equivalent.

When we turn deliberately from Santayana on Lucretius
to Van Wyck Brooks on Henry James, we turn from the
consideration of the rational ulterior purpose of art to the
consideration of the irrational underlying predicament of

the artist himself, not only as it predicts his art and is reflected in it, but also, and in effect predominantly, as it represents the conditioning of nineteenth-century American culture. The consideration is sociological, the method of approach that of literary psychology, and the burden obsessive. The conversion is from literary to biographical values. Art is taken not as the objectification or mirroring of social experience but as a personal expression and escape-fantasy of the artist's personal life in dramatic extension. The point for emphasis is that the cultural situation of Henry James's America stultified the expression and made every escape ineffectual—even that of Europe. This theme—the private tragedy of the unsuccessful artist—was one of Henry James's own; but James saw it as typical or universal—as a characteristic tragedy of the human spirit—illustrated, as it happened for him, against the Anglo-American background. Brooks, taking the same theme, raises it to an obsession, an omnivorous concept, under which all other themes can be subsumed. Applied to American cultural history, such obsessive thinking is suggestive in the very exaggeration of its terms, and applied to the private predicament of Henry James the man it dramatically emphasizes —uses for all and more than it is worth—an obvious conflict that tormented him. As history or as biography the book is a persuasive imaginative picture, although clearly not the only one to be seen. Used as a nexus between James the man and the novels themselves, the book has only possible relevance and cannot be held as material. *Hamlet,* by a similar argument, could be shown to be an unsuccessful expression of Shakespeare's personality. To remain useful in the field of literary criticism, Brooks's notions ought to be kept parallel to James's novels but never allowed to merge with them. The corrective, the proof of the gap, is perhaps in the great air of freedom and sway of mastery that pervades the Prefaces James wrote to his collected edition. For James art was enough because it molded and mirrored and valued all the life he knew. What Brooks's parallel strictures can do is to help us decide from another point of view whether to choose the values James dramatized. They cannot affect or elucidate but rather—if the gap is closed by will—obfuscate the values themselves.

In short, the order of criticism of which Brooks is a masterly exponent, and which we may call the psycho-sociological order, is primarily and in the end concerned less with the purposes, ulterior or not, of the arts than with some of the ulterior *uses* to which the arts can be appropriately put. Only what is said in the meantime, by the way—and does not depend upon the essence of argument but only accompanies it—can be applied to the arts themselves. There is nothing, it should be added, in Brooks's writings to show that he believes otherwise or would claim more; he is content with that scope and degree of value to which his method and the strength of his mind limit him; and his value is the greater and more urgent for that.

Such tacit humility, such implicit admission of contingency, are not immediate characteristics of Granville Hicks's *The Great Tradition,* though they may, so serious is his purpose, be merely virtues of which he deliberately, for the time being and in order to gain his point, deprives himself of the benefit. If that is so, however expedient his tactics may seem on the short view they will defeat him on the long. But let us examine the book on the ground of our present concern alone. Like Brooks, Hicks presents an interpretation of American literature since the Civil War, dealing with the whole body rather than single figures. Like Brooks he has a touchstone in an obsessive idea, but where we may say that Brooks *uses* his idea—as we think for more than it is worth—we must say that Hicks is victimized by his idea to the point where the travail of judgment is suspended and becomes the mere reiteration of a formula. He judges literature as it expressed or failed to express the economic conflict of classes sharpened by the industrial revolution, and he judges individual writers as they used or did not use an ideology resembling the Marxist analysis as prime clue to the clear representation of social drama. Thus Howells comes off better than Henry James, and Frank Norris better than Mark Twain, and, in our own day, Dos Passos is stuck on a thin eminence that must alarm him.

Controversy is not here a profitable exercise, but it may be said for the sake of the record that although every period of history presents a class struggle, some far more acute than our own, the themes of great art have seldom lent themselves to propaganda for an economic insight, finding, as it happened, religious, moral, or psychological —that is to say, interpretative—insights more appropriate impulses. If *Piers Plowman* dealt with the class struggle, *The Canterbury Tales* did not, and Hicks would be hard put, if he looked sharp, to make out a better case of social implication in Dostoevski than in Henry James.

What vitiates *The Great Tradition* is its tendentiousness. Nothing could be more exciting, nothing more vital, than a book by Hicks which discovered and examined the facts of a literature whose major theme hung on an honest, dramatic view of the class struggle—and there is indeed such a literature now emerging from the depression. And on the other hand it would be worth while to have Hicks sharpen his teeth on all the fraudulent or pseudo art which actually slanders the terms of the class and every other struggle.

The book with which he presents us performs a very different operation. There is an initial hortatory assumption that American literature ought to represent the class struggle from a Marxist viewpoint, and that it ought thus to be the spur and guide to political action. Proceeding, the point is either proved or the literature dismissed and its authors slandered. Hicks is not disengaging for emphasis and contemporary need an ulterior purpose; he is not writing criticism at all; he is writing a fanatic's history and a casuist's polemic, with the probable result—which is what was meant by suggesting above that he had misconceived his tactics —that he will convert no one who retains the least love of literature or the least knowledge of the themes which engage the most of life. It should be emphasized that there is no more quarrel with Hicks's economic insight as such than there was with the insights of Santayana and Van Wyck Brooks. The quarrel is deeper. While it is true and good that the arts may be used to illustrate social propaganda —though it is not a great use—you can no more use an economic insight as your chief critical tool than you can make much out of the Mass by submitting the doctrine of trans-substantiation to chemical analysis.

These three writers have one great formal fact in common, which they illustrate as differently as may be. They are concerned with the separable content of literature, with what may be said without consideration of its specific setting and apparition in a form; which is why, perhaps, all three leave literature so soon behind. The quantity of what can be said directly about the content alone of a given work of art is seldom great, but the least saying may be the innervation of an infinite intellectual structure, which, however valuable in itself, has for the most part only an asserted relation with the works from which it springs. The sense of continuous relationship, of sustained contact, with the works nominally in hand is rare and when found uncommonly exhilarating; it is the fine object of criticism: as it seems to put us in direct possession of the principles whereby the works move without injuring or disintegrating the body of the works themselves. This sense of intimacy by inner contact cannot arise from methods of approach which hinge on seized separable content. We have constantly—if our interest is really in literature—to prod ourselves back, to remind ourselves that there was a poem, a play, or a novel of some initial and we hope terminal concern, or we have to falsify facts and set up fictions[6] to the effect that no matter what we are saying we are really talking about art after all. The question must often be whether the prodding and reminding is worth the labor, whether we might

[6] Such a fiction, if not consciously so contrived, is the fiction of the organic continuity of all literature as expounded by T. S. Eliot in his essay, "Tradition and the Individual Talent." The locus is famous and represents that each new work of art slightly alters the relationships among the whole order of existing works. The notion has truth, but it is a mathematical truth and has little relevance to the arts. Used as Eliot uses it, it is an experimental conceit and pushes the mind forward. Taken seriously it is bad constitutional law, in the sense that it would provoke numberless artificial and insoluble problems.

not better assign the works that require it to a different category than that of criticism.

## III

Similar strictures and identical precautions are necessary in thinking of other, quite different approaches to criticism, where if there are no ulterior purposes to allow for there are other no less limiting features—there are certainly such, for example, for me in thinking of my own. The ulterior motive, or the limiting feature, whichever it is, is a variable constant. One does not always know what it is, nor what nor how much work it does; but one always knows it is there—for strength or weakness. It may be only the strength of emphasis—which is necessarily distortion; or it may be the worse strength of a simplifying formula, which skeletonizes and transforms what we want to recognize in the flesh. It may be only the weakness of what is unfinished, undeveloped, or unseen—the weakness that follows on emphasis; or it may be the weakness that shows when pertinent things are deliberately dismissed or ignored, which is the corresponding weakness of the mind strong in formula. No mind can avoid distortion and formula altogether, nor would wish to; but most minds rush to the defense of qualities they think cannot be avoided, and that, in itself, is an ulterior motive, a limiting feature of the mind that rushes. I say nothing of one's personal prepossessions, of the damage of one's private experience, of the malice and false tolerance they inculcate into judgment. I know that my own essays suffer variously, but I cannot bring myself to specify the indulgences I would ask; mostly, I hope, that general indulgence which consists in the task of bringing my distortions and emphases and opinions into balance with other distortions, other emphases, and better opinions.

But rather than myself, let us examine briefly, because of their differences from each other and from the three critics already handled, the modes of approach to the act of criticism and habits of critical work of I. A. Richards, Kenneth

Burke, and S. Foster Damon. It is to characterize them and
to judge the *character* of their work—its typical scope and
value—that we want to examine them. With the objective
validity of their varying theories we are not much here concerned. Objective standards of criticism, as we hope them
to exist at all, must have an existence anterior and superior
to the practice of particular critics. The personal element in
a given critic—what he happens to know and happens to be
able to understand—is strong or obstinate enough to reach
into his esthetic theories; and as most critics do not have the
coherence of philosophers it seems doubtful if any outsider
could ever reach the same conclusions as the critic did by
adopting his esthetics. Esthetics sometimes seems only as
implicit in the practice of criticism as the atomic physics is
present in sunlight when you feel it.

But some critics deliberately expand the theoretic phase
of every practical problem. There is a tendency to urge the
scientific principle and the statistical method, and in doing
so to bring in the whole assorted world of thought. That
Mr. Richards, who is an admirable critic and whose love
and knowledge of poetry are incontestable, is a victim of the
expansiveness of his mind in these directions, is what characterizes, and reduces, the scope of his work as literary criticism. It is possible that he ought not to be called a literary
critic at all. If we list the titles of his books we are in a
quandary: *The Foundations of Aesthetics, The Meaning of
Meaning* (these with C. K. Ogden), *The Principles of Literary Criticism, Science and Poetry, Practical Criticism,
Mencius on the Mind,* and *Coleridge on Imagination.* The
apparatus is so vast, so labyrinthine, so inclusive—and the
amount of actual literary criticism is so small that it seems
almost a by-product instead of the central target. The slightest volume, physically, *Science and Poetry,* contains propor-
tionally the most literary criticism, and contains, curiously,
his one obvious failure in appreciation—since amply re-
dressed—, his misjudgment of the nature of Yeats's poetry.
His work is for the most part *about* a department of the
mind which includes the pedagogy of sensibility and the
practice of literary criticism. The matters he investigates are

the problems of belief, of meaning, of communication, of the nature of controversy, and of poetic language as the supreme mode of imagination. The discussion of these problems is made to focus for the most part on poetry because poetry provides the only great monuments of imagination available to verbal imagination. His bottom contention might I think be put as this: that words have a synergical power, in the realms of feeling, emotion, and value, to create a reality, or the sense of it, not contained in the words separately; and that the power and the reality as experienced in great poetry make the chief source of meaning and value for the life we live. This contention I share; except that I should wish to put on the same level, as sources of meaning and value, modes of imagination that have no medium in words—though words may call on them—and are not susceptible of verbal re-formulation: the modes of great acting, architecture, music, and painting. Thus I can assent to Mr. Richards' positive statement of the task of criticism, because I can add to it positive tasks in analogous fields: "To recall that poetry is the supreme use of language, man's chief co-ordinating instrument, in the service of the most integral purposes of life; and to explore, with thoroughness, the intricacies of the modes of language as working modes of the mind." But I want this criticism, engaged in this task, constantly to be confronted with examples of poetry, and I want it so for the very practical purpose of assisting in pretty immediate appreciation of the use, meaning, and value of the language in that particular poetry. I want it to assist in doing for me what it actually assists Mr. Richards in doing, whatever that is, when he is reading poetry for its own sake.

Mr. Richards wants it to do that, too, but he wants it to do a great deal else first. Before it gets to actual poetry (from which it is said to spring) he wants literary criticism to become something else and much more: he wants it to become, indeed, the master department of the mind. As we become aware of the scope of poetry, we see, according to Mr. Richards, that "the study of the modes of language becomes, as it attempts to be thorough, the most fundamental and extensive of all inquiries. It is no preliminary or preparation for other profounder studies. . . . The very formation of the objects which these studies propose to examine takes place through the processes (of which imagination and fancy are modes) by which the words they use acquire their meanings. Criticism is the science of these meanings. . . . Critics in the future must have a theoretical equipment which has not been felt to be necessary in the past. . . . But the critical equipment will not be *primarily* philosophical. It will be rather a command *of the methods of general linguistic analysis.*"[7] I think we may take it that *Mencius on the Mind* is an example of the kind of excursion on which Mr. Richards would lead us. It is an excursion into multiple definition, and it is a good one if that is where you want to go and are in no hurry to come back: you learn the enormous variety and complexity of the operations possible in the process of verbally describing and defining brief passages of imaginative language and the equal variety and complexity of the result; you learn the practical impossibility of verbally ascertaining what an author means—and you hear nothing of the other ways of apprehending meaning at all. The instance is in the translation of Mencius, because Mr. Richards happens to be interested in Mencius, and because it is easy to see the difficulties of translating Chinese; but the principles and method of application would work as well on passages from Milton or Rudyard Kipling. The real point of Mr. Richards' book is the impossibility of understanding, short of a lifetime's analysis and compensation, the mechanism of meaning in even a small body of work. There is no question of the exemplary value and stimulus of Mr. Richards' work; but there is no question either that few would care to emulate him for any purpose of literary criticism. In the first place it would take too long, and in the second he does not answer the questions literary criticism would put. The literal adoption of Mr. Richards' approach to literary criticism would stultify the very power it was aimed to enhance—the power of imaginative appre-

[7] All quoted material is from the last four pages of *Coleridge on Imagination.*

hension, of imaginative co-ordination of varied and separate elements. Mr. Richards' work is something to be aware of, but deep awareness is the limit of use. It is notable that in his admirable incidental criticism of such poets as Eliot, Lawrence, Yeats, and Hopkins, Mr. Richards does not himself find it necessary to be more than aware of his own doctrines of linguistic analysis. As philosophy from Descartes to Bradley transformed itself into a study of the modes of knowing, Mr. Richards would transform literary criticism into the science of linguistics. Epistemology is a great subject, and so is linguistics; but they come neither in first nor final places; the one is only a fragment of wisdom and the other only a fraction of the means of understanding. Literary criticism is not a science—though it may be the object of one; and to try to make it one is to turn it upside down. Right side up, Mr. Richards' contribution shrinks in weight and dominion but remains intact and preserves its importance. We may conclude that it was the newness of his view that led him to exaggerate it, and we ought to add the probability that had he not exaggerated it we should never have seen either that it was new or valuable at all.

From another point of view than that of literary criticism, and as a contribution to a psychological theory of knowledge, Mr. Richards' work is not heretical, but is integral and integrating, and especially when it incorporates poetry into its procedure; but from our point of view the heresy is profound—and is far more distorting than the heresies of Santayana, Brooks, and Hicks, which carry with them obviously the impetus for their correction. Because it is possible to apply scientific methods to the language of poetry, and because scientific methods engross their subject matter, Mr. Richards places the whole burden of criticism in the application of a scientific approach, and asserts it to be an implement for the judgment of poetry. Actually, it can handle only the language and its words and cannot touch—except by assertion—the imaginative product of the words which is poetry: which is the object revealed or elucidated by criticism. Criticism must be concerned, first and last—whatever comes between—with the poem as it is read and as what it represents is felt. As no amount of physics and physiology can explain the *feeling* of things seen as green or even certify their existence, so no amount of linguistic analysis can explain the *feeling* or existence of a poem. Yet the physics in the one case and the linguistics in the other may be useful both to the poet and the reader. It may be useful, for example, in extracting the facts of meaning from a poem, to show that, whether the poet was aware of it or not, the semantic history of a word was so and so; but only if the semantics can be resolved into the ambiguities and precisions created by the poem. Similarly with any branch of linguistics; and similarly with the applications of psychology —Mr. Richards' other emphasis. No statistical description can either explain or demean a poem unless the description is translated back to the imaginative apprehension or feeling which must have taken place without it. The light of science is parallel or in the background where feeling or meaning is concerned. The Oedipus complex does not explain *Oedipus Rex;* not that Mr. Richards would think it did. Otherwise he could not believe that "poetry is the supreme use of language" and more, could not convey in his comments on T. S. Eliot's *Ash Wednesday* the actuality of his belief that poetry is the supreme use.

It is the interest and fascination of Mr. Richards' work in reference to different levels of sensibility, including the poetic, that has given him both a wide and a penetrating influence. No literary critic can escape his influence; an influence that stimulates the mind as much as anything by showing the sheer excitement as well as the profundity of the problems of language—many of which he has himself made genuine problems, at least for readers of poetry: an influence, obviously, worth deliberately incorporating by reducing it to one's own size and needs. In T. S. Eliot the influence is conspicuous if slight. Mr. Kenneth Burke is considerably indebted, partly directly to Mr. Richards, partly to the influences which acted upon Mr. Richards (as Bentham's theory of Fictions) and partly to the frame of mind which helped mold them both. But Mr. Burke is clearly a different person—and different from anyone writing today;

and the virtues, the defects, and the élan of his criticism are his own.

Some years ago, when Mr. Burke was an animating influence on the staff of *The Dial*, Miss Marianne Moore published a poem in that magazine called "Picking and Choosing" which contained the following lines.

> and Burke is a
> psychologist—of acute and raccoon-
> like curiosity. *Summa diligentia;*
> to the humbug, whose name is so amusing—very young and
> very rushed, Caesar crossed the Alps on the 'top of a
> *diligence.'* We are not daft about the meaning but this
> familiarity with wrong meanings puzzles one.

In the index of Miss Moore's *Observations,* we find under Burke that the reference is to Edmund, but it is really to Kenneth just the same. There is no acuter curiosity than Mr. Burke's engaged in associating the meanings, right and wrong, of the business of literature with the business of life and vice versa. No one has a greater awareness—not even Mr. Richards—of the important part wrong meanings play in establishing the consistency of right ones. The writer of whom he reminds us, for the buoyancy and sheer remarkableness of his speculations, is Charles Santiago Saunders Peirce; one is enlivened by them without any *necessary* reference to their truth; hence they have truth for their own purposes, that is, for their own uses. Into what these purposes or uses are it is our present business to inquire.

As Mr. Richards in fact uses literature as a springboard or source for a scientific method of a philosophy of value, Mr. Burke uses literature, not only as a springboard but also as a resort or home, for a philosophy or psychology of moral possibility. Literature is the hold-all and the persuasive form for the patterns of possibility. In literature we see unique possibilities enacted, actualized, and in the moral and psychological philosophies we see the types of possibility generalized, see their abstracted, convertible forms. In some literature, and in some aspects of most literature of either great magnitude or great possibility, we see, so to speak, the enactment or dramatic representation of the type or patterns. Thus Mr. Burke can make a thrilling intellectual pursuit of the sub-intelligent writing of Erskine Caldwell: where he shows that Caldwell gains a great effect of humanity by putting in *none himself,* appealing to the reader's common stock: i.e., what is called for so desperately by the pattern of the story must needs be generously supplied. Exactly as thrilling is his demonstration of the great emotional role of the outsider as played in the supremely intelligent works of Thomas Mann and André Gide. His common illustrations of the pervasive spread of symbolic pattern are drawn from Shakespeare and from the type of the popular or pulp press. I think that on the whole his method could be applied with equal fruitfulness either to Shakespeare, Dashiell Hammet, or Marie Corelli; as indeed he does apply it with equal force both to the field of anarchic private morals and to the outline of a secular conversion to Communism—as in, respectively, *Toward a Better Life* and *Permanence and Change.*

The real harvest that we barn from Mr. Burke's writings is his presentation of the types of ways the mind works in the written word. He is more interested in the psychological means of the meaning, and how it might mean (and often really does) something else, than in the meaning itself. Like Mr. Richards, but for another purpose, he is engaged largely in the meaning of meaning, and is therefore much bound up with considerations of language, but on the plane of emotional and intellectual patterns rather than on the emotional plane; which is why his essays deal with literature (or other writings) as it dramatizes or unfolds character (a character is a pattern of emotions and notions) rather than with lyric or meditative poetry which is Mr. Richards' field. So we find language containing felt character as well as felt co-ordination. The representation of character, and of aspiration and symbol, must always be rhetorical; and therefore we find that for Mr. Burke the rightly rhetorical is the profoundly hortatory. Thus literature may be seen as an inexhaustible reservoir of moral or character philosophies in action.

It is the technique of such philosophies that Mr. Burke

explores, as he pursues it through curiosities of development and conversion and duplicity; it is the technique of the notions that may be put into or taken out of literature, but it is only a part of the technique of literature itself. The final reference is to the psychological and moral possibilities of the mind, and these certainly do not exhaust the technique or the reality of literature. The reality in literature is an object of contemplation and of feeling, like the reality of a picture or a cathedral, not a route of speculation. If we remember this and make the appropriate reductions here as elsewhere, Mr. Burke's essays become as pertinent to literary criticism as they are to the general ethical play of the mind. Otherwise they become too much a methodology for its own sake on the one hand, and too much a philosophy at one remove on the other. A man writes as he can; but those who use his writings have the further responsibility of redefining their scope, an operation (of which Mr. Burke is a master) which alone uses them to the full.

It is in relation to these examples which I have so unjustly held up of the philosophical, the sociological or historical, the tendentious, the semasiological, and the psychological approaches to criticism that I wish to examine an example of what composes, after all, the great bulk of serious writings about literature: a work of literary scholarship. Upon scholarship all other forms of literary criticism depend, so long as they are criticism, in much the same way that architecture depends on engineering. The great editors of the last century—men such as Dyce and Skeat and Gifford and Furness—performed work as valuable to the use of literature, and with far less complement of harm, as men like Hazlitt and Arnold and Pater. Scholarship, being bent on the collection, arrangement, and scrutiny of facts, has the positive advantage over other forms of criticism that it is a co-operative labor, and may be completed and corrected by subsequent scholars; and it has the negative advantage that it is not bound to investigate the mysteries of meaning or to connect literature with other departments of life—it has only to furnish the factual materials for such investigations and connections. It is not surprising to find that the great schol-

ars are sometimes good critics, though usually in restricted
fields; and it is a fact, on the other hand, that the great
critics are themselves either good scholars or know how to
take great advantage of scholarship. Perhaps we may put it
that for the most part dead critics remain alive in us to the
extent that they form part of our scholarship. It is Dr. Johnson's statements of fact that we preserve of him as a critic;
his opinions have long since become a part of that imaginative structure, his personality. A last fact about scholarship
is this, that so far as its conclusions are sound they are subject to use and digestion not debate by those outside the
fold. And of bad scholarship as of bad criticism we have
only to find means to minimize what we cannot destroy.

It is difficult to find an example of scholarship pure and
simple, of high character, which can be made to seem relevant to the discussion in hand. What I want is to bring into
the discussion the omnipresence of scholarship as a background and its immediate and necessary availability to
every other mode of approach. What I want is almost anonymous. Failing that, I choose S. Foster Damon's *William
Blake* (as I might have taken J. L. Lowes's *Road to
Xanadu*) which, because of its special subject matter, brings
its scholarship a little nearer the terms of discussion than a
Shakespeare commentary would have done. The scholar's
major problem with Blake happened to be one which many
scholars could not handle, some refused to see, and some
fumbled. A great part of Blake's meaning is not open to
ordinarily well-instructed readers, but must be brought out
by the detailed solution of something very like an enormous
and enormously complicated acrostic puzzle. Not only earnest scrutiny of the poems as printed, but also a study of
Blake's reading, a reconstruction of habits of thought, and
an industrious piecing together into a consistent key of thou-
sands of clues throughout the work, were necessary before
many even of the simplest appearing poems could be ex-
plained. It is one thing to explain a mystical poet, like
Crashaw, who was attached to a recognized church, and
difficult enough; but it is a far more difficult thing to explain
a mystical poet like Blake, who was so much an eclectic in

his sources that his mystery as well as his apprehension of it
was practically his own. All Mr. Damon had to go on besides the texts, and the small body of previous scholarship
that was pertinent, were the general outlines of insight to
which all mystics apparently adhere. The only explanation
would be in the facts of what Blake meant to mean when
he habitually said one thing in order to hide and enhance
another; and in order to be convincing—poetry being what
it is—the facts adduced had to be self-evident. It is not a
question here whether the mystery enlightened was worth
it. The result for emphasis is that Mr. Damon made Blake
exactly what he seemed least to be, perhaps the most intellectually consistent of the greater poets in English. Since the
chief weapons used are the extended facts of scholarship,
the picture Mr. Damon produced cannot be destroyed even
though later and other scholarship modifies, re-arranges, or
adds to it with different or other facts. The only suspicion
that might attach is that the picture is too consistent and
that the facts are made to tell too much, and direct, but
instructed, apprehension not enough.

My point about Mr. Damon's work is typical and double.
First, that the same sort of work, the adduction of ultimately
self-evident facts, can be done and must be done in other
kinds of poetry than Blake's. Blake is merely an extreme
and obvious example of an unusually difficult poet who hid
his facts on purpose. The work must be done to the appropriate degree of digging out the facts in all orders of poetry
—and especially perhaps in contemporary poetry, where we
tend to let the work go either because it seems too easy or
because it seems supererogatory. Self-evident facts are
paradoxically the hardest to come by; they are not evident
till they are seen; yet the meaning of a poem—the part of it
which is intellectually formulable—must invariably depend
on this order of facts, the facts about the meanings of the
elements aside from their final meaning in combination. The
rest of the poem, what it is, what it shows, its final value as
a created emotion, its meanings, if you like, *as* a poem, cannot in the more serious orders of poetry develop itself to the
full without this factual or intellectual meaning to show the

way. The other point is already made, and has been made before in this essay, but it may still be emphasized. Although the scholarly account is indispensable it does not tell the whole story. It is only the basis and perhaps ultimately the residue of all the other stories. But it must be seen to first.

My own approach, such as it is, and if it can be named, does not tell the whole story either; the reader is conscientiously left with the poem with the real work yet to do; and I wish to advance it—as indeed I have been advancing it *seriatim*—only in connection with the reduced and compensated approaches I have laid out; and I expect, too, that if my approach is used at all it will require its own reduction as well as its compensations. Which is why this essay has taken its present form, preferring for once, in the realm of theory and apologetics, the implicit to the explicit statement. It is, I suppose, an approach to literary criticism—to the discourse of an amateur—primarily through the technique, in the widest sense of that word, of the examples handled; technique on the plane of words and even on linguistics in Mr. Richards' sense, but also technique on the plane of intellectual and emotional patterns in Mr. Burke's sense, and technique, too, in that there is a technique of securing and arranging and representing a fundamental view of life. The advantage of the technical approach is I think double. It readily admits other approaches and is anxious to be complemented by them. Furthermore, in a sense, it is able to incorporate the technical aspect, which always exists, of what is secured by other approaches—as I have argued elsewhere that so unpromising a matter as T. S. Eliot's religious convictions may be profitably considered as a dominant element in his technique of revealing the actual. The second advantage of the technical approach is a consequence of the first; it treats of nothing in literature except in its capacity of reduction to literary fact, which is where it resembles scholarship, only passing beyond it in that its facts are usually further into the heart of the literature than the facts of most scholarship. Aristotle, curiously, is here the type and master; as the *Poetics* is nothing but a collection and explanation of the facts of Greek poetry, it is the factual aspect that is invariably produced. The rest of the labor is in the effort to find understandable terms to fit the composition of the facts. After all, it is only the facts about a poem, a play, a novel, that can be reduced to tractable form, talked about, and examined; the rest is the product of the facts, from the technical point of view, and not a product but the thing itself from its own point of view. The rest, whatever it is, can only be known, not talked about.

But facts are not simple or easy to come at; not all the facts will appear to one mind, and the same facts appear differently in the light of different minds. No attention is undivided, no single approach sufficient, no predilection guaranteed, when facts or what their arrangements create are in question. In short, for the arts, *mere* technical scrutiny of any order is not enough without the direct apprehension—which may come first or last—to which all scrutinies that show facts contribute.

It may be that there are principles that cover both the direct apprehension and the labor of providing modes for the understanding of the expressive arts. If so, they are Socratic and found within, and subject to the fundamental skepticism as in Montaigne. There must be seeds, let us say —seeds, germs, beginning forms upon which I can rely and to which I resort. When I use a word, an image, a notion, there must be in its small nodular apparent form, as in the peas I am testing on my desk, at least prophetically, the whole future growth, the whole harvested life; and not rhetorically nor in a formula, but stubbornly, pervasively, heart-hidden, materially, in both the anterior and the eventual prospect as well as in the small handled form of the nub. What is it, what are they, these seeds of understanding? And if I know, are they logical? Do they take the processional form of the words I use? Or do they take a form like that of the silver backing a glass, a dark that enholds all brightness? Is every metaphor—and the assertion of understanding is our great metaphor—mixed by the necessity of its intention? What is the mixture of a word, an image, a notion?

The mixture, if I may start a hare so late, the mixture, even in the fresh use of an old word, is made in the preconscious, and is by hypothesis unascertainable. But let us not use hypotheses, let us not desire to ascertain. By intuition we adventure in the preconscious; and there, where the adventure is, there is no need or suspicion of certainty or meaning; there is the living, expanding, *prescient* substance without the tags and handles of conscious form. Art is the looking-glass of the preconscious, and when it is deepest seems to participate in it sensibly. Or, better, for purposes of criticism, our sensibility resumes the division of the senses and faculties at the same time that it preens itself into conscious form. Criticism may have as an object the establishment and evaluation (comparison and analysis) of the modes of making the preconscious *consciously* available.

But this emphasis upon the preconscious need not be insisted on; once recognized it may be tacitly assumed, and the effort of the mind will be, as it were, restored to its own plane—only a little sensitive to the tap-roots below. On its own plane—that is the plane where almost everything is taken for granted in order to assume adequate implementation in handling what is taken for granted by others; where because you can list the items of your bewilderment and can move from one to another you assert that the achievement of motion is the experience of order;—where, therefore, you must adopt always an attitude of provisional skepticism; where, imperatively, you must scrutinize and scrutinize until you have revealed, if it is there, the inscrutable divination, or, if it is not, the void of personal ambition; where, finally, you must stop short only when you have, with all the facts you can muster, indicated, surrounded, detached, somehow found the way demonstrably to get at, in pretty conscious terms which others may use, the substance of your chosen case.

1935

# 17. Lord Tennyson's Scissors: 1912–1950

## I

I hope these reflections on the mother tongue of poetry during the last forty years may be, like their subject, inescapably frivolous and indestructibly serious. Poetry is a game we play with reality; and it is the game and the play—the game by history and training, the play by instinct and need—which make it possible to catch hold of the reality at all. Thus there is intimacy and irresponsibility, menace and caress, escape and aspiration, indigestion and sudden death: all this is in the play. I suppose Eliot meant something like this when he called poetry a superior form of amusement; Yeats something like this when he hoped his poems would wither into the truth; and I am sure that Falstaff had no less a message in mind when, in his dying, he babbled of green fields. Poetry is as near as words can get us to our behavior: near enough so that the words sing, for it is when words sing that they give that absolute moving attention which is beyond their prose powers. It is behavior, getting into our words, that sings. It may be only barely song as in Eliot's lines in "The Dry Salvages":

> The salt is on the briar rose,
> The fog is in the fir trees.

Here is the salt of death and of truth and of savor, the salt in our souls of that which is not ours, moving there. The salt is on the wild and thorny rose grappling in the granite at sea's edge, grappling and in bloom, almost everblooming; and it is the rose which was before, and may yet be after, the rose of the Court of Love, or the rose of the Virgin. It is the rose out of the garden which includes the rose in the garden. There is in Eliot's line (alien but known to our line that we read) also all the roses that have been in his life, as in the next line is all the fog. The fog is another salt as the fir trees are another rose. It is all there is in fog that lowers, covers, silences, imperils, menaces and caresses; but in it, as it is in them; there is the slowed apparition, coming up under an island, of evergreen struggling, tenacious life. The two together make an image, and in their pairing reveal, by self-symbol declare, by verse and position unite, two halves of a tragic gesture.

> The salt is on the briar rose,
> The fog is in the fir trees.

I do not see that any other illustration is needed of how behavior gets into the words of the full mind, and how, a little beyond the time that it is there, it sings. It may have only a brusque lilt:

> I sing because I like to sing
> And not to hurt a living thing.

So the old song says, and it is enough till memory brings another song which shows that nothing is ever quite enough, either to say or sing. It may sing music not its own.

> Sweetheart, do not love too long:
> I loved long and long,
> And grew to be out of fashion
> Like an old song.

The author of those lines thought half the time that the poet had to choose between life and work, but when he looked at verse itself the occasion and the need for *that* choice had evaporated—true but gone—like a water-stain on stone; or had disappeared—true but changed—a snowflake in the river. This author—it was of course Yeats—sometimes resumed that self which is beyond choice by quoting lines made by a friend from the Irish: in song of a lifetime.

> When I was young,
> Who now am young no more,

> I did not eat things picked up from the shore:
> The periwinkle, and the tough dog-fish
> At even-tide have got into my dish.

At other times he found that unchoosable self as near at hand as the nearest door, or the clock's tick: in the song of the gathered moment.

> My fiftieth year had come and gone,
> I sat, a solitary man,
> In a crowded London shop,
> An open book and empty cup
> On the marble table-top.
>
> While on the shop and street I gazed
> My body of a sudden blazed;
> And twenty minutes more or less
> It seemed, so great my happiness,
> That I was blessèd and could bless.

The truth of such a man—he is dead; and we may say it—is that neither his vices nor his poetry ever quitted him;[1] and when we say that I think we have touched the quick and very membrane of style; or at any rate we have the gasp and thrill with which we respond to such penetrations: that is, with added song.

> Shakespearean fish swam the sea, far away from land;
> Romantic fish swam in nets coming to the hand;
> What are all those fish that lie gasping on the strand?

Style is the quality of the act of perception but it is mere play and cannot move us much unless married in rhythm to the urgency of the thing perceived: or until—to say it again —behavior gets into the words and sings. Style, if you like, is how that kind of song is read; and it is sometimes, as a shudder may become a blush and a blush may drift into vertigo, by this sort of reading that the urgency of substance is found. There is a zero quality in style by which it seems to project, as it contains, the infinity of numbers. For example: Pound's "Medallion": a song of syllables.

---

[1] Eliot, thinking of Yeats, once cited La Rochefoucauld's aphorism: If you say of a man that he has quitted his vices, watch out! the vices may have only quitted him.

Luini in porcelain!
The grand piano
Utters a profane
Protest with her clear soprano.

The sleek head emerges
From the gold-yellow frock
As Anadyomene in the opening
Pages of Reinach.

The name of Reinach's book was Apollo, and Apollo was Lord of the Lyre and Lord of the Light's Edge; in fact, Leader of the Muses, Apollo Musagete. Pound was not worried by all this; he grew up with Reinach, and by that and other hard training got to play a very complicated stylistic game by ear. Whatever words themselves can woo into being is wooed in his words. So to speak, he settled for what came from the conjugation of the spontaneous and the arbitrary through the mind's last mode of beautiful sound. I suppose this was one of the reasons why Eliot made Pound *il miglior fabbro*. "O brother," the lines go in Dante, "this one whom I distinguish to you with my finger, was a better craftsman of the mother tongue." This is too much to say of Pound (as it was not of Arnaut Daniel)—too much to say of anyone except in those moods when the mere movement of words in pattern turns the shudder of recognition into a blush and the blush into vertigo. Vertigo is one of the conditions in which we recognize our behavior. This is what Baudelaire only reminds us of when he says he was forever haunted by vertigo. Let it be, then; there is a true vertigo to be found through the exercise of the craft of the mother tongue. It is the naked voice that sings:

*What are all those fish that lie gasping on the strand?*

## II

Forty years of poetry took their rise in Eliot, Yeats, and Pound. Each of them in his own way understands what

Tennyson meant when he said he knew the quantity of every English vowel except those in the word scissors—where each vowel is enclosed and made of uncertain quantity by two consonants. Most of their successors do not understand what Tennyson meant and many of them would repudiate the statement not for its arrogance but for its irrelevant nonsense. W. H. Auden would be an exception, and the knowledge is patent in some of his verse. There are other exceptions but they do not seem to me able to get their knowledge into their verse as a regular thing. This is the chief indictment against that aspect of our poetry which we call verse. Syllable and stress are not enough to make a metric into a style, although they are quite enough to make a doggerel. It only strengthens the indictment when we remember that between 1912 and 1922 Yeats, Pound, and Eliot won their own battle against doggerel and deliquescence and reached their heights of style and idiom. 1922 seems the great year of our time—especially if you let the months run a little both ways—for it holds a good many of Yeats's Tower poems, Pound's first eight Cantos, and Eliot's *The Waste Land*, not to mention *Ulysses*, the finishing of *The Magic Mountain*, and the beginning of *The Counterfeiters*. The year 1922 is almost inexhaustible in all the arts. But here we are concerned directly only with the triumphant style and idiom in our three poets: with their victory, finally achieved, in the revolution of 1912. In their different ways, "Prufrock," "The Second Coming," and *Hugh Selwyn Mauberley* released the expressive burden of sensibility into forms which were suddenly available for everybody for the whole period between the wars of 1914 and 1939. These poems are now the commonplace of our meeting and are known like afterthoughts in the blood-stream. At the time they were thought "new" and were mistaken, like any instinct in the process of formation; they assaulted the sensibility, either investing it or sacking it. As a result there came into print and gradually into reading and meaning many other poets new, and difficult, and damned, and denied who are now blessed and used, if they have not been forgotten. This is what is meant by the triumph of style and idiom; and it is almost as useful to say that this is what is meant by the defeat—temporary and precarious—of doggerel.

The history of any period of poetry seen from the point of view of its verse is the history of its struggle to prevent Language from becoming a new form of doggerel or—equally a hard job—to prevent an older form of language from relapsing into the basic doggerel of the mother tongue; just as, from a social point of view, it is the history of readers catching on to new rhythms or new relations between rhythm and meter. This is not a superficial but a primary interest. The business of rhythm is to move perception into meaning, and so to move meaning into words. The business of meter (the quantitative or numerical measure of words prescribed by laws only partly known) is to keep meaning in motion by giving the rhythm foot and hand holds on the up and down (the up *or* down) of the rock-face to be climbed or descended to reach the theoretic form of life we call poetry. Prosody—the precise and loving care of the motion of meaning in language—is of first but not necessarily conscious importance.

The general prosody of the 'teens and 'twenties had equally little to do with the practice of Yeats, Pound, and Eliot (which as I say understood Tennyson on scissors) and with the practice of the old conservatives. The general prosody was perhaps the weakest and least conscious in English since the dead poetry of the mid-sixteenth century. It ran, under various guises and doctrines, toward a combination of absolute doggerel and absolute expressionism. Ezra Pound was as responsible as anyone for this condition, not by the progress of his own work but by the procession of manifestoes which he promulgated by letter and print. His doctrine, however it may have promoted the incentive of writing, only got in the way of full work and when it got stronger, deeply damaged, though it never destroyed, his expressive powers. We see this if we trace the connection (it would be worth somebody's study in detail) between the Imagism of 1912, which was a mere lively heresy of the visual in the verbal, and the full doctrine of the Ideograph which seems to have undermined the structure of the later

Cantos. The ideograph is actual picture-writing in verbal signs and although it has an attractive rationale in languages built upon it, it becomes an irrational agent in the languages of the West. In English, unless taken only as analogy like any other material of poetry, the ideograph destroys the composing power of the rational imagination because it can neither grasp nor replace the rational needs of the language. The procedure is very tempting, always, to get rid of what is behind one and what is ahead of one, neither by capitulation nor by mastery, but by declaring an arbitrary substitute. Then expression becomes immediate, which is good, and spontaneous, which is not; for spontaneity is the curse of poetry to at least the same degree that neologism is the curse of language. But the temptation is very deep; Art, as Maritain says, Art bitten by poetry longs to be freed from reason, but so long as nothing is substituted for reason the longing is not fatal and may indeed promote a fresh and rejoicing sense of disorder, as *The Waste Land* did, or a new underground for reason, as the work of Valéry and Mallarmé did.

Nor should Pound be blamed too much; the heresiarchs were everywhere; all that is known as semantics, semasiology, and semiotics was in the air, and it did no good but worse harm to replace these with Basic English, as Ogden and Richards did, for Basic English makes reading as well as writing an unbearable bore. What, should we get rid of our ignorance, of the very substance of our lives, merely in order to understand one another?

The poets did not think so either. They took both the ideograph and the semiotics (in the guise of free verse and the vade mecum of deliberate ambiguity, which is sometimes called irony or paradox) and made out of them a defense of absolute self-expressionism. The idea was that of absolute style (identity or abolition of form and content), which is all very well in a sacred book, after it has been made sacred, but which otherwise runs the risk of becoming absolute doggerel. *What are all those fish that lie gasping on the strand?*

What they did was to make just enough of a prosody to

heroize the sensibility and not quite enough to make a heroic statement. Just enough meter to make a patter, just enough rhyme to make a noise, just enough reason to make an argument; never enough of anything to bind together what came out of the reservoir of their extraordinary sensibility into possible poetry. I refer, of course, to the bad poetry of the time and to the bad poetry which is called modern: to what Yeats meant when he said that the bad poet does with no trouble at all what the good poet does with great difficulty: that is to say, by prosody, by expertness, conscious or not. This bad poetry is not worth reference in itself; it is here only to represent the condition of the language and the state of ambition in which an unusually large amount of good—or partly good—poetry got written. It is here because, outside Yeats who had other wounds, hardly a good poet or a good poem but shows the permanent and somewhat crippling scars of these diseases. To heroize the sensibility is to heroize the very spontaneity which is the enemy of poetry.

Pound (out of Ford Madox Ford) had the cure for this heroism: in his notion of the Prose Tradition in Verse, where the edict was that verse ought to be at least as well-written as prose. But the cure was either unacceptable because of ignorant superstitions about inspiration or because, being by nature allergic to it, the patient would die of the cure. For the most part the bottle was bought but never used after the first gagging dose. Besides, it was seldom taken as it should always have been, along with another of Pound's prescriptions, and without which it could never do anything but harm. Verse should be written, said Pound, not to the metronome but in the sequence of the musical phrase. The prose tradition alone produces flatness, inhibits song, and excludes behavior; and I see no sense in welcoming these disorders, as Eliot has done in parts of the Quartets and as Schwartz has done in all but his earliest work, as other and desirable forms of order. I do not refer to careless writing but to deliberate flatness: which is only the contemporary form of Georgian deliquescence. Pound was right; never mind the metronome, which is the measure of doggerel; the necessity is absolute to compose in the sequence of the musical phrase. That is the difference between writing verse with only the care that goes with prose and writing verse better than prose. What is better is that words written in the prose tradition *and* composed in the sequence of the musical phrase become their own meaning: the meaning which, as Eliot says in prose, persists after the words have stopped; that very meaning of which he says in the better writing of verse: "you are the music while the music lasts." What could be better than that?

Who knows? It is always interesting to consult the two geneses of poetry in prose and in doggerel. In the prose lies the sensibility, in the doggerel the hope, of poetry. The curious may consult Yeats's *Autobiographies* and the versions of "Sailing to Byzantium" printed since his death; both the doggerel and the prose for many poems are there. So with Pound, there is the *ABC of Economics* and the Canto on Usury; and with Eliot there are the deep parallels between the series of essays and the series of poems. In each case the poems are better than the prose because in each the doggerel whether of the verse or of the mind has been lifted into composition in the sequence of the musical phrase; and in each the sensibility has been freed from the heroism of the spontaneous—the merely self-expressed, or the merely argued—and become in some sense an incarnation of actual behavior: so that you are the music while the music lasts.

Of course we have been talking about the history of poetry, not about the history of sensibility except as it affects poetry. Perhaps only because it is our own age and we have a kind of disadvantageous intimacy with it, it seems to have been an age when the sensibility took over much of the task of poetry. That is why we have created so many private worlds each claiming ascendancy over the real world about which nothing, or nearly nothing got said. That is why, too, Yeats and Eliot (though not Pound, except rarely) were almost alone able to express a version—an actual form—of the real world. In each the sensibility had other grounds than itself; the ground of beseeching, history, faith or momentum and the other ground, no less important to poetry, of prosody. To combine words of each poet in a single question, in

> A woman drew her long black hair out tight
> And fiddled whisper music on those strings—

> O body swayed to music, O brightening glance,
> How can we know the dancer from the dance?

I submit that in these lines the sensibility has disappeared into the words and the words have disappeared into what is sung, and nothing forgot. *Nothing forgot* because the meter is so united with the rhythm that the quality of the act of perception is united with the urgency of the thing perceived.

## III

I suppose that all these words so far make up to an odd way of following Arnold step by step on his touchstones, but I hope the pace is lighter and comes out in another world than his, though I do not know what world because I trust it is the world in which we live. They are meant to give us, these stepping stones, points of perilous vantage from which to estimate the work of other poets *as poets,* and not only the poets who worked under their influence but also those who worked under the influence of other and as some say older parts of the traditions of poetry in English. If we think of Yeats, Pound, and Eliot—each with his pair of Lord Tennyson's scissors—it becomes easy to cut our way through the whole field. We see at once, for a rather lumped-up example, that only at a relatively low level did meter and rhythm unite in Housman, De la Mare, and Masefield; only at rough and uneven levels in Frost and Robinson; only at difficult and precarious levels in Empson and Auden; at faltering and ragged levels in Graves and Marianne Moore; at a chastened level in H. D. Similarly, in the metric of Sturge Moore there is a kind of woolly desperation, in Herbert Read, a brittle desperation, and a mechanical, relaxed desperation, striking idly on under-water objects, in Hardy.

Desperation is the quality of action at some critical point unsuccessful because the right equipment is lacking. None of these poets in the bulk of their verse—though all of them by exception—took enough stock in the music of the muse. Hence there is not often enough the steady pressure of cohesion, speed, and exigence. But all of them are better than the flannel-mouthed inflation in the metric of Robinson Jeffers with his rugged rock-garden violence.

None of these men are bad poets; all of them require reading. I only say that what impedes full reading is a faulty relation between language and sensibility, between meter and rhythm. Their engines are inefficient; and they should have been either Keatsed or Vergilianized; where to Keats means to blush at language found and not to blush until it is found, and where Vergilianize means so to see things bound together in words that they build into permanent structures of the mind, that is, into statement: into reason that sings in the nerves because built into the body of the language.

But think—still with the scissors for hand-run reading—of the parallel Old-Timers' school, what we might call the school of Chaucer and the Ballad; think of Hardy, Housman, Robinson, and Frost: Frost with his close piety to experience; Robinson with his combination of Browning and New England; Housman with the movement of Herbert and the temperament of Hardy; Hardy with his country piety, emotional distrust, and Comtean positivism: each with his view and sense of nature, man, and God. The scissors tell us that the reputation of these men may improve, if not absolutely then relatively to Yeats and Eliot. Reading them, we see why Pound does not occupy a first position, but a position on one side. The superlative metric of Pound may be a clue to their weakness but it would never furnish an understanding of their imperfect strength. Their work stands ready to infect the work of young men who have not yet found a form for their ambition and who can no longer, since they apprehend what has happened to it, heroize their sensibility. At least I should suppose there might be a coming race of poets who would want to reverse Maritain's phrase and say Art, bitten by reason, longs to be freed from poetry: from the spontaneous and the private and the calculated public worlds. There might be a race of poets, that is, who would woo the excited miracles of absolute statement, not as a refuge, but to get their work done. For such a race, Hardy, Housman, Robinson, and Frost would be not masters but the nearest exemplars of the line of work into which the work, itself superior to theirs, of Yeats, Eliot, and Pound would disappear. It is with such an attitude in mind that the work of Lorca becomes important; it permits access without overestimation into the late school of Chaucer.

These young men—the next thing that happens, whatever it may be—would gain little but reaction from the works of the Apocalyptic or Violent school: a school that seemed so lively, so menacing to others, and so destructive of themselves, only twenty years ago—a school that now seems dead, with two exceptions. Here is where we find the remains of Vachel Lindsay, the evangel of enthusiastic rebirth; Robinson Jeffers, the classical Freudian; Roy Campbell the animal, authoritarian evangel of anti-culture; Carl Sandburg, the bard of demagogic anti-culture; and of course others. Perhaps they have partial heirs in Kenneth Patchen who has a kind of *ex cathedra* automatism, Kenneth Fearing who envisages a city without a polity, and Kenneth Rexroth who sees anarchy as the form of culture. All of these stem poetically and emotionally from Whitman-Vates: and all are marked by ignorance, good will, solipsism, and evangelism. Lord Tennyson's scissors can find nothing but cloth in them to cut; nor should we think of them even so briefly as more than false alarms if it were not for the two extraordinary talents that must be grouped with them. With modifications because of their extreme eccentricity of vision or genius, their self-willed marvels of craft, and because of their absolute flair for meaning by rhythm, D. H. Lawrence and Hart Crane belong here. Each is a blow in the face but neither can hit you twice. Both left lasting poems naked as the sensibility itself, dark as their own rebirths in the darkness of blood. But it is Lord Tennyson's scissors, and not any other instruments of insight, that tell us sadly both Lawrence and Crane were outside the tradition they enriched. They stood at the edge of the precipice which yawns to those who lift too hard at their bootstraps.

Besides the Apocalyptic school, and related to it closely, there was another school of anti-intelligence (pro-culture and self-verbal varieties) who filled the little magazines of the 'twenties and early 'thirties, together with the attics and bars, with their random spontaneity and arbitrary rites on words. They got rid of too much of their reason, and as a result they effervesced rather than expressed, and what is left is flat. Nameless they shall be here; they belonged only to their principal journal *transition*. What was wrong with them is clear when you see how weak is their imitation of Apollinaire, Aragon, Cocteau, Soupault, and how great their misunderstanding of Mallarmé, Rilke, Joyce, Kafka, and Pirandello: all men who longing to be freed from reason had a kind of bottom supply of it. Neither the English nor the Americans have ever been very good at this sort of thing. Let us say that we have not so much of reason that we can afford to lose any of it; we need it to make our nonsense real as well as genuine; and one would say that in this respect prosody was a form of reason.

Prosody as reason is what the central school of the time characteristically has over and above our two anti-intelligence schools. This is the school of Donne into which the largest number of individual writers of good verse fall when shaken up and let settle. If we generalize them, they are difficult in style, violent in their constructed emotions, private with actual secrecy in meaning. There is in their work a wrestling struggle toward statement, a struggle through paradox and irony (forms of arrogance and self-distrust), and the detritus of convictions. The statements are therefore impossible to make, but the effort to make them is exciting because genuine and because, in the best poems, there is an emotion created in parallel to the undeclarable intent. Their language has flesh and nerves and is recurrently on the verge of voice.

One does what one can. John Ransom and Allen Tate, for example, around the gaps of the unstateable tremendous, are models of the uncontrollable in pseudo-control. John

Wheelwright had again and again the frightening stroke of direct wit on the thing itself unsaid, just as Empson can press his meters on the unsayable until it almost bursts into being. Hugh MacDiarmid is another, in his non-political poems, who has the force of immanent statement. Anybody can make his own list, or consult the anthologies; for it is at this point we see the great tide of talent whirl up individual after individual till the unlike is lost in the like.

*What are all those fish that lie gasping on the strand?*

The school of Donne; we call it that as a counter in exchange, and a counter of only generally determined value. Like any counter it tells a lie; but it would be a worse lie if we called it the school of Blake. We must tell two lies together. Both intellectually and prosodically we have the right. The general poetry at the center of our time takes the compact and studiable conceit of Donne with the direct eccentricity, vision, and private symbolism of Blake; takes from Hopkins the incalculable and unreliable freedom (which cost him so much, too) of sprung rhythm, and the concentration camp of the single word; and from Emily Dickinson takes spontaneous snatched idiom and wooed accidental inductableness. It is a Court poetry, learned at its fingertips and full of a decorous willfulness called ambiguity. It is, in a mass society, a court poetry without a court. There were some of course who believed there was a court, but they produced very little poetry, or at least very little with the infectiousness of authority. I mean poets like Robert Bridges, Yvor Winters, and Howard Baker. It is not authority one gets from their work but strictures: the impossible effort of the bootstrap-will to remake one's time in accord with one's sense of its defects of sensibility and form. This is the heresy as ancient as that of direct inspiration or (as Winters named it) expressive form: the notion of *a priori* correct form.

Not so much the opposed as the counterpart heresy is William Carlos Williams' notion, which rises from his intense conviction that the only value of sound or sense is in direct perception, that forms are themselves incorrect when they are not unique. To him beauty is absolute and falls like the rain, like the dream of rain in a dry year. He is, if you like, the imagism of 1912 self-transcended. He is contact without tact; he is objectivism without objective; *l'anima semplicetta* run wild, with all the gain in the zest of immediate wonder, with all the loss that strikes when memory and expectation, the double burden of the true music, are both gone. The neo-classicist and the neo-barbarian are alike in this: their vitality is without choice or purpose. *Wind shrieked, and where are they?*

The aghast cry is from Yeats; but the scissors of Eliot or of Pound could have shorn as close. There is in poetry no shearing power so great as the living twist of things called idiom caught on to that qualifying act of perception called style. This, as we hear it, is the music of Lord Tennyson's scissors.

It is a music involved here so that we may remind ourselves how differently, and in what varied voices, it may be heard at one time: all modes being approximations of truth. There are Wallace Stevens, Marianne Moore, and E. E. Cummings, to be invoked here so that we may more richly hear Yeats, Eliot, and Pound. Each, so to speak, is full of syllables where the others are full of words. Each is a kind of dandy, or connoisseur, a true mountebank of behavior made song. I do not know that there is precedence among them; let us say they make an equilateral triangle of three styles hung like a pendant from the three major styles. Each is much interested in prosody at the executive rather than the constructive level: each decorates and expands existing prosody. So with words, each is interested in refinements, recollections, and modifications of major meanings. None of them could ever so penetrate either their prosody or their words that their poems become their own music or their own meaning. It is always a haunting "other" music that you are while the music lasts. That is why each of them has so often been an immediate influence on younger poets and why none of them has ever been a permanent or protracted influence. Each is too remote from the urgency of perception.

Wallace Stevens is a dandy and a Platonist, he darlings the syllables of his ideas: it is the stroke of platonism on prosody that produces Euphues, wit with a secret, ornament on beauty. You need an old dictionary and an old ear to get his beauty: as if he had to find an unfamiliar *name* before the beauty of his perception could emerge; and it is along these lines that you have to think of the French symbolists' influence upon him. They taught Eliot the anti-poetic and the conversational style; Stevens they taught the archaic and the rhetorical; that is, Eliot and Stevens saw the one prosody running in opposite directions. But Stevens is in essence of a very old tradition, French and Platonic, working on a modern substance. He is a troubadour, a poet of the Court of Love, and his badge is *Trobar Clus;* he has a bias for the hermetic, for the complex and ornamented protection of complex and violent perception—which is his way of heroizing the sensibility. I would think that he has all his life wanted to make supreme statements discreetly, so that their beauty would show before their force. He should have lived in the age of Pope; with his sensibility and his syllables he could have made rational statements with more beauty than that age was capable of. But as it is, he is "the tranquil jewel in this confusion."

Marianne Moore is a syllabist too, for she has written the most complex syllabic verse of our time: as if she brought French numbers to English rhythms with no principle of equivalence. But she is not the syllabist as dandy but as connoisseur; she is the syllabist of the actual, the metrist of the immediate marvel—the small animal, the close perception, the fragment of phrase; and at her best all these small things move in a momentum, like the El Greco "brimming with inner light" of which one of her poems speaks. But almost everywhere she finds, chooses, refines sophisticated *forms* of simple perceptions which return upon their simplicity and their limits. There is a correspondence here to the coerced heightened perception (the forced close observation) in the painting of still-life. Poetry is to her, as she says, an imaginary garden with real toads in it. She knows all about the toads because she has imagined the garden; as you look suddenly everywhere there is the disengaged leap of a green or a brown toad, all warts, all soft, all leaping, all real. If there is not much other reality there, and there seldom is in a connoisseur's garden, you bring her, or ignore, the life she hasn't got just because what she has got is so real: you bring or ignore as with a shut-in whom you love. While you are with her reading, you wonder what reality can be when her remote refinement of it is so genuine in plain American that cats and dogs can read. You wonder, stop wondering, and are for the moment content with the game and the play that are there.

Perhaps this is the best thing that can be said of E. E. Cummings, too. Certainly when you want to read him for what is there you can neither argue with him nor about him; his emotions, feelings, attitudes have all the direct indignation, the natural blasphemy, the lyric purity, and all the sporadic high jinks of a serious child. He is Dante's *anima semplicetta* running into difficulties, but still running and still singing. He is the child turned poet, the child with *that* terrifying and incomplete dimension. Otherwise put, Cummings is the traditionalist who insists on the literal content of his tradition without re-understanding its sources: this is, of course, the easiest form of eccentricity and the most human form of fanaticism. He is St. Francis turned Unitarian and "candid-shot" honest. Nobody could be more direct and more conventional—and for purity of motive more admirable—in his basic perceptions than he. He has too little a developed self ever to escape from it except waywardly, when you want either to console him or beat him. His verse, oddly, is less direct and even more conventional than his perceptions. He was educated by Edmund Spenser, the English sonneteers, Keats, Swinburne, the funny-papers, and John Bunyan; but perhaps he was most educated by the things that were left out that would have gone to make a structured mind. All he knows is by enthusiasm, habit, and aversion. He refuses the job of the full intelligence, preferring intimacy with what he loves and contempt for what he hates; and he accepts what love and hatred give as if they made the music of a full mind. The gifts are great but they beat as well as console each other; and if he were not part of a going concern larger than he, he would be nothing. Here again is a case where prosody is an instrument of reason. Like the wilder currencies in the age of Veluta (or like the seried marks of Hitler) Cummings' experimental typography depends on the constant presence of the standard it departs from and would be worthless if not measured against it. Indeed it is precisely in the lyric quality which is his highest worth that the old meters break through. Like a roller coaster his thrill lets you drop. It is the mountebank in him that makes the vulgar motions, but it is also the mountebank that plays— the child turned poet—the most serious game in the world.

## IV

It is thinking of these others under the aegis of Yeats, Eliot, and Pound that makes us realize the everlasting need of keeping Lord Tennyson's scissors sharp. *What are all those fish that lie gasping on the strand?* No doubt they all came out of a common pool, but it is just to observe the order of their apparition, and it is rewarding to guess at those still far from land. The general absence of decorum in metrics and syntax and the general presence of heroized sensibility and private symbolisms only make it plainer (I mean because of the conscious struggle against them) that the work of Yeats, Eliot, and Pound belongs in the full tradition of literature. It is they who stand between the Victorians and Romantics and whatever it is that comes after them. They made form and substance possible. They made possible the further development and release, still inchoate to these observations, of the doomed school of Auden about 1930. The deliberate approach to doggerel through Skelton, the Ballads, the immediate situation, and the multi-valenced distrust of self combined to produce the new flat style on the one hand (as in Auden) and on the other hand (as in Dylan Thomas) what you might call the yelling, swinging style. In between lie many possibilities, not so far satisfied, or if so not so far seen.

Auden alone has all the interest and variety and learning that go with being a true poet, and it would seem that it is something in the age rather than something in himself or the condition of poetry that has kept him from proving the truth. It is as if his crankinesses, his ups and downs, were not what he ate when young but what he picked up on the shore.

> The periwinkle, and the tough dog-fish
> At even-tide have got into my dish.

Auden is not yet through; he has had his first rushes, indeed several of them, his rallies and relapses, and his ventures into taxonomies of all sorts. But he remains quick and perceptive even in the flaccid verse of the *Age of Anxiety;* he has an ear as true as any, the beginnings of a style and the earmarks of an idiom. He has the capacities but not yet the achievements of a great poet. But he is in his middle forties: the climacteric is not yet.

It is all the more reason to think so when we look at the generation born between 1913 and 1918: Shapiro, Barker, Schwartz, Thomas, Berryman, Manifold, Lowell, Betjeman, Meredith, and Reed. I would not say that any of these men have managed the full creation, but they have the enormous advantage over their predecessors that there is an idiom ready for them to develop according to their own needs.

> The salt is on the briar rose,
> The fog is on the fir trees.

They have more than a chance—it is half done for them—to develop out of personality the most objective of all creations, the least arbitrary and spontaneous, a style. This they are aware of. They are more open, more freed, nearer both statement and song than their predecessors. They began nearer the prose tradition and the sequence of the musical phrase. We might have a great age out of them yet. What more do you want? Only that it is by prosody alone—by the loving care for the motion of meaning in language—that a poet may prove that he "was blessèd and could bless." That thought is the music of Lord Tennyson's scissors.

1951

# ANCHOR BOOKS

THE AENEID OF VIRGIL—C. Day Lewis, Trans., A20

ALCOOLS: POEMS 1898–1913—Guillaume Apollinaire, William Meredith, trans., notes by Francis Steegmuller, A444

AMERICAN POETRY AND POETICS—Daniel Hoffman, ed., A304

AN ANTHOLOGY OF FRENCH POETRY FROM NERVAL TO VALERY IN ENGLISH TRANSLATION: With French Originals—Angel Flores, ed., A134

ANTHOLOGY OF SPANISH POETRY FROM GARCILASO TO GARCIA LORCA: With Spanish Originals—Angel Flores, ed., A268

ANTIWORLDS AND "THE FIFTH ACE"—Poetry by Andrei Voznesensky—A Bilingual Edition—Patricia Blake and Max Hayward, eds., A595

ASTROPHIL AND STELLA—Sir Philip Sidney, A581

BRATSK STATION AND OTHER NEW POEMS—Yevgeny Yevtushenko, A558

CANTERBURY TALES OF GEOFFREY CHAUCER—Daniel Cook, ed., A265

COLLECTED POEMS—Robert Graves, A517

THE COMPLETE ENGLISH POETRY OF JOHN MILTON—John T. Shawcross, ed., AC2

THE COMPLETE POEMS AND SELECTED LETTERS AND PROSE OF HART CRANE—ed. with an Introduction and Notes by Brom Weber, A537

THE COMPLETE POETRY OF HENRY VAUGHAN—French Fogle, ed., AC7

THE COMPLETE POETRY OF JOHN DONNE—John T. Shawcross, ed., ACO-11

A CONTROVERSY OF POETS: An Anthology of Contemporary American Poetry—Paris Leary and Robert Kelly, eds., A439

THE ECLOGUES AND GEORGICS OF VIRGIL—In the Original Latin with Verse Trans. by C. Day Lewis, A390

EMILY DICKINSON'S POETRY: Stairway of Surprise—Charles R. Anderson, A487

# ANCHOR BOOKS

# FORM & VALUE
# IN MODERN POETRY

## R. P. BLACKMUR

"Few if any critics live who write better criticism than Mr. R. P. Blackmur; I mean subtler and deeper criticism, and sounder. He probes the poem with a keen instrument, and his judgments, so far as such an adjective is ever applicable, are close enough to infallible."

John Crowe Ransom

If poetry is life named, arranged, and transfixed through art in language, then the essential problems of the poet concern the techniques by which he can best express the particular form and value he finds in his experience. Thus the best approach for a critic of poetry is technical, in the broadest sense of the word. This is the position of R. P. Blackmur, the most perceptive and thorough critic of poetry writing in America today. These seventeen essays, selected from his *Language as Gesture*, represent his most characteristic work. He examines modern poetry in its most significant aspects, relating its linguistic techniques to its intellectual and emotional form. The poets whose work he discusses here are Thomas Hardy, W. B. Yeats, Ezra Pound, T. S. Eliot, Wallace Stevens, Marianne Moore, D. H. Lawrence, Hart Crane, and E. E. Cummings. He includes, too, his famous essays, "A Critic's Job of Work" and "Lord Tennyson's Scissors."

A DOUBLEDAY ANCHOR BOOK